EDWARD STANLY:
Whiggery's Tarheel "Conqueror"

EDWARD STANLY:

Whiggery's

Tarheel "Conqueror"

NORMAN D. BROWN

Southern Historical Publications No. 18

The University of Alabama Press
University, Alabama

FOR BETTY, DAVID, And TRACY

6/17/8 2

086996

Contents

	Preface	*vi*
1.	The Ancient Standard of Federalism	1
2.	Encounter With a Connecticut Nightingale	30
3.	The Little Conqueror	46
4.	On, Stanly, On!	58
5.	The War With Captain Tyler	75
6.	Apple of Discord	94
7.	A Most Extraordinary Course	126
8.	Stanly and the Party Divided	157
9.	In the Land of Gold	171
10.	Mission of Love	201
11.	A Barren Sceptre	230
12.	An Inveterate Old-Line Whig	254
	Notes	277
	Bibliography	333
	Index	351

Preface

This biography of Edward Stanly relates the major political events of his life: his emergence, while still in his twenties, as a fiery and controversial leader of the Whig Party in North Carolina; his role as one of the ablest champions of Whiggery in the United States House of Representatives, 1837-1843, 1849-1853; his candidacy for governor of California on the Republican ticket in 1857; his appointment by President Abraham Lincoln as military governor of North Carolina in 1862; and his support in California of President Andrew Johnson's Reconstruction policy.

Many details of Stanly's private life have been lost because none of his family letters have so far been found; these might have enriched his portrait, but would not, I believe, have changed it appreciably. The strongest single influence in molding his character and politics was undoubtedly his father, John Stanly, a Federalist congressman and eminent lawyer and orator. For this reason, I have devoted much of the first chapter to an account of the elder Stanly's brilliant and sometimes tragic career.

Raised under the "Ancient Standard of Federalism," Edward Stanly was a southern nationalist in the tradition of the two great Virginia Federalists, George Washington and John Marshall. An outspoken opponent of the nullification and secession doctrines, as a party leader he fought hard to maintain the dominance of party over section in national politics. He was the respected friend of John Quincy Adams, William H. Seward, Robert Winthrop, and other northern anti-slavery men in Congress, and was one of President

Zachary Taylor's few southern supporters during the congressional debates on the Compromise of 1850. Historians have written extensively about the principles and spokesmen of state rights and secession in the Old South. Stanly's career offers a corrective view of ante-bellum southern politics. I have also tried to shed some new light on such topics as abolitionism and party politics in the 1830s; the Henry Clay-John Tyler struggle; and the southern Whigs in relation to the Wilmot Proviso, the Compromise of 1850, and the presidential elections from 1840 to 1852.

At the state level, I have described in some detail the national and state issues and personal rivalries which divided North Carolina Whiggery during its ascendency and contributed to its ultimate decline. I have also emphasized Stanly's six congressional campaigns as they vividly illustrate the intensity of two-party politics in the South at the grass roots after the rise of the Whigs. Party lines were drawn with the utmost stringency, and Stanly was frequently supported by state rights Whigs who did not agree with his nationalist views.

Stanly moved to California in 1853 and his unsuccessful candidacy for governor of that state is a little known chapter in the early history of the Republican Party on the Pacific slope, a history obscured until now by the famous rivalry within the California Democracy of William Gwin and David Broderick.

Reconstruction in the South began soon after Fort Sumter, not after Appomattox; yet historians have given the 1861-1865 period much less attention than the post-Appomattox years. And even those who have dealt with the war years are usually unaware that with Abraham Lincoln's appointment of Stanly as military governor of North Carolina in May, 1862, the Old North State had an early experiment in presidential reconstruction. Thus Professor E. Merton Coulter writes in *The South During Reconstruction, 1865-1877* (Baton Rouge, 1947), that "Lincoln had in 1862 tried to re-establish Federal authority in Tennessee, Louisiana, and Arkansas by appointing military governors." The probable explanation for this oversight is that while Lincoln had some nominal success in reconstructing the above states, the experiment failed in North Carolina and was abandoned for the rest of the war after Stanly's resignation in January, 1863. North Carolina was not one of the President's "ten percent" states. Stanly's first attempts to implement the Administration's vague directives aroused abolitionist hostility and influenced the debate in Washington on reconstruction policies; his ultimate failure demonstrated the near impossibility of reuniting the nation by negotiation.

I owe a debt of gratitude to the staffs of more than two score libraries and manuscript depositories from which I have sought information on Edward Stanly. Particular notice is due those persons who have given the most substantial aid in this respect: former director Dr. James Welch Patton and the staff of the Southern Historical Collection, University of North Carolina at Chapel Hill; Dr. Charles L. Price, director of the East Carolina Manuscript Collection, East Carolina University, Greenville, North Carolina; and the staffs of the Manuscript Department, Duke University Library, Durham, North Carolina; the State Department of Archives and History, Raleigh, North Carolina; the Library of Congress and National Archives, Washington, D. C.; the California State Library, Sacramento, California; the Bancroft Library, University of California at Berkeley; and the Church Historical Society, Austin, Texas. (Later acquisitions have increased the size and scope of some manuscript collections beyond the figures given in the bibliography.) Dr. Fletcher M. Green of the University of North Carolina at Chapel Hill, under whose direction this book was begun, was a constant source of guidance and encouragement. Mrs. John Treanor of Los Angeles, California, kindly provided a photograph of Edward Stanly. Former congressman Lindsay C. Warren of North Carolina sent me a copy of his useful pamphlet on Beaufort County. Dr. H. Wayne Morgan of the University of Oklahoma gave valuable advice on a number of occasions. The University of Texas Research Institute and the Office of the Graduate Dean provided timely financial assistance.

The word "Tarheel" used in the title is probably of Revolutionary War or earlier origin; however, it was Civil War governor Zeb Vance who gave it prominence as testifying to the steadfast courage of North Carolina troops. While the word was rarely used during Stanly's political career, I feel his life-long devotion to his state's interests warrants this posthumous designation. He would have worn it with pride.

Austin, Texas   NORMAN D. BROWN

EDWARD STANLY:

Whiggery's Tarheel "Conqueror"

1

THE ANCIENT STANDARD OF FEDERALISM

"EDWARD STANLY, a member of the House from North Carolina, called to take leave," former President John Quincy Adams noted in his diary on September 16, 1841, at the close of the special session of the Twenty-Seventh Congress. "He has excellent principles, and a lofty spirit, with a quick perception, an irritable temper, and a sarcastic turn of mind, sparing neither friend nor foe. He is the terror of the Lucifer party, and Wise made that desperate attempt last week to scale him on the floor, by which he only succeeded in flooring himself."[1]

This incident between Stanly and Henry A. Wise, a fiery state rights Whig from Virginia, had occurred on September 9, 1841, during a House debate on an appropriation bill for American diplomats. Stanly, a Whig serving his third term, made some "cutting remarks upon Wise," the leader of President John Tyler's "corporal's guard" of followers in the House. The two men had formerly been warm personal and political friends, but when Tyler, by vetoing the national bank bill, left the Whigs, he carried Wise with him; and the tall, spare Virginian's friendship with Stanly was changed into a bitter enmity. As debate continued, Wise went to Stanly's seat, "began by hectoring and finished by insulting him—whereupon Stanly called him a LIAR." Wise aimed a blow at Stanly's face, who instantly met or returned it. As the two men grappled, there followed what an observer described as "a scene of mingled uproar and *fight*, such as the Reporter in many years experience has never witnessed on the floor of the House. . . ." Members rushed to the spot, piling themselves one on the other, although it was difficult to say whether to separate the combatants or to take sides with them. A reporter saw several canes "raised up as if in the act of striking." Representatives Thomas Arnold of Tennessee and William O. Butler of Kentucky struck and grappled with each other. The Speaker resumed the chair informally and roared "Order! Order!" Members cried out in vain for the Sergeant-at-Arms. Meanwhile, the door-keeper was trying to close the doors and windows against the crowd outside, which wanted to rush into the chamber. After several minutes of uproar, Dixon Hall Lewis of Alabama, a man of huge bulk, succeeded in separating Wise and Stanly by holding one at each arm's length like two terriers.

Wise returned to his seat and told the Speaker he was "perfectly cool," and "most humbly begged pardon of the House." He had gone over to remonstrate with Stanly, words had ensued, until Stanly had applied a word to him which he could not permit, and he had struck him. Stanly, on his part, declared that he would not ask the House's pardon; in the course of their conversation Wise had said to him, "I warn you." To which he had rejoined, "I want none of your warning." Wise then invited Stanly to come to the door. "I refused. He then said 'you deserve my contempt.' To which I replied 'you are a liar.' He tried to strike me but was prevented from so doing, and if the House had not prevented me, I would have given him such punishment as he deserved." A committee of seven was appointed to investigate what was officially termed "the recontre." The next day, William Cost Johnson of Maryland announced to the House that the "transient difference" between Wise and Stanly had been entirely adjusted by their common friends, to their mutual satisfaction, and that their former friendly relations had been restored.[2]

This fight with Wise was only one of several personal encounters in which Stanly took part during his five terms in the House of Representatives (1837-1843, 1849-1853). Called by historian Arthur C. Cole "one of the ablest champions of whiggery in Congress,"[3] his wit and satire were very clever, but frequently so caustic as to easily arouse anger. On one occasion in the 1850s, while the North

Carolina Supreme Court was in session in Raleigh, Stanly was dining
with other lawyers at the Guion Hotel. Hugh Waddell of Orange
County exclaimed, "I don't understand. I can't understand why the
court dismissed my bill. I was so careful when I drew it that I had
the book of precedents before me and drew it from the book."
Stanly instantly quipped: "Ah! But Mr. Waddell, perhaps you drew
the wrong precedent!" Waddell rose, "quite flushed and angry," and
there would have been a "difficulty" if friends had not interfered.[4]
And this was a mild witticism compared with those Stanly often
made in the House chamber! A Democrat, John H. Wheeler, who
Stanly once sharply lashed in a House speech, wrote later that he
was considered a "decided party leader in Congress, and acquired an
unhappy reputation for an overindulgence in vindictive feelings and
ultra denunciations of his political opponents."[5]

Stanly's personal appearance belied his fiery nature. A "full
blonde," he was below average height, with a small face, and a high,
large forehead.[6] One acquaintance, after their first meeting,
described him as "a very plain man."[7] Yet like many passionate
natures, he had the ability to make warm friends as well as bitter
enemies; and during his later years in Congress, he exercised great
influence with northern Whigs.[8] His manners were genial, even
courtly. "Mr. Stanley [sic] makes a better show than most of our
representatives," a North Carolina woman remarked in 1850. "He is
so perfectly gentlemanly in his appearance and manners."[9] He was
not sensitive himself about titles, but in introducing others, always
stated what they were and if they had a title he would prefix it to
the name.[10]

Stanly's family had been eminent in North Carolina affairs for
two generations, and there was a family tradition that the immigrant
ancestor was John Stanley, a younger son of that seventh Earl of
Derby executed by Oliver Cromwell at Bolton in 1651. The story
was that Charles II gave to the eighth Earl at the Restoration only a
small part of the family estates and the younger brother came to
Maryland in disgust.[11] Other and more reliable evidence indicates
that John Stanley was the son of William and Mary Stanley and
came with his parents from Virginia to Maryland about 1663.
William Stanley, who first appears in the Maryland court records as a

"soapboiler," is described as a "planter, of Talbot County," in a deed conveyance of November 29, 1666. He died in 1680.[12] John Stanley prospered in Lord Baltimore's colony. He was appointed a provincial surveyor in 1680; served as a member of the lower house of the Assembly (1689); and was Captain of Troops in Talbot County (1680), becoming a Major in 1692, and dying in the same year. His eldest son John married into the well-connected Dancey family of Virginia.[13]

John Wright Stanly,[14] Edward Stanly's grandfather, was said by William Gaston to have been "a merchant of the greatest enterprise and most extensive business ever known" in North Carolina.[15] Born in Charles City County, Virginia, December 18, 1742, the eldest son of John Stanley's grandson, Dancey, a lawyer, and Elizabeth Wright Stanley, he was a merchant in Nova Scotia and Kingston, Jamaica, and was falsely imprisoned for debt by his partner in Philadelphia in 1768-1769. Stanly gave his side of the controversy in *A State of the Accounts and Disputes Betwixt Jonathan Cowpland and John Wright Stanly*; *Remarks on Scurrility and Oppression*; and *John Wright Stanly's Reply to a Few Observations, Lately Published by Jonathan Cowpland*. After a trip to the Caribbean, Stanly decided to return to Philadelphia, collect his resources, and settle in Charleston, South Carolina. But on his return southward in 1773, a Cape Hatteras gale forced his vessel to run into Beaufort, North Carolina, where he accepted the invitation of John Sitgreaves, a fellow passenger, to visit the colonial capital, New Bern. Attending the Governor's Ball, he met Ann Cogdell, the daughter of the prominent merchant, Richard Cogdell, and the two were married soon after. Stanly then established himself successfully in the West Indian trade.[16]

During the American Revolution, Stanly supported the patriot cause; a member of the New Bern committee of safety, he showed himself "a steady, invariable and generous Friend to the Liberties of America."[17] He also became the most famous revolutionary shipowner in North Carolina. He was a commissioner in December, 1775, to fit out an armed vessel for the state, and as early as August, 1776, asked for letters of marque and fitted out a number of privateers to prey on English commerce. During the war, he held an interest as part or sole owner in eleven Pennsylvania letters of marque, and he was probably the principal owner of the North Carolina sloops *Lydia* and *Success*, the brigantine *William*, brig of war *Sturdy Beggar,* and the privateers *Nancy, Bellona,* and *General Nash*. In 1780, the latter vessel, under the command of his brother, Wright Stanly, captured two enemy brigs, reportedly the most valuable prizes ever carried into a North Carolina port.[18]

This commerce raiding and the sale of war supplies to the state and to the Continental armies made Stanly a very wealthy man. His property in New Bern in 1779 was valued at 140,950 pounds, on which he paid a tax of 201 pounds. His children said that he loaned General Nathaniel Greene a large sum of money for the southern army which was never repaid and for which a claim was later unsuccessfully brought against the state of Georgia. William Attmore, a Philadelphia merchant who visited New Bern in 1787, noted in his journal that Stanly, "by a Series of fortunate events in Trade during the War," had acquired "a great property, and has built a house in Newbern where he resides, that is truly elegant and convenient; at an expense of near 20,000 Dollars—He has a large Wharff and Distillery near his house; upon Neuse River side of the Town—and a fine plantation with sixty Slaves thereon."[19]

Stanly acquired a reputation in the town for his generosity. In 1773, he made a contribution to the Masons, which their minutes "gratefully acknowledged . . . tho' [he was] not a member of the Lodge" at the time.[20] William Attmore said of him:

> One circumstance deserves to be recorded to his honour—
> Altho' brought to Philadelphia from Honduras a prisoner
> arbitrarily; and on his arrival sent to the Gaol by the person
> who brought him by force yet upon his getting into affluent
> circumstances, he generously relieved the pecuniary distresses
> of that very person afterwards; the more meritorious, as upon
> a settlement of Accounts with that Man, it was found that he
> owed him nothing, but on the contrary that person was in his
> Debt.[21]

However, Stanly suffered heavy losses in the war. Jacob Gooding, a clerk in the office of Stanly's partner, Thomas Turner, stated that Stanly lost fourteen armed vessels, in addition to some burned at his wharves in New Bern. In August, 1781, he visited Philadelphia at Robert Morris' request to consult on government finances. The British and Tories under Major James H. Craig made a raid on New Bern from Wilmington that month, one of their objectives being to capture Stanly, and not finding him, sacked and burned his property along the Neuse River. John D. Whitford commented that "if he had lived longer, there is every reason to believe his fortune would have been retrieved by his business capacity, his intrepid exertions."[22]

Towards the end of the Revolution, Stanly wrote that the approaching peace "has inclined me to devote my whole attention to the winding up of my concerns in Trade and preparing for a more general and extensive Feild [*sic*]."[23] Did a political career beckon? If so, he was destined for disappointment. In 1785, he was nominated but failed of election, in the first of several attempts, to the North Carolina Council of State. However, he held several appointive local offices, serving as a trustee of the New Bern Academy and as one of five commissioners of navigation charged by the General Assembly with ordering surveys and erecting beacons. At the time of his death, he was "Judge of the Maritime and Mercantile Court of Port Beaufort."[24]

Stanly died suddenly of yellow fever on June 1, 1789, at the age of forty-six, and was buried by the Masons of St. John's Lodge, No. 2, "accompanied by a number of visiting Brothers, and followed by a large concourse of inhabitants of the town." The Edenton *State Gazette of North Carolina* described him as having been "amongst the foremost in the late revolution as a warm and steady patriot," with a heart "ever touched with the most tender sympathy for the indigent and distressed" and a hand "ever open for their relief."[25] His wife Ann, only thirty-four, died of the fever a month later (July 2, 1789). Six children were left orphans: John, Ann, Richard Dancy, James Green, Margaret Cogdell, and Thomas Turner. The eldest John, born April 9, 1774, was a lad of fifteen; the youngest, Thomas Turner, a babe in arms.[26]

This double calamity interrupted John Stanly's academic studies, which were never regularly resumed. The orphans were left in greatly reduced circumstances, and John became a clerk for his father's partner, Thomas Turner. In 1795, at the age of twenty-one, he began a brief career as a merchant in a small house on the corner of Middle and Pollock streets in New Bern. That year he married Elizabeth Franks, who inherited from her father, Martin Franks, large estates in Jones County which "laid the foundation of Mr. Stanly's prosperity."[27]

Association with prominent New Bern lawyers, particularly Benjamin Woods and Thomas Badger, and an appointment as a district court clerk and master in equity led Stanly to study law without any regular instruction, and in 1799, "after a mysterious disappearance of a few days from the town," he returned with a license to practice.[28] Endowed with both mental and personal gifts, by diligent study he remedied the defects of his academic and professional education and soon attained high rank in a Bar which numbered William Gaston, Edward Graham, Abner Nash, and Richard Dobbs Spaight among its members. "Small in stature, neat in dress, graceful in manner, with a voice well modulated, and a mind intrepid, disciplined and rich in knowledge, he became the most accomplished orator of the State."[29] In the courtroom, his quick perception, retentive memory, keen wit, and bitter invective made him a formidable opponent. "In repartee and sarcasm I never saw his equal," said a man who viewed him often in court. "His efforts in that line were absolutely withering. The composure of no suitor, witness or rival advocate could survive his pungent criticism. Ever bold and fearless, he at once rose to the breadth of the occasion, always wielding a polished scimitar with the energy of a giant and the skill of an artist."[30]

Stanly once appeared against Vine Allen in a case respecting the interpretation of a will. Allen in his argument said that "in addition to the testimony submitted to the Court for a change of the will, he happened to visit the deceased a week or two before he died and was then told by him of the alteration desired and he intended to make." In reply, Stanly stated "he could with equal truth assert he, himself, had also visited the deceased who told him he wanted no alteration in his will and could not have changed his mind as immediately, after that, turned right over and died." After this rebuttal, Allen's case was gone.[31]

Stanly was equally at home in private conversation. Chief Justice

John Marshall wrote Archibald Murphey that while he had never heard him in court: "I have known him . . . in private, and it was not possible to be in his company, without noticing and being struck with his general talent, and most especially his vivacity, his wit, and his promptness. He appeared to be eminently endowed with a ready elocution, and almost intuitive perception of the subjects of discussion."[32] This pleasing effect was heightened by Stanly's courtly manners, a family trait, and one which made him "a favourite with all the ladies."[33]

Stanly devoted the best of his energies and much of his life to politics. William Gaston, one of his warmest friends, testified that "public interests seemed to afford to his ardent mind that peculiar excitement in which he delighted, and to give it that full employment without which it was ill at ease."[34] Entering public life in 1798 as an "uncompromising Federalist," Stanly succeeded Edward Graham as New Bern's representative in the North Carolina House of Commons, and was reelected the following year. In 1800, despite the general southern enthusiasm for Thomas Jefferson, the North Carolina Federalists elected four congressmen, including Stanly— then but twenty-six—who defeated the ailing incumbent Richard Dobbs Spaight by a 856 vote majority in the New Bern district.[35]

General Spaight had been a close friend of Stanly's father, visiting often in his home and serving as one of his executors, but there was for some unknown reason bad blood between him and the younger Stanly. "I have before been informed that Mr. Stanly would be my opponent," the General had written a friend from Washington. "I indeed understood as much before I left home. I make no doubt he will use every means in his power to accomplish his views—but even putting myself out of the question, I could not wish him success, because I think him an improper Character but that is not likely to have any weight with the electors in the district, & they may probably elect him—Froth you know always swims on the surface."[36]

Stanly later mortally wounded Spaight in a duel growing out of their continuing political quarrel and forced by the latter. On August 8, 1802, Spaight, who had just been reelected to the State Senate, was told by William Smyth that Stanly had stated publicly that morning that "though he Mr. Spaight was a Republican, the Federalists could always command his vote, or when they were hard run could always get Mr. Spaight's vote." Labeling these reported remarks "a direct attack on my character, and one that I will not suffer any man to make with impunity," the General the next morning sent Stanly a challenge. Stanly immediately offered an explanation. Spaight was not satisfied and Stanly, wishing to avoid a duel, wrote a second and third letter. The last was accepted on condition that the correspondence be published. Stanly agreed and left town on August 10 for the Jones County court. In his absence, it was reported in New Bern that Spaight had challenged him, that he had refused a duel, and had made humiliating concessions. In the next New Bern *Gazette*, the General published the correspondence, but accompanied it with Smyth's certificate (a man Stanly thought of "no character"), with the comment that "whether Mr. Stanly, or Mr. Smyth, is more worthy of credit, it is not for me to say." Stanly then published certificates from "gentlemen of Respectability" supporting his recollection of the conversation in question.[37]

There now began between Spaight and Stanly what the latter called "a paper war,"[38] that continued in every issue of the *Gazette* until the duel. Finally, on September 4, Stanly published a handbill in which he pictured the General as attempting "to play the hero, to strut the bravo, to ape the duellist," and concluding: ". . . as to Mr. Spaight's epithets, of which he seems to have good store, I have only to pronounce that they betray a malicious, low, and unmanly spirit." Spaight replied with a "redhot" handbill that evening, calling Stanly's style "billings-gate . . . extremely indecent and impertinent throughout," deriding his "*meek* and *calm*" spirit as cowardice, and ending by inviting a challenge. "I must now gentlemen, declare to you, that in my opinion Mr. Stanly is both a liar and a scoundrel; and that although I hold his character in so contemptible a point of view, yet as he had the confidence of the people of this District, I shall always hold myself in readiness to give him satisfaction—and to assure him, that if he asks for it once, he shall not be under the necessity of doing it a second time."[39]

The next day, Sunday, September 5, Stanly challenged Spaight and the latter immediately accepted. The two men and their seconds

(Edward Graham for Stanly and Edward Pasteur for Spaight) met the same day about 5:30 p.m. on the outskirts of New Bern. At first the General shot nearer the mark than Stanly. His second pistol ball passed through the younger man's coat; another cut off a cedar twig from a bough a few inches above his hat. Some of the large number of witnesses wanted to interfere, but Pasteur threatened to shoot anyone who tried to do so. At the fourth exchange, Spaight received a wound in his right side. Carried to his town house, he died the next day. On September 7, his remains were deposited in the family vault at his country estate near New Bern, "with expressions of universal sorrow and all those testimonials of respect which were due to his acknowledged merit." The widow's kinsmen threatened criminal proceedings against Stanly, but upon his petition, Governor Benjamin Williams pardoned him.[40] Spaight's death caused great excitement throughout North Carolina and the legislature passed an anti-duelling law; however, it could be easily evaded by going outside the state to fight.

Stanly was a candidate for reelection to the House of Representatives in 1803; his opponent was William Blackledge, "a gentleman," sneered Stanly, "who however otherwise deficient, possesses all the democrats require in their representatives, a belief in the infallibility of Mr. Jefferson."[41] The congressional elections were waged on the question of whether the state legislature could rightfully instruct senators and representatives in Congress. The four Federalist representatives, Stanly, William Barry Grove, Archibald Henderson, and William Henry Hill, had refused to heed the General Assembly's instructions to vote for the repeal of the Federal Judiciary Act of 1801. Stanly had grimly warned that repeal would be "the first link in that chain of measures which will add the name of America to the melancholy catalogue of fallen Republics." Despite the united support of their party on the instruction issue, all four lost their seats to Republican opponents. Blackledge's majority over Stanly was 877 votes, 2,653 to 1,776. The state's most prominent Federalist, William R. Davie, had consented to run for Congress in the Halifax district but was denounced "as a monarchist, and the intended King of the Federalists to the Southward," and was defeated by the incumbent, Willis Alston. The Federalist Party in

North Carolina, nearly crushed by this disaster, was never successfully rehabilitated.[42]

In 1805, Davie retired to his plantation, "Tivoli," on the Catawba River in South Carolina. He had little sympathy with efforts by younger Federalists like Stanly to revive the party. "The Federal Party is in fact *dead and buried*, and ought to be so considered even by its warmest friends," he wrote in February 1808. "No good can arise from any attempts towards its resurrection, therefore the policy of individuals of that description, for it is no longer a party, will, or ought, certainly to be . . . to take no active part, and give their votes to the least exceptionable of the republican candidates."[43]

Davie's obituary was a little premature, as even he soon realized. North Carolina Federalists staged a revival in 1808, when they capitalized on popular discontent with Jefferson's Embargo to win three electoral districts (New Bern, Fayetteville, and Moore) for their party's presidential candidate, Charles Cotesworth Pinckney of South Carolina. The other eleven electoral votes went to Republican James Madison. The Federalists also captured three congressional seats, those of the New Bern, Fayetteville, and Salisbury districts. William Tatham, an engineer appointed by Jefferson to survey the North Carolina coast, had written the President on May 6, 1808, after visiting New Bern, that "the Commercial interests of that Place seem to be very generally opposed to the present administration, . . . & Mr. Stanly (one of your inveterate [o] pposers) is pushed against Mr. Blackledge. So far as I can judge, the Majority of our Citizens in Town are as loyal subjects to John Bull, in their hearts, as any about St. Jame's; and would willingly mark similar lines of distinction in Society." Stanly's majority over Blackledge was 187 votes.[44]

In the Eleventh Congress, Stanly was an outspoken opponent of the Madison administration and the so-called "*War* men," who were advocating the strongest retaliatory measures against Great Britain for her violations of American neutral rights. He was one of five North Carolina representatives to vote for a new charter for the Bank of the United States. The bill lost narrowly in the House and a separate measure in the Senate by the Vice-President's casting vote. In a House speech on the Bank (January 24, 1811), Stanly warned that the "inevitable effect" of a revived non-intercourse with Great Britain and the destruction of the Bank in a time of danger from abroad "must be to let loose a torrent of overwhelming calamity, the extent of which you cannot estimate, and the force of which you cannot stay. The consequences are awful, and the responsibility serious. Let gentlemen look to it."[45] Stanly's remarks were noticed in a letter from Washington to the editor of the *Virginia Patriot*: "Mr. Stanly made the best speech that has been witnessed on the subject: cool, ready, impressive, argumentative: his language pure, and his metaphors unstrained and beautiful."[46]

North Carolina Federalists took great pride in Stanly, pointing out that northern papers praised him and printed his speeches, while generally ignoring his Republican colleagues. The New Bern *Carolina Federal Republican* quoted the New York *Evening Post*'s remarks that "Mr. Stanly is a true Washingtonian federalist, a man of sterling talents, a stateman and an orator. Such men are scarce especially on the floor of Congress." The Raleigh *Star*, in printing one of Stanly's speeches, declared: "Federalists will rejoice that their principles are advocated with such ability and Republicans will feel proud that their state is distinguished by the employment of such talents."[47]

Stanly for private reasons was not a candidate for reelection in 1810, and Blackledge was again returned to Congress, winning over Federalist William Gaston by a 483 vote majority, 2,781 to 2,298.[48] The Federalists were very much disappointed in Gaston's defeat. Their bitterness may be judged by the regret expressed by J. A. Cameron who wrote his brother Duncan:

> with yourself, every rational man, everyone who regards the prosperity of the nation, must sincerely lament the issue of the New Bern election. When worth and talents such as Gaston's are postponed for the bloated ignorance, the arrogant presumption and the poisoned politics of Blackledge, well may the friends of order inquire into the dangers of their situation. . . . French politics have so far gained the ascendancy that the godly precepts of Washington are no longer remembered.[49]

In August, 1812, Stanly was one of sixty Federalists elected to the General Assembly, representing New Bern in the House of Commons. The 1811 state law repealing the district system of choosing electors and giving the choice to the Assembly on joint ballot had angered the voters. Also, the declaration of war against Great Britain in June, 1812, gave the Federalists a potent weapon to wield against their Republican opponents. Gaston was elected to the House of Representatives in 1813 by a huge 1,820 vote majority, 2,763 to 943, over Blackledge, a reluctant candidate who entered the contest only a few days before the election. In a circular to the district's voters, Gaston had declared that the war "was forbidden by our *Interest*" and "from the *honour* and fair character of the Nation, nothing could be more abhorrent." He saw nothing to hope and everything to fear from the war's continuance and avowed himself "the earnest the anxious FRIEND OF PEACE."[50]

Twelve years of Republican ascendency in the nation did not dim Stanly's Federalism. He promoted party organization as best he could, and contributed to the support of the Federalist press. When northern Federalists showed a determination to support DeWitt Clinton of New York, an anti-Madison Republican for President in 1812, Stanly expressed a preference for a distinct Federalist candidate. "I should prefer to erect the ancient Standard of federalism," he wrote Gaston in August, 1812, "its principles are understood & hallowed by the precept & example of our father, Washington. Surely we can say the federalists of this State will support John Marshall—or Pinkney [*sic*], or if no federalist any mortal not the Vice regent of the Devil himself, Bonaparte, in preference to Madison."[51] But he acquiesced in the Federalist's informal choice of Clinton, serving as an elector on the Clintonian ticket in North Carolina. On joint ballot the General Assembly chose the Madison electors by a vote of 130 to 60.[52]

The "ancient Standard of federalism" was thus still flying bravely above the handsome Stanly home in New Bern, where Edward Stanly was born on January 10, 1810.[53] In 1779, John Wright Stanly had purchased four lots at Middle and New Streets from the merchant Thomas Ogden, and erected the mansion at a cost of $20,000, probably under the direction of John Hawks, the supervising architect of Tryon's Palace. A special Federalist aura surrounded the northeast room on the second floor in which President George Washington had found "exceeding good lodgings" during his visit to New Bern in 1791.[54]

Unfortunately, little information has been preserved concerning Edward's childhood, but he did not lack for companions at home. John Stanly and his wife Elizabeth had fourteen children, five of whom, four daughters and a son, died in infancy. There were eight living sons: John, Alfred, Frank, Edward, Alexander Hamilton, Fabius Maximus, Marcus Cicero, and James Green. The eldest, John, was idiotic from birth and was confined in the Stanly home, "helpless as an infant," until his death at eighteen. Elizabeth Mary Stanly, the only daughter to reach adulthood, married Captain Walker Keith Armistead, a West Point graduate, against her father's wishes. A son, Lewis Addison Armistead, was born to the couple in New Bern, February 18, 1817. He was to fall at Gettysburg on July 3, 1863, while leading the remnants of Pickett's division into the Union lines at "the Angle."[55]

Mrs. John Stanly is a shadowy figure. Stephen Miller, who spent several years in New Bern in the early 1820s, describes her rather unkindly as a "country heiress without cultivation or opportunity...." According to Miller, Stanly's "nature did not harmonize with the taste of his wife; for she was a shouting Methodist, and he a staid Vestryman of the Episcopal church."[56]

Edward was three years old when a tragic event cast a pall of grief over the Stanly family. John Stanly's youngest brother, Thomas Turner Stanly, while attending a supper given by William Gaston in February, 1813, playfully tossed a piece of cake across the table to attract the attention of a young lady opposite him. The cake fell in a cup of tea and spattered her dress. Thoughtlessly, she turned to Lewis Henry, a classmate of Stanly's at Princeton, who was seated beside her, and exclaimed: "Do you stand that?" Somehow, from this trivial incident, Henry sent a challenge which Stanly, on the advice of his brother John, accepted. The two men crossed into Virginia (to avoid the penalties of the North Carolina anti-duelling law), and met on February 14, 1813. At the first fire, Thomas Stanly was shot through the heart. Mrs. Lydia Badger, a kinswoman, noted in the family record: "A promising young man much lamented and never to be forgotten." This incident, coming after the death of another brother, Richard Dancy Stanly, about 1808 in a duel in the West Indies, fastened upon the Stanly family an unenviable, if not undeserved, reputation as a hot-tempered and fighting clan of the "Hotspur" type.[57]

In 1814, when the war with Great Britain was going badly, delegates representing the Federalist controlled states of Massachusetts, Connecticut, and Rhode Island met in convention at Hartford, Connecticut. Republicans feared the meeting was preparatory to the formation of a northern confederacy, and in North Carolina, many Federalists shared their alarm.[58] These Federalists were critical of "Mr. Madison's War"; but unlike their dissatisfied northern brethren, they considered disunion a greater curse than the evils of Republican rule. As John Stanly wrote Gaston when word of the convention reached New Bern:

> The severance of the Union is an evil of such magnitude, that I cannot apprehend any man of standing & influence will meet the responsibility of recommending such a resort—weighty as are the evils & curses of Madison's administration, those of disunion would be so much more awful, that I will not yet believe that the patriots of New England contemplate any such resort.[59]

Yet despite their loyalty to the Union, the North Carolina Federalists, *as a party*, shared some of the odium which fell on the New England Federalists in their twilight years as a consequence of the Hartford Convention. No talented Federalist in the state could aspire either to the governorship or the United States Senate, and few were elected to the House of Representatives. Unquestioned devotion to Jeffersonian principles was the *sine qua non* of political advancement. When Senator David Stone submitted his resignation to the legislature in 1814, an unwilling Francis Locke, one of six Republican nominees, was chosen 104 to 75 on the eleventh ballot over Stanly, the only Federalist contender. To succeed Locke the General Assembly of 1815 picked Nathaniel Macon over John Branch, 101 to 59 with 27 scattered. The Federalists were determined to block Branch, the caucus choice, and Stanly said to Weldon Edwards, a Warren County neighbor of Macon's: "Edwards, I am convinced we cannot elect one of our own party, therefore, we will assist you to elect a man we will all know where to find."[60]

Judge Duncan Cameron, in declining to be a candidate for the Senate in 1816 to succeed James Turner, succinctly stated to Archibald Murphey the hopelessness of the Federalist cause: "Of this I feel very certain, that however wide the schism may be among the friends of the democratic candidates for the appointment of Senator; yet they will unite in solid column against any and every federalist who may be put in nomination for that office. If so, the result cannot be doubtful." He advised Murphey: "You must take the best of *their* men; for that office, you cannot get one of *your own*."[61] Yet North Carolina Republicans also paid a price for their dominance. They were by-passed in the selection of cabinet officers (none before 1829) or foreign ministers, because their state was regarded as a political appendage of Virginia, whose lead she would always follow.

Although his Federalist principles barred John Stanly from the highest political offices, he remained a power in state affairs. New Bern annually sent him to the House of Commons in 1798-1799, 1812-1815, 1817-1819, and 1823-1827. In 1821 he was one of the Craven County members in the House. Stanly seldom had opposition. A brief press announcement of candidacy a week before the August election—"We are authorized to state that JOHN STANLY, Esq. is a candidate to represent this town of Newbern in the next General Assembly"—sufficed.[62] There were about three hundred voters in New Bern, and of these fifty or more were free Negroes, "who generally voted, without exception, for him."[63]

In 1818, Gaston offered for the Senate, Stanly for the New Bern seat. Abner Neale and Richard Dobbs Spaight, Jr. were proposed for the Craven County seats in the Commons. "If no opposition is made to Gaston, there will be none to Neale & Spaight," Stanly revealed to General Samuel Simpson, "—but if they will oppose Gaston, we must 'win the horse or lose the saddle'—& oppose them too—"[64] However, to the town's surprise, Spaight "boldly" came out in opposition to Stanly himself! "Some think it will be a hard Poll," wrote local Republican leader John West, "but I suspect Stanly has been too long in the service to be out polled by a youth; indeed I have long been of opinion that no man could beat him in Newbern." A postscript confirmed West's prediction. "Stanly is elected by a majority of 42 votes—Spaight had 108 and Stanly 150—"[65]

Stanly was twice elected Speaker of the House of Commons, in 1825 and 1826, after Federalist proscription had eased. Possessing "an eye like Mars, to threaten and command," he "held a rod pickled in . . . Sarcasm" over the western members in the House.[66] Nor did easterners escape. In the General Assembly of 1823, a member reported that "There is a little County Court Lawyer here from the Town of Halifax—[Jesse A.] *Bynum*, who is nothing but food for Stanly's wit & sarcasm—very much to the amusement of the House and spectators."[67] William Gaston relates that when General Lafayette was expected to visit the state, certain "economists and calculators" in the House opposed a resolution authorizing funds for a fitting reception. Stanly rose, "his clear blue eyes bright with unusual fire," and declared that any "miscreant" who opposed the resolution would be "gibbeting his name high on the pillory of infamy." Not a word more was said. "The question was taken and all. . . recorded their votes in favor of the resolution."[68]

Stanly won high praise as Speaker. Former State Senator John H. Bryan of Craven reported after his first election in 1825 that "Mr. Stanly presides in the H of C with great dignity & grace and the members appear well satisfied with their choice." David F. Caldwell, attending the Commons from Salisbury, wrote Willie P. Mangum: "Mr. Stanly whom I fear you are not partial to presides over us with impartiality, dignity & ability. He certainly gives a dignity to the deliberations of the Commons, & preserves a degree of decorum which I have never witnessed."[69]

On the most important political issue dividing the eastern and western parts of the state, Stanly was decidedly an "Eastern" man. The Constitution of 1776 gave the East a majority in the General Assembly, each county being allowed one senator and two members of the House of Commons, and with certain towns receiving individual representatives in the House. The West, whose population was increasing more rapidly than the East, had larger counties and consequently fewer representatives. About 1820 the West began to demand the calling of a constitutional convention to adopt an equitable apportionment. In a debate on the convention question in the House of Commons in December, 1821, Stanly argued from

"ELEMENTARY PRINCIPLES OF SOCIETY" against any change in representation. Society was not formed, he said, merely to protect personal liberty but also property. "The rich are *people*, as well as the poor, and the right of property, whether large or small, is alike sacred." It was a fundamental principle in government, "that barriers should be erected for the security of property; that the possessors of the property of a State, or of a District, should have a weight in its affairs, proportioned to the contribution they make to its support, and to the stake which they have placed upon its prosperity." The majority in every country were men without property; if numbers alone should decide, the greater number would take the property of the less. Certainly, no government could be free or enjoy constitutional liberty, which excluded the people, however poor, from a share in its administration; "yet assuredly all power of government is not to be trusted, uncontrolled, in such hands. In every age, and in every climate, man is the same;—unchecked, he is found unjust, tyrannical and cruel." The rights of the propertied minority must be protected by giving property its weight and influence in the government.

Stanly calculated that upon the basis of property and taxation, the eastern half of the state would be entitled to thirteen more representatives than the western half, and the growing value and improvement of the eastern section would continue to increase the difference in its favor. Under the present constitution, wealth, taxation, and population each had its influence in representation. "For the opposite claim, that population alone should govern representation, and give laws to the State, there was no pretence of reason and no sanction of authority." North Carolina, he hoped, "would not be the first to fall into a fanciful experiment, at the sacrifice of a principle of the utmost magnitude." The House defeated the convention resolution eighty-one to forty-seven, and for fourteen years longer, the East staved off the West's demand for reform.[70]

Stanly used geographical and economic differences in the state as an argument for the selection of its presidential and vice-presidential electors by the district system. The eastern section of the state had commercial interests while the western section was more exclusively devoted to agriculture. How could they see eye to eye on the selection of a president? In the legislature of 1812 Stanly urged repeal of the recent bill vesting elector selection in the General Assembly for the benefit of those who could not "look with complacency on the destruction of commerce." Eleven years later, in arguing for a district system instead of the general ticket then in use, Stanly returned to the subject of eastern versus western interests. Easterners, he said, "were cursed with a large slave population, the possession of which gives a considerable addition to the number of our votes for electors. The people of the west have fewer slaves; the curse bears more lightly on them; the price of the increased number of electors is paid by the East, why then should we not have them?"[71]

If Stanly was a conservative when dealing with political reforms, he could be progressive on other state issues. As early as 1790 a few leaders had advocated a penitentiary system to ameliorate the sanguinary criminal code. Speaking in the House in the 1817 session, Stanly admitted that he had formerly approved the old system and had doubted the need for change; "but he congratulated himself that he had been enabled to take a clearer view of the subject," and he was now convinced that the existing barbarous system of public and severe punishment, "originating in ages but half civilized," was "ineffectual, repugnant alike to justice, humanity and religion, and ought to be abolished." The House of Commons passed a penitentiary bill on second reading by a large majority but the bill was lost in the Senate by a vote of thirty-four to twenty-seven, and the movement was successfully defeated throughout the ante-bellum period.[72]

Stanly was not unmindful of the friendly support he received at the polls from the free Negro voters of New Bern. In the assembly of 1825, a bill was introduced to prevent free Negroes from migrating into North Carolina and regulating the conduct of those already in the state. The measure passed the Senate, but in the House of Commons it was debated for two days in committee of the whole; "and after a most able discussion as to the constitutionality of the bill," a motion to strike out the first section (equivalent to rejection) was carried fifty-six to forty-seven. William Watts Jones, David L.

Swain, and James Iredell spoke for the bill and Stanly, George E. Spruill, and A. H. Shepperd against it. State Senator Bartlett Yancey complained that "the infernal spirit of emancipation," generated by colonizing and emancipating societies, was greatly felt in the state, and "so is the free negro suffrage in many Counties & almost all the towns." He warned:

> If the people of this State are not more awake to their rights and interest on this subject, a few years more will produce an influence here, greatly to be lamented & feared. . . . In the discussion in the legislature, upon the Bill to prohibit the migration into the State of free negroes, Stanly supported the principle of the proposition of Mr. [Rufus] King, openly in debate, declaring 'that negroes had the same God, & the same Redeemer the white has'., which though literally true, serves to show you the *slang* employed on the question.[73]

During the years when John Stanly was adding to his laurels in the House of Commons, his son Edward was growing to manhood in New Bern—a town whose galaxy of able men had earned it the name of a modern Athens. John Stanly, William Gaston, Edward Graham, Vine Allen, John H. Bryan, Francis L. Hawks, John R. Donnell, Richard Dobbs Spaight, Jr., and Wright Stanly (John's cousin) were all living in New Bern at the same time, competing with one another in the courtroom.[74]

On the square beyond the Presbyterian church, which stood opposite the Stanly house and law office on New Street, was the square, two storied brick New Bern Academy building, erected in 1806. In the belfry hung a small bell with which the local boys would, "on the first peep of the rising sun out of the woods beyond the broad Neuse, ring in the 'glorious fourth' with hearts ablaze 'with patriotic fire.'" Edward Stanly attended the Academy, and in the examinations, he and Charles Shepard, later a political rival, were among the first and about equal in scholarship. Examinations were rigorous and the discipline strict. Wrote John D. Whitford: "If a pupil would not keep up otherwise and without much persuasion or coxing he was flogged up at school and at home."[75]

All was not seriousness in New Bern, however; the town boasted a theatre in the basement of the handsome brick Masonic building, and a "Thespian corps" was organized, with Edward's uncle, Richard Dancy Stanly, in the lead as an actor and manager. Coming after Stanly and his associates were John Hawks, Francis L. Hawks, John H. Bryan, and James C. Stevenson, followed later by James W. Bryan, Charles Shepard, Edward Stanly, and Cicero Hawks.[76]

In 1822, Edward, then a lad of twelve, must have witnessed the "very animated canvass" for state senator from Craven County waged by his father and the incumbent, Richard Dobbs Spaight, Jr. Spaight was reelected, 297 to 251, owing mainly, it was believed, to a broadside issued by Stanly in which he righteously declared that "though five hundred gallons of Rum should be started in opposition to me, I will not treat" the voters. He continued: "Who, in his calm moments, can look without grief and shame, upon the picture of an election scene, in which the Candidate with his jug, and the Voter with his glass, perhaps reeling together, belch forth their patriotism and fidelity! Such scenes are the opposite of everything manly and honorable." On election night, the Spaight party held a victory procession in New Bern, complete with music and banners. On one of the latter Stanly was represented as stricken down by the Goddess of Liberty, who held a drawn sword over him. The thirsty marchers were refreshed after the parade with a "great abundance of punch" at the Spaight home.[77]

At sixteen, Edward, having completed his Academy work, was sent to the University of North Carolina, at Chapel Hill, to continue his studies. On August 4, 1826, he appeared before the University faculty and after "an approved examination" was admitted to full standing in the Sophomore class. He was enrolled in the Philanthropic Society on September 6, 1826. Edward did well in his studies—an indication both of native ability and thorough preparation at the Academy. On the basis of the semiannual examinations in December, the faculty judged him one of the seven best scholars in the Sophomore class.[78]

Despite this fine beginning, Edward did not return to the University for the spring term. Still another family tragedy interrupted his studies. On January 16, 1827, John Stanly, who was serving as Speaker of the House of Commons, suffered a paralytic stroke while speaking in the Committee of the Whole. According to the Raleigh *Register*, "he had proceeded but a few minutes, when his voice failed him. He asked for water, and after drinking a little attempted to proceed; but he had uttered but two or three sentences before he said, 'My voice fails me, from some cause, I cannot proceed.'" A motion was immediately made and carried for the Committee to rise. Stanly with difficulty reached the Speaker's chair, and after adjourning the House, was carried off in the arms of his friends.[79]

Twenty-four hours after the attack, Stanly still had his senses and could speak so as to be understood, but his doctors saw no improvement and doubted he would survive. "The affection seems confined to one side of his body but the whole face is affected," an observer reported. "His mouth is drawn up & his eyelids have lost in a great degree their muscular power." Some of the doctors were "of opinion that there is a suffusion of blood on the brain, by the rupture of a blood vessel."[80] He remained in a very critical state for weeks, and friends were distressed at the complete prostration of his once powerful mind. "I apprehend now that the disease is taking the worse type it can assume," William Gaston wrote on February 5, "and that quitting its fury on his physical frame, it is reducing his mind to the most lamentable imbecility." Pious men saw in this "calamitous" case the inscrutable working of Divine Providence. "What poor creatures we are!" Gaston exclaimed. "How mysterious the ways of Heaven!"[81]

Stanly's health improved somewhat in the summer of 1827 as he traveled to Warm Springs in Buncombe County, and to Virginia; while still paralyzed on his left side, his mind cleared and he was able to walk around his room with a little assistance. The presidential election of 1828 was in full swing and he gave a limited support to Andrew Jackson's candidacy. In 1824 he had supported the People's Ticket while stating a preference for John C. Calhoun or John Quincy Adams. A Jackson meeting at the New Bern Courthouse, November 24, 1827, appointed him to the Committee of Correspondence. (His friend Gaston took President Adams' side.)[82] But in January, 1828, a New Bern resident reported his health was "very feeble" and it was supposed he could not survive for long; "he however endeavors to appear cheerful and wishes every person to believe that he is recovering."[83] Gaston, who had been elected to fill Stanly's seat in the House of Commons at a special election on December 7, 1827, now also replaced him as president of the Bank of New Bern—a position he had held since 1817.[84]

Stanly's friends, as a complimentary gesture, placed his name before the General Assembly in 1828 as a candidate for governor and he received 21 votes on the first ballot to 66 for James Iredell, 60 for Richard Dobbs Spaight, and 24 for William Polk. On the second ballot, his name was withdrawn; and on the third ballot, Iredell was elected with 104 votes to 80 for Spaight, Polk withdrawing. In January, 1830, the legislature paid him the further compliment of placing his portrait in the House of Commons. Said the New Bern *North Carolina Sentinel*: "This well-merited tribute of respect, must yield a high gratification to the family of this gentleman, as well as to the numerous friends who lament his protracted indisposition."[85]

In May, 1827, when his father's life was no longer in any immediate danger, Edward left New Bern to enroll in Captain Alden Partridge's American Literary, Scientific and Military Academy, then located in Middletown, Connecticut. A cousin, Harvey Stanly, had entered in 1825. Partridge, a graduate of West Point, first established his academy at Norwich, Vermont, in 1819, but moved it to Middletown in 1824. Courses were offered in engineering, military science, agriculture, bookkeeping and accounting, and the arts and sciences. Each student was allowed to progress as rapidly as possible in his studies and was presented with a certificate of graduation when he had completed the prescribed course. No student was received for less than a year, and was required to be at least nine years of age, of good moral character, and able to read and spell correctly and write a "fairly legible" hand. The students were organized into a cadet battalion and were required to wear a uniform dress, preferably of "domestic manufacture."[86]

Edward entered the Academy in 1827 and graduated in 1829; beyond this nothing is known concerning his activities.[87] However, his education at the Academy must have "tended to strengthen his Federalism."[88] He also received his first taste of Washington society at this time. On March 5, 1828, he was in the national capital and

went with General John Wool and Augustine H. Shepperd to the
home of Secretary of State Henry Clay. They met John H. Bryan, a
member of Congress from the New Bern district, and visited in the
drawing room with the other guests. "We had a great crowd," Bryan
informed his wife the next day. "I introduced Edward to several of
the dignitaries, and he seemed to be much delighted & surprised at
the show."[89]

John Stanly, meanwhile, lingered on, "sinking day by day in
mind and body, strength and intellect."[90] Stephen F. Miller, during
a visit to New Bern from Georgia in February, 1829, found his
"noble features" distorted by his affliction. "He tried to converse in
his former commanding way, but failed." Too ill to attend church,
Stanly received communion in his sick chamber from the Reverend
John R. Goodman, rector of Christ Church.[91] Yet in a surviving
letter from this dark period, his old asperity shines out. On March 4,
1829, he wrote John H. Bryan expressing dismay at Jackson's
reported cabinet:

> If he should go to the interior of N. Carolina to seek a
> gentleman to take charge of our navy, surely he could not in
> the town of Halifax have overlooked the celebrated character
> Willis Alston who in all the virtues which distinguish Govr.
> Branch is very little inferior to him... Nor can I discover why
> Genl. Jackson should ride from the Hermitage to Washington
> overlooking all the good Ten. riflemen to look for a county
> court lawyer in Mr. Ingham of Pa for the Treasury. I am sure
> Sir, it is all a *lie*. If however it should prove to be true I shall
> not hold myself responsible for any act of Genl. Jackson's
> *republican* administration.[92]

During Stanly's long illness, his financial affairs became disor-
dered, reportedly because his sons were improvident. Creditors
pressed claims, and only William Gaston's intervention saved the
Stanly mansion from sale. The Bank of New Bern brought a debt
suit against Stanly, and he ceded the Bank about 1,700 acres of land
in Jones County, which it offered for sale in August, 1831. The
remainder of the plantation, about 2,500 acres, which Stanly had
ceded to his son, Alfred, the latter offered for sale "upon a liberal
credit" in October, 1831. Stanly's brother, James Green Stanly, and
a cousin, Wright C. Stanly, were forced to sell their plantations to

satisfy debts. Mrs. Stanly suffered the humiliation of being forced to place the following advertisement in the New Bern *Spectator*:

MRS. JOHN STANLY

Is prepared to accomodate a few Boarders, at her house on Middle-Street. Further information, if wanted, can be obtained upon inquiry at her house. 5th Oct. 1832.93

John Stanly's neighbors considered his sons, except Edward, to be "unpromising"; and, with the exception of Fabius Maximus, who had a distinguished career in the United States Navy, rising to the rank of Rear Admiral, their later lives bore out this opinion. Both John H. Bryan and William Gaston thought highly of Edward, who was evidently expected to follow in his father's footsteps.[94] He was selected in 1831 to read the Declaration of Independence at the Fourth of July celebration in the Presbyterian church and delivered what the *North Carolina Sentinel* termed "some appropriate and excellent prefatory remarks. . . ." "This is our 'Pillar of fire by night, our cloud by day,'" Edward said of the Declaration, and with the South Carolina nullification doctrine in mind, declared in a tired metaphor: "Follow this, and it will safely lead us by the Scylla of Disunion, the Charybidis of Nullification."[95] Here, in his first public address, he expressed Unionist sentiments that were to be the guiding principles of his political life.

In September, 1831, Edward announced for the New Bern seat in the House of Commons, after the death of the incumbent, Charles G. Spaight, stating, however, that he would withdraw if Gaston would agree to serve. When Gaston consented to run, Edward published a card in the New Bern *Spectator*, three days before the election, withdrawing from the canvass. "Although fully convinced of the certainty of my election," he declared, "I cannot, without a total disregard of the opinions and wishes of many of our oldest, best citizens, whose characters I respect, whose age I venerate, and to whose judgment and experience the most implicit deference is due, consider myself any longer a candidate." Gaston was narrowly elected, polling 146 votes to 145 for young Charles B. Shepard.[96]

The fifty or more free Negro voters in New Bern had apparently gone heavily for Gaston, for Shepard published a card in the *North*

Carolina Sentinel thanking the townsmen for their "very flattering support" in the poll and expressing his pride "that a majority of the free white men of the town have given him their support, and although their votes have been overruled, the result is highly gratifying to his feelings." In December, 1831, 164 white New Bern citizens petitioned the General Assembly to deny free Negroes the suffrage. The *North Carolina Sentinel* declared that the petition "meets the hearty concurrence of two-thirds at least, of the free white voters of the town" and said caustically that "the member elect [Gaston], in his desire to promote the wishes of his constituents, will doubtless use his endeavors to effect the object of the Petitioners."[97] The General Assembly took no action. The next year Charles Shepard was again a candidate for the New Bern seat and according to his brother-in-law, John H. Bryan, "is violently opposed by the free negroes, and Messrs. Alfred and Edward Stanly—They have been very anxious to bring out Mr. [Matthias E.] Manly in opposition and I think it is very probable they will vote for him, whether he is a declared candidate or not."[98] Shepard, however, was elected without opposition.

In the Constitutional Convention of 1835, the free Negro was denied the ballot by the close vote of sixty-six to sixty-one, over the objections of Gaston, representing New Bern. He argued eloquently that "a person of that class, who possessed a freehold, was an honest man, and perhaps a Christian, he did think should not be politically excommunicated, and have an additional mark of degradation fixed upon him, solely on account of his color."[99]

Meanwhile, Edward had decided to become a lawyer, and after a brief period of study and service as the clerk of the Craven County Superior Court was admitted to the Bar in 1832. Two years earlier he had become engaged to Julia Jones, one of the four daughters of Doctor Hugh Jones of Hyde County. According to John D. Whitford, "these ladies were highly educated, and, as a rule, their business capacity and experience in that line, were far in advance of the ladies generally then around them. . . ." The couple were married on April 24, 1832, in New Bern, and went to live in Washington, North Carolina.[100] Washington was the county seat of Beaufort County, and while there was considerable litigation in the area, the local Bar did not offer as much competition for a struggling young attorney as in New Bern. In 1847, Stanly formed a partnership with Thomas Sparrow, a New Bern native and Princeton graduate, who had read law with William Gaston. A profound student, Sparrow was a forceful debater and orator whose appealing personality gathered men around him.[101]

John Stanly was now confined to bed, and his sister, Ann Taylor, wrote on April 18, 1833, that "all hope of his improvement in health has fled—in his present state he must remain until removed to another & we trust better world."[102] The end finally came on August 2, 1833, when Stanly was fifty-nine. State leaders paid tribute to his character, talent, and public services. William Gaston presided over a memorial meeting of the New Bern Bar, published an eloquent tribute in the New Bern papers, and composed an epitaph for Stanly's tombstone. "He was indeed a great man," Gaston wrote later, "distinguished pre-eminently for acuteness of intellect, rapidity of conception, a bold and splendid eloquence. How unfortunate it has been for his family that he lived so much for others and so little for himself!"[103]

This man of splendid ability, whom a contemporary, Weldon Edwards, called "the great wit, the scathing satirist, and the unequaled orator in his generation in North Carolina,"[104] had a deep and abiding influence on the character and principles of his most talented son. Edward Stanly shared his father's strong passions and intellect, and although not his equal in formal oratory, was to display a genuine ability in political debate; while at caustic repartee, he was to prove a master.

A more fundamental legacy from his father was an undeviating devotion to the American Union. John Stanly remained an unreconstructed Federalist to the end. "For myself," he declared proudly in 1824, when the party's organization was just a memory, "I thank God, I can say I am still a Federalist."[105] But his Federalism was not the sour, parochial New England variety of a Fisher Ames or Timothy Pickering. Rather, it was Federalism in its finest flowering—the nationalistic Federalism of George Washington and John Marshall. Stanly was an implacable foe of John C. Calhoun's nullification doctrine and the "right" of secession, and he taught

Edward to abide by the teachings of Washington's farewell address, to love the Union, and to shun any movement tending to its destruction. "I have from my earliest youth," the latter declared in 1851, "regarded our Union as full of inestimable blessings to us and all mankind."[106] John D. Whitford wrote many years later of his friend Edward:

> His hostility to secessionist and disunionist was implanted in his bosom by his father when the son was a youth and it grew with his years and strengthened with his age. He believed in the right of rebellion, never in the right of secession. It was foreshown by him what would be the result of the war in the event of a conflict between the north and south years before it occurred, that chivalry could not overcome numbers and almost endless resources whatever politicians might say from sinister motives to the contrary; and too he was consistent throughout his political career in holding to every line of Jackson's Proclamation against the nullification acts of South Carolina.[107]

John and Edward Stanly were both devoted to their native state and to the advancement of her interests and prosperity. They were angered by her political subordination to Virginia, the citadel of Republican state rights. In 1824, John Stanly denounced those North Carolinians who, as "puppets in the hands of Virginians," had brought their state "almost to a condition of vassalage, and humbled . . . once proud and independent . . . North Carolina, to the lowly rank of a colony of Virginia."[108] Edward Stanly shared this hostility toward the Old Dominion and extended it in full measure to South Carolina, the home of John C. Calhoun and his "abominable" nullification doctrine. In a speech in the House of Representatives in 1841, Stanly likened North Carolina to a Mount Ararat between Virginia and South Carolina—"a distinguished land-mark in the desert, to which the weary pilgrim who may be lost in clouds of metaphysical sophistries, in the impenetrable bogs of Jeffersonian abstractions and 'strict constructions,' may turn his eyes with undoubted confidence that in her borders he will find comfort and repose."[109] His love for North Carolina was no less fervent than his hostility towards her "immediate neighbors." Said the Raleigh *Register* in 1850: "Mr. Stanly possesses one trait . . . which should always propitiate for him the calm and unbiased judgment of every true hearted North Carolinian:—we allude to his constant and unceasing devotion to his native state."[110]

A moderate who too often spoke immoderately, Stanly in his public career was to denounce with equal fervor the extremists of both the North and South. Refusing to place sectional interests before national and party loyalties, he sought a union of hearts in an indissoluble Union. His political and personal friendships transcended sectional lines and embraced all parts of the country. Congressional service dispelled "ridiculous prejudices" and enabled him "to remove prejudices from the minds of others." He found in the Yankee character as represented by New England congressmen of the Whig persuasion an "absence of all assumption of superiority, . . . combined with elevated patriotism, sound sense, and solid merit."[111]

The shrines of the American Revolution, North or South, were sacred because they symbolized the common revolutionary experience and national spirit. "If I live I must visit Mass.," he declared in 1844. "I shall not feel qualified to serve the public, until I shall have been in Fanueil Hall—It ought to be considered an indispensable requisite, that every member of Congress should go there—would that they all cherished a respect for it."[112]

Because Stanly freely expressed these "honest feelings" in Congress and on the stump, his political enemies called him "a Southern man, with Northern principles." Yet his constituents sustained him with their votes in all but one of six congressional campaigns. A southerner who often stood against the dominant views and policies of his region, the significance of his life is to be found in his unwavering devotion to his state and to the Union—twin loyalties which were to cause him much anguish during the Civil War, when as President Abraham Lincoln's military governor in North Carolina he tried to reestablish federal authority in the state.

2

ENCOUNTER WITH A CONNECTICUT NIGHTINGALE

EDWARD STANLY once declared that he had come among the people of Washington, North Carolina, "without fortune, without the patronage of the influential, relying only on my own efforts and their generosity."[1] This statement was not altogether accurate. True enough, Stanly was "without fortune" when he moved to Washington in 1832, but as the son of John Stanly he was not without influential friends. This was demonstrated in November, 1835, when he was a candidate before the General Assembly for the office of state solicitor in the second judicial district. Wilson B. Hodges of Washington County wrote Ebenezer Pettigrew, a wealthy and respected planter of Tyrrell County, requesting that he use his influence with the representatives from the "Nags Head" country in behalf of "our mutual friend Mr. Edwd. Stanly," who "you know is a gentleman well qualified for the office and stands high among all classes who know him best."[2]

The balloting took place on November 26, and Stanly defeated the veteran incumbent, General Stephen Miller, by 28 votes, 107 to 79. Both Pettigrew and Matthias Manly, New Bern's representative in the House of Commons, used their influence in his behalf. His friends felt that the fees of the office would enable him to maintain his family while the job itself would introduce him to other business.[3]

Among those who congratulated Stanly upon his victory was William Gaston, the man to whom Stanly looked most frequently for advice after the death of his own father. Gaston gently advised him not to disappoint "public expectation" by his conduct as solicitor. Stanly replied that he entertained the highest respect for Gaston's opinion, "and there is no one, who will more gladly follow any suggestions of yours, or more highly prize anything coming from you, than myself." He was fully aware of his obligations and for the sake of his father's good name, if there were no other consideration, "I should exert myself . . . with all the ability I possess, and with the consciousness, of the importance of the office, to which I am elected."[4]

Stanly could not have chosen a wiser or abler counselor than Gaston, who stood in the first rank of the country's lawyers. A native of New Bern, educated at Georgetown and Princeton, Gaston, like John Stanly, began and ended his political career as one of, in his own words, "the proscribed sect of Federalists." The brilliant Federalist leader, Alexander Hamilton, was his political pope. Gaston served in the state senate from Craven County in 1800, 1812, 1818-1819, and represented New Bern in the House of Commons, 1808-1809, 1827-1828, 1831. He was a member of Congress from 1813 to 1817, and was called by Daniel Webster "the greatest man" in the War Congress. One of a small political minority during the last twenty years of his life; according to David L. Swain, "during that period he was the favorite of the State above all others, for any position to which he chose to aspire." In 1833, without any solicitation on his part, he was elected to the North Carolina Supreme Court by the General Assembly and served until his death in 1844.[5]

Gaston was strongly nationalistic in his political opinions, cherishing the Union as "the best patrimony which we have received from our ancestors, and . . . [the] most precious inheritance for our children." He contemptuously dismissed John C. Calhoun's nullification doctrine as involving "glaring and impractical absurdities."[6] When the Nullifiers sneered at North Carolina as the Rip Van Winkle of the South, Gaston retorted that better "sleep on than wake to treason or disunion; better be the Rip Van Winkle of the South than the Cataline of the historian, or the Bobadil of the poet."[7] Friendship with such a man strengthened Stanly's already strong nationalism.

While Stanly was beginning his law practice in "Little Washington," national events foreshadowed the formation of the party in
which he was to become, while still a young man, a recognized state
and national leader. The virtual disintegration of the National
Republican Party after the presidential election of 1832, and the
failure of the Anti-Masonic Party to increase its strength, pointed up
the need for a new party that could rally the opponents of
Jacksonian Democracy into some semblance of political order. Just
such an anti-Jackson coalition emerged in the spring of 1834.
Adopting the name "Whig" because of its opposition to the tyranny
of "King Andrew," the new party included the great majority of
National Republicans and Anti-Masons, as well as Democrats who
opposed Jackson's executive "usurpations" or his war on the United
States Bank. Calhoun and the Nullifiers maintained a tenuous
connection with the Whigs. Members of the new party could be
found among all social classes, but its nucleus in the North was the
merchants, manufacturers, and professional men, together with a
respectable number of commercial farmers.[8]

The Whig Party in the South was controlled by urban commercial
and banking interests, supported by a majority of the planters, who
were dependent on the towns for banking and trade facilities. Across
the lower South from Georgia to Louisiana, most fertile "black belt"
counties gave Whig majorities, while the hill or frontier counties of
small farmers tended to be Democratic. Nevertheless, the Whigs were
no more exclusively the patrician party than the Democracy was the
plebeian party.[9] In North Carolina the Whigs drew strength from the
back country and mountainous areas, while the Tidewater, with the
exception of the region of the Albemarle and Pamlico Sounds, was
Democratic. According to the leading state history, the Whig Party
"was strongest wherever slaves were fewest. It was preeminently the
party of the democratic small farmers, merchants, and business men
who desired the economic development of the state. Its leaders were
not champions of democracy but rather men of wealth, education,
and aristocratic philosophy, often interested in railroads and manufacturing."[10]

The Whigs received the major credit in the West for the constitutional reforms adopted by the Convention of 1835 favorable to that section.[11] They also gained support by championing the distribution to the states of the proceeds from federal land sales. It was a popular issue, particularly in the West, where internal improvements were desperately needed to promote economic prosperity, and in the counties adjoining the Albemarle and Pamlico Sounds, where there was a demand for an ocean inlet at Nags Head. Although North Carolina had a long Atlantic coastline, inferior harbors had retarded commercial growth. The Democrats opposed distribution, contending that it was unconstitutional and meant a high tariff, but their arguments brought them only odium. The Democratic Party's refusal to support annual distribution, more than any other measure, caused its downfall in the state. In addition, President Jackson's strong stand against nullification and his war on the Bank of the United States brought disgruntled Democrats into the Whig ranks.[12]

Stanly was too young to play an important role in the formation of the Whig Party in North Carolina, but his support of Whiggery was a near certainty. The Jackson party in the state, dominated by aristocratic eastern planters, was the lineal descendant in its strict construction principles of the Jeffersonian Republican Party, opposed so vigorously by his father. Nathaniel Macon, the state's most powerful representative during the Jeffersonian era, was still the titular leader of the Democracy there, and kept the bulk of the party in line for Jackson and the Force Bill during the nullification crisis.[13] The opposition of the Democrats to a national bank and internal improvements at federal expense, and their "do-nothing" program at the state level, was not appealing to a man of Stanly's Federalist antecedents. In April, 1836, he complained to Ebenezer Pettigrew, his representative in Washington, that Congress would not give North Carolina "a little of the land money" to build a hospital at Ocracoke on the Outer Banks; "it has been greatly wanted there of late, and would be highly beneficial to a large part of our State.—But I suppose the 'Pets' have other uses for the money."[14]

Stanly expressed his dislike for Jackson and the Democratic Party in the most vehement language, his youth and ardent temperament giving full rein to his pen. Writing Ebenezer Pettigrew, shortly before Jackson left office, he declared hotly:

I still hope after Jackson is dead, and the reptiles who have crawled into power during his reign will have lost his influence, that the eyes of a deluded people will be opened, and all things come right again—I do not wish the death of Andrew Jackson or any other living creature, but I believe the Country will lose nothing by it, and if he is to retire on the 4th March next, I wish the people of Beaufort, to celebrate his retirement with 'bonfires and illuminations' and to have a day of public prayer, to thank Heaven, his reign is over. . . Was there ever a parcel of greater fools and knaves, than those who now control our financial matters?[15]

In 1836, Stanly, in common with the Whigs generally throughout the state, supported Hugh Lawson White of Tennessee for the presidency, although his new duties as state solicitor kept him "more busily engaged than . . . ever before."[16] At a public meeting of the citizens of Beaufort County, held in Washington on May 5, 1836, he was one of a six-man committee appointed to draft resolutions endorsing White for President and John Tyler of Virginia for Vice-President.[17] In April, he had written Pettigrew that while Edgecombe County would vote for Van Buren, "the rest of the district, I think, will give a strong vote for White."[18]

The state elections in August, 1836, resulted in a victory for the Whig gubernatorial candidate, Edward B. Dudley of New Hanover County, over the incumbent, Richard Dobbs Spaight, Jr., and the election of a Whig Senate. But the national election was a different story. There was really only one issue in the presidential election— Andrew Jackson. His name, and the exertions of the Democratic organization headed by Macon, carried the day for Martin Van Buren by a popular majority of 9,240 votes. This election represented the "expiring flicker of Jacksonian Democracy in North Carolina national elections."[19] Not until 1852 would the Democrats again carry the state in a presidential election. In 1838 the Whigs reelected Governor Dudley over John Branch by a vote of 34,329 to 20,153 and won both houses of the legislature, which increased state aid to railroads and enacted, in 1839, a law for the establishment of a state free public school system.

In 1837, Stanly's good friend, Ebenezer Pettigrew, serving his first term in Congress, was so disgusted with the turmoil in the

House chamber that he declined to be a candidate for reelection. His withdrawal left the Whigs in his district no choice but to seek a new candidate.[20] Henry Toole of Washington was "anxious to offer," but the "better opinion" feared he would be badly beaten.[21] A district Whig convention met in Washington on April 7, 1837, and selected Josiah Collins, a state rights Whig planter, as the party's candidate for Congress. When he declined the nomination, the convention reassembled in Washington (May 4) and unanimously recommended "Edward Stanly, Esq" to the electorate "as a fit and suitable person to represent them in the 25th Congress of the United States."[22]

The speed and unanimity with which Stanly's nomination was carried in the convention indicates that the local Whig leadership, as was the usual practice, had agreed upon his selection prior to the meeting. Although only the third choice of the Whigs, after Pettigrew and Collins, his nomination at the youthful age of twenty-seven was a tribute both to his own ability and to the fame of the Stanly name.

In accepting the nomination, Stanly said he had neither solicited nor expected it, since there were so many "older and abler soldiers" among the Whigs. However, he could not disregard the wishes of those whom he respected, nor be so ungrateful as to refuse his assistance in advancing and supporting correct principles. He approved of distribution and promised, whether in public or private life, "promptly to resist the slightest interference with the peculiar institutions of the south." During the coming months, he would acquaint the people of the district with his political opinions, "as far as I can gratify them."[23] Stanly's nomination was cordially received by the Whig press in the state. Said the New Bern *Spectator*: "If talents, integrity, and unbounded devotion to our country, her interests and laws, be recommendations, the choice of the Third District has been eminently successful."[24]

The Democratic Party in the Third District also had some difficulty in finding a suitable congressional candidate. A portion of the party in Edgecombe County met on April 8, and approved a former incumbent, Doctor Thomas H. Hall, an old-line Republican, who had been defeated for reelection by Pettigrew in 1835. When

Hall declined to run because of opposition within his own party to his nomination, the New Bern *Spectator* predicted that Stanly would be allowed "'to walk over' the congressional course" in the Third District. Stanly, however, was not so sanguine. *"Dr. Hall has declined*; and thus far I have the field to myself," he informed Pettigrew on May 20, but he added that "Edgecombe will hardly rest satisfied with this."[25] He was right. The Democrats finally prevailed upon Louis D. Wilson of Edgecombe to take the field; a party wheelhorse, he had represented his county in the constitutional convention of 1835.

During the campaign, the "spirited little" Washington (N.C.) *Whig* published dispositions implicating Wilson in what the paper considered shady western land speculation. The New Bern *Spectator* declared that if the charges were true, it was "little short of degradation on the part of a high-spirited and honorable son of John Stanly to enter into any contest whatever with such a man as Wilson is represented to be." The Tarborough *Scaevola* retorted that the dispositions "was [*sic*] got up by an unprincipled band of Shin Plasters, some seven or eight years ago, for the purpose of defeating Gen. Wilson in an electioneering campaign."[26]

In the final analysis, the election came down to a contest between Edgecombe and the other five counties in the Third District. Edgecombe, the "Tenth Legion" of the North Carolina Democracy, had given Van Buren the largest majority of any county in the state, 1,175 votes, and Hall had carried it in 1835 by a margin of 1,245 votes.[27] The Whig candidate's task was to offset this huge Democratic vote in the other counties of the district. This Stanly accomplished. The election was held in Edgecombe, Pitt, Beaufort, Washington, and Hyde on July 27, 1837, and in Tyrrell in early August. Stanly's majority in the former counties was 377 votes, and Tyrrell's Whig faithful gave him a final winning margin of 666 votes, 2,842 to 2,176; he carried every county except Edgecombe, which gave Wilson 1,167 votes to 78 for Stanly. The total vote was 583 less than in 1835.[28] Stanly polled fewer votes than had Pettigrew in Beaufort, Hyde, Washington, and Tyrrell; gained three in Edgecombe; and brought Pitt into the Whig camp.[29]

"Hurra for the Patriots of the third Congressional District!"

exulted the Washington *Whig*, when Stanly's victory was assured, "who *have elected* STANLY *by a majority of about* 700; left Wilson at home to console the Scaevola, and to learn his own weakness among free men."[30] Overall, North Carolina Whigs gained one seat in the congressional elections, electing eight members to five for the Democrats.[31]

On May 15, 1837, President Martin Van Buren had issued a call for an extra session of Congress to cope with the financial problems growing out of the "Panic of 1837." Pursuant to his call, the first session of the Twenty-Fifth Congress assembled in Washington on September 4. As the House was unorganized, it was called to order by Walter S. Franklin, the clerk of the previous Congress. The Democrats had a majority, but the margin was so narrow that James K. Polk of Tennessee took great precautions to insure his reelection as Speaker. He was successful, winning over John Bell of Tennessee, 116 to 103, with 5 votes scattered. However, a Whig-Conservative coalition of Whigs and New York state bank, paper money Democrats elected Thomas Allen, editor of the conservative Washington *Madisonian,* House Printer, over Gales and Seaton of the *National Intelligencer* and Blair and Rives of the *Globe.*[32]

Polk chose his committees with great skill to avoid a Whig-Conservative Democratic union that could control the House. "The Speaker appears to have had some difficulty in getting clear of all the Whigs," one newspaper correspondent noted; "they are becoming almost too many for him."[33] Minor committees were crammed with Whigs and Conservatives, while "rank Van Burenites" were given safe control of the more important ones.[34] The Administration enjoyed a healthy majority on the Ways and Means Committee, which was headed by Churchill Cambreleng of New York, a hard money Democrat and close friend of the President. Stanly, as a Whig and new member, was placed on the relatively unimportant Invalid Pensions Committee.[35]

Van Buren's message to Congress blamed the depression on overbanking and overtrading, and suggested certain relief measures, chiefly designed to see the government through the financial crisis. He proposed a law throwing into bankruptcy banks which suspended specie payment; postponement of the distribution of the surplus still

in the Treasury (to cover the estimated deficit for 1837); postponement of payment of bonds posted for duties by the merchants of
New York and other ports; an issue of Treasury .notes to meet
current expenses; and the passage of a law providing that the
government keep its own funds, thus divorcing its fiscal operations
from private or state banks. Finally, he warned citizens looking to
the government for relief. The Founding Fathers had "wisely judged
that the less government interferes with private pursuits the better
for the general prosperity."[36]

On September 15, Cambreleng reported a bill from the Ways and
Means Committee "imposing additional duties as depositories in
certain cases on the public officers and for other purposes." "This is
the famous Sub-Treasury scheme," Representative John Quincy
Adams noted caustically in his diary, "which is to be the panacea for
all the diseases of the country." The bill ordered collectors of customs,
postmasters, and other receivers of public money to hold their
receipts until ordered to pay them out or transfer them. The
Secretary of the Treasury was ordered to withdraw the government's
funds as quickly as possible from the pet banks and place them in
depositories established by the act. The bill was read twice and
referred to the Committee of the Whole on the State of the
Union.[37]

On September 27, 1837, Stanly submitted a resolution to the
House requesting the Secretary of the Treasury to furnish a statement of the number of Sub-Treasuries which would be required if
the bill should become a law; how many new offices must be
created, if any; how many new buildings erected; "and what will be
as nearly as he can estimate, the annual expense of the system; what
the salaries to be paid the officers, and what will be the commissions
to which they will be entitled." Two days later, on Stanly's motion,
his resolution was taken up, considered, and adopted. On September
30, Polk laid Secretary of the Treasury Levi Woodbury's reply
before the House. Aware that the Whigs hoped to charge the
Administration with extravagance during a depression, Woodbury
minimized the estimated cost of the Sub-Treasury system; he would
not feel authorized to appoint any new officers since the bill merely
imposed additional depository duties on existing officers. No new

buildings were contemplated. The only additional expense would be for clerks, fire-proof chests, or vaults, "or other necessary expenses of safe-keeping, transferring, and disbursing said moneys." He estimated the "whole additional expense" under the bill at not more than $25,000 yearly.[38]

Whigs denounced the Sub-Treasury, or Independent Treasury, as a hindrance to recovery, since by removing specie from circulation, it would force banks to curtail loans and thus accelerate the deflationary trend. Despite Woodbury's assurances that no new officers were contemplated, the Whigs charged it would fasten a horde of new office-holders on a long-suffering people and foster peculation. Senators Henry Clay and Daniel Webster, the two great leaders of the Whig Party, argued for the re-establishment of a national bank as an essential relief measure. Speaking in the Senate on September 25, Clay remarked that the President had no more right to infer from his election that the people were opposed to a national bank "than he had to infer that the people considered a little man of five feet, with red face, sandy-colored whiskers, head inclined to baldness, and a downcast look, a model of human perfection."[39]

The most momentous event of the special session was John C. Calhoun's decision to support the Independent Treasury bill. He agreed to do so after Administration leaders incorporated in the Senate bill his amendment, known as the "specie clause," which provided that after January 1, 1841, all funds received or disbursed by the government should be in gold or silver, or in notes, bills, and paper issued under the authority of the United States. This action signified his separation from the Whigs and his return to a party whose strict-construction views were more akin to his own.

Calhoun's defection surprised and angered the Whigs. His fellow senator from South Carolina, William Preston, charged him with desertion. In the House, Waddy Thompson of South Carolina refused to follow the Nullifiers into the ranks of "Benton and Co."[40] Stanly wrote Pettigrew:

Calhoun's course has filled all with surprise, and his friends with deep mortification—he is openly in favor of the subtreasury scheme, and thinks he sees some great commercial

benefit, to the South hereafter, while he admits, it must injure
the North.—He is too metaphysical for me, he sees too far and
too much for a man of common sense to comprehend him—I
cannot go with him, his South Carolina friends will not
support him—only part of them.

Stanly thought it was ridiculous to hear men talk of the "divorce
of Bank and State" while they were willing to place the whole
money of the country under the President's entire control. "We
shall—we must have, an United States Bk—we cannot do without
it—and I believe with Clay, 'our Union, as one people depends upon
it.'"[41]

Calhoun's zealous support suffised to carry the Sub-Treasury
through the Senate, but in the House, the Whig-Conservative coalition was too strong to be overcome during the short extra session.
The Administration finally agreed to table the bill so that it could be
taken up at the regular session. The vote on the tabling motion was
120 to 107. North Carolina's delegation voted along party lines, the
Whigs favoring and the Democrats opposing the motion. The Whigs
on their part lacked the strength to carry a new national bank bill;
on October 5 a resolution "that it is inexpedient to charter a
national bank" passed the House, 122 to 91.[42]

The Van Buren leadership did push through, over Whig objections, a bill to postpone the payment of the fourth installment of
the surplus to the states until January 1, 1839. No one in Congress,
however, expected that the fourth installment would ever be paid.
"Postpone means . . . to *repeal* the Law," Representative James
Graham wrote his brother William. "The Bill was passed by the
destructives and nullifiers their new allies."[43] Congress also passed a
bill authorizing the government to issue $10,000,000 in Treasury
notes bearing interest at not more than six percent.[44]

To carry these measures through the House, the Van Burenites
held frequent night sessions. Writing Pettigrew from the House
chamber during one such session, Stanly complained that he was
"'tired sleepy' and sober, and wish I was abed." "Johnny Q" (John
Quincy Adams?), at his left hand, had assured him that the House
would probably adjourn at six the next morning; "he says it is a
pretty sight to see day breaking through the windows, and gradually

eclipsing the candles!" It was a sight Stanly did not wish to see, but duty must be performed, "and if these rascals will not go home, I can stand it." The Van Buren men were "forcing matters through.— We cannot adjourn—What a wretched slave a public man is."[45]

The special session ended on October 16, 1837, and the weary congressmen were free to return home for a brief rest before the regular session met in December. Stanly went to North Carolina to attend the Beaufort County Superior Court.[46] He had voted consistently against Administration measures, but had not delivered a set speech on any subject. As befitted a new and inexperienced congressman, he had kept a curb on his tongue, gaining the floor only to submit his Sub-Treasury resolution and to present memorials and bills from the Invalids Pension Committee.

When Congress reassembled on December 4, Van Buren again urged passage of the Sub-Treasury bill, noting that since the banks had suspended specie payment, the government was already keeping its own funds. Calhoun's specie amendment was stricken out in the Senate to secure Conservative support, the bill passing by a narrow margin with Calhoun in opposition. Even thus modified, it failed in the House by a vote of 111 to 125 (June 25, 1838), the Calhoun men deserting to the Whigs.[47]

In the early days of the session, William Slade, a Vermont abolitionist, stirred up a stormy slavery debate in the House by presenting several abolition petitions and following them up with a withering attack on the South's "peculiar institution." Until 1836, such petitions, praying the abolition of slavery and the slave trade in the District of Columbia, had been referred without serious dissension to the standing Committee on the District. But the increasing number of these petitions had led southern members to urge their exclusion from the House; and in May, 1836, that body adopted the so-called Pinckney "gag rule," providing that "all petitions, memorials, resolutions, propositions or papers relating to the subject of slavery or the abolition of slavery, shall, without being printed or referred, be laid upon the table and that no further action whatever shall be had thereon."[48]

This "gag rule" had not been reenacted when Slade presented his petitions, and Polk upheld his right to the floor despite frequent interruptions by angry Southerners. At a meeting of southern representatives that evening, there was a talk of disunion, while Calhoun called for a convention of the southern states. But more moderate counsels prevailed, and it was decided to enact a more stringent gag rule.[49] On December 21, John Patton of Virginia introduced the following resolution in the House:

> Resolved, that all petitions, memorials, and papers, touching the abolition of slavery, or the buying, selling, or transferring of slaves, in any State, District, or Territory, of the United States, be laid on the table, without being debated, printed, read or referred, and that no further action whatever shall be had thereon.

The rules were suspended to receive the resolution, and it was adopted 122 to 74, Stanly voting with the majority. When John Quincy Adams' name was called, the fiery old man rose and declared, "amidst a perfect war whoop of order": "I hold the resolution to be in violation of the Constitution of the United States."[50] The next day, Stanly wrote Pettigrew, calling his attention to the congressional proceedings on abolition and slavery. Said he: "We out of doors have agreed that the slave holding states appoint one from each, to consult upon what shall be done for our future direction."[51]

In the Senate, Calhoun introduced on December 27, six resolutions defining his position on slavery and the annexation of slaveholding territory. These declared that the states had acted "as free, independent, and sovereign states" in adopting the Constitution; that they retained "exclusive and sole" control of their domestic institutions; that slavery was not to be attacked or interfered with; that the federal government, as the agent of the states, was bound "to resist all attempts by one portion of the Union to use it as an instrument to attack the domestic institutions of another"; that any effort to abolish slavery in the District of Columbia or in the territories would be a "direct and dangerous attack" upon southern institutions; and that to refuse to annex slaveholding territory would, in effect, disfranchise the slaveholding states and prove detrimental to the Union.[52]

The Senate debated Calhoun's resolutions from January 2 to 12,

1838. Most southern senators disapproved of their introduction, but the gaunt South Carolinian went his own way. Stanly termed them an "apple of discord," to disturb the peace and harmony of the whole country. They could do the South no good, he told Pettigrew, "and Patton's resolution, according to the understanding of the southern members, was to settle the matter for the present."[53] The Senate modified the resolutions by striking out the reference to annexation and to the federal government's duty to safeguard state institutions. Even so, they remained a stern admonition to the abolitionists. They passed by large majorities.[54]

In February, 1838, Congress and the nation were electrified by the fatal outcome of a duel between a Maine Democratic represent-ative, Jonathan Cilley, and a Kentucky Whig, William Graves, arising out of a trivial controversy. The two men met on the Marboro Pike, near Washington, with Henry Wise, a Virginia Whig, acting as Graves' second and George Jones, the territorial delegate from Wisconsin, as Cilley's. The duel was fought with rifles at eighty yards, and Cilley fell mortally wounded at the third fire.[55]

The affair was widely denounced, and a select House committee was appointed to investigate the tragedy. Chairman of the com-mittee was Isaac Toucey of Connecticut, a Democrat, as were three of the six other members. On April 21, 1838, the four Democrats submitted a majority report recommending the expulsion of Graves from the House and the censure of Wise and Jones. Toucey moved that the report be printed and that its consideration be postponed for two weeks.[56]

The Whigs saw in this report and motion a Democratic attempt to make party capital out of the duel by blackening the reputation of Wise and Graves. John Quincy Adams declared that the committee had "entirely transcended its powers," since the House had no power to delegate any authority to the committee to try any member. Every member had the privilege to be heard and tried by the House itself. On April 27, Toucey retorted sharply to Adams, insinuating that he had seen his "better days." He considered Adams' attack on the committee to be a greater breach of privilege than had been committed by "those whose hands were imbued in blood"—a patent reference to Wise and Graves.[57]

On the following day, April 28, Stanly gained the floor and condemned Toucey's warm language, particularly in referring to the deed in "sepulchral tones," as that of a man "'embruing [*sic*] his hand in his brother's blood.'" This alone showed that Toucey had exhibited a warmth of feeling that militated against his impartiality as a judge. The committee was a "packed jury," with previously formed opinions, and they had no right to try the men they had arraigned before them. Noting Toucey's allusion to Adams' "better days," Stanly declared he was surprised to hear such language applied to an old man—"to one who had been the First Magistrate of the first nation in the world." What did Toucey mean by his "better days?" Adams' better days were *now*, the days of his old age; "his mind grows stronger . . . as his body decays." He was ready to believe that Toucey's words had escaped him in the heat of debate and that upon reflection he would regret them.[58]

Toucey, however, would not let the matter drop, and he accused Stanly of going out of his way to "interfere" between himself and Adams, who had made a violent attack on the committee; the member from North Carolina, he sneered, "had seen fit to raise his puny voice, and to banish [*sic*] his dagger . . . on this occasion."[59]

When Toucey had taken his seat, Stanly again obtained the floor. He denied any intention to "interfere" between Adams and Toucey—"this modest chairman, who deems himself his match." He had only exercised his privilege of replying to remarks made in House debate, remarks "sprung from a disappointed, malignant ambition, in a committee-room, and . . . nurtured in the bitterness of party spirit." Toucey had seemed to take great offense at the reference to the sepulchral tones of his voice; those "doleful sounds" that had fallen upon Stanly's ear and attracted his attention; very well, he might believe, if he pleased, that he had a nightingale's voice: "I will call him the Connecticut nightingale, and tell him that he has a powerful and melodious voice." Stanly concluded witheringly:

It is in Aesop's fables, if I remember right, that a certain animal, conceiving he had a fine voice, and, like this chairman, proud of it, put on the skin of a noble beast, and by the exertions of a voice (not to be compared with this nightingale's) frightened all the beasts of the forest; they expected he really was a lion ... And ... if this nightingale chairman from ... Connecticut ... will excuse me for the comparison, I was, like the beasts of the forest, disappointed; for all that came from him was 'nothing but voice.' And when he rose to 'notice' me, I thought, from the pompous elevation of his sepulchral voice, I should at least hear a roar; but, if he will excuse me for saying so, I heard only a bray—a melodious bray.[60]

Stanly's severe rejoinder surprised the House. The Washington correspondent of the Baltimore *Patriot* declared that it had been "as pointed and effective" as any heard there for some time: "He speaks in a very low tone, and the members finding from the looks of those around him, he was using edged tools, came down from their seats into the arena and aisle in his vicinity."[61] Another observer reported to the New Bern *Spectator* that "our young countryman" had come down on Toucey "with a bolt of keen, bitter irony and sarcasm, which made his complacent assailant start up from his dream of victory."[62] Stanly boasted that "when I made a *direct* personal attack upon him, he shrunk away like a whipt hound—I think he is better behaved *since*."[63]

The importance of this "Connecticut Nightingale" speech to Stanly's political career was out of all proportion to the issues involved. In an age when keen repartee was inordinately admired, his speech catapulted him out of obscurity, and made him instantly a well known, if not yet prominent, figure in the House. A correspondent of the New Bern *Spectator*, who had been acquainted with Congress for ten years, declared that no young member during that period, "has, by a single effort, placed himself as high as Mr. Stanly has by this complete overthrow of the phlegmatic chairman of the Duelling Committee."[64] Thereafter, Stanly would ever be in the public eye, and would come to enjoy a reputation as one of the "most effective and ready debaters" in the House.[65]

3

THE LITTLE CONQUEROR

AS THE CONGRESSIONAL SESSION neared the end of its sixth month, Stanly became restless and anxious for home. "I wish I was sitting in your porch," he wrote Pettigrew wistfully on May 30, "looking on the 'glad waters' of Lake Phelps and listening to the gentle sighing of the summer breeze, through your sycamores, for a few hours,—how much more delightful than the yelping of these hounds of party." His irritable comments on the Administration were almost venomous. Secretary of the Treasury Levi Woodbury of New Hampshire was "Wood*bug*"—a "poor Devil" who was afraid to resign, and yet knew he would fall into deeper and deeper ruin if he stayed—"Like the ass between the two stacks of fodder,—though he has feathered his nest vastly well, out of Uncle Sam's stack I suspect." The more he thought of "these rascals," the "worse I hate them—and the more I write, the more I have to write about them." To discuss the characters of such men was like shingling an old house, for every old shingle you tore off, there was another which needed mending. [1]

Despite his often expressed desire for the "glad waters" of Lake Phelps, Stanly was already looking ahead to the congressional election of 1839. When he heard there was danger of a split in the Whig ranks in the Third District over the "infernal" Sub-Treasury, he wrote Pettigrew in some alarm that he did not differ more widely with the Nullifiers now, than when first elected; and he could not believe that they would prefer a "Van Buren, whole hog, expunging

. . . Jackson man" to himself. Yet, if they would have a *Whig* sub-treasurer, he was prepared to yield his pretensions, sooner than divide the Whigs and again raise up the Edgecombe supremacy—"to gratify the county pride of a single county, and raise the spirit of Rip Van Winkle over our whole district again."[2]

Upon his return to North Carolina, after the adjournment of Congress in July, Stanly ventured into Edgecombe County, speaking at a militia review in Tarborough on September 29, 1838. He strongly advocated a national bank, arguing for its constitutionality under the provisions to regulate commerce; to coin money and regulate the value thereof, and of foreign coin; and the "necessary and proper" clause. He condemned the Sub-Treasury scheme as "being fraught with innumerable evils," and charged the Jackson and Van Buren administrations with extravagant expenditures. He was answered by Thomas Hall, who argued in favor of the Sub-Treasury and against a national bank. Stanly made a favorable impression on his predominantly Democratic audience; but the *Taboro' Press* expressed the opinion that Edgecombe Democrats could not be induced to forego their hostility to a national bank.[3]

When the Twenty-Fifth Congress assembled for its third and final session on December 3, 1838, the "gag rule" was among the first items of House business. Democratic leaders held a pre-session caucus in Speaker Polk's apartment and carefully drafted a new set of gag resolutions. While denying the Congress the right to interfere with slavery in the states, the resolutions avoided the constitutional question as to the territories or the District of Columbia. Every "petition, memorial, resolution, proposition, or paper, touching or relating in any way" to slavery or its abolition, "on the presentation thereof," was to be laid on the table, without any further action, and "without being debated, printed, or referred."[4]

On December 11, these resolutions were introduced in the House by Charles Atherton of New Hampshire, and by a persistent application of the previous question, were pressed to a vote and passed without debate. Henry A. Wise, Daniel Jenifer of Maryland, and Stanly refused to vote on the resolutions because they yielded the right of petition ("on the presentation thereof") and dodged the question of slavery in the territories and the District of Columbia.

Wise charged that "these are not Southern resolutions, and I repudiate them as such . . . It is a plot sprung upon the South."[5] Stanly tried to state his reasons for wishing to be excused from voting; but Polk directed him to take his seat. "I obeyed," Stanly informed Pettigrew, "but told him, 'I had no doubt, he like the rest, had received his orders from his *master at the palace*, and was bound to obey.'" To avoid any breach of the rules, which required every member to vote who was in his seat, Stanly stood outside the bar while the resolutions were being voted upon.[6]

Stanly was particularly angry because the Atherton Resolutions had been drafted in a secret Democratic caucus from which the Whigs had been excluded. It had been "outrageous, in these scoundrels," he complained to Pettigrew, "to constitute themselves the exclusive guardians of Southern interests"; it had been "mean" of the Van Buren men from the South to exclude their own people from deliberations on such a subject. But they had missed their aim. The objection had instantly been made that Atherton's resolutions yielded the right of petition, as they certainly did. What then could southern men say who had gone into a caucus and admitted that fanatics had the right to petition upon this subject? "They are caught in their own trap, I hope and believe." Some Southerners, he noted, thought it would be better to receive abolition petitions and to report against them in mild yet firm language. This might have been productive of good formerly, but circumstances had changed; they now petitioned for too much:

> They—the North—are proving stronger than we, and the sooner we teach them to let us alone, the better. I think it is our duty and interest to refuse to receive their petitions absolutely; and we can do this, with good argument. The constitution gives the people a right to petition for grievances, but what grievance is it, to a man in New Hamshire [*sic*] or Maine, if I own a thousand slaves?[7]

Stanly attempted to introduce a set of resolutions designed, he said, to supply the omissions in the Atherton "caucus" resolutions. These declared that all attempts on the Congress' part to abolish slavery in the District of Columbia, or in the Territories, or to regulate the internal slave trade, were "in violation of the Constitution, destructive of the fundamental principle on which the Union . . . rests, and beyond the jurisdiction of Congress"; and that, as such, "no petition, memorial, resolution, proposition, or paper touching or relating in any way, or any extent whatever," to slavery or its abolition, "shall be entertained or considered by this House." Polk ordered these resolutions laid on the table without being considered.[8]

These extreme resolutions were, in part, a manifestation of youthful zealousness, but they also reflected Stanly's fear that his constituents would construe his refusal to vote for the Atherton Resolutions as an indication of hostility to slavery. On December 14, in a public letter to the editor of the Washington *National Intelligencer*, he promised the voters of the Third District that in a leisure hour he would fully inform them why he had refused to vote for the resolutions. Said he: "I have good reasons for refusing to join in the miserable farce which has been played by the instruments of party in the house of representatives during Tuesday and Wednesday last."[9]

Stanly's most acrimonious controversy during the session was with Alexander Duncan, a Democratic representative from Ohio. The Democratic press in the southern states was representing the northern Whigs as acting in collusion with the abolitionists to oppose Administration measures. According to the Raleigh *Register*, the chief Whig paper in North Carolina, one Van Buren paper had gone so far "as to assert the imprudent falsehood that 'no Abolitionist was ever the candidate of the Democratic Party.'"[10] When Duncan expressed similar views in a House speech, Stanly gained the floor and read extracts from a recent anti-slavery letter written by Duncan in Ohio. This letter had been handed him on the House floor by William Slade, the Vermont abolitionist. In the letter, Duncan had termed slavery "one of the greatest evils that exists on the face of the earth" and had called down a curse on the heads of those who sustained such an institution. No abolitionist, said Stanly, had ever uttered sentiments of a more venomous malignity; and yet who was Duncan? Why he was the "very personification of locofoco democracy—the 'dear sir' of Amos Kendall and Levi Woodbury—the beloved defender of the measures of Martin Van Buren!" Van Buren professed to be a great friend of the South, but he loved those who abhorred slavery and the abhorrers loved him. Did this not strengthen the already strong evidence that the President was but

> A hovering temporizer that
> Can'st with thine eyes at once see good and evil,
> Inclining to them both?[11]

Duncan, while admitting authorship of the letter, denied he was an abolitionist. Any person or newspaper making such a charge was a "vile calumniator." But he admitted, under Stanly's cross-examination, that he was opposed to the admission of any more slave states into the union and believed in the right of petition on the slavery question. Stanly then told the House that he had succeeded in showing in its true light to the country the character of the Van Buren democratic friendship for the South.[12]

The matter did not end there. Stanly wrote out his remarks and published them in the Washington *National Intelligencer* on February 4, 1839. Duncan then charged in a letter to the Washington *Globe* that the speech as printed had never been delivered in the House, or any other place, except through "the polluted columns of the corrupt, bank bought, servile, and degraded sheet, through which it makes its appearance." He produced affidavits from Democratic representatives testifying that Stanly had not spoken more than fifteen minutes in the House—"a short time in which to make a speech occupying four and a half columns of one of the largest newspaper sheets." Terming the speech a "tissue of misrepresentations, unmanly insinuations, and low vulgarity," Duncan applied such epithets to Stanly as "foul calumniator," "base liar," and "mean poltroon." He charged that he and Slade had been in "*cahoots*" to expose the "dangerous tendencies" of what had been merely an expression of hostility to slavery in the abstract, and its effects, without regard to time or place.[13]

Stanly's Whig colleagues in the House immediately rallied to his defense. On the morning of February 20, the day after Duncan's letter appeared in the *Globe*, Seargent S. Prentiss, Whig of Mississippi, handed Stanly a letter signed by thirteen representatives affirming the correctness of his published remarks in the *National Intelligencer*.[14] Some of the Whigs, led by Prentiss, were prepared to carry the controversy into the House itself. On February 21, Prentiss moved that Duncan be expelled from the House for "grossly indecent, ungentlemanly, disgraceful, and dishonorable conduct," as the author of the letter in the *Globe*. Later he consented to change his resolution to one of censure. The Democrats succeeded in defeating this modified resolution, which was laid on the table by a vote of 117 to 94.[15] Writing Pettigrew from the House while the debate was in progress, Stanly declared that Duncan "has been punished enough," adding later: "the resolution about Duncan is laid on the table—this is probably the best course as it is so late in the Session."[16]

The Whig papers in North Carolina were lavish in their praise of Stanly for the "castigation" he had administered to the "bully of the House," Duncan of Ohio. "Dr. Duncan may take our word for it," declared the Raleigh *Register*, "he will make nothing out of Mr. Stanly, in any way; for . . . he is neither to be run over, rode down, scared off, or *butted* off." The Raleigh *Star* said Stanly was adding new laurels to the high fame he had already acquired in Congress; during the present session, he had exposed the "Atherton Plot against Southern liberty" and literally "used up" the "Abolitionist Van Buren *'howler'*" from Ohio. "The voice of his constituents; the voice of North Carolina is, 'well done good and faithful servant.'" The Whig press thought his remarks evidence enough to satisfy anyone of the vile falsehood propagated by the Van Buren party, of a coalition between the Whigs and the Abolitionists.[17]

Whig ranks in the North Carolina delegation were thinned at this session by the defection of Charles Shepard to the Van Buren party. He distrusted the slavery views of the northern Whigs, thought the South and its institutions in the "greatest danger," and refused to "entangle" himself in party politics. "Let this currency-question be settled to their satisfaction," he warned John H. Bryan in July, 1838, "& a violent crusade will commence against us: Rely on what I say, the South is in jeopardy."[18] By the winter of 1838-39, he had left the Whig for the Democratic ranks, "frightened off," John Quincy Adams remarked sarcastically, "by the bugbear of abolition."[19] Stanly saw him go more in sorrow than in anger, but Shepard was vehemently hostile to his former academy classmate:

"He is a *small* man—more bigoted in politics than any other man at Washington." Part of his dislike stemmed from Stanly's friendship for John Quincy Adams.[20]

On January 10, 1839, Stanly clashed with Shepard during a debate in the House on a bill for the construction of a dry dock and other improvements at the Brooklyn (N.Y.) Navy Yard. Shepard, who had the floor, declared that for every thousand dollars appropriated for internal improvements in the South, one hundred thousand was appropriated for the North; when appropriations were to be made, all parties in that section went "in mass, in solid column." Stanly took exception to the remarks of his colleague, "now emphatically on the other side"; they were in bad taste from a man who had once entertained more liberal views. He for one disapproved of this "eternal thundering" from certain southern members against what they pleased to call the "miserable local appropriations" of the North. It was probably true that northern congressmen were more attentive to their section's interests and understood "ciphering" better than their southern brethren, but justice must be done them. "As far as my experience goes," said Stanly, "I have never known any Northern man to oppose any appropriation for the Southern country, because it was for the Southern country."

Why then did the South have so little public money expended for its advantage? It had been the policy of many southern "economical Democrats," not only to refuse to ask for any appropriations, but to refuse to take them when they were offered. One might admire this class of politicians who opposed federal improvements within their states on constitutional grounds; "but then it comes with an ill grace from us to censure others for the consequences of our own conduct." Stanly concluded this remarkable speech with his most statesmanlike remarks of the session:

> Mr. Chairman, I am a Southern man. I thank my God that I am. Next to learning the Lord's prayer and the ten commandments, I was taught to venerate the character, protect the interests, and defend the honor of North Carolina. I still cherish the recollections of these early lessons. They 'grow with my growth, and strengthen with my strength.' And, sir, I regard it as a duty I owe to my State and my country to avoid creating sectional feelings. In doing so, we forget the advice of

the Father of his country, and the dignity which becomes the Representatives of sovereign States.[21]

Here Stanly revealed that despite his occasional gasconading on the slavery question his views on internal improvements at federal expense were those of a nationalistic Whig. He deprecated sectional feelings and was ready to concede the North's fairness on the matter of appropriations. Nor was he loath to accept federal funds for improvements in his own district. At the previous session, he had secured $5,000 for the removal of a sand shoal in the Pamlico River near Washington. He had also introduced a resolution requesting the Committee on Roads and Canals to investigate the building of a canal to connect the waters of Albemarle Sound with the Atlantic Ocean.[22]

In the spring of 1839, Stanly was heartily endorsed for reelection to the Twenty-Sixth Congress by Whig meetings in his district. Resolutions declared him to be "decidedly at the head of the North Carolina delegation" (Hyde County) and "in the ranks of the foremost men of the country" (Pitt County). The Whigs of Beaufort County expressed their approval of his fearless independence "in unmasking democratic abolitionists." "The great body of the people of the district are with him," said the Washington *Whig*; "a number of gentlemen opposed to his political creed are also with him, because they admire the consistency, stern integrity, and lofty independence of the man. The efforts, therefore, of the opposition to defeat the reelection of a gentleman who is worthy of their support will be utterly unavailing."[23]

Democratic delegates from Edgecombe, Pitt, and Beaufort met in Washington on April 15 and nominated William L. Kennedy of Beaufort for Congress. The Raleigh *Register* sarcastically proclaimed it an "excellent nomination for *defeat*." Kennedy, however, declined to run, and the *Tarboro' Press* issued a call for "A TRUE REPUBLICAN" to take the field against Stanly. On May 1, a Democratic meeting in Washington unanimously nominated "the *old Republican wheel-horse*" Doctor Thomas H. Hall. In accepting the nomination, Hall gave his unqualified endorsement to the "Constitutional Treasury," as the Democrats termed the Sub-Treasury scheme. The Washington *Republican* defined the "*true issue*" of the campaign to its own satisfaction when it asked the people of the Third District if they were prepared to be governed by "that Arch Apostate, *Henry Clay*," with his "fifty million Northern Bank," to be "'hewers of wood, and drawers of water'" for northern money-kings and task-masters. "The Federal Whigs are for a National Bank; the Republicans are for a Constitutional Treasury. *That is the true issue*."[24]

On his part, Stanly waged a vigorous stump campaign all over the district, even going into Edgecombe to deliver a speech at Tarborough in late May. His remarks on this occasion infuriated the Democratic faithful. The *Tarboro' Press* hotly charged that during his speech he had "pompously claimed" that he came to Edgecombe "not . . . as a supplicant, but in the spirit of a Conqueror."[25] The Whigs, in turn, accused the *Tarboro' Press* and the Washington *Republican* of misrepresenting Stanly's remarks to injure him with the people. Stanly gave his own account of the incident to Pettigrew:

> The remark at which they were offended was this. I told them, I came there out of respect to them, and from self respect. I came not as a supplicant begging them for votes, that I was assured already of success. I came more in the spirit of one certain he would conquer, and not in the spirit of a supplicant. This intimation to their own faces, that their power was at naught enraged them furiously.[26]

The North Carolina Democratic press assailed Stanly for his refusal to support the Atherton Resolutions; he had opposed them in order that his party might avail itself of abolitionist numbers to carry out their political designs and to seize political ascendency. "A Countryman," writing in the *Tarboro' Press*, declared that Stanly, though perhaps detesting the abolitionists in his heart, had made himself "the ardent apologist" of dangerous and murderous fanatics, who were using all means to carry fire, desolation, and ruin into the peaceful abodes of the southern people. Another Democratic letter-writer proclaimed Stanly "the little favorite of the two great chiefs of the 'negro party' in Congress, Adams and Slade."[27] The object of this abuse wrote Pettigrew in some amazement that the Democrats did not charge him with any neglect of duty, breach of promise, or change of opinions—"the only charge yet brought forward is—you did not vote for Atherton's resolutions (which I am proud of)—and therefore say the Edgecombe 'wheelhorses'—you are an Abolitionist!"[28]

The campaign grew even hotter in the last weeks as both sides sought to rally their full strength to the polls. In urging Pettigrew to "bring out the people" in the lower counties, Stanly asserted "that no man was ever more bitterly opposed by the party in and out of the district than I am."[29] Pettigrew, finding that Hall was "making head" in Tyrrell, took the stump against him at Cool Springs and Columbus. "I have never known such exertions made before as has been for the van candidate," he wrote a friend, "such lying is monstrous, among them such as this, that I had gone over to Dr. Hall and would carry over 250 votes in my section, which I had to contradict with all dispatch that it might not have its effect in distant parts of the district."[30]

Election day in the district was July 25, except in Tyrrell, where the polls opened on August 1. Both parties brought their voters to the polling places amidst great enthusiasm. Wilson B. Hodges wrote Pettigrew that he had been at a great many elections, but had never before witnessed such a warmly contested one as at Germanton in Hyde County:

> I got in the Village early in the morning. Two handsome flags, with Stanly and Liberty hoisted—a fine dinner was prepared, and a plenty of the *ardent* set out—(we *the people* of Hyde, would not suffer the little 'conquorer' [*sic*] to be at any expense.) After the Polls were opened, the Hall gentry began to rave curse and threaten. I took my station at the ballot box—determined to see that there was no foul play. I kept my station until the Poll was closed. The patent democrats were routed—they beat a retreat; and a considerable number of them were found lying along the road—while the friends of Stanly returned to their homes rejoicing.[31]

One Stanly partisan had predicted before the election that his majority in the Third District would be five hundred votes, and the returns bore him out.[32] Stanly carried every county in the District except Edgecombe (which went heavily for Hall) and received a majority of exactly 500 votes, 3,058 to 2,558.[33] The Third District voted earlier than the other congressional districts; and as soon as

Stanly's victory was assured, word was sent to Raleigh, so that the Whigs elsewhere might take heart. The Raleigh *Register* issued an extra on July 31, proclaiming Stanly's victory "THE FIRST GUN!" in the North Carolina elections. It noted that the most vigorous and determined efforts to defeat him had been made by the administration party in his district, but in vain. "THE PEOPLE HAVE SUSTAINED HIM. Whigs of the whole State, take counsel from their example, and victory is ensured."[34]

Even in distant New England, Stanly's victory occasioned rejoicing. The Boston *Atlas*, spokesman of New England Whiggery, reported that the success of the "intrepid, gallant and high-minded Stanly" had been received by Boston Whigs "with feelings of no ordinary exultation." Hundreds of inquiries had been made, "and the anxiety with which the question was put showed how strong was the apprehension that government influence had been too powerful for him to overthrow." The *Atlas* thought North Carolina Whigs would be happy to learn that there was a kindling glow of patriotic sympathy with their success pervading the bosom of every Whig in New England.[35]

In North Carolina, Whig rejoicing was considerably muted by the party's failure to make anticipated gains in the other congressional districts. The most bitter disappointment was the victory of Charles Shepard, as a Democrat, over Samuel S. Biddle of New Bern. The Whigs had spared no expense or effort to defeat him, and news of his election fell on them "as a showerbath in December."[36] Over all, North Carolina elected five Whigs and eight Democrats to the Twenty-Sixth Congress. "To say that we are not disappointed at this result would be disingenous and untrue," the Raleigh *Register* admitted. The Whigs had expected better things, and had a right to expect them.[37]

Despite the generally unfavorable result in the state as a whole, Stanly could take solid pride in his reelection. His margin of victory, while less than in 1837, had been gained against the most desperate opposition.[38] The voters had approved his congressional course. In only two years, the "little Conqueror" had become one of the brightest new stars in the Whig firmament. At the age of twenty-nine, he could reasonably look forward to a long political career, with even higher office as the reward for talents and diligent service to his party.

4

ON, STANLY, ON!

ON DECEMBER 4, 1839, a "Democratic Whig National Convention" assembled in Harrisburg, Pennsylvania, to select a standard bearer for the 1840 presidential campaign. Henry Clay, General Winfield Scott of the regular army, and General William Henry Harrison of Ohio were the leading contenders for the nomination. The popular Clay had a plurality of the delegates, but they were largely from states which were not likely to vote for any Whig candidate. Certain party leaders, notably the wily Thurlow Weed of New York, believed that he lacked "availability" because of his firm stand on public questions about which Whigs disagreed. For this reason it would be difficult for the diverse elements in the party to unite on him. The delegates from Pennsylvania, Ohio, and Indiana said flatly, "We can carry our States for General Harrison, but not for Mr. Clay."[1] Accordingly, the Kentuckian was passed over by the convention in favor of Harrison, an elderly and amicable military hero of the War of 1812 who had few political enemies and had run well in 1836. To balance the ticket and conciliate the disgruntled Clay men, John Tyler of Virginia was persuaded to accept the nomination for Vice-President. A state rights Whig, he was popular with southern members of the party and had worked hard for Clay's nomination.

Clay's southern supporters were sorely disappointed at his defeat. They believed that Harrison was unsound on the slavery question and that his nomination would result in the Whig Party's rout in the

South. Governor James Barbour of Virginia, who presided with great dignity over the convention, lamented: "We shall be defeated, in all probability, but we must stand it. There is not much hope for us; we shall have to take the thrashing after all our trouble."[2] Efforts were made during the last hours of the convention to awaken some enthusiasm for the ticket. "But the deep mortification of the friends of Mr. Clay rendered those efforts but partially successful," wrote Thurlow Weed. "The delegates separated, less sanguine than usual of a united and zealous effort to elect the ticket."[3]

In North Carolina, the Raleigh *Register* confessed that nine-tenth's of the Raleigh Whigs had been disappointed, if not dissatisfied, at the General's selection. "We had set our hearts upon the elevation of that 'noblest Roman of them all'–HENRY CLAY." But upon mature reflection, the *Register* had decided that the nomination was a judicious one, "and promised a surer guarantee of success than any other would have done." It predicted North Carolina Whigs would go for the cause and not the man and zealously sustain the nomination.[4]

Seeing the enthusiasm that Harrison's name aroused among the people, southern Whigs were soon actively campaigning for "Tippecanoe, and Tyler too!" Many years later, Henry W. Hilliard of Alabama recalled that from the evening hour in Harrisburg when a flag bearing a portrait of General Harrison, "in full uniform, surrounded by the insignia of war," was displayed to a cheering crowd, "I caught the inspiration of coming victory; I recognized in the heroic face of General Harrison a leader who would be followed by a great and generous people, who would bear his standard with resistless ardor to a splendid triumph. From that hour, throughout the wonderful canvass that followed, I never swerved from his support, and never lost heart. Young, ardent, and fearless, with full faith in the Whig cause, I did not believe defeat possible."[5]

Stanly was one of the first Clay men in the South to "break ground" for Harrison in Congress. On December 21, he declared in the House that the General's candidacy would be "like wildfire in the prairies–it would advance and extend until it embraced the great portion of the Union in its influence." Turning to the Democratic members in the chamber, he called on them to "'Mourn, sinners, mourn'; your time is at hand, and if you do not retrench and reform, an abused and insulted people will soon call you to account."[6]

In the House, when it assembled on December 2, 1839, were 119 Democrats and 118 Whigs. Five New Jersey Whigs held certificates from the governor of that state, but their seats were contested by Democrats, and they were not allowed to vote for the Speaker. The Democrats at first generally supported John W. Jones of Virginia and the Whigs, John Bell of Tennessee; when neither man could muster a majority, the nod went to Robert M. T. Hunter of Virginia on the eleventh ballot. Although a Democrat, Hunter's "moderate Whiggish proclivities" made him acceptable to that party. In organizing committees, Hunter gave the Democrats a majority where the committees were connected with the executive departments, and the Whigs a majority where the committees were investigatory in character. Stanly was appointed chairman of the Committee on Expenditures on the Public Buildings.[7]

On January 28, the House added the so-called "21st rule" to its standing rules, by a vote of 114 to 108. Sponsored by a Maryland Whig, William Cost Johnson, it declared against the *reception* of abolition petitions, thus meeting one of Stanly's objections to the Atherton Resolutions. Johnson wanted to test the northern Democrats to see to what extent they would follow southern Whig leadership. The Washington *Globe* interpreted his move as designed to help Harrison in the South and to embarrass northern Democrats, but expressed satisfaction that enough of the latter (twenty-seven members) went with southern Whigs and Democrats to adopt the rule and thus defeat Johnson's strategy.[8]

During debate on this "gag," Polk's successor, Harvey Watterson, made his maiden speech, "the drift of which," according to John Quincy Adams, "was that the Whigs of the South were all abolitionists, and the Administration party of the North all against them."[9] Stanly had heard *that* story before, and struck back with a familiar weapon. He charged that Representatives Henry Williams and William Parmenter of Massachusetts and Marcus Morton, recently elected governor of that state, were all "Van Buren abolitionists," and read extracts from their "abolition letters" to prove his contention. Parmenter, who was present, objected that in reference to Morton, Stanly had failed to draw a distinction between anti-slavery and abolitionism—one was "a mere opinion—a senti-ment"; the other the policy of a party that was ready to carry its measures against the Constitution. Morton was an anti-slavery man, but not an abolitionist. Stanly then asked Parmenter if *he* was an abolitionist, and Parmenter said no. Very well, Stanly replied, let the Speaker and the advocates of the humbug Atherton resolutions read the letters of these "'anti-slavery' men," these "true Van Buren men," and then tell him what *they* thought of the distinction. The gentleman would be famous for the clearness of his distinctions. "He will deserve to have it said of him—'He could distinguish and divide, a hair, 'twixt south and southwest side.'" Stanly would send these definitions to his constituents and let them judge of their sin-cerity.[10]

Because Harrison was on record as favoring a federal appropria-tion to secure emancipation through colonization, Southerners distrusted his views on slavery. "General Harrison's sentiments were understood to be hostile to slavery," Henry W. Hilliard remembered, and "it was supposed that he had sympathized with those who favored emancipation in Virginia, his native State, some years previously . . . He had been for years a resident of Ohio, a State that already exhibited a tendency to encourage the growth of free-soil ideas."[11] Yet a lengthy defense could be made of the old General's anti-abolitionist speeches at Cheviot, Ohio (July 4, 1833) and Vincennes, Indiana (May 25, 1835). At Vincennes, he had termed the abolitionist measures "weak, presumptuous, and unconstitutional," and had declared that even the right of petition was unjustified as used by the abolitionists.[12]

At one time Stanly was among those who feared that the General was under abolitionist influence, but he was "gratified to find" that they were "bitterly opposed to him."[13] On April 13, 1840, during debate on the Civil and Diplomatic Appropriation bill, Stanly gained the floor to deliver a major speech defending Harrison against the charge of abolitionism. He quoted from abolitionist papers to show that his nomination had met with their "decided and irreconcilable hostility," and defied any Van Buren men in the House to produce evidence to the contrary. He reminded his audience of Alexander

Duncan's 1838 anti-slavery letter and "deeply scored" Benjamin Tappan, the "Van Buren Senator from Ohio," who was reported to have expressed a willingness to give $500 "to purchase arms and ammunition to put in the hands of the blacks that they might free themselves." Stanly then reviewed Harrison's record on the slavery question, quoting extracts from his Cheviot and Vincennes speeches. He was willing to regard his opinions in these speeches as being his opinions now. Abolitionists who were determined to oppose Harrison regarded his "'infamous'" Vincennes speech as the Whig Party's ultimatum on the subject of abolition. He, for one, had no objection to this.

Stanly held Van Buren responsible for the agitation of the slavery question. His official organ, the Washington *Globe*, incessantly tried to excite the South upon this subject and spared no pains to create sectional differences. If the President thought there was any danger, why did he not speak out against the abolitionists as Harrison had done at Cheviot and Vincennes? Stanly himself had never apprehended any danger from them, and had always told his constituents so. "I believe a large majority of our Northern people are devotedly attached to our glorious Union; I believe a large majority are disposed to protect our constitutional rights; I *know* they are. The subject gives me an uneasiness. The people cannot always be duped."[14]

The election of 1840 has gone down in history as the "log-cabin, hard cider" campaign. An unlucky sneer in a Democratic paper that Harrison would be content with a $2,000 pension, a log cabin, and a barrel of hard cider was seized upon by the Whigs who represented General Harrison as the "log-cabin" candidate, the common man's friend. In contrast to this rustic life, "Sweet Sandy Whiskers," as the Whigs derisively dubbed Van Buren, was depicted as living in great splendor, dining from massive plate and crystal goblets, and all at the taxpayer's expense! The worst example of this foolishness was a speech delivered in the House by Charles Ogle of Pennsylvania. Entitled, "The Royal Splendor of the President's Palace," it was widely reprinted and served as a campaign textbook for Whig orators.

During a House debate on the expediency of abolishing the

branch mints at Charlotte, North Carolina, Dahlonaga, Georgia, and New Orleans, Louisiana, Stanly did a little "Ogleing" of his own, charging that John H. Wheeler, a Democrat and Superintendent of the Charlotte mint, had purchased in November, 1838, with public funds, "218 dollars worth of trees and flowers for the branch mint," including such exotic varieties as the *Morus Multicaulis*, the *Chacorus Japonica*, and the *Lonicera Fluxuosa*. He moved to reduce Wheeler's salary to not more than $1,500, since he had "wasted the public money, and been more anxious to secure his own comfort then to serve his country."[15] According to John Quincy Adams, Stanly's bill for the flowers and trees "caused great discomfiture in the ranks of the Administration Democracy."[16]

In May, Stanly and some of the other Whig "*young men*" in the House journeyed to Baltimore to attend a "Whig Young Men's Convention," called to ratify the Harrisburg nominations and stir up enthusiasm for the campaign. On May 4, the jubilant Whigs held a great parade, complete with bands, banners, log cabins, cider barrels, and raccoons, symbols all of resurgent Whiggery. James Graham reported there were "about *Twenty thousand Gentlemen* marching in one line of Procession with Banners and Badges and Motto's indicating the States, Districts & principles of those whose divisions marched under them." The North Carolina delegation bore a banner of the arms of the State, upon which was the motto, "On, Stanly, on!" Stanly was one of the Whig leaders who spoke to a huge crowd in Monument Square on May 5, and "after a stirring address of an hour," the cry was again "On, Stanly, on!"[17]

During the spring and summer of 1840, Stanly, as a member of the Whig Central Committee in Washington, franked thousands of Whig campaign documents for distribution in the southern states. The Huntsville (Alabama) *Democrat* complained that he had "literally flooded the whole South with his incendiary documents." No less than a thousand of his franks had reached a single county in Mississippi! He had scattered them also throughout Alabama; and even in Huntsville, his friends were supplied with large numbers.[18] Of course Stanly had another view of the matter, writing Pettigrew that he was "trying to supply Van Buren districts with a little light." The labor of franking was immense and his correspondence very heavy. He had no doubt of Harrison's election, although the Whigs faced a hard fight. "The spoilers are fighting for life, and for bread."[19]

In 1807, Harrison, as Governor of Indiana Territory, had approved a law which provided that any person convicted of a minor offense, if unable to pay the fine and court costs, could be hired out to service to any person who would pay the fine and costs, for such time as the court deemed reasonable. On June 8, 1840, two Democratic representatives from North Carolina, William Montgomery and Micajah T. Hawkins, issued a circular accusing Harrison, under this law, with approving the sale of poor but respectable white men and women as slaves to free Negroes. Four North Carolina Whig congressmen, Stanly, Lewis Williams, Edmund Deberry, and Kenneth Rayner, replied with a circular, drawn up by Stanly, in which they charged Montgomery and Hawkins with misrepresenting the facts by leaving out that section of the law which specifically forbade a Negro, mulatto, or Indian to purchase a servant "other than their own complexion." Montgomery and Hawkins then admitted their error in a second circular.[20]

The Whigs, in turn, made much of the fact that in 1839 one George Mason Hooe, a Lieutenant in the United States Navy, had been court-martialed and convicted, in part upon the testimony of two free Negroes. Hooe had appealed to the President, calling attention to the Negro testimony, but Van Buren had refused to interfere with the court's action. The Whigs declared that the President had been "*fishing for Abolitionists* with abolition *Bate* [*sic*]" and raised the cry "No Negro Testimony!" Stanly's June circular urged the "log cabin men" to come to their country's rescue and "save us from the disgrace of being punished by the testimony of negro servants."[21] This kind of demagoguery on the touchy slavery question was all too common on both sides during the campaign.

Congress adjourned on July 21 after a seven-month session in which the presidential election had overshadowed every other question. Despite the confusion and jockeying for political advantage, the Administration at last succeeded in driving the Independent Treasury bill through both houses. Van Buren signed the measure into law on July 5. The editor of the Washington *Globe*, Francis Preston Blair, joyously hailed the bill as a second Declaration of Independence.[22]

Great Whig rallies were a prominent feature of the Harrison campaign. The most eloquent Whig orators in the country were asked to address these meetings and traveled from point to point. Such "Whig champions of the Old South" as Stanly, Seargent S. Prentiss of Mississippi, Hugh Swinton Legaré and William C. Preston of South Carolina, and Henry Wise and William C. Rives of Virginia, were much in demand in the northern states, to emphasize Whig solidarity behind "Old Tippecanoe." After Congress adjourned, Stanly, accompanied by his wife Julia, took the stump in New York State and spent two days with the young Whig governor, William H. Seward. "Few persons, entire strangers to each other, have so great curiosity concerning one another," Seward wrote later of this visit. "Mr. Stanley [*sic*] and I had each been assured that the other was his counterpart in person. For myself, I was quite desirous to see how I did look, since my unfortunate person had brought me so many ungrateful attentions, in opposition newspapers and speeches."[23] According to Seward's son, Frederick, mutual acquaintances saw a striking resemblance between the two men at the time:

> Stanley [*sic*] was about the same height, of rather slighter frame, with hair and features resembling Seward's....This resemblance grew less marked in later years though both had the same genial manner and winning address, and their views on political questions corresponded more nearly than was usual at that time among the Whigs of the North and those of the South.[24]

Stanly and Seward became good friends, and remained so for the rest of their lives. The New Yorker would later describe Stanly as "an agreeable and excellent man, modest and moderate in his aspirations."[25] They were destined to act together more than once in times of crisis.

In the last month before the election, Stanly went to North Carolina to aid the Whig cause there. The state elections in August had resulted in a Whig victory, with John Motley Morehead of

Guilford elected governor by a margin of 8,581 votes over his opponent, Romulus Saunders. A Whig legislature was also chosen. Although defeated, the Democrats did not slacken their efforts, and Saunders remained on the stump until November. The Whig state campaign against Van Buren followed the national pattern. In Raleigh, a huge log cabin was erected, called Harrison Hall, where the Tippecanoe Club held semi-weekly meetings; smaller "log-cabins" were erected in towns throughout the state. General Harrison was lauded as the simple "Farmer of North Bend," while the President was denounced as a heartless aristocrat. As evidence of Van Buren's unfitness for office, Charles Manly, in a debate with Saunders, made three damning charges against the President: "1, with riding in a splendid carriage drawn by four houses; 2, with sending to the post office for his mail instead of walking to get it himself; and 3, with wearing silk stocking."[26]

To keep up interest in the campaign, the Whigs held a convention in Raleigh on October 5, with delegates present from all parts of the state. The Third District Whigs had appropriate banners and badges; the Beaufort County group wore a handsome badge with the words "Stanly's Home" on it. "Pettigrew cleared the way," said the Pitt County banner, "Stanly keeps it open. On, Stanly, on!" John Owen presided over the meeting and ten prominent North Carolina Whigs made speeches, including Stanly, Daniel M. Barringer, George E. Badger, Lewis Williams, and Kenneth Rayner. Stanly spoke twice, at the beginning of the convention and again, by popular request, immediately before its adjournment, when he delivered what the Raleigh *Star* called "one of the most eloquent and effective speeches we have heard on any occasion."[27]

Learning that Stanly had accepted an invitation from the "spartan band" of Wayne County Whigs to visit them on October 29, the Craven County Tippecanoe Club invited him to address the citizens of New Bern on October 26. Stanly accepted and spoke for nearly *four hours* before a large audience in the Courthouse. He had been present earlier in the day when the apostate Whig, Charles Shepard, addressed his "new democratic allies" and had taken notes of his speech; and, said the *New Bern Spectator*, "the way he 'used it up' should be a caution to all public men who have no fixed political principles." Shepard himself had been present during the "dissection." The *Spectator* declared that it had never seen more delight manifested, then appeared among Stanly's audience as he spoke:

> But a few years ago, he left this, his native town, little more than a mere boy, either in age or worldly experience. Now he comes amongst us *a man* in every sense of the word—a patriot—a most prominent and able defender of our country's laws and liberties—and one of the most fearless and efficient opponents of governmental tyranny, corruption and misrule![28]

The local boy had made good, at least by Whig standards!

A Philadelphia Whig wrote Stanly just before the election that Pennsylvania was *"safe"* for Harrison and would give him up to a six thousand majority.[29] In fact, not only the Keystone State but the national election as well was "safe" for the old General. He carried nineteen of twenty-six states, including seven southern states, and every northern state except New Hampshire and Illinois. North Carolina went for Harrison by a 13,141 majority. His popular majority, however, was only 146,843 out of 2,408,630 votes cast. The anti-slavery Liberty Party, making its first appearance in a national election, polled 6,225 votes for James G. Birney, a former slaveholder.[30]

After the presidential election, North Carolina Whigs again turned their attention to state politics. The Whig majority in the General Assembly had the pleasant task of selecting two United States senators to replace Democrats Bedford Brown and Robert Strange, who had resigned their seats after a conflict with the legislature over the instruction issue. Two factions existed within the Whig Party in the state and each had several favorites for the two places. The "Federal Whigs" supported William Gaston, George E. Badger, Lewis Williams, John H. Bryan, and William A. Graham, while the "Republican Whigs" favored former senator Willie P. Mangum, William B. Shepard, and former governors John Owen and Edward Dudley. "So far as definite action was demanded, the Federal Whigs wished support of the United States Bank made a test, while the Republican Whigs thought the senators should be left free to act as the occasion seemed to demand."[31]

There was not much question that Mangum would be elected to the long term and for the remainder of Brown's term, since the Whigs believed their victory would not be complete until he was restored to his seat. Mangum had resigned from the Senate on November 24, 1836, in a controversy with the Democratic legislature, who had earlier instructed him to vote for a motion expunging the resolution of censure against Jackson for removing the deposits. William Gaston could have had the second seat for the asking, but preferred to remain on the state bench.[32]

George Edmund Badger, a favorite with the Federal Whigs because of his genial manners and great legal ability, was a maternal first cousin of John Stanly. Born in New Bern in 1796, he had attended Yale for two years and then returned home to study law under Stanly. By inheritance and temperament a Federalist, he supported Jackson in 1828, and was mentioned for a cabinet post. Joining the Whig Party, he emerged from political retirement in 1840 to campaign for Harrison, and his powerful services had placed the party in his debt. A rival for the Senate seat, William B. Shepard of Camden County, wrote Ebenezer Pettigrew that Badger was making "great exertions to be chosen & I suppose will endeavor through his relative Stanly to procure the votes of the members from this district." Shepard complained that his brother Charles' political course was used against him, "as if I could control it or had anything to do with it. And I have no doubt from what I have heard [that] Stanly would take great pleasure in defeating me."[33]

When the General Assembly met, the Whig members held a caucus to reach agreement on the two Senate seats. After much sharp discussion and many meetings, it became apparent that neither Shepard nor Badger could be chosen. The caucus then endorsed William A. Graham for the short term and Mangum for the long term; and they were easily elected over Strange and Brown. The Whigs generally accepted these elections, although there was some grumbling, particularly in the East, because both senators were from Orange County.[34]

North Carolina Whigs were very anxious to place one of their number in the Harrison cabinet to "give the state some character abroad," and the Whig legislative caucus recommended Badger for

Attorney General. Stanly wrote David L. Swain that North Carolina might secure a place, "if our friends do not differ as to the man. If they do, she will not have a cabinet office, I think."[35] In January, 1841, it was rumored in Washington that Stanly himself would be Secretary of the Navy. A correspondent of the Harrisburg *Daily Telegraph* noted that he had been the first southern man to break ground for Harrison in Congress and was favorably known throughout the country for his fearless and successful exposure of the corruption and profligacy of the Van Buren administration. The objection had been raised that he was a young man, but, said the correspondent, "he is nevertheless a discreet one, and has proved himself a useful one; and youth is a fault unlike many others, which mends every day."[36]

By the time Harrison reached Washington on February 9, the cabinet was complete with the exception of the Navy portfolio, which he promised to whomever the delegations from the South Atlantic states could agree upon. A series of stormy caucuses followed, "until, on the morning of February 12, Stanly . . . finally brought about the selection of his relative, George Badger, who had been mentioned for the place only the day or two preceding."[37] The North Carolina delegation, excepting Stanly, had first nominated former governor John Owen for the Navy Department. However, members from other states assailed him as an inferior man, and Harrison intimated he would prefer Badger. They therefore joined in recommending him. There was no serious expectation of Stanly's own appointment, although his wife Julia had "set her heart upon it."[38]

Badger was reluctant to accept the Navy portfolio, fearing that "honest motives & ill assured exertions" would prove inadequate to the task. He wrote William A. Graham that Stanly's nomination would have been "a very good one," and would have been welcomed by the Whigs of the Old North State. The "notion about *age*" he did not regard as a matter worthy of attention. "He who has passed thirty is fit for most things for which he is likely to be. But that is, I suppose, out of the question."[39] Badger's objections were overcome, and contrary to his early fears, he found the Navy post to his liking. "Sec. Badger is quite devoted to his Department," Graham observed in June, 1841, "and I think he gives general satisfaction."[40]

The second session of the Twenty-Sixth Congress, which began on December 7, 1840, and lasted until March 3, 1841, was largely empty of accomplishment. The Democrats were disheartened by their recent defeat, while the Whigs wished to mark time until Harrison's inauguration. On December 9, John Quincy Adams made another foray against the "gag" by moving to rescind the 21st rule. His motion was tabled by a vote of eighty-two to fifty-eight, Stanly voting with the majority. A Whig effort to repeal the Independent Treasury Act failed in the House, seventy-nine to eighty-seven.[41]

The Administration did introduce a bill authorizing the government to issue $5,000,000 in interest-bearing treasury notes to relieve its financial distress. Many Whigs, among them Stanly, favored tariff legislation as a more permanent and effective remedy. On January 19, 1841, he gave notice that when in order he would move to amend the treasury note bill by placing duties ranging from ten to twenty percent ad valorem on a variety of milk goods, wines, and bleached and unbleached linens, "the foregoing duties being in accordance with the terms and spirit" of the Compromise of 1833. However, Stanly was absent from the House on February 5 when the bill came up for its third reading and his amendment was withdrawn, the bill passing under a rigorous application of the previous question.[42]

At an evening session of February 18, during debate on the General Appropriation bill, Stanly gained the floor and announced he would say something about the tariff—a word which caused certain southern gentlemen "to start from their seats with affected dismay, as if they beheld some spirit bringing 'blasts from hell,' which were to desolate their country." He argued at length in favor of laying duties on luxuries to meet necessary government expenses, contending that such duties would not constitute a violation of the Tariff of 1833. He denied that the compromise of that year had abandoned the principle of protection, and made it plain that the word *protection* held no terrors for him. A tariff would protect southern commerce and agriculture as well as northern manufactures; and should the day come when Texas or Indian cotton threatened southern markets in the North, he thought it "very probable the South would not very strongly object to a little protection." The time might also come, as he hoped it would, when North Carolina, having turned to manufacturing, would demand protection from the government. And when that time arrived; yes, before then, if any great branch of American industry required protection, he would not be deterred from supporting its claims by any fear of the measure's unpopularity.[43]

In connection with his remarks on the tariff, Stanly had an exchange with Robert Barnwell Rhett, a "Hotspur politician" from South Carolina, who was the advocate of an alternate revenue proposal, "direct taxation." Stanly now charged that this scheme was only advocated by "those . . . who have advocated or do advocate a dissolution of the Union." When challenged by Rhett, Stanly retreated slightly; he would not charge the South Carolinian and his friends with "wantonly" desiring to dissolve the Union, but they were advocating opinions which must inevitably lead to disunion if they were received favorably by any respectable portion of the country. What did Rhett mean by saying his constituents would not "submit" to a protective tariff? What if Congress refused to heed such threats?

Rhett dodged by asking Stanly what *he* would do if Congress passed an unconstitutional law which was unequal and unjust in its operations. The latter replied without hesitation that he would abide by the decision of the Supreme Court. "I should hold myself unworthy a seat on this floor if I impudently endeavored to excite civil war because my opinion upon a constitutional question was overruled by a majority of Congress and by the Supreme Court of the United States."[44]

Stanly then read several resolutions of the South Carolina legislature denying the constitutionality of the protective tariff and warning that when such a case occurred, "the several States will decide for themselves the mode and measures of redress." Terming these resolutions "the most insolent" ever presented to Congress, he declared that they should have been treated like abolition petitions and rejected without being read or referred. The people of South Carolina were as high-minded, brave, and patriotic as any other people, but they did not possess any peculiar virtues which made them superior to citizens of the other states.[45]

In concluding this remarkable address, Stanly urged that the proceeds from public land sales be given to the states for schools and internal improvements. Let every man learn to read his Bible "and the farewell address of the Father of his country." As for his own state, which had never been shaken in her attachment to her sister states, he wished to make her like New York in internal improvements; like Massachusetts and Connecticut in schools and charitable institutions. "I wish her to imitate her sister states in this exhibition of true Yankee feeling and spirit; the true American spirit which in war shows itself at the point of a bayonet, not in words; in peace, in cultivating the arts and promoting the good of the whole people."[46]

Stanly's tariff speech, with its plea for "Union and Progress," and contempt for disunion, was the most important statement to date of his ardent nationalism.[47] But as he must have anticipated, his gibes at the proud Palmetto State infuriated her House delegation.[48] The next morning, Francis Pickens of South Carolina alluded to Stanly's speech and sneered that he had shot his "dreaded arrows" at the state with about as much effect as the savage who let fly his arrows at the sun. Stanly's course reminded him of the nursery rhyme: rhyme:

> "Who shot cock robin?
> I, said the *sparrow*,
> With *my* bow and arrow,
> I shot cock robin."

Stanly retorted sharply that "as a sparrow from North Carolina," he was able, anywhere, "to put down a dozen such cock robins" as Pickens. "Come one, come all, ye South Carolina cock robins, if you dare; I am ready for you," he taunted. Pickens, stung, wrote out a challenge, but friends interposed and averted a possible tragedy.[49] John Quincy Adams, returning that afternoon to the House chamber, found George Evans of Maine "cooling down" the two men. "They finally agreed to consider it on both sides as *ridicule*"[50]

Harrison was inaugurated on March 4, 1841, amidst the rejoicing of the Whigs, who were at last in power. The day of "mis-rule" was over, and the country could look forward to better times. "General Harrison is in fine health and spirits," Stanly informed Pettigrew on February 25. "A plain old farmer in his manners, retaining full possession of his mental faculties. I confidently hope we shall have a glorious administration."[51] However, the "plain old farmer" was soon faced with a rift in the victorious Whig ranks over the question of a special session of Congress. Clay, with whom the President was already at odds over cabinet appointments, insisted that one be held to charter a national bank, enact distribution, and consider tariff reform. According to William A. Graham, "general sentiment" favored such a session, although Henry A. Wise and a "few other busy Whigs" were opposed.[52] Secretary of State Daniel Webster was also cool to the idea, since if Clay were absent from Washington until the regular session in December the ambitious Secretary could consolidate his own position with the President. But Clay was not to be denied, and on March 17, Harrison summoned Congress into special session on May 31, 1841.[53]

In North Carolina, Governor Morehead ordered the congressional elections held in May rather than in August, as would normally have been the case. The North Carolina banks had suspended specie payments in March, and this was expected to benefit the Whig cause. Moreover, six of the state's Democratic representatives, John Hill, Charles Shepard, William Montgomery, Charles Fisher, Henry Connor, and Jesse Bynum, declined to seek reelection.[54]

Stanly also considered leaving Congress, writing Pettigrew that he was "heartily sick of public life," and suggesting that Josiah Collins come to Washington in his place. He was persuaded to take the field again, this time without regular opposition.[55] The Whigs remained on guard, wary of some Democratic stratagem. Stanly darkly warned Pettigrew that "Locofocoism" never slumbered; "It is the very spirit of evil, and ought always to be watched."[56] A week before the election, a correspondent of the Washington (N.C.) *Whig* reported that the district Locofoco leaders had agreed in a secret conclave to bring the "whole Loco Foco forces" to the polls on election day, hoping to take Stanly's friends by surprise and defeat him. Fortunately, someone had talked and thus thwarted this "nefarious" scheme "to retire our faithful and intrepid representative."[57]

Despite Whig fears, the election passed off quietly. The Democrats generally voted for Henry I. Toole of Pitt County, who received 1,149 votes to Stanly's 2,469. It was a thumping vote of confidence in the "little conqueror." The Whigs scored gains elsewhere in the state, taking three additional seats.[58]

Whig rejoicing over these victories was muted by the sudden death of President Harrison only one month after taking office. The elderly chief executive's strength had been sapped by the hordes of office seekers who descended upon Washington and overwhelmed him with their importunities. On April 1, he became ill after going out bareheaded and without an overcoat to do the White House marketing, developed pneumonia, and died early on the morning of April 4.

Two days later, John Tyler took the oath of office as the tenth President; at fifty-one, he was the youngest man to attain that high office. Genial in manners and very popular in the party, his public record was that of a consistent state rights, strict constructionist. He had voted against the bank recharter bill in 1832 and had been driven into the Whig ranks only by his distrust of Andrew Jackson. Nationalistic Whigs had well-founded fears concerning his future political course. "No one can foresee all the consequences of this national calamity," Stanly wrote Pettigrew after learning of Harrison's death. "I have great confidence in Tyler, and his cabinet: though I fear his opinions are too much like those of the Virginia 98 & 99 abstractionists. We must hope for the best."[59]

5

THE WAR WITH CAPTAIN TYLER

WHEN THE SPECIAL SESSION of the Twenty-Seventh Congress convened on May 31, 1841, the Whigs enjoyed a nominal majority of seven in the Senate, where Clay assumed control as chairman of the Finance Committee, and twenty-eight in the House, with twelve vacancies. A strong Clay man, John White of Kentucky, was elected Speaker of the House, and Clay's friends dominated the important committees. Stanly was appointed to the Committee on Naval Affairs.[1] Adams again moved to rescind the "gag rule," and this time the House voted to sustain him, 112 to 106 (Stanly voting no), but later reversed itself after angry debate and rejected the rescinding resolution, 110 to 106. On this reconsideration, Stanly, who had private misgivings about slavery, voted with Adams in favor of the resolution and in opposition to a continuation of the gag—an act of political courage for a slave-state representative.[2]

On June 7, Clay outlined his legislative program for the session in a series of resolutions which he introduced in the Senate. He called for the repeal of the Independent Treasury Act; the "incorporation of a bank adapted to the wants of the people, and of the government"; a tariff adjustment to provide more government revenue; a temporary loan to cover the public debt created by the previous administration; and provision for the distribution of the proceeds from public land sales.[3]

The most important measure in this program was the establishment of a new national bank. On June 12, in pursuance of a Senate resolution, Secretary of the Treasury Thomas Ewing reported a plan for the incorporation of a central "Bank and Fiscal Agent" in the District of Columbia with branches, or offices of discount and deposit, located in consenting states. The Cabinet had drafted "Ewing's plan" and it represented a compromise between their views and Tyler's strict construction opinions. The President disliked the provisions for discount and deposit, but probably would have approved the bill if it had been sent to him without undue delay or controversy.[4]

Moderate Whigs found the Ewing bill acceptable. *The Washington National Intelligencer*, press spokesman of the party, thought it a "well-considered project," and predicted its adoption would benefit the country. Before leaving home for the capital, Stanly had sketched a petition for a national bank which he asked Pettigrew to circulate for signatures. Therein he called for the chartering of "a national institution,—a specie paying Bank, bound to collect, transfer, and disburse the public money, and to regulate exchanges, as they were before, under the two former Banks, permanently to relieve the people and the Government." Now he found nothing in the Ewing plan that would forbid his support. "Mr. Ewing has sent in a plan of a Bank, which I think will be popular & carried through," he informed Pettigrew on June 14. "I sincerely hope so, for the sake of the Country."[5]

But the imperious Clay would have none of the Ewing plan, and on June 21 he reported his own Fiscal Bank Bill with an unlimited branching power. Thus early in the session a rift had developed in the Whig ranks. Writing Pettigrew two days after Clay reported his bill, Stanly still believed there would be a "U. S. Bank of some sort," although he feared it would be an imperfect machine. "The great difficulty with the President seems to be, that the States shall have the right to *refuse* to have branches." Unlike Clay and the "ultras," he was more interested in getting a bank than in defying John Tyler's constitutional scruples. Many of the Whigs, he noted, believed that to give in to the President would mean "giving up the whole ground." As for himself: "I do not like it much, but I shall take the best we can get, and trust to amending it hereafter."[6]

During June and July, the Senate struggled with Clay's bank bill. On July 1, William C. Rives of Virginia tried to substitute Ewing's bill for Clay's by an amendment requiring the assent of the state legislature to any branch of discount and deposit in the state, but providing that once established the branch could not be withdrawn without Congress' consent. This was the extreme concession of the Tyler Whigs, but Clay brought about its defeat. He finally accepted a modification of the bill permitting the states to prevent bank branches within their borders by allowing the state legislatures to "unconditionally dissent" at their first sessions after the bank bill had passed Congress. However, if Congress deemed it necessary and proper for the carrying out of its powers, it could still establish branches in any state. Tyler Whigs refused to accept Clay's amendment, and it barely passed the Senate on July 27, twenty-five to twenty-four. On the following day, the Senate accepted the amended bill by a three-vote margin, twenty-six to twenty-three. The House concurred, 128 to 97, on August 6.[7]

It was now up to Tyler to accept or reject the bank bill. For the moment he said nothing, and there was much speculation in Washington as to what action he would take. William A. Graham told his daughter Susan that the Cabinet had advised the President to sign, but his Virginia friends (Graham called them a "cabal") were urging him to stand firm against Clay and veto.[8] Thurlow Weed, who had been summoned to Washington to use his good offices in the dispute, reported to Seward that while the Cabinet faintly hoped, congressmen despaired; that he had been laboring all day to soothe excited feelings among the Whigs; that Stanly, "Stewart" (Alexander H. H. Stuart?), and John Minor Botts were trying to dissuade the President, but that a veto was inevitable.[9]

Tortured by indecision, Tyler finally resolved to veto the bank bill, since to sign it despite his known objections would seriously weaken his claim to party leadership. This was important to Tyler, as he hoped for the Whig nomination in 1844. By August 11, it was generally known in Washington that the President would veto the measure; this opinion was based on the sentiments expressed by Tyler's friends and by the Washington *Madisonian*, the administration paper. On the evening of August 15, Graham and several other gentlemen called at the White House and were told that a veto message would be sent in the next day. Graham could not foresee the consequences of this action, but he predicted they would be injurious to the country and the Whig Party.[10]

Moderate Whigs still hoped that despite Tyler's veto a compromise might be reached on the bank question. Tyler told Senator Rives that he still favored a fiscal agency, although one of more restricted powers than those proposed in the Ewing bill. It should be located in the District of Columbia, be authorized to establish branches with state consent, but should not have the power to make local discounts. Tyler consulted with the Cabinet and members of Congress, and a bill embodying these provisions was drafted. But at this point both Tyler and the Clay "ultras" were more interested in political maneuvering than in securing a compromise measure. The second bank bill passed the House, 125 to 94 (August 23), and the Senate, 27 to 22 (September 3). But even before the Senate acted, it was reported that Tyler was contemplating a veto. "If so," Graham declared privately, "a breach with him is inevitable."[11]

Stanly was one of the moderate Whigs who hoped to the very last that the rift between the President and the Whig Party might be healed and an acceptable bank bill passed. Among the Clay supporters in Congress, Thomas Arnold and John Minor Botts were particularly severe in their criticisms of Tyler. Botts, in his so-called "Coffeehouse Letter" of August 16, had predicted that "Captain" Tyler would veto the bank bill in an effort to curry favor with the Democrats. But "he'll be headed yet" and "will be an object of execration with both parties." This letter, sent to a Richmond coffeehouse, was published in the Washington *Madisonian* on August 21, and greatly offended the President. On August 25, Arnold delivered an hour-long "counterblast" against the "*base, miserable* wretch at the other end of the Avenue," accusing him of treachery to the Whig Party and of allying himself with the Locofocos.[12]

Arnold was followed by Stanly, who gave what John Quincy Adams called "a speech of sharp rebuke" to Arnold and Botts.[13] He declared that he saw no desire on the President's part to leave the Whig Party and did not know in what particular Tyler had abandoned his Whig principles. Arnold could not read him out of the "Whig Church"; he could not live in the Locofoco camp. "His heart is Whig." It was true, to be sure, that ninety-nine out of a hundred of the bank's friends would have preferred an old-fashioned United States Bank. However, said Stanly:

> This the President cannot agree to, but he is willing so far as appears to give us a bank, though it must not be a bank of discount. In his veto message he intimates that he can sign a bill for deposit and exchange; and why denounce him in advance, when he appears willing, as far as he can do it without a sacrifice of principle, to sacrifice his personal prejudices to the public wish and general prosperity?

Stanly confessed he had heard the attacks on the President "with many pangs of heart." He dismissed as "false as hell," the charge that Botts' coffeehouse letter expressed the Whig viewpoint. He had not heard a single Whig speak of it who did not disapprove of its spirit and tone. He regretted that some gentlemen, who had spoken of Tyler in terms of contempt, seemed ready to scatter disaffection and to sow discord among the Whig Party. Instead of pursuing so suicidal a course, the Whigs should unite themselves as a band of brethren in a broad and patriotic spirit. Let the old Whig banner "fly over a brave and united host," he pleaded, "and let our enemies tremble . . . as they read upon that triumphant flag the well known legend, 'Tippecanoe and Tyler too!'"[14]

Stanly was preaching peace where there was no peace. To his plea for party unity, Botts retorted that Tyler was guilty of the basest and vilest treachery to the Whig Party and "when that second veto should come, as come it must, he should be able to maintain this." Adams noted in his diary that evening: "The Whig Party is in the agonies of dissolution, and this day disclosed many symptoms of its approach. We are in the hands of a Being good and wise."[15] Four days after Stanly's speech, it was generally believed that Tyler would veto the second bank bill. Graham declared that such a feeling of distrust had grown up between the President and the Whigs that there could hardly ever be a cordial reconciliation.[16]

On September 9, Tyler returned the second bank bill to the House with his veto. An effort to override the veto failed. On September 11, the entire Cabinet, except Webster, sent in their letters of resignation. The Whigs charged Tyler not only with folly and imbecility but with treachery as well. Graham told James Bryan that the President had assented to the second bank bill before its introduction in the very words in which it was introduced and passed and had drawn the title in his own handwriting. Yet in his veto message he had disapproved of the title as well as the act itself. "The Cabinet have therefore not left him for mere disagreement on a measure, but for trifling and treachery towards them . . . They were not consulted about the last veto and never saw it until published."[17]

Tyler's reorganized Cabinet signalized his complete breach with the Whig Party. New members were Walter Forward of Pennsylvania, Secretary of the Treasury; John C. Spencer of New York, Secretary of War; Abel P. Upshur of Virginia, Secretary of the Navy; Charles A. Wickliffe of Kentucky (who was hostile to Clay), Postmaster General; and Hugh Swinton Legaré of South Carolina, Attorney General. Henry A. Wise was offered the post of Secretary of the Navy but declined it. Tyler's new advisers were Whigs who had originally been Jackson men. Clay Whigs believed it contained "strong Nullification tendencies" and that the President expected to build a third party on it with the aid of his "Corporal's Guard."[18] However, the great majority of the nation's Whigs rallied with unanimity around the Clay banner. On September 13 (the day Congress adjourned), some fifty or more Whig members of Congress held a caucus on Capital Square, presided over by Mangum, and adopted an address reading Tyler out of the party and disavowing any responsibility for his actions.[19]

Stanly's fight with Wise on the floor of the House, described earlier, on the very day Tyler sent in his second veto message (September 9), was symbolic of the schism in the Whig ranks. The two men, so alike in their fiery temperaments, although differing in their political philosophies, had stood shoulder to shoulder in the struggle against "Locofocoism." But with Tyler's accession their friendship had deteriorated as Wise assumed control of Tyler's friends in the House and worked at cross purposes with the rest of the party. As early as June 16, the two men had exchanged the following words in the House:

Mr. Stanly, I am glad to see my friend from Virginia—*personal*, not *political* friend, I mean; for . . . I do not recognize him as a political friend. I part with him, and if he embarrasses and opposes his friends as he has for the past fort-night, we had better not have his help.

Mr. Wise said he had never been the *political* friend of that gentleman.

Mr. Stanly. Mr. Speaker, I think that a matter of little consequence; but I have now excommunicated him first.[20]

Relations had continued to worsen; and now, at last, blows had been struck, and the word *liar* uttered.

Friends of the two men intervened and prevented a duel, and the next day, William Cost Johnson of Maryland reported to the House that the "transient difference" had been amicably adjusted. The House, meanwhile, had appointed a committee, headed by Charles J. Ingersoll of Pennsylvania, to investigate the fight. On September 11, it recommended that the written statements of the two parties and the committee report should be spread upon the House Journal as a reprimand; that in the future, if any member should strike another, he should be expelled; and that if any member should insult another, he should be fined $100. Lott Warren of Georgia then moved to substitute a resolution expelling Wise from the House. The Virginian, with what Adams described as "a forlorn and crafty affectation of humility," expressed the hope that the House would not censure Stanly and declared that he would submit to its judgment, "for there was but one man in the House whose judgment he was unwilling to abide by," and that was Adams. Refusing to be provoked into an intemperate retort, Adams disclaimed all personal hostility to Wise and advised against his censure. Alexander H. H. Stuart of Virginia finally moved that the report be recommitted, with instructions to report a resolution that as Wise had apologized to the House and Stanly, the House would take no further notice of the subject. Stuart's motion was adopted, 104 to 56.[21]

Wise and Stanly were now officially "reconciled," but it was a reconciliation in name only. Adams, going into the House chamber a few days later to claim his seat for the next session, met Stanly, "who was franking documents, and who thinks worse of Wise than I do."[22]

Out of the Congress, the aristocratic New York City diarist, Philip Hone, penned the following about Stanly on September 30:

> Mr. Stanley [*sic*], Wise's competitor in the disgraceful fracas which lately occurred in the House of Representatives, although a clever man and a good fellow, is fiery as a Loco-foco match, and as easily ignited by hard rubbing; and so small and boyish in his appearance that Pickens once contemptuously called him Cock-Robin, and he in return let out a broadside of cannon-balls, bomb-shells, and chain shot, each apparently larger than the calibre of the gun itself. It must have been funny to hear this little man with a big heart boast of the fisticuffs he inflicted upon Mr. Wise, and what he would have done if they had not been separated. These remarks are suggested by reading the following nursery lines, taken from a Western paper, as a sort of heading to an account of the congressional battle:

> > Stanley, you should never let
> > Your angry passions rise;
> > Your little hands were never made
> > To pummel Mr. Wise.[23]

The Whigs had not forgotten the remainder of Clay's legislative program during their futile struggle with Tyler over the bank. The repeal of the Independent Treasury act was carried through the Senate in June and the House in August. Clay's distribution and preemption bill passed the Senate and then the House, after Stanly led a "bold movement" which forced the measure out of the Committee of the Whole, where it had been debated for two weeks, and passed it under a rigorous application of the previous question, 116 to 108 (July 6).[24] To secure Tyler's approval for the bill, Clay had accepted an amendment suspending distribution if future tariff duties exceeded the final twenty percent level fixed by the tariff of 1833. The Whigs also passed a revenue bill, a bankruptcy act providing for both voluntary and compulsory bankruptcy, and a loan bill authorizing a government loan not in excess of $12,000,000.[25]

Stanly had pursued a moderate course during the session's hectic weeks. Adopting a pragmatic view of the bank question, he had worked to conciliate the discordant elements that were threatening to disrupt the Whig Party. "I have labored hard to reconcile conflicting opinions, and to sooth jealousies," he wrote William Gaston on July 29, "and I trust not without some effect."[26] During the session, a Washington correspondent of the Raleigh *Register* thought it necessary to reassure North Carolinians that Stanly's failure to play the partisan did not spring from apathy. "Mr. Stanly has done much good service in keeping the House at work . . . He has lost none of his former energy of character, though he makes less frequent displays of it than he did during the last Session."[27] Even his fight with Wise did not seriously tarnish his reputation, the general consensus being that he had acted "exactly right."[28]

Still, his efforts at conciliation had fallen short, and he was deeply discouraged by the division in the ranks of his beloved Whig Party. Adams observed that "Stanly's spirit is not to be subdued; but the thunderbolt of heaven has fallen upon the Whigs, and he, with all the honest men of the party, is disheartened and perplexed."[29] How often in these dark hours must he have thought back to the glorious "log-cabin" victory in 1840!

When the Twenty-Seventh Congress met for its second session on December 6, 1841, Stanly was made chairman of the important Committee on Military Affairs. He accepted the appointment without enthusiasm. "I suppose I ought to consider it an honor," he wrote Pettigrew. "I must for the sake of my constituents endeavor to do my duty creditably." Toward "Capt. Tyler," he was disposed to follow, as far as possible, a course of moderation and calmness.

He is already sinking fast & deservedly into irredeemable contempt. If we quarrel with a shadow, we drive a little strength & all his patronage into the ranks of the Locos.—By forbearance, we at least weaken our enemies, our natural enemies, the enemies of religion, peace, decency & laws—the loco-focos. I think we will be moderates as long as the fraility of human nature will allow. It is a hard task for me to suppress my indignation, but *I will try*.[30]

During the session, Stanly and Wise were continually quarreling with one another. "They will have to shoot each other yet, I expect," was the prediction of one observer.[31] Stanly must have had Wise in mind when he wrote Pettigrew in January, 1842: "We will not 'put any of these rascals to death'—because some public executioner will do it some of these days."[32] On January 24, when Wise declared in the House that members had some privileges, Stanly remarked: "*They do not deserve any*." Wise did not hear the comment at the time; but when it appeared in the *National Intelligencer*, he wrote Stanly asking "whether you did make that remark; and, if so, whether you intended it to apply to me particularly." A yes to the latter question would almost certainly have brought a prompt challenge from the hot-tempered Virginian. Stanly, however, briefly and coolly replied that his remark had not been intended to apply to any one individual "*particularly*."[33] The incident thus blew over harmlessly, but indicated how volatile relations had become between the two men.

These differences finally culminated on May 7, 1842, on the Washington race course road. Both men were present on horseback. Stanly's horse became frightened, bolted, and jostled Wise, who was riding ahead with a friend. Believing the contact to be deliberate on Stanly's part, Wise rode up behind him as he struggled to control his hard-mouthed horse, and struck him across the back of the head with a whale-bone walking cane. According to a report published in the Raleigh *Star*, Wise cursed and said, "'Now ride against me again.' Mr. Stanly replied, 'I did not see you.' Mr. Wise. 'Then I excuse you.' Mr. Stanly. 'You come up behind a man and strike him like a d---d coward.' Mr. Wise. 'Take that blow and the coward and make the most of them, d---n you.'" Wise's friend remarked that this was no place to settle such matters. Stanly replied "very well," and rode on. "It is said he intends to challenge Mr. Wise."[34]

On May 9, Stanly sent Senator Willie P. Mangum to see Wise with an invitation to meet him at Barnum's Hotel, Baltimore, on May 18, at 12 noon, "when and where he (Mr. Stanly) desires to open the discussion of . . . unpleasant personal matters."[35] News of the impending duel was soon abroad; and on May 11, a district judge issued warrants for the arrest of both Stanly and Wise on a charge of contemplating a breach of the peace by fighting a duel. Stanly left the District before he could be arrested and went to Baltimore where his friend, Senator Reverdy Johnson, took him in custody. Wise was arrested and placed under a $3,000 bond to keep the peace and not leave the District to fight a duel with Stanly.[36]

Mangum, considering the matter settled and without consulting his principal, then conditionally recalled the "invitation" of May 9. When Stanly repudiated this action, Mangum withdrew as his intermediary. The former, meanwhile, went to the country where he practiced firing at a mark under Reverdy Johnson's instruction. He had earlier written Mangum that "there never was a fellow going to be hanged, who had better spirits than I have."[37]

On May 18, Stanly's new intermediary, John M. McCarty of Virginia, met in Baltimore with William Cost Johnson, representing Wise, who was still under bond in Washington. The genial McCarty, familiarly known as Colonel Jack McCarty, had the undeserved reputation of being a "fire-eater," from a duel fought in 1819 with muskets at a few feet distance, in which he killed his kinsman, Armistead T. Mason. In a letter to Wise, handed Johnson by McCarty, Stanly declared that the collision with Wise had been entirely accidental, his horse having bolted; but since he had received no "reparation or atonement for this outrage," his only recourse was to demand satisfaction. Johnson replied that if this letter was withdrawn, its explanation of the collision would warrant him as Wise's authorized friend, to express the latter's "regrets that his not being aware of Mr. Stanly's intention to apologize for the collision caused him to assail Mr. Stanly." McCarty found this satisfactory, the letter was withdrawn, and the correspondence ended with Johnson expressing his "heartfelt pleasure at the amicable adjustment."[38]

After the settlement Stanly boasted to Pettigrew that he was glad the affair had been amicably adjusted, because while he "*might*" have been hurt, Wise "*must*" have been. "I was right, he was wrong. I had acquired skill in the use of the weapon, & confidence that I could use it well, and though I may be afraid of other men, I did not fear Captain Tyler's Cur."[39]

Brave words, but the "Conqueror's" reputation did not escape unscathed from this second violent encounter with Wise. Washington gossip said he had not acted "as a man of honor ought to have acted" in settling the affair without bloodshed after a blow had been struck.[40] An Arkansas observer wrote Graham that Stanly should neither have apologized nor accepted an apology. "*His distinguished Sire could not have acted thus.*"[41] Stanly threatened to reinstate the duel if the "slightest imputation" was attached to his name, but the damage was already done. Even Ebenezer Pettigrew confessed that he would have disliked to take the blow, "without killing or at least trying to kill him."[42] The Wise affair, by reflecting on Stanly's courage, unquestionably hurt him politically, and was later used against him by his enemies in and out of the Whig Party.

Stanly further injured his popularity at home by voting for the Whig tariff of 1842, which restored duties to the general level of 1832. At first he declined to vote favorably upon a measure so unpopular in his state, but he did not wish to see the bill defeated; and when it appeared that it would be lost by the casting vote of the Speaker, 103-103, he and Landaff Andrews of Kentucky, who had also abstained, voted yes and secured its passage.[43]

Eliza Gaston, who saw Julia Stanly on August 27 "& heard her talk politics," reported to William Gaston that she seemed to feel rather uneasy about her husband's vote for the tariff. "His popularity is very dear to her & . . . she hates him to lose any of it at home though she of course approves of every act of his."[44] Mrs. Stanly's apprehensions were well founded. The Raleigh *North Carolina Standard*, chief paper of the Democratic Party in the state, was quick to note Stanly's evasive action and to place the responsibility for the tariff squarely on his shoulders. It declared:

> *Edward Stanly* has been the means of passing this high protective Tariff. What will the honest farmers of this State say to this?—Do they not see every day and in every development, a violation of their trust—and that they have been betrayed by those who made so many promises in 1840, and who now violate every one of them.[45]

Having voted for the tariff, Stanly tried to put the best possible face on his action. He told the House on August 29, 1842, that he had felt a patriotic duty to protect northern laboring men from the ruinous competition of European pauper labor. His own constituents were intelligent, fair, and generous men, and when he saw them again, he would tell them, "without hesitation or disguise, that he blessed God he had been spared to live, and had breath to lisp the word 'ay' on the passage of the tariff bill." It was an upright act, if he ever performed one, and far from blushing at the remembrance, it would be the pride and consolation of his future days.[46]

After Congress adjourned on August 31, Stanly returned home for the first time since the beginning of the special session in May, 1841. When the Washington (N.C.) *Republican* reported his friends and neighbors had coolly received him, "Many Whigs" replied indignantly in the Washington *Whig* that no man, returning after a long absence, could have met with a more cordial reception than Stanly. He stood as high as ever in the confidence and esteem of his neighbors and, if anything, could increase their regard for him, it was the "fiendish abuse, which, from the lying secrecy of their closets, a cabal, in this town, continue to hurl at him through the Republican." According to "Many Whigs," William Blount Rodman, a Washington lawyer and Democratic leader, was the author of the secret slanders that had been uttered against Stanly and his friends, and particularly the recent *Republican* editorials commencing the attacks on Stanly.[47]

Whig overconfidence after the 1840 victories led to a relaxation of effort in the state elections of August, 1842, with the result that, while Governor Morehead was narrowly reelected, the Democrats won the legislature. They thus controlled not only the election of a United States senator to succeed Graham, but also the redistricting of the state under the 1840 census. North Carolina had lost four seats under the new apportionment, and the Democrats redistricted to assure themselves at least five of the nine remaining seats. In a frank attempt to gerrymander Stanly out of Congress, Craven, Carteret, Greene, and Nash Counties, the last a Democratic citadel, were added to his district. The Raleigh *Register* later estimated the normal Democratic majority in this new Eighth District at four or five hundred votes.[48]

In February, 1843, William Washington of Craven having declined a reelection, the Raleigh *Register* took it for granted that Stanly would again take the field and gallantly uphold the Whig banner. If the district was thoroughly canvassed, the *Register* did not fear the result, "however strongly Locofoco the Legislature endeavored to make it."[49] But Stanly, who had returned to the capital in

December, 1842, for the third and last session of the Twenty-Seventh Congress, publicly stated in March, 1843, that he did not wish to seek reelection, although he probably was not averse to a draft. On March 10, he wrote Pettigrew a letter intended for publication, informing him that through his own efforts and those of Rayner and Graham, an appropriation had been obtained for a survey to ascertain the practicability of opening an inlet at Nags Head. While he did not wish to be a candidate again, he begged the people of Washington and Tyrrell Counties to take care of their own and their country's interest, "by sending no politician of the Edgecombe regency school to Congress, who will oppose this noble undertaking." It depended upon the people themselves whether or not an inlet was begun.[50]

In a covering note to Pettigrew, Stanly said that he had sent one hundred lithographed copies of the letter to Washington and Tyrrell. "Whether I am a candidate or not, and I hope not to be, I want in parting to say a word against Edgecombe politics."[51]

Some of the Whig leaders in his old district were more than willing to take Stanly at his word. Joseph Beasley of Washington County told William Pettigrew that the Washington Whigs would prefer Josiah Collins to any other nominee. If Stanly received the nomination, he could not be elected. "His course in Congress has lost him the confidence & esteem of the Whig party in this district. And I should feel less willing to trust our chance of success in his hands, than in those of any other prominent man in the district."[52]

No one, however, wanted to take up the seemingly impossible task of overcoming the heavy Democratic majority in the Eighth, and once more the party turned to the "Conqueror." Meeting in Washington on April 6, the Whig district convention unanimously nominated Stanly "amid lively evidences of the approbation of every member." Stanly was out of town when the nomination was tendered, but accepted it upon his return. "I have not the slightest doubt of success," he declared, "if every Whig will do his duty, as I shall try to do mine." The Whig press in the state hailed his nomination and dutifully predicted victory in spite of the Democratic gerrymander. "Unless we are greatly deceived," said the Raleigh *Register*, "they will find they have 'dug a pit for themselves.'"[53]

The Democratic press in the Eighth District professed great scorn for the Whig nomination. The *Tarboro' Press* sneered that the party had nominated the "same old coon" because no one else could be found reckless enough to undertake the hopeless task "to beguile and mislead the honest yeomanry of the district." The Washington *Republican* suggested that the "Whig nag" was too stiff in the joints to run against the well trained courser on the other side. "The 'Democratic Nag' will be at the winning post in due time to take the prize!"[54]

The "Democratic Nag" opposing Stanly was Archibald H. Arrington, a large landowner in Nash County, who had served without distinction in the previous Congress. He was nominated by a Democratic convention in Washington on March 28, 1843, over Henry I. Toole of Pitt County. The Washington *Republican*, a supporter of Toole, admitted that "a great portion of the Democrats" had been disappointed, even mortified, with Arrington's nomination but expressed support for his candidacy. Arrington's political views were orthodox strict construction, appropriately summarized in the motto: "Free trade; Low Duties, No Debt; Separation from Banks; Economy; Retrenchment; and a strict Adherence to the Constitution."[55]

Stanly and Arrington stumped the district, appearing in joint debates at Greenville, New Bern, Washington, and elsewhere. As usual, each side claimed its own champion had the best in these encounters. "A Voter" in the *Tarboro' Press* reported that at Greenville, Arrington had acted in a manner "becoming a gentleman of good taste," while Stanly had looked and acted like an angry man. "A man that has never seen a 'conqueror' would think he had a legion of devils in him." At Washington, Stanly held a candle near Arrington's face that every one might see him and then "poured out, for nearly an hour, a torrent of sarcasm and ridicule which seemed to wither the subject of them into nothingness, while the whole audience, democrats and all, were convulsed with laughter."[56]

Stanly had been warned that he would not be allowed to speak in Nash County, but at once announced a speaking date in Stanhope. Facing a largely hostile crowd, he declared: "I realize that I am facing the unterrified Democracy of Nash County, but I want you to know and to bear witness that I face you unterrified." Thereafter the phrase, "The unterrified Democracy," became a part of the period's political vernacular.[57]

The Democrats, in their eagerness to defeat Stanly, brought every conceivable accusation against him. He was bitterly denounced for his vote in favor of the tariff of 1842, "a bill of abominations," said one Democratic writer, "Civis," that "like the Simoon of the desert" would "blast the fairest portion of our country" and "stagnate the streams of Southern enterprise and industry."[58] He was damned as the "most haughty and confirmed aristocrat in North Carolina," the "dear friend and 'cousin'" of George E. Badger, himself the "very pink and personification of Federal aristocracy."[59] Labeled a "Southern man with Northern principles," Stanly's friendship with John Quincy Adams and opposition to the Gag Rule was pronounced unworthy of a southern representative. It was even charged that during the Twenty-Seventh Congress, he had exceeded his legal mileage allowance by $53.00![60]

In July, a scurrilous handbill, originating in Raleigh, appeared in the campaign. Entitled *The Campaigns of a Conqueror; Or the Man "Who Bragged High for a Fight,"* and signed "Chester," it was a thinly veiled accusation of cowardice on Stanly's part during some eight encounters ("Campaigns") in Congress and elsewhere with members of the opposition. Said Chester of Stanly's affair with Wise in 1842: "Thus closed the campaign of our 'Conqueror'—the man 'who bragged high for a fight'—commencing with the motto, 'On, Stanly, on!' but which was *Wise*–ly changed to 'Run, Stanly, run.'"[61] Such charges came with ill grace from an anonymous author, as the Whigs were quick to point out. The Whig young men of New Bern called Chester a "Raleigh dastard," "base liar," and "sneaking coward," who would rather "jump over the falls of Niagara than send a copy of this tissue of malignant falsehoods, with his proper name annexed to Mr. Stanly."[62]

Early in the campaign, Stanly had written James W. Bryan that he had the "most gratifying intelligence" from all parts of the district—"even in Nash, I have warm friends, and Arrington has many enemies, among the democrats." "I have no doubt I shall be elected," he confided to Ebenezer Pettigrew on May 15.[63] However, despite heroic Whig efforts, Stanly was badly beaten at the polls. He carried seven of the ten counties in the district, but Nash and Edgecombe together gave Arrington 2,363 votes to his own 177 votes—an almost insurmountable lead. Even in the counties of the old Third District, Stanly's vote dropped sharply, his margin there being only sixty-one as compared to five hundred two years before. The total vote was 4,813 for Arrington to 4,265 for Stanly, a Democratic majority of 548 votes.[64]

The Democratic press in the district rejoiced mightily over Stanly's fall: "548 MAJORITY, Over the 'Conqueror,' who did 'not feel like one who had an opponent,'" exulted the *Tarboro' Press*. "A GLORIOUS VICTORY! The *'Conqueror' conquered*!!" proclaimed the Washington *Republican*, adding that Stanly had been "compelled to submit (though unwilling) to the decision . . . of the 'unterrified Democracy' of the Eighth District."[65]

The Washington *North State Whig* attributed Stanly's defeat to two factors: (1) "the falsehoods concerning him that have been scattered, broadcast, over the district . . . which Truth, slower, in his motions, has not had time to override and correct"; and (2) "The rain . . . which poured down in almost ceaseless torrents during the day of election, . . . keeping from the polls, the aged, the infirm, and the lukewarm." In the eight lower counties five hundred votes at least had been lost from this one cause alone. The Whigs also claimed that while Stanly had refused to spend one dollar in buying votes, by "treating," Arrington must have spent at least $5,000.[66]

Stanly himself attributed his defeat to his vote for the tariff of 1842 and the gerrymander.[67] However, there was another cause that neither he nor any other Whig mentioned publicly, but which must have had its weight with the voters—the innuendo that Stanly was a coward. A Tyrrell County Whig informed Ebenezer Pettigrew that the "fight between Wise and Stanly caused him to lose his election— that was one time when fighting was necessary."[68]

The "Conqueror" took his defeat calmly. Resuming the practice of law at home, he was "much encouraged," considering the hard times. "Sitting by my own fire, I feel grateful to a kind providence for its favors, & am as independent a fellow as you ever saw," he wrote Leverett Saltonstall, a Massachusetts representative. Thinking back over his six years in Congress during which he had labored "with ardor" in the Whig cause, he was not without consolation: "My efforts may have been abortive, my intentions were good, & the acquaintances I made, especially with my New England friends, will long afford me many pleasant recollections."[69]

Stanly struck a less cheerful note when he unburdened himself on the "alarmingly painful subject" of slavery. A slaveholder, owning a few Negroes as house servants, he cherished no warm attachment for the institution. Indeed, Rufus Barringer, a North Carolina Whig leader, believed that he was "always at heart an anti-slavery man."[70] Yet like many thoughtful Southerners who privately disliked slavery, he saw no immediate way to safely abolish it, and concluding that the abolitionists were doing more injury than good with their agitation, he had denounced them in Congress. Now he lamented to Saltonstall:

> They do not know, the harm they have done to the cause of emancipation. God knows, I love liberty, as much as any man, but what are we to do? What is a man to do, who makes sacrifices to buy a poor negro, for the sake of preventing the separation of families and then when he keeps them from feelings of kindness, to be denounced as a 'man stealer, robber, &&'—To allow them to remain here, free, is impossible.—Their masters, who are attached to them,—the slave-holders, could not protect them. To send them, *at once*, to Liberia, is equally impossible.—We know the evils, we have hearts, and souls, and bibles and consciences, & deserve anything else, but crimination from the free States.—If we had been let alone, at this day, Ky: Md: & Va: would have been free States, & we should have followed. I have not time to express all I feel, on this alarmingly painful subject. You can better decide how to manage the mistaken philanthropy of the North, so that our country may not be injured. I should not have spoken as freely, but to a friend.[71]

Stanly's years in Congress had been exciting and contentious ones; he would later look back upon them with some regret as his "boyish days of 1837—& 1840" and "the days of my wicked folly." Writing to Robert Winthrop of Massachusetts in 1865, he recalled that:

With most of the So: Car: members, on account of my often
expressed hatred of the treason of secession, & the absurdity
of their State-rights, I had no social intercourse whatever: the
aversion was mutual & so strong, as sometimes . . . to threaten
a resort to the 'code of honor.' I did not for years pay Mr.
Calhoun the respect of a visit, because I had spoken of him as
a traitor.[72]

And yet if his caustic tongue had made him one of the most
cordially detested Whigs in Congress and in his own state, it had also
gained him a national reputation as an able and tireless champion of
Whiggery. He had gone down the line for the Whig program in the
House, even voting for the tariff of 1842.[73] Most important of all,
his congressional service further strengthened his already strong and
fervent nationalism. At first somewhat suspicious of the North, he
said in 1844 that these "ridiculous prejudices" had been dispelled
from his mind, and he had learned to love his own country more.[74]
He was thus better prepared to cope with anti-northern sentiment in
his state and section. This was to be particularly important in
coming years as the slavery question became more and more
inflamed and angry men began to speak openly of secession.

6

APPLE OF DISCORD

EIGHTEEN FORTY-FOUR was a national and state election year in North Carolina, and as early as January, 1843, the Whigs began to search for a suitable candidate to succeed Governor John Motley Morehead. Among those mentioned for the nomination were Stanly, William A. Graham, Charles Manly, John H. Bryan, and Kenneth Rayner. Graham, who was about to end his short term in the United States Senate, was the favorite of the Raleigh Whigs, with Manly as the second choice. The Whigs in the legislature held a caucus on January 20, 1843, and although no nomination was made for governor, Graham was told that he would be urged to accept it.[1]

Following his defeat for reelection in August, 1843, Stanly's friends brought his name forward as a suitable gubernatorial candidate for 1844, and in September the *Newbernian* published an article by co-editor Dr. Lawrence Scott nominating him. The Raleigh *Register* took note of this eastern movement for Stanly with the comment that he was "a whole-souled, go-the-whole figure Whig," who the paper would most heartily support if the state Whig convention should nominate him. But it cautioned that it was only right and proper that the names of other prominent Whigs should be brought before the public, and its pulse felt, in order to more certainly concentrate on the strongest candidate.[2]

Stanly's cousin, George Badger, was particularly anxious for his nomination. On a visit to Beaufort City, Stanly told James W. Bryan that Badger had written him on the subject, stating that he (Stanly) would receive the nomination and "must buckle on his armour" for the contest. Bryan expected "great exertions" would be made for Stanly by his immediate friends, but had heard many Whigs expressing dissatisfaction at the prospect of his nomination. He thought that Graham would run better than Stanly and that Badger had given the latter "bad counsel" in urging him to be a candidate.[3]

Richard Hines of Raleigh, for many years the Whig state chairman, admitted to Mangum that Stanly had "many and strong claims" on the Whig Party; but it was urged against him that he was too young, rash and indiscreet, and not a successful campaigner, his vote in the old Third District having fallen off sharply at the recent election. Moreover, said Hines:

> The Quakers with many moderate Whigs would not vote for him on account of his violence, and his nomination would bring out every loco vote in the state and cause one of the most bitter contests every [*sic*] witnessed at any election. It is also believed by many that he would lose many votes in the western part of the state on account of the old Federal politicks of his father[,] his own partiality for J. Q. Adams and his father's uniform opposition to the west and many personal enemies he made whilst in the legislature. For these and other objections it is feared his nomination might endanger that triumphant success important at all times but particularly so at present as all eyes will be turned to us being the first to elect in the great presidential campaign.[4]

This combination of his own and his father's political sins was too much for Stanly to overcome. County meetings in the Eighth District endorsed him, but his campaign never gained much momentum.[5] When the Whig convention met in Raleigh on December 7, 1843, Graham was nominated without opposition—another victory for the Raleigh Whigs, who dominated the party's state organization. As a face-saving gesture, a letter from Stanly to the Beaufort delegation declining the nomination in the interest of party harmony was read to the delegates. The convention endorsed Clay for the Whig presidential nomination, and the platform declared for a national bank, distribution, tariff duties as opposed to direct taxation, and incidental protection. Badger and Edward B. Dudley were chosen as delegates at large to the national convention.[6] Stanly accepted his failure to win the gubernatorial nomination without apparent resentment, writing Mangum that he was doing well in his profession and should remain at home for a year or two. "Graham you will have seen, is to be our Gov: all right: it would have ruined me."[7]

Henry Clay's visit to North Carolina in April, 1844, was the event of the year for the state's Whigs. Stanly was elected an honorary member of the "Wake Clay Club" and was invited to be in Raleigh on April 12 to greet the Whig chieftain. Earlier, the Whigs of the Eighth District had appointed him to represent them at the Whig National Convention in Baltimore on May 1, 1844. Like the overwhelming majority of the party leaders and rank and file, he was solidly behind "Harry of the West" for the Whig presidential nomination, labeling the coming national conclave "the *Clay* National Convention."[8]

Whigs from all over the state poured in to Raleigh to see the magnetic Clay. On the night before his arrival, several thousand persons assembled at Capitol Square, under the enlivening strains of the Salem Band, recalling to some the "glorious scenes of 1840." The Raleigh *Register* reported that soon a "shout that fairly rent the air, conveyed the intimation that the Hon. Edward Stanly was on the ground, and an irresistible call was made upon him for a speech." He complied and his arguments, said the *Register*, "fell with the weight of a battleaxe." Henry K. Nash and William G. "Parson" Brownlow, editor of the Jonesboro (Tenn.) *Whig*, also spoke to the crowd. The next day Clay was welcomed at the Capitol by Badger and Governor Morehead, and delivered an address in support of Whig principles.[9]

The most important issue in national politics was the annexation of Texas. The Tyler Administration was ardent for expansion and had concluded a treaty with the Lone Star Republic by which Texas was to enter the Union as a territory; its public lands were to be ceded to the United States, which in turn would assume up to ten million dollars of the Texas public debt. On April 22, 1844, Tyler submitted the treaty to the Senate for ratification.

The proximity of the national election made the acceptance or rejection of the treaty a political question, since the position of the two major parties would figure in the campaign. From Raleigh, Clay sent his friend John J. Crittenden a letter on the Texas question which he wanted to have published in the Washington *National Intelligencer*. "In my opinion, it is my duty to present it to the public," he said. "And in that Badger, the Governor [Morehead] & Stanly (to whom I have confidentially read it) concur."[10] Despite the disapproval of some of his Washington friends, Clay's "Raleigh Letter" was published in the *Intelligencer* on April 27, 1844, the day after he arrived in the Capital. His position on Texas annexation was summed up in one sentence:

> I consider the annexation of Texas, at this time, without the assent of Mexico, as a measure compromising the national character; involving us certainly in war with Mexico, probably with other foreign powers; dangerous to the integrity of the Union; inexpedient in the present financial condition of the country; and not called for by any general expression of public opinion.[11]

Martin Van Buren, the leading contender for the Democratic nomination, also opposed immediate annexation; a letter indicating his disapproval appeared in the Washington *Globe* on the same day as Clay's Raleigh letter. Suspicion immediately arose of collusion between the two men because of an earlier Kentucky meeting, and it is certain that each candidate knew the other held similar views and thus hoped to eliminate annexation from the campaign. Yet, it is impossible to find definite evidence of agreement, while the circumstantial evidence is inconclusive.[12]

The Whig convention met in Baltimore amidst the greatest enthusiasm on May 1, 1844. John M. Clayton of Delaware served as president, and twenty-five vice-presidents were selected (one from each state), with Stanly receiving the honor for the Old North State. Clay was unanimously nominated for President with Theodore Frelinghuysen of New Jersey as his running mate. The convention resolutions called for a "well-regulated currency," but avoided any specific recommendation of a national bank; nor was there any reference to expansion. Stanly was called upon for some remarks after the resolutions were adopted, and "expressed himself delighted with the scene before him and with the glorious Whigs around him."

He was more than satisfied with the nominations, and predicted North Carolina would stand by them.[13]

On May 2, ten thousand Whigs, described by Philip Hone as a "great mass of noble, fine-looking fellows, from the granite hills of New Hampshire to the green prairies of the great West," held a ratification parade in the streets of Baltimore, each state under its own banner, with flags and badges and patriotic devices, and then marched to the Canton race course outside the city, where Daniel Webster and other Whig notables addressed a great unity meeting in behalf of the "people's candidate." After participating in the day's exciting events, Stanly dined in the evening at the home of his friend, Senator Reverdy Johnson, along with Webster, Hone, Benjamin Watkins Leigh, John M. Berrien, Thomas Ewing, John J. Crittenden, Francis Granger, Thomas Butler King, and others of "the great genii of the Whig party." "I was never concerned in a more jovial affair," wrote diarist Hone after he returned to his quarters, "and never heard more small shot fired from big guns. I was eight hours on my legs in the morning of this great day, and eight hours seated at the table, and shall now get eight hours sleep, if I can."[14]

The Democrats also met in Baltimore. Martin Van Buren's opposition to annexation cost him the Democratic nomination, and he was passed over in favor of James Knox Polk of Tennessee, an ardent expansionist who enjoyed the confidence of the still influential Andrew Jackson. The platform, reflecting the rising expansionist fever in the South and West, demanded "the reoccupation of Oregon and the reannexation of Texas at the earliest practicable period."

In North Carolina, the Whigs generally opposed and the Democrats favored annexation. When the Texas treaty was overwhelmingly defeated in the Senate on June 8, 1844, Mangum voted against it and William Haywood, the Democratic senator, for it. The Raleigh *Register*, in opposing annexation, declared that the true policy of the United States was to be the "mother of Republics" on the North American continent, surrounded by "Republican daughters" and united with them by treaties of amnity and commerce. Expansion was the chief subject of debate in the gubernatorial campaign, with Graham speaking against, and his opponent, Michael Hoke of Lincoln County, for, annexation.[15]

Polk's nomination for the presidency was welcomed by North Carolina Democrats because of his North Carolina birth and education at the University. The Whigs called attention to his relative obscurity before the Democratic national convention (Who is James K. Polk?), termed him a small man unfit for the heavy duties of the presidential office, and charged that his grandfather, Ezekiel Polk, had been a Tory in the American Revolution. The Democrats retorted that Ezekiel had signed the Mecklenburg Declaration of Independence, a claim indignantly denied by the Whig press.[16]

In June, 1844, a "trial of strength" was held at Greenville, in Pitt County, between Stanly and Romulus M. Saunders, the "Goliath of Democracy" in North Carolina. An assiduous office-seeker, Saunders had been his party's gubernatorial candidate in 1840 and was an effective public speaker, despite carelessness and inaccuracy in the use of words. As a delegate to the Democratic national convention, he had moved the adoption of the two-thirds rule which defeated Van Buren and became a permanent part of the Democratic nominating machine until 1936. Both men spoke at length upon such now familiar subjects as a national bank, distribution, and the protective tariff (all of which Saunders opposed and Stanly favored), but annexation was the topic of greatest interest.

Saunders, who spoke first, contended that annexation was the all absorbing question; that everything else was swallowed up in it; that every section of the country was interested in "*immediate*" annexation; that to the South particularly, it was a matter of life and death; and that the "foul spirit of abolitionism" was the only cause which prevented the immediate annexation of Texas.

Stanly said he occupied the same ground on Texas as Clay. He was against the treaty, but not against Texas being received into the Union, "when a majority of the American people said so—when she can do it without a violation of our solemn treaty with Mexico, or a forfeiture of our national honor." He denied that annexation was a party question, since both Van Buren and Senator Thomas Hart Benton of Missouri were against the treaty. Indignantly scouting Saunder's charge that the "foul spirit of abolitionism" had induced the Whigs to oppose annexation, he pointed out that two delegates to the Democratic convention, Marcus Morton and Robert Rantoul of Massachusetts considered slavery a curse and believed that Congress had the power to abolish it in the District of Columbia. Stanly also denounced the disunionists of South Carolina, who had recently called for Texas or disunion, and appealed to every man present to stand by the Constitution, "to say whether he would make himself a party to this *treasonable scheme* of annexation or disunion!"[17]

The Whigs hailed Stanly's speech at Greenville as a masterly one, "the best, perhaps, he ever made."[18] Saunders was said to have remarked that "he had come down to Pitt to do the people some good—to brush the dust out of their eyes—but his friend *Stanly brushed it all back again and a little more*, and he must leave them as he found them."[19] When Saunders failed to keep an appointment at Washington, the *North State Whig* declared that the "valorous General" had "*backed out*" because he knew his cause to be a rotten one which could not stand before the light of truth. "Hence his determination to get away where he could have the field to himself."[20]

The state elections in August, 1844, brought a narrow Whig victory, Graham's majority over Hoke being about 3,153 in a total vote of 82,019. The Whigs controlled the legislature, although they had only a two-vote majority in the Senate. Stanly was elected to the House of Commons from Beaufort County, with a comfortable 332 vote majority (871-539) over his Democratic opponent.[21]

Both parties continued their efforts in the presidential campaign, the Whigs hoping to give Clay a much larger majority than that achieved for Graham in the state election. In this they failed, for Clay's margin of victory was only 3,390 in a vote of 62,488, slightly more than Graham's. The total vote was almost twenty thousand less than in the state elections, each party losing about the same number of votes. Stanly's electioneering was curtailed, after the state elections, when he was upset in a gig, leaving him "much lamed" and in need of relief at the seashore.[22]

The Whig victory in North Carolina was not repeated nationally. As the campaign progressed, Clay realized that he had underestimated annexation sentiment in the South, but the more he tried to hedge on the issue the worse off he became. New York was the key state, and there the 15,814 votes cast for the Liberty Party, coming largely from anti-slavery Whigs, gave the state and the election to Polk. He received 170 votes in the electoral college to 105 for Clay, but had a popular majority of only 32,367 votes. Whigs everywhere were disheartened by the narrow defeat of their beloved chieftain, and none more so than Stanly, who told Mangum that in "these gloomy times" the Whigs were "still unconquered & feel unconquered: though heart stricken for our country & our glorious 'old chief'—dearer to us now than if he had been successful."[23]

When the General Assembly met in Raleigh on November 18, 1844, Stanly was chosen as the Whig nominee for Speaker of the House of Commons, for him a particularly desirable honor since his father had twice held that office. He was elected, receiving sixty-eight votes to forty-eight for Calvin Graves of Caswell. Upon taking the chair, he pledged that the powers of the office would to the best of his ability be exerted with impartiality—a pledge, one suspects, received with some incredulity by House Democrats. The Raleigh *Register* declared that his election had given the Whigs of North Carolina much satisfaction and had infused "gall and bitterness" into the cup of Locofocoism. The honor, however, had been eminently his due:

> He now fills the seat, where his honored father fell, in the discharge of his duties as a Representative of the People—a consideration which must, in his estimation, greatly enhance the dignity of the position which he occupies.[24]

Stanly's pledge of impartiality did not make him less a partisan out of the chair. On December 10, he reported to Mangum that the Whigs in the legislature were disinclined to pass political resolutions because they did not have a safe majority in both branches, while he was of the opposite opinion: "We ought to give 'line upon line & precept upon precept': to let the people understand that Whig principles still exist."[25] The House of Commons finally adopted resolutions condemning annexation, although many Whigs in the state were resigned to it. Stanly was not one of them. "We ardently hope the Senate will save us from Annexation—with Texas," he wrote Mangum on February 10, 1845.[26] However, Tyler persuaded both Houses of Congress to pass a joint resolution for the admission of Texas as a state. This resolution made unnecessary the two-thirds vote required in the Senate for ratification of a treaty. On March 3, 1845, the President offered statehood to Texas. Polk accepted this action, and by the end of the year Texas was in the Union.

Stanly kept his pledge to preside impartially over the House, and at the end of the session on January 10, 1845, the customary resolutions of thanks to the Speaker were passed unanimously amid "long and loud continued plaudits" from Democrats as well as Whigs. Stanly, usually collected, was moved to tears as he briefly but eloquently expressed his appreciation to the members for the warmth of their approval and thanked them for their forbearance and good will.

> Let it be our part gentlemen, [he concluded], to prove to our constituents, as we have to each other, that we feel it a sacred duty, to keep the honor of the State untarnished, to protect with unfaltering determination the public faith, to exercise charity one towards another, so that we may be always . . . able to say, with pride and thankfulness—*We are North Carolinians*.[27]

The impartiality with which Stanly had presided over the House surprised the Democrats, who had considered him one of the most rabid Whig partisans in the state. The Raleigh *Register* declared that "many and many a member, who came to the legislature with feelings full of bitterness towards him, have returned home to sound his praises and cherish him in their heart of hearts." An exaggeration, but even the Raleigh *North Carolina Standard* admitted he had deserved the unanimous vote of thanks. Charles R. Kinney, an Elizabeth City lawyer, said he had never known a Speaker who had given such universal satisfaction as had Stanly; a "leading" member of the Democratic Party told him he would prefer Stanly for Speaker "to any man of his own party."[28]

Content for the time being with his General Assembly service, Stanly was not a candidate for Congress in the election of 1845. The Whigs of the Eighth District selected young Richard Spaight Donnell of Beaufort County as their standard bearer. Donnell was a "well tried and faithful" Whig, although his father, uncle (ex-Governor

Richard Dobbs Spaight), and brother-in-law (Charles Shepard) were leaders in the Democratic Party. Stanly thought his prospects were favorable. As he explained to Ebenezer Pettigrew: "Nash & Edgecombe cannot be brought out, as they were against me, with the vote for the Bk-rupt law, the Tariff, & the 'Conqueror' speeches. I think the women & children of Edgecombe cannot all vote this year, & certainly will not vote *twice*, as they were said to have done before."[29]

Donnell's opponent was Henry S. Clarke of Beaufort County, who was selected in a Democratic district convention over the incumbent, Archibald Arrington, and Henry I. Toole. The Raleigh *Register* said in July, 1845, that Donnell's election prospect was "very flattering", but he was beaten even more badly than Stanly two years before, falling 641 votes behind Clarke. Edgecombe and Nash, Stanly's prediction to the contrary, delivered their usual heavy majorities for the Democratic candidate, who also ran well in the lower counties, receiving a particularly heavy vote in Hyde.[30] In the state as a whole, with Texas and the tariff as the chief issues, the Democrats won six districts to three for the Whigs, a gain of one.

In January, 1846, Stanly attended the Whig state convention in Raleigh as a delegate from Beaufort. William A. Graham was unanimously renominated for governor. The platform opposed the Sub-Treasury scheme, declared for incidental protection and distribution, and demanded Oregon without war. Stanly addressed the convention twice and confessed that in his younger days he had felt and expressed some bitterness toward the Democrats; but "what gall he had, had been long ago spent." He had done them wrong so far as North Carolina was concerned. Almost his first acquaintance with the Democratic Party had been in Congress, where Democracy and Locofocoism were synonymous, or rather, Locofocoism there was "progressive Democracy 'full blown.'" The Democracy of North Carolina, he was happy to say, was merely progressive, and he prayed before it attained its full-blown honors that it might receive a "blight and a blast that should crush it beyond resuscitation."[31]

Stanly's confession of past error occasioned some merriment among the Democrats. "A LOOKER ON" wrote the Raleigh *North Carolina Standard* that Stanly's "tours" through Nash and Edgecombe counties had "smoothed him down, and given him quite a polish." He had said he now had some respect for the Democrats—indeed, he believed there "were a good many of them who would not steal a sheep under any circumstances." He had been well received, and "seemed tolerably comfortable in his new *trowsers* of charity and politeness."[32] The "trowsers" had probably been donned because Stanly realized after his failure to win the Whig nomination in 1843 that his reputation for violent abuse of his political opponents had alienated many moderate Whigs and was injuring his political career.

Graham's opponent in the gubernatorial contest was James Biddle Shepard of Wake County. Stanly, who was a member of the Central Whig Committee of North Carolina, warned Mangum that the "Locos" would make a desperate effort to carry the state against Graham. The Whigs must work if they expected to win.[33] Shepard waged an active campaign, going first to the East, where he debated with Stanly at New Bern on April 25, and later to the West, meeting Graham a number of times in joint debate.[34]

Two developments during the campaign injured the Democratic cause. The first was the outbreak of war with Mexico in May, 1846. Although the Whigs did not actively hinder the prosecution of the war, remembering the fate of the Federalist Party in the War of 1812, they could and did charge that it was unnecessary and had been brought about by President Polk's rashness. On June 3, Stanly wrote Governor Graham to request a field officer's appointment for his brother, James G. Stanly, Jr., in one of the North Carolina regiments. "There is very little War feeling among us," he said. "Politically, we go on smoothly."[35]

The second event was the sudden resignation of Senator William H. Haywood. A man of independent views and a close friend of the President, Haywood, in accordance with the Democratic doctrine of senatorial responsibility, resigned rather than vote for the Walker Tariff of 1846. His resignation—praised by the Whigs—hurt the Democratic Party in the campaign.[36]

Graham was reelected by a majority of 7,859 votes, and both Houses of the legislature were Whig. Stanly was again elected to the House of Commons from Beaufort, this time without regular opposition. The *North Carolina Standard* attributed Shepard's defeat to "base, secret, and abominable Whig lies and Whig slanders"; Haywood's resignation; the Mexican War; and the dissatisfaction of some Democrats with Shepard's selection as the party's nominee.[37]

When the General Assembly met on November 16, 1846, Stanly was again chosen Speaker, defeating Daniel W. Courts of Rockingham County, sixty-five to forty-seven.[38] The first concern of the Whigs in the legislature was the election of two United States senators; Mangum was assured of reelection to his own seat, but several candidates were suggested for the senate seat vacated by Haywood. Thomas Clingman of Buncombe County, young and able, was the favorite of the western Whigs and was anxious for the honor, while the Raleigh Whigs favored George E. Badger or John Motley Morehead. In the east, state rights Whigs pressed the claims of William B. Shepard of Camden County and the Federal Whigs, those of Stanly. The New Bern *Newbernian* told the Whigs in the legislature that it would not be wise to disregard Stanly's claims, while the Washington *North State Whig* also called for an eastern senator, without mentioning Stanly by name.[39]

However, the Whig caucus selected Badger for the vacant seat, over Shepard, and he was elected, defeating Asa Biggs of Martin County. Mangum was reelected over James J. McKay of Bladen. Badger was called the harmony candidate because his political views, kinship to Stanly, and previous association with the East made him acceptable to the eastern Federal Whigs, while Clingman in the West admitted his claims.[40]

The *North Carolina Standard* saw an opportunity to sow disaffection among the rival Whig princelings and their followers, and insisted that both the East and the West had again been slighted by the central Whig clique in Raleigh. Whig papers in those areas would have the "'proud satisfaction'" of waiting two more years for a senate seat and then perhaps witnessing the election of Governor Graham to succeed Badger. "For what Federalist dare deny that Orange is the State, or that the Central Clique have the power to produce *'harmony' by sending their own men to the Senate*?"[41]

The *Standard*'s party purpose was obvious, but its charge contained a large measure of truth. Since 1840, the Whig Party's senatorial and gubernatorial candidates had been men from the center part of the state favored by the Raleigh Whigs. Mangum and Graham were from Orange County, Morehead from Guilford, and Badger from Wake. The eastern and western Whigs quite correctly felt they had been slighted and their resentment was growing.

The General Assembly also had to elect a state attorney general for a four-year term, and Stanly was one of those spoken of for the office before the legislature met. [42] When the two houses began to ballot on December 2, 1846, Stanly, Spier Whitaker (Democrat), and Benjamin F. Moore (Whig) were the leading contenders, but none could get a majority of the whole numbers of votes cast. Finally, on December 12, the Democrats broke the deadlock by withdrawing their present candidate, Duncan McRae, and voting generally for Stanly, who was elected. The Raleigh *Register* attributed his many Democratic votes to the impartiality with which he had presided over the House. [43]

The Whigs used their legislative majority to redistrict the state to give the party six and possibly seven of the nine congressional seats. This was done under the leadership of Kenneth Rayner of Hertford County, and the Democrats coined the word "Raynermander." Nash and Edgecombe were removed from the Eighth District and Wayne, Greene, and Jones were added. The Democrats complained bitterly, the *Standard* declaring that Wayne and Lenoir, with their lumber and turpentine interests, had been made to "lean over and kiss the distant fish-ponds and corn-fields of Hyde and Tyrrell!" But the Whigs were quick to remind the Democrats that they had gerrymandered Stanly out of his seat in 1842, and even boasted of it. [44]

The Whig gerrymander resulted in the election of six Whigs and three Democrats in the congressional elections of 1847. In the Eighth District, Richard S. Donnell was again the Whig candidate and this time was victorious, defeating William K. Lane of Wayne by 369 votes. [45]

With the congressional elections safely passed, the Whigs turned their attention to the choice of a candidate for governor in 1848. Many names were mentioned, including Stanly, Richard Hines, Andrew Joyner, John Kerr, James W. Bryan, William B. Shepard, Kenneth Rayner, and David L. Swain. Kerr, Bryan, and Rayner refused to be considered, the latter giving as his reasons ill health and agricultural interests in the Southwest which necessitated frequent absences from the state.[46] It was generally understood in Raleigh that someone from the East would be selected, and William A. Graham told James W. Bryan that the delegates to the convention from that region would have the choice "very much in their power," if they could agree on a candidate. He added that at Raleigh the name of Andrew Joyner of Halifax County had been the most conspicuously mentioned in conversation.[47]

Stanly was asked by Fenner B. Satterthwaite, a Whig leader in Pitt County, if he would accept the Whig nomination for governor if tendered to him. Stanly, then in Raleigh attending the Supreme Court, replied on January 15, 1848, that "if the nomination is conferred on me, I must accept it." At the same time, he wanted the convention's choice to fall on someone more worthy of it, and more able to wear its honors than himself.[48] This letter was not intended for publication, but could be shown privately to interested parties.

The Whig convention met in Raleigh on Washington's birthday, February 22, and organized with Richard Hines as president. Hugh Waddell of Orange County moved that the selection of a candidate for governor be referred to a committee representing the congressional districts in attendance at the convention. Satterthwaite spoke in opposition to this resolution and Kenneth Rayner in its favor and it was then passed. The next day, Waddell announced that the Committee had unanimously agreed to report the name of Charles Manly of Chatham County as the Whig gubernatorial candidate, and his nomination was carried unanimously.[49]

Manly's selection surprised the state, for he was one of the few well-known Whigs who had not been mentioned for the nomination. At this time, he was secretary of the University trustees, county attorney for Chatham, bank attorney, attorney for the Literary Board, attorney for a life insurance company, member of the Literary Board, and clerk of the House of Commons. Eastern Whigs were angry because a candidate from their section had once more been passed over in favor of an "office-holding lawyer" associated with the Raleigh Clique. The *North State Whig* declared hotly that Manly's nomination had been brought about by "a nefarious plot of the political jugglers" who had mocked and scorned the claims of the East.[50] Some of Stanly's friends were critical of Satterthwaite's course in the convention, and in self-defense he wrote Henry Dimock of the *North State Whig* on March 8, 1848, requesting the editor to publish Stanly's letter of January 15. Satterthwaite noted that he had talked to Stanly before the Whig convention, and the latter had urged him to procure the nomination of Andrew Joyner or some other eastern man. Said Satterthwaite:

> I thought that Mr. Stanly possessed, in an eminent degree, all the qualities requisite for the station; and for that reason I desired his nomination. But when I saw there were a few *Politicians* opposed to his nomination, I determined to act according to his instructions, and withdrew his name, stating to the Committee my reasons for doing so, and at the same time reading the enclosed letter, which, though not intended for publication, I have taken the liberty of making public, as a justification to Mr. Stanly's friends of my course in the Convention.[51]

Neither the *North State Whig* nor Satterthwaite, in the interest of Whig harmony, identified the "political jugglers" or "few *Politicians*" who had prevented Stanly's nomination, but the *North Carolina Standard* correctly reported that Kenneth Rayner and "a few leading Whigs about Raleigh" had carried the day in the Whig convention.[52] What did happen there can be pieced together from private letters at the time and from letters and newspaper comments in 1853, when Rayner was a candidate before the General Assembly for the United States Senate. In sum, Rayner opposed Stanly's nomination because he did not like him personally and feared his selection would prejudice his own political claims.

Rayner had declined to be a candidate for governor in November, 1847, but David Outlaw, a representative from North Carolina's Ninth District, who talked with him in Washington before the Whig convention, thought he regretted having declined the nomination and would now accept it if tendered. "There is, as is easy to be perceived, no good blood, between him and Stanly," Outlaw informed his wife. "Rivalry among politicians is very apt to destroy their friendship for each other."[53]

While in Washington, Rayner was told by Thomas L. Clingman that Badger had said to him that Stanly ought to accept the nomination for governor because the end of his second term of office would coincide with the termination of Mangum's senatorial term, and he would then be ready to take his place. According to Outlaw:

> this disposing of offices so far ahead, was not particularly agreeable to Clingman who has aspirations himself, nor to Mr. Rayner, as he also is looking in the same direction. This conversation was repeated in Raleigh and is supposed whether justly or not I do not know, to have had some influence in defeating Stanly's nomination.[54]

The *North State Whig* claimed in 1853 that this story, made up falsely by Clingman, had been circulated by Rayner among the convention delegates "to excite prejudice," since it was known that Badger and Stanly were cousins, "and of course the convention would not like to have two members of the same family in the Senate at the same time." The *Whig* added that by "some extraordinary or unfair means," otherwise not specified, the convention had agreed to be "Raynerized"—to vote by congressional districts, "and although it was known that Mr. Stanly was the choice of a majority of the convention, by hook or by crook he was not nominated."

The *Whig* also claimed that when Stanly's friends had asked Rayner why he was opposing his nomination, he replied in substance: "*If Mr. Stanly is elected Governor, it will put him ahead of me.*" The *Whig* said Rayner would not deny this, since there were witnesses alive to whom he had made this "pitiful declaration." Rayner did deny the charge, but admitted that his reasons for opposing Stanly's nomination "were of a private nature, growing out of our peculiar relations."[55]

What Governor Graham termed "quite a difference" arose between Stanly and Badger on one side and Clingman and Rayner on the other, owing to the latter's opposition to Stanly's nomination.[56] Badger denied that he had used such language as ascribed to him by Clingman; whereupon Clingman wrote to Rayner reaffirming it and authorizing the use of his name as the source of the story. Outlaw told his wife that no bloodshed would result, for Badger, both from principle and constitutional aversion, was a noncombatant; but he was satisfied there was "no good feeling" between Rayner and Badger.[57]

Writing Thomas Sparrow in April, 1856, Stanly recalled that he was ready for months to make an issue with Rayner over his conduct at the State Convention; but when Rayner disclaimed having cast any "personal imputation," he forgave him and paid him a visit of "respect and courtesy" in Raleigh. Continued Stanly:

> You remember when sitting with you in your office, on the day the Convention met that nominated my estimable friend Gov. Manly I remarked to you that I would bet you a glass of lemonade that Col. Joyner would be nominated because his friends would be numerous in Raleigh and because Mr. Rayner would not be there to advocate my 'claims'—I was unconscious of ever having given him any cause of offence—I never did. Was always true to him; never omitted an opportunity of placing him ahead of and above me in public opinion: tried for years to make [him] Govr: I begged him to be a candidate: but I repeat I forgave him this. His jealousy was a weakness.

Subsequently, during his last term in Congress, Stanly learned from Reverdy Johnson that in his controversy with Henry Wise, Rayner's conduct, while presumably acting as a friend, *"had been anything but what a gentleman and a friend had a right to expect!"* More than this Stanly would not tell Sparrow, except to ask: "Could any man act more unworthily than Mr. Rayner did to me?"[58]

In April, 1848, Stanly told Graham that he would resign as Attorney-General at the close of the circuit because he did not wish to live in Raleigh and thought he should not hold the office unless he did so. When he resigned in May, the *North Carolina Standard* reported that his Beaufort County friends intended to run him for the legislature and would no doubt bring his name prominently forward to replace Badger in the Senate. Badger's term expired in 1849, and the next legislature would have his place to fill. The *Standard* predicted that Rayner, having defeated Stanly in his aspirations for the Whig nomination for governor, would not stand by quietly and see his rival sent to the Senate: "Trouble is brewing in the *Whig*-wam. Look out, about the 1st day of December, 1848, for warm work in the Legislature between the Rayner and Stanly branches of the 'great Whig party'—provided the Whigs should carry a majority of that body."[59]

North Carolina Whigs had not only a governor and legislature to elect in 1848, but a president as well. State leaders were divided in their sympathies for the Whig nomination between Henry Clay and Generals Zachary Taylor and Winfield Scott, the two heroes of the Mexican War; and the Whig state convention, with a fine impartiality, endorsed all three. Stanly supported Taylor, who had reluctantly admitted he was a Whig, but not an "ultra Whig."[60] At the Whig national convention in Philadelphia on June 7, 1848, Taylor was nominated on the fourth ballot. John Motley Morehead served as convention president, and Stanly was a delegate. There is a tradition that Kenneth Rayner came near receiving the nomination for Vice-President instead of Millard Fillmore of New York.[61]

Meanwhile, the state campaign had opened, with Manly opposed by David S. Reid, a young Rockingham lawyer, who had just completed two terms in Congress. Reid was a hard campaigner of excellent ability and almost unerring judgment; Manly, while a man of great charm and considerable ability, was said by Graham to be "by no means well informed in politics"; moreover, his nomination had not been acceptable in many quarters.[62] Manly attempted to wage the campaign on national issues, but in the first joint debate at New Bern, Reid called for the abolition of the fifty-acre freehold qualification required of a voter for state senator. The next day at Beaufort City, Manly came out against "free suffrage," as Reid had termed it, arguing that one might as well abolish the Senate itself as extend the privilege of voting for senators to those who had no land. The Whig leaders agreed with Manly, proclaiming "free suffrage" to be the worst sort of "demagoguical [*sic*] doctrine."[63] Stanly debated the issue with Reid at Washington on May 22 and declared the latter had "mounted the hobby of free suffrage" to lead the people astray. He thought it a Republican principle that taxation and representation should go together. He had heard only one other man beside Reid denounce the fifty-acre qualification, and he, when last heard of, was in jail, "where he would not have been, if he had worked honestly for 50 acres of land to qualify him to vote for the Senate."[64]

Toward the end of the state campaign many Whigs, particularly in the West, openly began to favor free suffrage, while the party press tried to ignore the issue wherever possible. Reid waged a strong campaign, ably seconded by William Holden, editor of the *North Carolina Standard*, and only the strength of the Whig party organization saved the Whigs from defeat—Manly's majority was just 854 in a total vote of 84,218. The General Assembly was equally divided in both houses. Stanly was elected to a third term in the House of Commons from Beaufort.[65]

After the state elections, attention centered on the presidential race, where Whig prospects were considerably brighter. The Whigs asserted that Lewis Cass of Michigan, the Democratic nominee, was unsound on the slavery question and a perennial office-seeker, "often found at the foot of power vilely seeking favor." The Democrats, in turn, decried Fillmore as an abolitionist and proclaimed Taylor unfit for public office. The Whigs lauded Taylor's military record in Mexico, calling him "The Hero of Buena Vista," and dwelled upon his honesty, integrity, and soldierly sense of duty. "He is plain old Zach Taylor," said the Raleigh *Register*, "honest and incorruptible—the man whom the People delight to honor!"[66] Stanly was a Taylor elector and stumped the Eighth District in opposition to Asa Biggs of Williamston, the Cass elector.[67]

For the first time, the entire nation went to the polls on the same day, November 7. Taylor won over Cass by 140,000 votes, carrying eight slave states and seven free states with 163 electoral votes to 127 for Cass. The fact that Taylor was a Southerner and a slave-owner helped him in the South, and he lost only Virginia, Mississippi, and Alabama. North Carolina went for him by a margin of 8,154 votes in a total vote of 81,280. The vote cast in New York for Martin Van Buren, the candidate of the new Free-Soil Party, came largely from the Democrats and gave the state and the election to Taylor. The Free Soilers also elected nine congressmen to the House of Representatives where they might hold the balance of power, so evenly divided were the two major parties.[68]

Just at the time when a rejuvenated Democratic Party was challenging Whig supremacy in North Carolina, the Whigs there were faced with the potentially divisive issue of slavery in the territories.

In August, 1846, David Wilmot, a free soil Democrat from Pennsylvania, had introduced an amendment to an appropriation bill in the House which would have prohibited the introduction of slavery into any territory that might be acquired from Mexico. The House adopted this "Wilmot Proviso," the Senate rejected it. In North Carolina, both parties opposed the Proviso, the Raleigh *Register* going so far as to declare that on this issue, it was "time for party distinctions to sleep, and for the South to present a united front."[69]

North Carolina Democrats were almost unanimous in denying that Congress had any constitutional right to exclude slavery from the territories, but the Whigs were divided on this question, although united in opposition to the *exercise* of any such power by Congress. In July, 1848, the Senate debated the so-called "Clayton Compromise" bill, which expressly prohibited the legislatures of New Mexico and California from passing laws respecting the establishment or prohibition of slavery and referred all questions in these territories growing out of the institution of slavery to the United States Supreme Court. During the debate, Senator Badger declared that whether slavery was introduced into the territories acquired from Mexico or its exclusion continued under Mexican law depended upon the will of Congress. "If nothing be done by Congress it remains excluded, and their power over the subject is complete and perfect."[70] Whig representatives Richard S. Donnell, Nathaniel Boyden, and David Outlaw held similar views, as did Stanly. But Mangum, representing the views of the state rights wing of the Whig Party in North Carolina, denied that Congress had any constitutional right to exclude slavery from the territories. He voted for the Clayton Compromise, as did Daniel Barringer, Shepperd, Clingman, and Outlaw in the House. Badger, Donnell, and Boyden voted against it. The Senate accepted the Compromise, but the House rejected it; and New Mexico and California remained unorganized and under military authority.[71]

The term for which Badger had been elected in 1846 expired on March 4, 1849. His opposition to the Clayton Compromise and his belief in the exclusive control of Congress over slavery in the territories alienated the state rights wing of the Whig Party in North Carolina, and several Whigs came out in opposition to him. William

H. Washington wrote James W. Bryan that both Clingman and Daniel M. Barringer had "put in" against Badger for his seat, while Stanly, Rayner, Graham, Morehead, and William B. Shepard were also in the field. Washington did not think Badger could be elected because some of the state rights Whigs in the legislature would vote against him because of his opposition to the Clayton bill. It was doubtful who could be elected, but he thought Shepard stood the best chance.[72] Badger himself thought his reelection "very doubtful—the chances against it."[73]

More than just the slavery question was involved in Whig opposition to Badger. Personal ambition and jealousy were important factors. Clingman warned Mangum before the presidential election that if Taylor was elected, Badger would seek a cabinet office for himself and a foreign mission for Stanly, which would about absorb North Carolina's share of the offices abroad. "It is obviously proper therefore for all those who do not intend that the Whig party of the State shall be the mere property of one family to show a proper feeling of indpendence [*sic*] as we shall soon be a minority in the State."[74]

The Whig caucus selected Badger as the party's nominee for the full six-year term; and on December 12, 1848, the General Assembly began balloting. On the first ballot, Badger received fifty-eight votes in the House; his two nearest Democratic rivals, James B. Shepard and James McKay, obtained fifteen and ten votes respectively. Clingman had three votes. In the Senate, Badger had twenty-four votes; Weldon Edwards and McKay eight each; Clingman three; the rest scattered. Every Whig member in the Assembly voted for Badger except William B. Shepard, who voted for Rayner, and Atkin of Buncombe and Farmer of Henderson, who voted for Clingman. Badger's eighty-two votes were just one short of a majority, and one of the three errant Whig votes would have elected him. The legislature balloted again on December 16, and once more Badger fell short with eighty-two votes to seventeen for William Shepard, seventeen for James B. Shepard, and fourteen for Clingman, with the rest scattered. After this vote, one observer reported that "It is now very certain that Mr. Badger cannot be elected Senator and very probable that Mr. W. B. Sheppard [*sic*] can and will."[75]

Clingman, meanwhile, had been fishing for Democratic votes; and when on December 18 a committee of Democratic members asked him for an expression of his political views, he replied in writing that he was opposed to a national bank, opposed the repeal of the Walker Tariff of 1846, and considered the Wilmot Proviso unconstitutional.[76] These answers satisfied most Democrats, and on December 20, when the Assembly balloted a third time, Clingman received forty-eight votes, while Badger held at eighty-two. After this ballot, Stanly gained the floor and, in obvious reference to the discussions between Clingman and the Democrats, remarked that the air was filled with rumors, rumors that gave the Whigs pain.

> We have heard sir, that the Democratic party are making propositions; that they have received favorable answers. We have heard also that the desperate spirit of party has been attempting to compel gentlemen on the other side to take up some one to whom hitherto opposed. . . Will gentlemen on the other side inform me how much of these rumors are true? Has any contract been made? Have the contracting parties agreed? How much remains to be done to complete the arrangement?

Although "much attached" to Badger and anxious to secure his election, Stanly was not willing to say "'that talked of Rome, that her wide walks encompassed but one man.'" Solely upon his own responsibility and without prior authorization, he proposed that all factions and parties unite to elect David L. Swain, "a favorite son of old Buncombe," to the Senate. Swain's nomination was seconded and notification sent to the Senate.[77]

On the fourth ballot, Badger's total dropped to seventy-five, as Swain received nine votes (including Stanly's) and Clingman climbed to fifty-five. But on the fifth ballot, Swain was dropped and Badger breasted the tape with eighty-three votes, a bare majority of the total votes cast. He received every Whig vote except those of Shepard and Atkin. As Badger explained to Senator Crittenden: "One of Clingman's men [Farmer] came over to me & thus gave the requisite majority & none to spare."[78]

The senatorial struggle left scars on the Whig Party in the state which were never healed and which contributed to its decline and eventual defeat. Thomas Clingman published an address defending

his action in consenting to be a candidate against Badger; "so far was
he [Badger] from being the choice of the State generally," Clingman
declared, "that the opinion was by no means uncommon at Raleigh
that he was not the first choice, even of a majority of the Whig
members, though nominated by the [caucus] system. . . ." He
blasted the Raleigh Whigs who depended upon the West for heavy
majorities but divided the spoils among themselves, and warned
darkly of a bolt if this "greedy rapacity" continued.[79]

The concern which some Whigs felt on the subject of slavery in
the territories was reflected in a series of resolutions which Walter L.
Steele, a state rights Whig from Richmond County, introduced into
the House of Commons on November 27, 1848. The resolutions
declared that the territories were the common property of the states;
that Congress had no right to pass any law making any discrimination between the states by which any one of them would be
deprived of its full and equal right in any United States territory;
and that the enactment of any law directly, or by its effects,
preventing the citizens of any state from emigrating with their
property into the territories, would be "a violation of the Constitution, and the rights of the states . . . and in derogation of that
perfect equality which belongs to them as members of this Union,
and would tend directly to subvert the Union itself."[80]

Stanly and Kenneth Rayner led the Federal Whigs in opposing the
Steele resolutions. Stanly, speaking on December 7, urged the House
to attend to the pressing needs of the state rather than enter into
idle debate to gratify the ambition of fifty young gentlemen, on
both sides, under twenty-five, who were "panting for an opportunity
of 'fleshing their maiden swords' in political controversy." The
presidential election was over; the people of the country were worn
out and tired of the noise and confusion of the campaign, while
nothing new could be said on the subject of the Wilmot Proviso.
What possible good, then, could result from the introduction of this
"pestiferous question," this "apple of discord?" Let the "trumpeters
of party strife" be still, at least until the session's important business
had been transacted. His appeal failed, and he was unsuccessful in an
attempt to table the resolutions. On December 14, they were
referred to a House committee for study.[81]

A series of resolutions introduced into the Senate on January 15, 1849, by William B. Shepard were later substituted for the Steele Resolutions. These resolutions declared: (1) "that the states came into the Union as equals, and that the citizens of each state are entitled to equal rights, privileges and immunities under the Constitution"; (2) that the framers of the Constitution had incorporated "into the instrument distinct and ample guarantees of the rights of the slaveholder"; (3) that the legislature viewed "with deep concern and alarm the constant aggressions on the rights of the slaveholder, by certain reckless politicians of the North," and that the recent congressional proceedings on slavery were "fraught with mischief, well calculated to disturb the peace of our country, and should call forth the earnest and prompt disapprobation of every friend of the Union"; (4) that the exclusion of slavery from any of the territories "will be an act not only of gross injustice and wrong, but the exercise of power, contrary to the true meaning and spirit of the Constitution, and never contemplated by the framers thereof"; (5) that for the sake of preserving the peace and the Union, the legislature was willing that the Missouri Compromise line be extended to the Pacific, without conceding that Congress had the constitutional power to prohibit slavery in any of the territories; and (6) that copies of the resolutions be forwarded to North Carolina's representatives and senators to be laid before their respective houses.[82]

Stanly announced to the House that he would not vote for Shepard's resolutions and would oppose some of them. He had evidence they were advocated because it was believed they would embarrass "a distinguished gentleman in the Whig Party [Badger]." The third resolution, moreover, contained a "sly threat of disunion" which he did not like and hinted at Nullification "in a parenthesis." If this resolution meant to say that North Carolinians would for a moment think of disunion because "slavery is, or shall be," excluded from the southwestern territory, then it was a gross misrepresentation of the feelings and opinions of nine-tenths of the people in the state. "Whether the Wilmot Proviso should be adopted or not, the people of North Carolina will stand by the Union."

The fourth resolution, Stanly continued, could have been so

worded as to admit of a vote on the constitutional question separate from that of the injustice of legislating slavery from the territories. This had been done because of a desire to embarrass the Whig Party. It was well known that many Southern men of intelligence agreed with Badger as to the constitutional *power* of Congress to pass the Wilmot Proviso.

> To say that Congress will do an act of gross injustice and wrong, is one thing; but to say this same act [is] unconstitutional is quite another thing....I am willing to say it is wrong to exclude the Southern people from the Territories; wrong to abolish Slavery in the District of Columbia; but I cannot say it is unconstitutional.

The fifth resolution was the most pitiful of all. If Congress, under the extension of the Missouri Compromise line, could prohibit slavery north of 36°30', what man of sound mind could say that it did not also possess the same power *south* of that line? It seemed too clear for argument. The legislature had better leave the question to be settled by Congress, under the administration soon to be in power.[83]

During his remarks, Stanly introduced a resolution, written in the language of Washington's Farewell Address, as an amendment to Shepard's Resolutions. It resolved that "the people of North Carolina of all parties are devotedly attached to the Union of the United States . . . [and] believe it is the duty of their public servants to discountenance whatever may suggest even a suspicion that it can in any event by abandoned." Stanly's resolution was adopted, fifty-six to thirty-one, and he exultingly declared that he would not further delay passage of the Shepard Resolutions, having sent "the bane and antidote together," and taken the "poison from the arrow." However, he would vote against the third, fourth, and fifth resolutions.[84] On January 20, 1849, the Shepard Resolutions passed the House by heavy majorities. Stanly, Satterthwaite, and John Y. Hicks submitted a written "Protest" against them which was ordered printed in the *House Journal*.[85]

Stanly charged during his speech on the Shepard Resolutions that their author ("Mr. Senatorial") in introducing them had been motivated by his personal dislike of Badger, rather than by any

desire to rebuke Northern fanaticism. He also suggested that Shepard
hoped to force Badger to resign from the Senate and then take his
place with the aid of Democratic votes. Shepard denied the accusation and the two men exchanged angry letters in the Raleigh
Register. Shepard finally asserted that Badger was a "Southern man
with Northern principles," and Stanly retorted hotly that the former
had a "Senate-mania." He warned Shepard that if he did not change
his course, and continued to give "unbridled license to his angry
feelings," he must "hereafter remind us of Goldsmith's Elegy on the
death of a mad dog—a part of which he will pardon me for quoting:

> "This dog and man at first were friends,
>   But when a pique began,
> The dog to gain his private ends,
>   Went mad and bit the man.

> "Around from all the neighboring streets,
>   The wondering neighbors ran,
> And swore the dog had lost its wits,
>   To bite so good a man.

> "The wound it seemed both sore and sad,
>   To ev'ry christian eye,
> And while they swore the dog was mad,
>   They swore the man would die.

> "But soon a wonder came to light
>   That showed the rogues they lied;
> The *man* recovered of the bite.
>   The *dog* it was that died.[86]

The Assembly also concerned itself at this session with the
question of internal improvements. Poor roads forced many Pied-
mont and western North Carolinians to trade in Virginia and South
Carolina. Governor Graham, in reply to a senate resolution, sent a
special message to the legislature on November 27, 1848, urging the
construction with state aid of a railroad from Raleigh to Charlotte
by way of Salisbury.[87] The Charlotte and Danville (Va.) Company
was offering to build a railroad between these two cities with only a

"naked charter" and no state aid of any kind. According to Rufus Barringer, one of the House leaders in the fight for the "naked charter," Stanly was the "most determined, ever ready, outspoken opponent" of the "Danville Connection," as it was called. He feared that a railroad connecting western North Carolina with Virginia and South Carolina, rather than with the eastern part of the state, would place the West in economic and political bondage to the two neighboring states. He sneeringly referred to Richmond as only a "Great Slave Mart," and to Charleston as "surviving solely on past pretensions." Barringer then offered to support any fair and feasible North Carolina system. Stanly sprang to his feet and pledged his support and that of his eastern friends to a bill introduced by Senator W. S. Ashe of New Hanover County if Barringer would do likewise. This provided for a state subscription of $2,000,000 to build a railroad from Charlotte to Goldsboro, two hundred and thirty miles, provided that $1,000,000 was privately subscribed. Barringer agreed to Stanly's proposal, and the Ashe bill was pushed through the House, sixty to fifty-two, and the Senate by Speaker Calvin Graves' casting vote.[88]

In addition to the Ashe bill, the General Assembly passed several other internal improvement measures and authorized the construction of a state hospital for the insane. North Carolina had entered a new era; and as Stanly had long hoped, seemed about to cast off the derisive appellation of the "Rip Van Winkle" state. The people sensed the change. "All of the Internal Improvement schemes have passed," Charles L. Hinton informed Governor Graham from Raleigh on January 26. "Last night there was great rejoicings, the crowd seemed to think the State was redeemed."[89]

Meanwhile, it was understood in the state that North Carolina would receive an important foreign mission from the Taylor administration; and Stanly, Hugh Waddell, and Daniel M. Barringer were candidates for the appointment. In January, 1849, Badger wrote John J. Crittenden, one of Taylor's original supporters: "Dont forget our friend Stanly."[90] At the end of February, Mangum, who was committed firmly to Waddell, talked with Badger for the first time on the subject, and reported to Graham that Badger favored Stanly for Spain and Waddell for Mexico and would push in a peremptory manner for both; but "he cannot get both & possibly, not to say probably, will fail for both."[91]

The struggle continued until May, with great uncertainty as to who would finally get the prize. Badger continued to press Stanly's name, and Mangum that of Waddell, and the inability of the two senators to agree upon one name finally led the Administration to offer William A. Graham the Spanish mission. As Mangum explained to him: "The Senators are understood to have made a *point* of this matter & the admn are unwilling to make a *point* with either." When Graham declined the appointment despite his friends' entreaties, it was given to Daniel M. Barringer, who had many friends among the original Taylor men.[92]

The Democrats were prepared to wage the congressional elections of 1849 with the protection of "Southern Rights" as their major issue. The Eighth District Democratic Convention, meeting in New Bern on May 17, resolved that it would support no man for Congress who did not believe that the Wilmot Proviso was directly at variance with the spirit and intention of the Constitution. When the delegates nominated William K. Lane of Wayne County, who had contested the district with Donnell in 1847, the Raleigh *North Carolina Standard* said that "above and beyond other considerations, *he is sound to the core on the Slavery question*; and the rights of the slaveholder, in every crisis and under all circumstances, will be safe in his hands."[93]

The Whig press in the state denounced the Democratic efforts to agitate the slavery question and reaffirmed its devotion to the Union. The Raleigh *Register* thought the dogmas contained in the Steele resolutions of "little practical importance" since it took it for granted that no one would ever think of taking a slave to California or New Mexico, for purposes of profit, "though he might be ever so free to do so."[94] Nor did the people seem concerned lest slavery be excluded from the territories.[95] Badger echoed the sentiments of many Federal Whigs in the state when he declared privately:

I am a friend to the Union—I have sworn to support the constitution & will never concur in any movement which may however remotely endanger its continuance—certainly not for the privilege of carrying slaves to California or keeping up private gaols by slaveholders in this district.[96]

When Richard S. Donnell declined to be a candidate for reelection, the Whigs of the Eighth District, meeting in Washington on May 24, unanimously nominated James W. Bryan of Craven County as the Whig candidate for Congress. Bryan reluctantly accepted the nomination, but almost immediately withdrew from the canvass because of feeble health. The convention then reassembled at Washington on June 19 and nominated Stanly.[97]

The Washington *North State Whig* reported that Stanly's nomination had kindled the "old Whig fires . . . in first-rate style" throughout the district. In Craven, it had been received "with great enthusiasm"; in Washington and Tyrell there was a "*cordial* and *undivided* support of the nominee." A Carteret Whig reported that no nomination could have been more acceptable to the Whigs in his county: "We love Stanly, and I predict for him the largest majority Carteret has ever given for any candidate."[98]

Whig papers outside the Eighth District also hailed Stanly's nomination, the Philadelphia *North American* terming it "an omen of good" in a time of national crisis. The Raleigh *Register* predicted he would bear the Whig banner—as always—"gallantly and nobly through the campaign." In Washington, D. C., the *Republic*, organ of the Taylor administration, declared:

> Mr. Stanly has already commenced the canvass with a spirit which cannot fail of success. We shall hail his return to the Congress of the United States with pride. He is one of the champions of the Whig cause, who has borne its banner highest when the tide of adversity was strongest. He is wanted here.[99]

The Democratic press bitterly assailed Stanly for what the Raleigh *North Carolina Standard* termed his "unwise and indefensible course upon the Slavery question, at the recent session of the Legislature." Not only had Stanly been the life and soul of the Badger party, but he had made every effort to defeat Steele's resolutions. "If *his* wishes had prevailed," said the *Standard*, "the voice of North Carolina would have been hushed into silence and these Resolutions of remonstrance against Northern aggressions would have been consigned to the sleep of death."[100]

The New Bern *Republican* declared that there was only one issue in the campaign—"the constitutionality or unconstitutionality of the [Wilmot] Proviso." Lane thought the Proviso unconstitutional and denied the right of Congress to pass it, or to abolish slavery in the District of Columbia. Stanly, although ostensibly opposed to the Proviso on the grounds of its injustice to the South, admitted its constitutionality, and the right of Congress to abolish slavery in the District of Columbia. Lane, therefore, was the safer man and occupied a more defensible position. Said the *Republican*:

> In our view, he who gives up the Constitutional objections gives up all; if the power is conceded to Congress to pass the Proviso, the whole question is yielded; it is only an acknowledgement of this power that is wanted by the North, and they will forthwith proceed to exercise it. Whatever may be Mr. Stanly's intentions, his position must be 'unsafe and dangerous' for the South.[101]

Speaking at New Bern on July 21, Stanly answered those critics who said he was unsound on the slavery question. He defended his opposition to some of Steele's resolutions, a number of which were "strongly tinctured with Calhounism," promoted agitation, and squinted at disunion. As for the Wilmot Proviso, he thought it unjust, abominable, and grossly offensive to the South; yet in all honesty, he could not deny the right of Congress to legislate upon the subject of slavery in the territories. The New Bern *Newbernian* quoted him as saying:

> He had considered the subject well—he had pondered it fully and the result was, his judgement forced him to admit that Congress *had* the right, although his early prejudices, education, interests and inclinations, were all opposed to that view. But while he admitted the right, no one was more opposed to its exercise than he was.[102]

Stanly assured the voters "that if elected to Congress, I shall oppose the Wilmot Proviso, the abolition of slavery in the District of Columbia, *and abolition in all its forms*."[103]

The "Conqueror" was elected, although his forty-seven vote majority was considerably less than Donnell's two years before. In fact, the final result was not known until it was learned that Stanly had received a 272 vote majority in Tyrrell County. The Whigs and Democrats were both mortified at the result—"The Whigs that the majority should be so small and the Democrats that they did not work *a little harder*."[104] However, the Whigs pointed out that Stanly's total vote was 694 more than Donnell's in 1847 and only 10 votes shy of General Taylor's count in the district. The closeness of the poll was due to the fact that the Democratic faithful had turned out *en masse* to battle their nemesis. Lane ran 1,016 votes ahead of his vote in 1847 and went 974 votes beyond Cass.[105]

The New Bern *Republican* concluded that Stanly owed his election, not to the endorsement of his views by the voters, but to the union of the Whig Party on him right or wrong. Party lines had been drawn with the utmost stringency: "There are many Whigs who voted for Mr. Stanly, and yet declared that they *did not approve* of his position."[106] There was some truth in this assertion. The New Bern *Newbernian* warmly advocated Stanly's election, although admitting later that it differed with him on the constitutionality of the Wilmot Proviso.[107]

As for Stanly, he congratulated James W. Bryan "on my ill-luck, for had I been beaten, you would never have been forgiven. You ought to have been the candidate, for I had every thing that the General Assembly did, or failed to do, to be blamed for—besides my own doings."[108]

The political complexion of the North Carolina delegation remained unchanged, as the Whigs elected six of the state's nine congressmen. The only thing the election showed was that both Whigs and Democrats were unequivocally opposed to the Wilmot Proviso. Party strength determined the result, not the candidates' attitude on the slavery and disunion issues.[109]

North Carolina Whigs remained divided on the constitutional issue of slavery in the territories, and state rights Whigs began to grumble that the Raleigh *Register* was not going far enough in its defense of Southern Rights. The Charlotte *Hornet's Nest*, the most ultra Whig paper in the state, even accused the *Register* of "Free-soilism." Thomas L. Clingman, who was slowly but surely drifting into the Democratic camp, wrote Senator Henry Stuart Foote of

Mississippi on November 13, 1849, that adoption of the principle of the Wilmot Proviso would be a violation of the Constitution, which he thought the southern states should resist. The abolition of slavery in the District of Columbia would be "an act of tyranny so insulting and so gross as to justify a withdrawal of confidence from such a government."[110]

The prospect of harmony among the Whig members of North Carolina's delegation to the Thirty-First Congress was very faint indeed, including as it did two such fiery and dissident spirits as Stanly and Clingman. Their rivalry, mingling as it did personal ambition and conflicting political principles, was a microcosm of the forces threatening to tear their party and their country apart.

7

A MOST EXTRAORDINARY COURSE

INITIALLY THE SOUTHERN PEOPLE had every confidence in Zachary Taylor's soundness on the slavery question. As a resident of Louisiana, owning a cotton plantation and over a hundred slaves in Jefferson County, Mississippi, he seemed to have a vested interest in the institution. But when Congress assembled in December, 1849, two original Taylor Whigs, Representatives Alexander H. Stephens and Robert Toombs of Georgia, were dismayed to find that Senator William H. Seward of New York, an anti-slavery Whig, had installed himself as the Administration's confidential friend. Stephens wrote later that Seward "as a charmer" had gained complete control of Secretary of the Navy William B. Preston of Virginia, one of the seven original members of the Taylor Club in Washington, and had convinced him that it would destroy the northern wing of the Whig Party to abandon the Wilmot Proviso; but that the vexing question could be got rid of by a policy of "non-action."[1]

This non-action policy, which so alarmed Stephens and Toombs, sought to bypass the question of slavery in the territories by admitting California and New Mexico immediately as free states while abstaining, as Taylor was to phrase it in his annual message, "from introduction of those exciting topics of a sectional character which have hitherto produced painful apprehensions in the public mind." In the spring of 1849, Taylor had sent Representative Thomas Butler King of Georgia to California as his special agent. King informed the Californians that the President was ready to protect them in the formation of any republican government which was the result of their deliberate choice. California shortly adopted a free-state constitution and applied to Congress for admission to the Union. In August, 1849, at Mercer, Pennsylvania, Taylor assured the North that it "need have no apprehension of the further extension of slavery." In November, Army Lieutenant Colonel George A. McCall was sent to Santa Fe, New Mexico, with an order to aid the people of the territory in taking steps toward securing admission as a state, if they so desired.[2]

The President's actions and Seward's influence in the administration convinced Stephens and Toombs that the New York senator intended to make the Whig Party the anti-slavery party to strengthen it in the North. They even came to believe that Taylor would sign the Wilmot Proviso if it should pass Congress. When Taylor refused to give private assurances to the contrary, Toombs, Stephens, and six other southern Whigs decided to insist that the Whig caucus in nominating a candidate for Speaker of the House "as a touchstone of party principle," should express strong opposition to the Proviso and to the abolition of slavery in the District of Columbia. A resolution to this effect was drawn up in Stephens' room and presented to the Whig caucus by Toombs on December 1, 1849. Its introduction caused intense excitement among the northern Whigs, which the more moderate southern members tried to allay by opposing the resolution, although acknowledging it expressed correct sentiments. Clingman said he was favorable to Toombs' resolution, and would vote for it if pressed to do so; but he regretted its introduction and hoped Toombs would withdraw it. On Stanly's motion, the resolution was laid on the table, whereupon Toombs, Stephens, and four other southern Whigs withdrew from the caucus. Robert Winthrop, a conservative anti-slavery Taylor Whig from Boston, who had served ably as Speaker in the previous Congress, was then selected as the Whig nominee for Speaker.[3]

The action of the insurgent Whigs was condemned by the vast majority of the party press in the South outside Georgia.[4] To moderate Whigs, the walk out portended the breakup of the Whig Party and even the disruption of the Union. David Outlaw, the conscientious and reserved Whig congressman from North Carolina, wrote his wife on the day after the caucus: "The future of the Whig Party and of the country is as gloomy and cheerless as this cold, cloudy snowy Decr. Day. The Slavery question constantly assumes a more portentious and threatening aspect—sectional bitterness and hatred is daily becoming more exacerlated [*sic*]."[5] Moreover, the "worst possible state of feeling" existed between the Whig members of the North Carolina delegation: "Mangum and Badger dislike and are jealous of each other. Clingman and Stanly are, or suppose they are rivals, and will do all they can to thwart each other."[6]

The House of Representatives began balloting for Speaker on December 3, with Winthrop as the Whig candidate and Howell Cobb of Georgia, minority leader in the previous House, as his chief opposition. On the first ballot, with 111 votes necessary to a choice, Cobb had 103, Winthrop 96, with 22 votes scattered. This tally revealed that nine Free-Soil representatives led by Joshua Giddings of Ohio and the Toombs-Stephens rump group held the balance of power in the House; either Cobb or Winthrop could have won with their help; but when they refused to support either man, a memorable deadlock ensued.[7]

During the next three weeks, the House took ballot after ballot without success. When Winthrop and Cobb fell short, northern Whigs generally sought an alternate candidate among their southern brethren, while southern Democrats looked north for their candidate. On the fortieth ballot (December 12), William J. Brown, an Indiana Democrat, received 112 votes, slightly below a majority, although exceeding the Cobb and Winthrop highs. Brown had secretly negotiated with the Free-Soilers for their support, promising to constitute the committees on the District of Columbia, the territories, and the judiciary in a manner satisfactory to them.[8]

Rumors of these negotiations had filtered into the House, and after the fortieth ballot Stanly moved to uncover Brown's scheme. He began by stating that the Government was not coming to an end yet, no matter what gentlemen might say about "Free Soilism, Wilmot Provisoism, and all such tomfoolery." There was no danger of that. "The Union could not be dissolved while Henry Clay and Thomas H. Benton were in the Senate, or Old Rough and Ready was at the other end of the Avenue." He wanted the House organized, but Brown was not acceptable to a considerable number, as the result showed. Moreover, there was "something wrong: something 'rotten in Denmark.' He looked upon his own side of the House without blushing; he blushed when he looked at the other side." Thomas H. Bayly of Virginia, after consulting with Brown, branded the "imputation . . . circulating in whispers . . . through this Hall" as having "no foundation in truth." However, despite Bayly's categorical denial, Brown's negotiations were soon exposed and Stanly's suspicions wholly confirmed. "This exposure has overwhelmed him," Outlaw said of Brown that evening. "He is beneath contempt and the democracy are ashamed of the figure which they have made before the country."[9]

Stanly was acceptable to many northern Whigs as a compromise candidate, and on the forty-sixth ballot his total, which had been rising steadily, reached sixty-seven (Linn Boyd of Kentucky, a Democrat, had eighty-five), held at sixty-six on the next ballot, and then dropped to three after Stanly requested that the members who had voted for him should discontinue doing so. "The cause of Boston is the cause of all," he said, referring to Winthrop. However, on the fifty-ninth ballot (December 20), he received seventy-five votes to fifty for William McClernand of Illinois, twenty-eight for Boyd, and thirteen for Winthrop. But he could not be elected, as Outlaw perceived: "He can get no democratic votes, nor all the Whig votes. Indeed I doubt very much whether Clingman would vote for him."[10]

After a joint Democrat-Whig conference which Stanly had suggested earlier as a means of resolving the deadlock, the House agreed on December 21 to ballot three more times, after which, if no member had a majority, "the roll shall again be called, and the member who shall then receive the largest number of votes . . . shall be declared to be chosen Speaker." Stanly and McClernand, who had received the largest number of votes of their parties on the previous ballot, withdrew in favor of Winthrop and Cobb.[11] Before the new rule went into operation, Stanly, Charles Conrad of Louisiana, and John Houston of Delaware "labored hard" with the five recalcitrant southern Whigs, pointing out to Toombs and Stephens in particular that Taylor had been their original choice for President, "and that,

by conniving at a Democratic Speaker, they were giving the administration a set-back at the outset, besides inflicting a profound and
perhaps irreparable injury upon the Whig party." There was "some
little wavering," but the "iron will of Toombs" held his associates
fast against Winthrop.[12]

Cobb took the lead on the sixtieth and sixty-first ballots;
Winthrop tied him on the sixty-second; but on the crucial sixty-
third, Cobb had 102 votes to Winthrop's 99, with 20 scattered. If
four of the disaffected southern Whigs had voted for Winthrop, he
would have been elected. Immediately after the roll was completed,
Stanly rose and offered the following resolution: "Resolved, That
the Hon. Howell Cobb, a Representative from the State of Georgia,
be declared duly elected Speaker of the House for the thirty-first
Congress." Despite the protest of one member that Cobb was *now*
the Speaker "by its own order and action, without any resolution,"
Stanly's resolution was adopted, 149 to 34, and Cobb was conducted to the Chair. The long agony was over at last, and the
Democrats now controlled both the House and Senate organizations.[13]

On Christmas eve, Taylor sent his annual message to the Congress.
He believed that the people of California would soon apply for
statehood, and should their constitution be comfortable to the
United States Constitution, he recommended their application to
Congress. This was point one of what came to be known as the
"President's Plan." Point two contemplated New Mexican statehood,
although the President was "content for the present to hint broadly
at it, leaving implementation for a later date."[14] Taylor also
recommended abstention "from the introduction of those exciting
topics of a sectional character which have hitherto produced painful
apprehensions in the public mind." He closed with a strong plea for
the preservation of the Union, pledging that "Whatever dangers may
threaten it, I shall stand by it and maintain it in its integrity to the
full extent of the obligations imposed and the powers conferred
upon me by the Constitution."[15]

Taylor's soldierly nationalism, so reminiscent of Andrew Jackson,
could not fail to stir men of his stamp who placed national loyalty
before sectional interests. As Stanly reported to John H. Bryan on

January 11, 1850:

> The President says, he is President for four years, from the 4th
> March last, & he does not intend the Union shall be despoiled
> while he is President. The laws must be executed, he has sworn
> they shall be &—He talks calmly, but he looks as I think he did
> when he sent the message to Santa Anna, that his 'proposition'
> was respectfully declined.[16]

The President's plan pleased few southern representatives, particularly those of the state rights school, who desired at the very
minimum an equitable distribution of the western territories and a
new and more stringent fugitive slave law. During January, Thomas
Clingman, James Seddon, Democrat of Virginia, and Volney E.
Howard, Democrat of Texas, spoke in the House against Taylor's
plan and helped arouse passions in the capital to fever heat.
Clingman discussed secession openly. "Do us justice," he declared to
the North, "and we continue to stand with you; attempt to trample
on us, and we part company."[17]

This gasconading, with its open threat of disunion, alarmed
moderate men in Washington. Outlaw lamented that at the very
moment when forbearance and conciliation were of the first importance "those cardinal virtues, so essential to the peace of the country
and the preservation of the Union, seem to have departed from the
legislative halls."[18] Stanly told John H. Bryan that Calhoun had
succeeded to a greater extent than ever before in exciting the
southern mind. Steps must therefore be taken in North Carolina to
see that the Old North State should be "right" on this question, for
her own sake and that of the country. "The papers in the west, if
you can so arrange it, ought to denounce the dissolution efforts of
the Chivalry destructionists of the South: I think the lead should
come from that part of the State, to prevent the outcry of the
Raleigh Clique."[19]

In North Carolina, the first effect of the events in Congress was a
renewed emphasis on the maintenance of Southern Rights within the
Union.[20] In October, 1849, the Mississippi legislature had issued a
call for the other southern states to send delegates to a convention in
Nashville, Tennessee. At the time, little attention was paid to this
summons in North Carolina; but in early 1850, the Raleigh *North*

Carolina Standard took the lead in urging that the state be represented. "Let our watchwords be:–'Equality or Independence'–the union of the South for the sake of the Union and of Southern Rights." The *Standard* claimed that three-fourths of the newspapers in the state wanted North Carolina represented; all the Democratic papers were in favor of it, together with such Whig journals as the Raleigh *Star*, Charlotte *Hornet's Nest*, Fayetteville *Observer*, and Goldsborough *Telegraph.*[21]

The conservative Whig press in North Carolina condemned the convention movement as a disunionist scheme. The Hillsborough *Recorder* declared flatly that disunion was "no remedy for any evil, present or prospective, real or imaginary. Our motto then is '*The Union, the Constitution, and the laws*!'" The Washington *North State Whig* denounced the policy of "Mr. Clingman and his coadjutors in disunion." The Raleigh *Register* had believed from the first that no good would result from a Southern Convention, and had been able to find nothing that would induce a change of opinion.[22]

As angry passions mounted, the venerable "Sage of Ashland," Henry Clay, came forward with a compromise plan by which he hoped to preserve the Union. He proposed that California be admitted as a free state; that the Southwest territories be organized without the Wilmot Proviso; that the United States assume the pre-annexation debt of Texas, in compensation for the territory added to New Mexico; that a more stringent fugitive slave law be passed; that the slave trade be abolished in the District of Columbia; and that Congress adopt a resolution denying its power to prohibit or obstruct the internal slave trade. These proposals did not originate with Clay, but he did pull them together in one grand compilation. On February 5 and 6, he defended his resolutions on the floor of the Senate, arguing that there was no need of the Wilmot Proviso since climate alone would effectively exclude slavery from the Southwest. He warned that secession was not a legal right and would be followed by a disastrous civil war. By a resolution of April 17, his proposals were referred to a Committee of Thirteen with Clay as chairman.[23]

In general, southern Whigs supported Clay's proposals, while northern Whigs favored Taylor's plan. Among the former group,

Stanly and Meredith Gentry of Tennessee in the House and John Bell of Tennessee in the Senate stood almost alone in support of the President's plan of admitting California separately.[24] Stanly said later that he objected to Clay's so-called "Omnibus Bill," because "I thought it was wrong to make the admission of California depend on the success or failure of other measures."[25] However, he would not support a resolution offered by Joseph Root of Ohio organizing the territory ceded to the United States by Mexico, with the exception of California, with slavery excluded.[26]

Toward the end of February, Stephens and Toombs conferred with Taylor and found him determined to adhere to his original policy. When they heatedly spoke of disunion, the President angrily retorted that the Union must be preserved, and that, if necessary, he was prepared to take the field at the head of the nation's armed forces to put down any attempt at disunion.[27]

The Taylor Whigs were particularly anxious to enlist the powerful oratory of the "Godlike" Daniel Webster in behalf of the President's plan. Shortly after Clay introduced his resolutions, Stanly went to Robert C. Winthrop, and, according to the latter, said substantially as follows:

> I am very anxious Webster should know that if he can see his way clear to indorse the plan of the Administration, Taylor's Southern supporters are prepared to do their best to make him the next President. We pressed Taylor two years ago merely because it seemed the best chance of ousting the Democrats, but he has no idea of running again, and Clay is too old to be considered, though he cannot be made to realize it. The extravagancies of men like Toombs and Stephens threaten to wreck the Party. We are ready to support Webster on a moderate platform.

Winthrop confidentially communicated Stanly's message to Webster, who replied that he had not pledged himself to support Clay's resolutions and thought well of the general drift of the President's policy. "In short," he finally said, "I am substantially with the President, and you can tell Mr. Stanly so."[28]

To the surprise of the Taylor Whigs, Webster's "Seventh of March" speech, although strongly Unionist in tone, made no men-

tion of the President's plan, and was generally considered a conciliatory plea in behalf of the Clay resolutions. Yet Webster stated he
favored Taylor's plan *after*, as well as before, his speech. On March
8, he told Winthrop he had omitted allusion to the President's plan
for want of time, and with the intention of making it the subject of
a separate speech later. Since Webster had led Clay to believe as early
as January 21 that he would support the Kentuckian, his remarks to
Winthrop seemed to lack candor.[29]

There is evidence that Stanly's colleagues, Badger and Mangum,
were measurably responsible for thwarting the hopes of the Taylor
Whigs. An anonymous "close observer" of these events wrote two
years later:

> Henry Clay had thrown himself into the breach but he was
> powerless without some efficient aid from the North. The
> leading Southern Whigs, such as Mangum, and Badger, and
> Dawson, rallied upon Mr. Webster, seized upon him, stuck to
> him, and finally brought him up to the mark. His speech on
> the seventh of March gave a new impulse to the compromise
> movement, and the whole country felt the danger was past.
> But it is notorious that, in the proceedings upon the report of
> the committee of thirteen, Mr. Webster wavered again, voting
> this way and that way, and was only held to his place by the
> unceasing vigilance of Messrs. Mangum and Badger.[30]

According to Augustine H. Shepperd, a member of the North
Carolina delegation, the opposing purposes of Stanly and Badger
"created no little surprise amongst those who knew their usual
coincidence of opinion."[31] The Omnibus Bill was the first important issue upon which the two men had differed during their
political careers.

On March 6, the day before Webster was to speak in the Senate,
Stanly delivered his major remarks of the session on the slavery
question. Members drew up their chairs near him, and the area was
crowded with listeners. He began by contending that much of the
hue and cry about northern aggressions against the South could be
explained by a malignant wish to embarrass Taylor and build up the
Democratic Party. This "new-born zeal" for fugitive slave legislation
was owing to Cass' defeat. He admitted that the North had acted
badly in not surrendering fugitive slaves, but he believed this abuse

would be remedied. Complaint was also made against the people of the North because they would not stop the agitation of abolition fanatics. But how could they stop them? Who could reason with fanaticism? "'You may as well go stand upon the beach, and bid the main flood bate his usual height' . . . as try and suppress fanaticism by reason or law." Nor should much importance be attached to these agitators; the great body of the northern people were not enemies to the South.

As for the Wilmot Proviso, although the constitutional question was worn out, the southern people believed, as he did, that to enact the Proviso would be "an act of gross injustice and wrong"; and if adopted, he thought the people of North Carolina would feel compelled to discuss in a state convention "if it is not time to inquire whether our northern brethren intend to regard us as equals, or to treat us with unkindness." After this mild warning, Stanly went on to say that he did not believe the House would enact the Wilmot Proviso as there was no need of it. "All admit that new States, after they are admitted, can either tolerate or prohibit slavery."

Turning to the question of California, Stanly argued that to reject her application for statehood would be "productive of the most calamitous consequences"; it would raise a sectional feeling throughout the land that might never be allayed. As a southern man, he wanted her admitted and the sooner the better. Nor did he see any danger to the South's existence in the admission of New Mexico as a free state.

Stanly saw no necessity for the proposed Nashville Convention and great reason why it should not be held. "If that convention meets," he declared in the most quoted words of his speech, "and a proposition is made to consider even whether the Union ought not to be dissolved, I hope the citizens of Nashville will drive every traitor of them into the Cumberland river."

In conclusion, he invoked the protection of the "great Jehovah" on the whole country, and declared in the name of the people of North Carolina that "this Union cannot be, shall not be destroyed. Those whom God hath joined together, no man or set of men can put asunder."[32]

The Washington *Republic* warmly praised Stanly's speech, des-

cribing him as "a national and catholic Whig," who in arraigning the
ultraists of both sections had hit the temper of the House "just
betwixt wind and water." His remarks should go into every home
from Passamaquoddy to San Francisco. However, the Washington
Union, Thomas Ritchie's paper, declared that Stanly had blown his
"war-trumpet" in the House and had succeeded in throwing that
body into an excitement which was only calculated to delay, if not
to counteract, the attempts being made by cooler and patriotic men
to compromise the agitating slavery question. The *Union* correctly
predicted that the speech would produce recrimination from his own
party and state.[33]

David Outlaw thought Stanly's speech "an unfortunate and
foolish one," adding that "it would have been supposed almost, that
he was a Northern and not a Southern representative."[34] His
reaction was mild compared to the abuse heaped on Stanly by the
pro-southern press in North Carolina. The Raleigh *North Carolina
Standard* predictably termed the speech a "tirade of insolence and
treason," while the New Bern *Eastern Carolina Republican* shrilly
urged Eighth District Whigs to "*sacrifice this traitor, and indignantly
bid him to resign the seat which he so ingloriously fills.*" Had he
lived during the American Revolution, said the *Republican*, "he
would have been a tory, and if caught by the patriots, they would
have hung him on the nearest tree." In the western part of the state,
the *Hornet's Nest* reported that Whigs about Charlotte were ashamed
to claim Stanly as one of their party.[35]

More surprising than these partisan outbursts was William A.
Graham's privately expressed belief that Stanly and Badger "are in
danger of injuring us, by not being zealous enough, for the right of
slavery, or at least by appearing too tolerant of the Abolition feeling
at the North."[36]

The conservative Whig press generally withheld comment on
Stanly's speech until it had been written out and published in
pamphlet form. The New Bern *Newbernian* then declared that the
southern people had nothing to complain of as there were numerous
passages in which Stanly had taken "strong Southern ground" and
administered a deserved rebuke to northern fanaticism. The Raleigh
Register commended it to the "careful perusal of all those who are

madly labouring to weaken the bonds of our Union." The Whig press also took up Stanly's charge that much of the slavery agitation could be traced to the desire of the Democratic Party to embarrass the Administration. "Party, party, party is at the bottom of all this," cried the Washington *North State Whig.*[37]

Meanwhile, the conservative Whigs continued their opposition to the Nashville Convention. Although Southern Rights meetings in Wilmington (March 11-12) and Charlotte (April 23) elected delegates to the convention, Clay's compromise measures took the steam out of the movement in North Carolina.[38] Stanly, although busy in Washington, urged his friends in the Eighth District to oppose the Southern Rights campaign. On April 6, he warned James W. Bryan that an attempt would be made, probably at the next court session in Jones County, to get up a Southern Rights meeting. If Bryan and Richard Donnell would exert themselves a little among the intelligent men of the county, they could put a stop to it.[39] Bryan assured Stanly that he would not be embarrassed by any slavery resolutions—"every body seems to be tired of the agitation and now that poor Calhoun is gone, we shall have peace and quiet in the land."[40] A Southern Rights meeting had been held in Washington, North Carolina, on March 18; but Stanly's "particular personal friends," Donnell, Satterthwaite, and Edward J. Warren had succeeded in rallying a small majority against the Nashville Convention.[41]

By late May, even William W. Holden, editor of the Raleigh *North Carolina Standard*, considered the convention a "dead question." When delegates from nine slave states met in Nashville in June, North Carolina was not represented.[42] The convention was more moderate than had been expected, and expressed a willingness to accept, as an extreme concession, the extension of the Missouri Compromise line to the Pacific.

On February 13, Taylor submitted a four line message to Congress transmitting the California constitution. Two weeks later, James Doty, a Wisconsin free-soil Democrat, introduced a California statehood bill in the House which was ordered printed and referred to the Committee of the Whole on the State of the Union. For the next four months, House debate was premised on this bill and Taylor's February 13 message. Stanly and other friends of the

Administration tried repeatedly to end debate and bring the Doty bill before the House for final action. Their efforts were frustrated by a coalition of Southerners and northern Democrats, aided by Speaker Cobb, who were determined to keep the bill in committee until a complete compromise scheme could be introduced and passed.[43]

Debate in the Senate from May through July was based on the Omnibus Bill reported from Clay's Committee of Thirteen on May 8. This measure called for the admission of California as a free state; the organization of New Mexico and Utah territories without the Wilmot Proviso;[44] adjustment of the Texas–New Mexico boundary; and assumption of the Texas debt. Kept separate was a more stringent fugitive slave law and a bill abolishing the slave trade in the District of Columbia. Astute observers considered the Omnibus Bill's fate in great doubt because of the united opposition of the ultras from both sections, and that of the Administration.[45] Stanly thought it would probably fail, "so that we shall fall back on the plan of the President, which though it is not all that we wish, is all we can get."[46]

The North Carolina delegation was sharply divided on the Omnibus. Outlaw reported on May 13 that Caldwell, Deberry, Shepperd, himself, and Mangum and Badger, would go for it, while Venable was understood to be opposed. Clingman would "probably recover his senses sufficiently to go for it." Outlaw did not know Ashe's or Daniel's views. As for Stanly, he was pursuing "a most extraordinary course":

> He ought to be from the North instead of the South side of Mason and Dixon's line. Unless I am greatly mistaken the curses both loud and deep of his constituents will be his reward. I think he is looking to some Executive appointment....It is supposed he will go against the compromise bill.[47]

Clay's relations with Taylor had been coldly civil for several months, but not until May 21 did the Kentuckian break openly with the President, rising in the Senate to compare unfavorably his plan with that of the Committee of Thirteen. "Here are five wounds," said Clay, "bleeding and threatening the well being, if not the existence of the body politic." The President's plan would heal only one, California, leaving "the other four to bleed more profusely." Taylor ought to put aside his own ideas and defer to the wisdom of Congress in this matter, "to permit us to consider what is best for our common country." To this appeal, the Washington *Republic* replied on May 27 with an editorial defending the President's plan. The paper argued that no territorial bill could pass Congress without bringing up the Wilmot Proviso and sowing the seeds of trouble broadcast over the free states. However, by admitting California and New Mexico as states, Congress could escape the necessity of legislating on the question of slavery in the territories.[48]

The split between Clay and Taylor posed a dilemma for North Carolina Whigs, as the astute William W. Holden was quick to discern. "Clay has just attacked Taylor in the strongest terms, and Whigs in this State *must* decide between the two," he informed David Reid, who was again a candidate for governor against Manly.

> Several Whig papers have already denounced Taylor; and next week the Raleigh Star will denounce Stanly, the North State Whig, and the Raleigh Times, in the fiercest terms. These things, all together, may not indeed give you any *Whig* votes, but they *must* produce lukewarmness in the Whig ranks—divisions...which cannot fail to *diminish* Manly's vote.[49]

Both Whig and Democratic papers in North Carolina favored the compromise, although the Raleigh *North Carolina Standard* complained it gave too much to the North and too little to the South. The Whig press, while endorsing the compromise as a measure that would give the country repose, professed to believe that Taylor, while preferring his own plan, would not act so unwisely as to try to defeat the other.[50] Yet there was no doubt that if a showdown came, the great bulk of the Southern Whigs would stand with Clay, as they had stood with him against Tyler. On June 24, Outlaw predicted that if the Administration persisted in its present course, it would be left without a "corporal's guard" in the southern states. He had just received a letter from North Carolina, which revealed that in the recent state Whig convention, of one hundred and sixty delegates, only three had opposed Clay's adjustment bill, and not one was in favor of the President's plan.[51]

Taylor, meanwhile, was mulling over a possible shakeup in the

Cabinet. Even among the President's friends, dissatisfaction had been expressed with some of its members. "We look upon disunion as at rather a low ebb," Stanly had informed James Bryan on April 6. "No one believes the Wilmot Proviso can pass. If we had a good cabinet we could get along, but with this cabinet we cannot get along." He hoped for some change.[52] Orlando Brown, a Taylor Whig from Kentucky, declared that in a praiseworthy effort to obtain a reputation as "a *working Cabinet*," the Secretaries had secluded themselves too much. "Not meaning to be offensive or impolite, they created that impression and had been struck by a volume of 'defamatory remarks.'"[53] The Cabinet's image was further tarnished in April by the disclosure that Secretary of the Treasury William M. Meredith, on the opinion of Attorney General Reverdy Johnson, had paid out $191,352.89 in interest on the so-called Galphin Claim, and that Secretary of the Army George W. Crawford, as agent for the Galphin's, would receive one half this amount. The Democrats immediately raised the cry of a Whig treasury raid and the House conducted an investigation.[54]

After lengthy debate, the House resolved that the Galphin Claim was not a just demand against the United States and that Meredith had acted without authorization in paying the interest. None of the cabinet officers were censured, not even Crawford.[55] Still, the Secretary of War had become a liability, as had, to a lesser extent, Meredith and Johnson. Taylor thought of Winthrop, Hamilton Fish, John Davis, and Stanly for places in his official family. Thomas Ewing and William B. Preston might have been retained.[56] According to Thurlow Weed, the President in late June selected Stanly as Crawford's successor. Taylor intended to call an extra session of the Senate the day after its expected adjournment in July, when he would nominate his new Cabinet.

> The cabinet-making business was to be kept profoundly secret. The President, however, allowed me to ask my friend Stanly, in the event of an early adjournment of Congress, to remain in Washington until I could see him, but without telling him why. Nor did Mr. Stanly know the President's intention to call him to the War Department until I met him some two years afterwards.[57]

It was probably just as well for Stanly that he was never tendered the War Office. His enemies had charged that he supported the President's plan because he hoped to get a foreign mission from Taylor. They would have seen in the offer of a Cabinet post a reward for what Outlaw contemptuously called "truckling and servility . . . to those in power." Moreover, Outlaw was pretty certain that if Stanly was nominated for an office, the Senate would not confirm him.[58]

Despite the united efforts of Clay, Webster, Toombs, Stephens, Cobb, and Senator Stephen A. Douglas of Illinois, among others, the Omnibus Bill was no nearer enactment in June than in February. Taylor remained steadfast behind his plan of statehood for California and New Mexico. Retaining the support of every northern Whig senator except Webster and James Cooper of Pennsylvania, he won over some northern Democrats who had formerly leaned the other way. Clay was helpless in the face of the President's veto power. He could never command a two-thirds majority of both houses to override a veto; it was even doubtful whether the compromise could be passed initially through the House.[59] Southern Whigs were desperate, believing like Outlaw, that if the Administration defeated the Omnibus Bill, it would have a "disastrous effect . . . to our party, in the South." Toombs and Stephens vainly remonstrated with the President, and "Little Aleck" spoke angrily to Preston of impeachment.[60]

Hope for the passage of the Omnibus Bill revived with the death of Taylor on July 9. The old soldier, already depressed by the Galphin revelations, succumbed to acute gastroenteritis, then called cholera morbus, after eating quantities of raw fruits and vegetables and iced milk on a blistering Fourth of July in Washington. His successor, Millard Fillmore, was Seward's rival in New York Whig politics and threw the prestige and patronage of the Administration behind the compromise measure. Texas bondholders were also at work on behalf of adjustment.[61]

Moderate Whigs like Stanly, who had loyally supported the President before his death, now had no heart to continue the struggle alone and moved over into the Clay camp. Augustine H. Shepperd wrote later that Stanly and Badger "differed on the

Compromise measures during the lifetime of Gen'l Taylor, but came together on Mr. Fillmore's succession."[62] Taylor Whigs Tom Corwin and John J. Crittenden entered the Cabinet "as a symbol of compromise unity."[63] Stanly joined with the other Whig members of the North Carolina delegation in recommending William A. Graham for a place in the Cabinet, and the former governor and senator was appointed Secretary of the Navy.[64] On August 2, Stanly declared in the House that if Joshua Giddings and his Free-Soil friends would not vote to attach the Wilmot Proviso to the territorial bills, "we can get through all our business—have California admitted and establish territorial governments—in less than three weeks, and go home."[65]

But it was not to be that easy. Even with Administration support, Clay failed in an attempt to push the Omnibus Bill through the Senate on July 31; after a wearisome day of voting, all that remained of the California, territorial, and Texas boundary provisions was the Utah bill, which passed on August 1. Exhausted by his labors, and discouraged by the wreck of the Omnibus, Clay left Washington and went to Newport, Rhode Island, to restore his health. In his absence, Stephen A. Douglas rallied the compromise forces, and taking up the measures one by one, pushed four of them through the Senate in less than a month. The abolition of the slave trade in the District of Columbia—the last compromise measure—passed the Senate on September 19. Many historians have given Whig leaders and Whig members most of the credit for the result. Actually, the "hard core and the greater number of Compromise votes" in the Senate were "Democratic in origin."[66]

The House united the Texas debt and boundary measure with the bill for the organization of New Mexico territory; this "little omnibus" bill passed on September 6 by a vote of 108 to 97. California statehood was carried 150 to 56 and the Utah territorial bill, 97 to 85, both on September 7. On September 12, the fugitive slave law went through 109 to 76, followed by the abolition of the slave trade in the District, 124 to 59, on September 17. Fillmore signed the various parts of the Compromise of 1850 into law; and on September 30, both houses adjourned *sine die*.[67]

The vote of the North Carolina delegation on the various

compromise measures "was for the most part pro-Southern."[68] In the Senate, Mangum and Badger voted against the abolition of the slave trade in the District of Columbia and did not vote on California statehood. Both voted for the fugitive slave law and the New Mexico territorial bill. Badger supported the Texas debt-boundary settlement and the Utah territorial bill, while Mangum was paired with no indication of a preference.[69]

In the House, the North Carolina members gave a majority of their votes for all the compromise provisions except the abolition of the slave trade in the District and California statehood. Only Stanly and Joseph P. Caldwell, a western Whig from Iredell County, voted to admit California. On the Texas-debt-boundary-New Mexico territorial bill, Stanly, Caldwell, Deberry, Outlaw, and Shepperd voted for it, and Clingman, Ashe, Daniel, and Venable against. On the bill organizing the territory of Utah, Clingman and Venable did not vote; the rest of the delegation supported the measure. Every member voted for the fugitive slave law, and, with one exception, against the abolition of the slave trade in the District; on the latter measure, Stanly was paired with an opponent of the bill. In general, the Whigs (except Clingman) were favorable to compromise, particularly on the crucial Texas-debt-boundary-New Mexico and Utah bills, while the Democrats, joined by Clingman, were opposed to most of the compromise measures.[70] However, this was not true of the Democratic representatives generally. In the House, as in the Senate, Democratic leadership and votes were mainly responsible for the Compromise of 1850.[71] It is interesting to note that Stanly, despite his initial opposition to the Omnibus, ultimately supported *more* of the compromise measures (if we include the pairing) than any other member of the North Carolina delegation in either the House or the Senate.

Stanly suffered some embarrassment at this momentous session as chairman of a House committee to inquire into the conduct of office-holders under the Polk administration. On April 22, William Richardson, an Illinois Democrat, had asked the House to appoint a committee to inquire and report what federal appointees of Secretary of the Interior Thomas Ewing were correspondents of newspapers, their salaries, and for what papers they edited or wrote. The

House readily agreed to this partisan attempt to embarrass the Taylor administration. On April 25, Stanly tried to "carry the war into Africa" by asking the unanimous consent of the House to offer a resolution instructing Richardson's committee to also inquire into the conduct of certain office-holders under Polk as correspondents and editors of newspapers; in particular, who was the author of the "Bundelcund" tariff essays that had appeared during the 1848 election, and what office he held; and whether during the election any of them were absent from their offices to make electioneering speeches or were called upon to subscribe money for Cass.

Robert W. Johnson, an Arkansas Democrat, objected to the resolution, remarking that he was opposed to the reception of any such "trash." Stanly retorted that his objection only proved that the Democratic Party was opposed to a fair investigation. Johnson, not daunted, again objected "to any such trash from that quarter." "If it is 'trash,'" Stanly replied, "it is such matter as the gentleman from Arkansas can appreciate." The Speaker interposed and ruled the resolution out of order since an objection had been made.

Stanly offered his resolution again on May 6. The Democrats voted him down, but offered to give him a committee of his own. The next day Cobb appointed a nine-man committee, five Whigs and four Democrats, with Stanly as chairman. On May 15, the House denied the committee a clerk (104-60), but authorized it to send for persons and papers.[72]

The Democratic press generally greeted Stanly's resolution with jeering contempt, the Philadelphia *Spirit of the Times* calling it "the most farcical effort to gratify spite which has ever been submitted to the American people."[73] The Washington *Republic* defended Stanly as "right in this matter,"[74] but his call for an investigation stirred no enthusiasm among the Whigs. It was David Outlaw's impression that none of these committees would result in any practical benefit. "They are generally designed to manufacture electioneering matter for one side or the other instead of being intended as they should be to correct existing abuses, where they are known to exist."[75] Edmund Burke, an editor of Thomas Ritchie's Washington *Union*, readily admitted that while serving as Polk's Commissioner of Patents he had written the "Bundelcund" essays at Ritchie's request, although not during office hours. He was gratified to know that Stanly and the House had vindicated the "high national importance" of his essays by ordering a solemn investigation into the fact of their authorship.[76]

The Stanly committee took testimony from a number of witnesses, including Thomas Ritchie. He was asked by Stanly what he knew relative to the several matters under investigation. Ritchie declined to give the name of his correspondents; because, he said, he "would not betray the secrets of our correspondents, and thus countenance an infringement of the immunities and liberty of the press." "How far can the press be considered *free*," he asked in a *Union* editorial, "when its editor is compelled to betray the confidence of his correspondents, and expose them to the proscription of men in power?" The Washington *Republic* dismissed this argument by noting: "It is the Locofoco liberty of the press that was in danger: when the Whig press was attacked, we heard no complaint from the Union."[77]

On August 28, Stanly reported to the House that Ritchie and C. P. Sengstack, former keeper of the District Penitentiary, had refused to answer relevant questions asked them by the committee. The committee therefore thought it proper to submit the matter to the House for its advice and order. Stanly himself believed the members should not waste valuable time in discussing the propriety of Ritchie's and Sengstack's conduct; "he would dismiss the whole matter from his thoughts." But when Democratic members prolonged debate and began to extol Ritchie as a defender of the liberty of the press and freedom of discussion, Stanly introduced a resolution ordering the two men to be brought before the House to answer for contempt. After lengthy debate, much relished by the Democrats, the resolution was easily defeated, 132-49, and the whole subject was laid on the table. Stanly had to be content with having the committee's report printed in the appendix of the *Congressional Globe*.[78] He was probably glad to be rid of the whole business as it was proving acutely embarrassing. The "Conqueror" had won no new laurels in this encounter with the venerable "Father Ritchie." The New Bern *Eastern Carolina Republican* accurately gauged the general opinion of the investigation when it labeled it "A piece of

'Tom-Foolery.'"[79]

In North Carolina most people were prepared to accept the Compromise of 1850, although the ultra-southern wing of the Democratic Party, led by Holden's *North Carolina Standard*, did not conceal its dissatisfaction. The Whigs were unusually vocal in their approval, and nowhere more so than in Stanly's own Beaufort County. On September 18, the Washington *North State Whig* proudly announced that "100 GUNS will be fired in this place this afternoon in honor of the passage of the Compromise Bills." In the evening, as bonfires burned in the streets, a large and joyous public meeting in the Court House unanimously resolved that the several compromise measures were "unjust to no section, but eminently wise, patriotic, constitutional and conservative"; and that the thanks of the whole country were due to the distinguished and patriotic statesmen who had accomplished the adjustment, among them "our able and efficient Representative in Congress, the Hon. Edward Stanly."[80]

Letters from North Carolina Whigs to Secretary of the Navy Graham give added evidence of the party's support of the Compromise. "I and the Whigs generally have been delighted at the passage of the compromise bills and the approval of the President," Raleigh leader, Richard Hines, wrote. "The Administration is gaining golden opinions *from the people* of all parties in this state." A Charlotte Whig reported that "99/100 of our population have but one sentiment, devotion to the Union and the Constitution." Whig leaders were already scheming to kill off those Democratic representatives in the North Carolina delegation who had voted against the Texas boundary bill.[81]

However, even conservative Whigs believed that the preservation of the Union depended upon the faithful execution of the new fugitive slave law. The Raleigh *Register* said flatly that "in the event of the continued nullification, or the repeal of the Fugitive Slave law, the Union *ought not* to stand." Richard Hines warned that if the law was repealed, "the South as one man would be in favor of a dissolution of the Union." "Will the Fugitive Slave Bill be repealed?" asked a worried American minister in Madrid, Daniel M. Barringer. "If the North should fail to execute in good faith and with efficiency the provisions of that Act, such neglect and disregard of duty on their part will do more to estrange the South and increase the sentiment in favor of separation than all other causes combined."[82]

The second session of the Thirty-First Congress, which began on December 2, 1850, passed off quietly after the previous session's turmoil. In January, 1851, Graham reported a general disposition on Congress' part to acquiesce in the Compromise. Seward and his faction were "disposed to apparent peace," and were secretly asking quarter in order to retain the offices they had acquired under Taylor. Graham thought that the Compromise and Fillmore's firmness in executing the fugitive slave law had given a "new lease" to slavery, and that kind of property had not been so secure for twenty-five years.[83]

Meanwhile, Stanly continued at every opportunity to disparage the idea of disunion. When an abolitionist wrote William Lloyd Garrison from Scotland that there was a growing conviction in Great Britain that slavery would never be abolished in the United States as long as the Union existed, Stanly obtained a copy of the *Liberator* containing the letter and sent it to Henry Dimock, the editor of the Washington *North State Whig*, with a request that he publish it. "My object," he explained, "is to enable my constituents to see how much reliance they can place on the friendship of England, if the crazy disunionists of the South should succeed in dissolving the Union." He wanted the people of North Carolina to know that English and American abolitionists believed that slavery would never be abolished as long as the Union existed. "When we remember the course of England to her West India possessions, and that of France to hers, who can think without horror of the condition of the Southern country, if our Union is dissolved, with war at home and an alliance with England?"[84]

Stanly had two personal encounters in Congress at this session, either of which might have had a fatal conclusion. On February 18, 1851, during a House debate upon the River and Harbor Bill, Thomas H. Bayly of Virginia charged that the measure was "sectional" in that the bulk of the proposed appropriations went to the northern states, a statement which Stanly immediately denied. If there was not a large appropriation in the bill for the southern states, it was the fault of southern congressmen. Because of constitutional scruples, they refused to call attention to their constituents' wants or to move appropriations for the benefit of their states; moreover, they were warmly opposing this bill. Personally, he earnestly hoped the bill would pass as it would greatly promote North Carolina's interest. It was another bond of Union. "And after the passage of the glorious compromise measures, give them this bill, and then a little improvement in the tariff, and it would be the cap-sheaf adorning the whole."

After Stanly took his seat, Samuel W. Inge, an Alabama Democrat, submitted an amendment providing for river improvement in Alabama and Mississippi, and in his remarks referred to Stanly's course and asked: "When did the gentleman from North Carolina ever perceive sectional injustice in the action of this Congress?" "If the South were to wait for that gentleman's warning," Inge continued, "she would sleep in eternal unconsciousness: it [*sic*] would sleep until every assault was perpetrated, and until her spoliation was complete. . . . It is not from him that I should expect admonitions of danger to the South."

Stanly was provoked to say that Inge had "little sense and less charity when he charges me with being unfriendly to the South." Inge replied that "that remark is ungentlemanly and unparliamentary, and comes from a blackguard." "Mr. Chairman," retorted Stanly, "he charges me with being a blackguard. He has just shown to the House and to the country that he is one." The Chairman said personalities were not in order. "No, personalities are not in order," Stanly concluded hotly:

> I am willing to let our conduct be judged of by the public; and let them estimate his character and mine. As to my friendship for the South, let the record and my conduct speak, whether I have not more friendship for the South than those noisy traitors who impeach others, and seek the applause of the grog-shops at cross-roads at home by their own professions of devotion, and by crying out eternally, 'there is danger, danger to the South!' Even those who voted with a majority of Southern members upon certain measures are uncharitably assailed. I regret I have been called on to say anything. I was

unconscious of giving any provocation. The gentleman cast the first stone, and he will make the most of what I have said. I shall hereafter treat remarks from that quarter with the contempt they deserve.[85]

This exchange led to a challenge from Inge which Stanly accepted as he thought "it was determined that I should be assailed by Southern disunionists."[86] On February 24, the two men and their seconds (Jefferson Davis for Inge and Charles Lee Jones for Stanly) quietly left Washington and crossed the Maryland line to Bladensburg. After an exchange of pistol shots in which neither man was hit, Jones went to Davis and suggested the affair be terminated. He stated that Stanly's remarks had been made in answer to what he considered a gross personal insult on Inge's part in his first remarks. Davis replied that those remarks had been "political" and not "personal" in their bearing—a nice distinction! Stanly then agreed to withdraw his remarks; and the difficulty being "honorably adjusted" in accordance with the duelling code, the parties returned to Washington that evening. This bloodless encounter was the last duel in the United States arising out of congressional debates. As the Raleigh *North Carolina Standard* sarcastically observed, it proved only that Inge and Stanly were "quite courageous—a fact well known before; and both to be 'bad shots'—a fact before unknown."[87]

In a letter to William A. Graham, Stanly defended his acceptance of Inge's challenge:

I would not engage in a contest which I knew was in many respects wrong, to gratify vengeance, or even redress personal wrong, but I was assailed as a Southern man, assailed for discharging conscientiously my public duties, and as a North Carolinian, I thought it due to my constituents to show my assailants that they might be mistaken in supposing a Union man wouldn't fight under any circumstances.[88]

Before the end of the session, Stanly also had a "scrimmage" with his bitter rival, Thomas L. Clingman. The Buncombe Whig came to Stanly's seat in the House and accused him of misrepresenting Clingman's remarks on the River and Harbor bill. According to the Raleigh *Register*:

Mr. Stanly said it was false. Mr. Clingman retorted by calling him a liar. Mr. S. then said that he gave the lie first. Upon which Mr. C. made a blow at M. S. and caught him by the neck, which was pretty severely scratched. Mr. Stanly attempted to strike Mr. Clingman, when the parties were separated. Great confusion prevailed for a few moments, but which was promptly and efficiently quelled by the Speaker.[89]

Friends of the two men settled the incident without a resort to pistols; but it was probably well for the fiery "Conqueror's" health that Congress adjourned soon after, affording him relief from his role as the House combustible.

In North Carolina, meanwhile, both parties were rallying their forces for the congressional elections of 1851. The Whigs had lost the governorship to David Reid in 1850 by a majority of nearly three thousand votes, and both houses of the legislature as well, and were determined to make a good showing. The Whig minority in the General Assembly had vainly offered resolutions approving the Compromise, but had to be content with defeating, with the aid of moderate Democrats, radical resolutions affirming the constitutionality of secession. The conservative Whigs now prepared to wage the campaign on the issues of the Compromise, Secession, and Disunion. The Raleigh *Register* set the tone on March 8, 1851, when it warned the friends of the Compromise that they must remain on the alert. "Secession is not yet dead. It will lift its poisonous crest again, when it is least expected."[90] The Whig strategy was to equate the *right* of secession with *actual* disunion. The "destructive doctrine of *Secession*," asserted the Raleigh *Register*, is "the Juggernaut of *Disunion*!" Secession meant disunion, nothing more or less—"a disruption of those ties which have bound us together as a free, glorious and *united* nation!" Would the South sustain the Compromise, by sustaining its defenders? "That is the question."[91]

A Craven County Whig expressed a similar sentiment more vividly in a letter to the *Register*:

In some portions of the country, where rattle-snakes abound, there is a poisonous sneaking reptile, that is said always to go before the bolder, but more terrible snake, called 'Pilot.' When you meet one, the other is close by. Honestly and seriously, my mind has come to regard this [Secession] doctrine as the

'Pilot,' that is leading the bolder but more to be feared rattle-snake, Disunion, into our political Eden.[92]

Stanly at first declined to be a candidate for reelection; because of pressing domestic affairs, he explained to Henry Dimock, and a conviction that the noisy agitators, North and South, would shortly be overwhelmed with public indignation.[93] A Whig district convention met in Washington on May 20, 1851, and nominated William H. Washington of Craven for Congress. However, he declined to run; and the Whig leaders, "at sea," cast about for another candidate. "Stanly, respected & beloved as he is, we were afraid to trust," one confessed. "At the last election, he only succeeded by 47 votes, when opposed by a very weak man, and when there was more perfect union among the Whigs. For these reasons it was thought prudent to run some other person."[94]

State rights Whigs in the district wanted to nominate Charles Pettigrew of Tyrrell, and Stanly reportedly sent him a message, urging him to become a candidate. Pettigrew was willing to run; but some of Stanly's friends about Washington, disliking his state rights opinions, objected to him; and he withdrew. Privately, the Pettigrews blamed Stanly for Charles' embarrassment. William Pettigrew believed that Stanly had only been "cajoling" his brother, "merely wished his support, and hoped to obtain it by flattery, having no idea he could be induced to declare himself." He had thus acted "any thing but creditably" in the matter. In any event, when Pettigrew declined, and "no better man" could be found, Stanly did agree to make the canvass.[95]

Stanly's opponent was Thomas Ruffin, a young Goldsboro lawyer, who was said by the Raleigh *North Carolina Standard* to be "*a Democrat of the best stamp, and warmly devoted to the Constitution and Southern Rights.*" Ruffin went into Washington and Tyrrell counties to speak before the Whigs had found a candidate to oppose him, but was met by Stanly at Washington, Plymouth, Skinnersville, and Cool Springs. Stanly took what the Plymouth *Villager* called "strong grounds for the Union of the States," and said there was no just cause at present for disunion.[96] After these first debates, but before formally announcing his own candidacy, Stanly wrote President Fillmore about the impending contest:

The Democrats scold me, yet profess their desire to abide by
the Compromise acts.—Their nominee dare not avow 'secession,'—but talks of 'Southern rights & Northern aggression'—
were he to avow opposition to the Compromise acts, or
advocate secession, he would be beaten more than a thousand
votes; with his dodging & equivocation he may deceive the
people. Though it will be a close contest—my majority before
was only forty-six [47] votes—'I will try Sir,' if no one else
will.[97]

The Whigs realized that Stanly faced an uphill fight for reelection,
since he had alienated other state rights Whig planters in the district
besides the Pettigrews. In Tyrrell County, he was expected to get the
"full vote of 1849," but the prospect was unfavorable in Washington
County. "There are many Whigs who are avowers of the right of
secession, and who have expressed themselves opposed to him,"
Hezekiah G. Spruill of Plymouth informed William A. Graham on
July 4. Overall, however, Spruill thought his prospects of success
were better than formerly. "I find that, since his visit here there are
persons who were openly opposed to him, and who are coming over,
& I believe, before the election, his Whig opponents will be few."[98]
James W. Bryan, after a visit to Pitt County to aid Stanly's cause
there, reported that he would be "sore pressed," but would probably
be elected by a small majority; "he was certainly the weakest
Candidate that could have come forward from among the prominent
Gentlemen in the Whig ranks," he added; "he is more cordially hated
and despised by the Locos, & has offended more Whigs, than any
politician in the Country." Stanly himself was sanguine of success,
and thought he would increase his vote in some parts of the district.
He had succeeded in some degree in making the issue of Union or
Disunion with Ruffin, and this brought several Democrats to his
side.[99]

Thomas Sparrow, as chairman of the Whig district committee,
became the manager of his law partner's campaign, and lost no time
in launching it. In a ringing appeal to the voters, prepared and signed
by him as chairman and by others, he roundly denounced Ruffin as
"a warm and ardent open advocate of the right of secession." He

warned that the next presidential election might be thrown into the House of Representatives and asked: "Who shall cast your vote for President of the United States—Edward Stanly, a Union Whig, or Thomas Ruffin, a locofoco secessionist?" And then Sparrow drove home the clinching argument:

> The abolitionists and secessionists continue to assail these [compromise] measures. The wise and patriotic policy of our conservative Whig President is bitterly denounced. South Carolina is on the eve of disunion. Finding no other state to join her, she threatens to secede alone. Nullification and secession, odius [sic] always and crushed in 1833 by General Jackson have been revived. If this doctrine is right, then South Carolina is right and our Government is wrong. If Stanly is defeated it will be proclaimed in all the land as a South Carolina victory in Stanly's district, in Union-loving North Carolina.[100]

The Whig press also waged an aggressive and effective campaign against the state rights views of Ruffin and the Democratic Party. The Goldsborough *Telegraph* charged that he was "an avowed, open, and strong secessionist," while the Washington *North State Whig* hammered home the point that Union or Disunion was the only issue in the election. "Secession is but another name for Disunion," it warned. "Let it be so regarded, before the people have eaten of the 'insane root.'"[101]

The Democratic papers in turn vigorously attacked Stanly for his denial of the right of secession. Thus, the Goldsborough *Republican and Patriot* asked the men of the Eighth District if they were willing to say "that in case you withdraw from the Union under the unconstitutional acts and intolerable oppression of the consolidationists and abolitionists, the Federal Government has the right . . . to whip you into subjection?" The voters must decide:

> On the one hand, Mr. Ruffin contends that a state has the right to withdraw from the Union as a last resort, peaceably if she can, forcibly if she must. On the other hand, Mr. Stanly contends that a state cannot secede from the Union for any cause whatever, only as rebels.[102]

Stanly and Ruffin held joint debates throughout the district before large crowds. The former defended his support of the compromise measures, denounced secession as "an abominable doctrine," and declared in favor of a force bill like Jackson's should South Carolina resort to extreme measures. In that event, he would send ships to collect the revenue, and would prevent South Carolina from seceding and forming an alliance with England, whose policy was universal emancipation, and who would eventually crush the state and her institutions. He admitted, however, that the repeal of the fugitive slave law would be an abominable act, "and would lead to 'Revolution'; whenever that hour came, he would be found acting with the sons of Carolina. He and Ruffin would be found side by side."[103]

Ruffin, on his part, denied that he was either a secessionist or disunionist, but acknowledged his belief that a state had the right to secede "for adequate cause." He believed, too, that the South had not received justice from the North in the Compromise; but as it was now the law of the land, and he wished to show his devotion to the Union, he would abide by it.[104]

It was a hard fought campaign. As the "Day of Battle," August 7, drew near, both sides redoubled their efforts. The Whigs printed several thousand copies of Jackson's proclamation against nullification and scattered them over the district. Thomas Sparrow, Edward J. Warren, Richard S. Donnell, and David M. Carter were all on the stump for Stanly, denouncing secession and breathing devotion to the Union. As one of the "spartan band" of Wayne County Whigs wrote Kemp P. Battle:

> Both parties are straining every nerve, exerting themselves to the very utmost in order to elect their respective candidates. Not content with the canvassing of the candidates themselves, friends of either side have taken the stump, and labour as if life & death were dependant [sic] on the issue. Perhaps this may be the case, for it appears to me, that if Ruffin and his antiunion doctrines are triumphant, there is no telling what will become of us. I know I never felt half the interest in any previous election that I do in this.[105]

The press of both parties made final appeals to the voters before election day. The Washington *North State Whig* urged the friends of the Union and Constitution to "shoot their little paper bullets" into the ballot box for Stanly and the Union. "That is the surest way to put down secession, and prevent the necessity of ever having to shoot leaden bullets at each other—as we shall have to do when Disunion comes." The Raleigh *North Carolina Standard* called upon the party faithful to "Rally for RUFFIN, the CONSTITUTION, and SOUTHERN RIGHTS," and warned that if Stanly were reelected, "the result will be regarded in the free states as a triumph of Freesoilism in the midst of a slaveholding people, and the freesoil organs will shout for joy."[106]

Then shout for joy they did. Stanly defeated Ruffin by 269 votes, carrying every county in the district except Wayne, Lenoir, and Greene. In Washington County, he gained forty-five votes over his 1849 total, despite the opposition of a half-dozen leading Whigs. "This is a great triumph," Hezekiah G. Spruill said of the result there, "as it was thought Ruffin would carry the county." Stanly's total vote in the district, 5,237, was the largest polled up to that time, exceeding General Taylor's total by 247 votes. Ruffin's 4,968 votes gave him only 28 more than Lane had received in 1849.[107]

Stanly regarded his victory as much more than a mere *party* triumph. "It is a victory of the friends of the Union," he told the citizens of New Bern. "It has proved that the people of this district condemn those who advocate even the 'abstract right of secession.' Nothing is more certain than that the word 'secession' is odious to the people of the good old North State of both parties."[108]

Of course the Democratic press did not agree with this view of the result. The Raleigh *North Carolina Standard* attributed Stanly's victory to the unfounded and false charge that the Democrats were disunionists, and to "an under current of *Abolitionism* in several of the Counties, which silently but surely augumented Mr. Stanly's strength." More reasonably, the Goldsborough *Republican and Patriot* contended that many Whigs had voted for Stanly although they believed in the right of secession and almost entirely disapproved his political course. "Party associations are too strong to be broken even when an important principle is at stake. Hence the re-election of Mr. Stanly."[109] Nevertheless, one must conclude that the district's voters either approved Stanly's strong Unionism or felt the Compromise was enough protection for Southern Rights.[110]

Taking the state as a whole, the political complexion of the North Carolina delegation was unchanged. Venable, Ashe, Daniel, and Clingman (who ran as a Southern Rights Whig) were all returned without much difficulty, while Outlaw, Caldwell, and James T. Morehead (who replaced Deberry) were unopposed. In the Third District, Alfred Dockery, a strong Union Whig, defeated Green W. Caldwell for Shepperd's seat.[111]

It was apparent that the people of North Carolina still clung to the Union "as it is" and were opposed to disunion; and the Whig press, eager to hoist the Democrats on their own petard, hit hard at the fact. The Raleigh *Register* warned that the Secessionist leaders would now attempt "*to take the back track*," and urged the friends of the Compromise and the Union to hold them to their doctrines. "Remember the 'Standard' has proclaimed that '*secession is a cardinal principle of the Democratic faith*!' Keep this before the People and we have them just where we want them."[112]

Not only in North Carolina, but throughout the southern states, the Compromise of 1850 was accepted as a settlement which obviated disunion. In Mississippi, Henry S. Foote, who endorsed the Compromise, was elected governor over Jefferson Davis, after John Quitman, an "ultra," withdrew from the contest. In Georgia, Whigs and Democrats disappeared, and a Union party led by Toombs, Stephens, and Cobb carried the day. A state convention endorsed the Compromise but warned that upon the faithful execution of the fugitive slave law depended the preservation of the Union. Even in South Carolina, the cooperationists, who favored secession only in cooperation with the other southern states, won the day over the immediate secession party headed by Robert Barnwell Rhett. For a time, at least, the Union was preserved, and moderates could hope that the Compromise of 1850 would give peace to a distracted people.

8

STANLY AND THE PARTY DIVIDED

WHEN THE THIRTY-SECOND CONGRESS met in December, 1851, the Whig House members caucused, with between fifty and sixty persons present, and decided in view of the large Democratic majority in the House not to make a nomination for Speaker, but to allow each member to exercise his own judgment. The Democrats easily elected Linn Boyd of Kentucky, who received 118 votes; among the Whigs, Stanly led with 21, followed by Joseph Chandler of Pennsylvania with 20, and Thaddeus Stevens of the same state with 16, and the rest scattered. Stanly voted for John L. Taylor of Ohio. Stanly's votes, except that of Alfred Dockery, came from northern Whigs, who admired his staunch nationalism and friendship for the North.[1]

Over the objections of Thaddeus Stevens and Orin Fowler of Massachusetts, the Whig caucus endorsed the compromise measures and declared "they ought to be adheared to and carried into faithful execution, as a final settlement, in principle and substance, of the dangerous and exciting subjects which they embrace."[2] But this action did not satisfy Robert Toombs and Alexander H. Stephens. They were convinced that the old parties must give way to a new "United National" party of Conservatives or Constitutional Union men who were sound on the slavery question. This new party would repeat on a national scale the Toombs-Stephens-Cobb party which had kept Georgia in the Union in 1850. "The Whig party is dead," Stephens wrote Cobb after the Whig caucus. "It made a galvanic

struggle in caucus, but it may be considered as disabandonned [*sic*].
I mean the national organization. There are a great many *sound men*
of that party now at the North who are ready for a new movement,
and in a few months many of the Democratic organizations will be
ready for the same."[3] Stephens viewed as *"tricksters"* those members of the Whig Party who wished to keep up the old organization.
To obtain this end, he wrote his brother Linton, they had taken
Toombs from the Ways and Means Committee and put Stanly in his
place. "It is thought *he* will keep up the fight on the old line."[4]

Stanly was indeed prepared to "fight on the old line"; the very
idea of breaking up the Whig Party was anathema to this staunchest
of southern Whigs. Toombs and Stephens would not work with
anti-slavery northern Whigs, no matter how moderate. Toombs
declared that the struggle between Charles Sumner, an anti-slavery
zealot, and Robert Winthrop, for the Massachusetts senate seat of
Daniel Webster, was a contest in which the "friends of the country"
had not the slightest interest. "The success of the principles of either
would be equally fatal to the safety and existence of the Republic."[5] Stanly, on the other hand, had no objection to working with
northern anti-slavery Whigs against the "Locos," so long as they
were not men of the Sumner or Giddings stamp. "I have looked with
great anxiety to the Mass: election & earnestly hoped you would be
triumphantly elected," he wrote Winthrop wistfully, after Sumner
had won the seat. "I shall miss you much in Washington."[6]

The subject uppermost in the minds of congressmen at this
session was the approaching presidential election. The leading candidates for the Whig nomination were President Millard Fillmore,
Daniel Webster, and General Winfield Scott. Fillmore, by his firmness and fairness, especially in the execution of the fugitive slave
law, had won the gratitude and confidence of the southern Whigs;
and they were almost unanimous in their determination to support
him for the nomination. "Were it left to the Whigs of the South to
say who should be the next President," said one observer, after a
tour of the southern states in 1851, "almost with one voice they
would say let the present Administration be continued."[7] Webster
was also popular with southern Whigs, but had little first-line
strength outside New England.

Scott was primarily the candidate of the northern Whigs, among them Thurlow Weed and William H. Seward, who were struggling with Fillmore for control of the Whig Party in New York. Although Scott had supported the compromise measures, most southern Whigs distrusted him because of Seward's backing.[8] The demand was therefore made that Scott cut loose from Seward and publicly and unequivocably endorse the compromise measures, including the controversial fugitive slave law. The state Whig convention in North Carolina resolved that no candidate for the Presidency or Vice-Presidency could obtain the vote of the Whigs in the state "unless he is, beyond doubt, in favor of maintaining the entire series of Compromise measures."[9]

Free-soil Whigs were equally determined that Scott should not give such a pledge. Senator Benjamin Wade of Ohio brought the northern Whigs to "a final and irrevocable decision" that the South should take Scott without sectional pledges. He had no fears for the loyalty of the southern Whigs in such a case. "They dare not go against us."[10] When William A. Graham learned of this decision, he declared privately that it "would be ruinous to us at the South."[11]

Only the most devoted southern Whigs could accept Scott on Wade's terms. Still, in January and February, 1852, a number of Whig congressmen from the upper South prepared to lend him their support. This small group included Stanly and Mangum of North Carolina, senators John Bell and James C. Jones of Tennessee, and Representative William T. Ward of Kentucky. To these men, Scott, a Virginian by birth, with a brilliant war record, seemed the best choice for a party which had never won the presidency except with a military hero.[12]

On April 6, 1852, Stanly wrote a letter to the Washington *Republic*, which was intended to overcome southern distrust of Scott. While Fillmore was unquestionably the first choice of the people of North Carolina for President, Stanly had never said, and would not say now, "that 'I can't and won't go for Scott.'" On the contrary, he had always said he knew Scott to be as earnest, ardent, and zealous a friend of the compromise measures as there was in the United States. "I *know, of my own knowledge, that he was so before their passage in Congress and afterwards*....I do not believe, at this time, there is one man in Congress . . . who does not know Gen. Scott is in favor of maintaining the Compromise acts."[13]

Mangum followed up Stanly's letter with a speech in the Senate on April 15 in which he came out openly for Scott, who, he said, possessed as "clean a bill of health" as Fillmore, Webster, and Clay on the Compromise. It had been his unwavering conviction for more than a year and a half that Scott was the only Whig in the country who could be elected President; and Mangum had little fear for the result if he should be the Whig nominee.[14]

This activity on behalf of Scott did not meet with the approval of most North Carolina Whigs. "You have seen the letter of Stanly, and speech of Mangum in favor of Gen'l Scott's nomination," Graham wrote James Bryan from Washington. "I think them exceedingly ill-timed, and they have produced much feeling among the National Whigs of the North."[15] The private observation of Edward J. Hale, the influential editor of the Fayetteville *Observer*, was bitingly caustic: "We are rather inclined to suppose, in these parts, that Mangum was not very sober when he commenced his speech, & that he was very drunk when he finished it."[16] But a few North Carolina Whigs were ready to follow Stanly and Mangum into the Scott camp. The Raleigh *Register*, while "earnest and ardent" for Fillmore, saw no reason why southern Whigs should hesitate to support Scott as the nominee, if by that time he had declared himself in favor of all the compromise measures.[17]

Meanwhile, a strategic move by House Democrats further widened the breach between the northern and southern Whigs that Stanly and Mangum were laboring to close. Two Georgia Democrats, Joseph W. Jackson and Junius Hillyer, introduced resolutions affirming the finality of the compromise measures. They were designed to show the southern Whigs that their northern brethren were unsound on the Compromise and admirably served that purpose. For the vote on the resolutions revealed that while two-thirds of the northern Democrats had voted in the affirmative, two-thirds of the northern Whigs had been opposed.[18]

Such southern Whigs as Humphrey Marshall of Kentucky, Meredith Gentry of Tennessee, and David Outlaw of North Carolina now determined to put the Whig Party to the test on the Compromise at the first opportunity. They decided to raise the issue in the Whig caucus which had been called for April 9 to decide on the time and place for the Whig national convention.[19]

The first caucus, presided over by Mangum, with fourteen senators and fifty-six representatives present, adjourned until April 20, without taking any action; but at the adjourned meeting, Mangum ruled out of order Marshall's resolution affirming the finality of the Compromise, and was sustained by a vote of forty-six to twenty-one. Marshall almost immediately declared that the caucus was no place for a Whig and left. Gentry, in a last attempt to preserve party unity, offered a resolution which declared that in fixing the time and place for the convention, the Whigs did not commit themselves to support the party's nominees unless they publicly and unequivocally endorsed the finality of the Compromise. Mangum also ruled this resolution out of order and was again sustained by vote of the meeting. Only six southern Whigs, including Stanly, opposed the Marshall and Gentry resolutions. One by one, Outlaw, Gentry, Clingman, and other southern Whigs, declaring that the rejection of the compromise resolutions was the same as throwing them out of the party, withdrew from the caucus. Mangum, Stanly, James Morehead, and Alfred Dockery were among the thirteen southern members who remained (Badger was absent). The rump caucus then selected Baltimore as the site of the Whig national convention and June 16 as the date.[20]

Stanly, Morehead, and Dockery stated in the caucus that unless the convention selected a candidate who would expressly support the compromise measures, he could not carry a single Whig state in the South; but unlike the seceders they were not ready to adopt a Compromise resolution; congressmen might be regarded as "impertinent" in attempting to instruct the people's representatives in a Whig convention. Stanly, although privately for Scott, expressed a preference for Fillmore, but said he would support Scott if nominated, since he knew him to be a "thorough Compromise man" and had no doubt he would avow his sentiments before he was nominated. According to one report, Stanly was "very severe on those who had withdrawn."[21]

The next day, Stanly declared on the floor of the House that

Scott was in favor of sustaining "*all* the compromise measures, the fugitive slave law included"; but Outlaw retorted that private assurances were not enough; when Scott made a public declaration, "he and everybody else would be able to judge how far he was committed to maintain them as a final settlement of the slavery question."[22]

The refusal of the southern Whigs to take Scott on faith convinced Stanly that the General must make known his opinions on the Compromise. On May 10, he warned William Schouler, editor of the Boston *Atlas*, and a Scott man, that if Scott did not write a letter "only admitting what his opinions have been & are now" the national convention would be called on to pass Compromise resolutions. "These will meet with opposition & then another secession will take place & every whig state of the South is gone." Southern Whigs deserved some sympathy. They were not all unreasonably arrogant; they had to fight the Secessionists at home upon the ground that northern Whigs were conservative. He could see no difficulty in Scott making known the opinions which the *Atlas* said he entertained:

> I want no pledges for vetoes, no notes of approbation of the provisions of the fugitive law. But when I *know*, serious efforts are making to make an Union party—to breakup the Whig party, by Toombs, Stevens [Stephens?], & such men, when I know the great excitement in the minds of our people, I want the Whigs of the North without sacrificing principle, to let us have the truth from Scott, & save the Country from 'Cass, Cuba' & all the horrors of Loco-focoism.[23]

However, despite Stanly's plea, no "truth from Scott" was forthcoming. Seward, Wade, and company kept the old General well muzzled.[24] On June 10, six days before the national Whig convention was to meet in Baltimore, Outlaw complained in the House that "we have yet no response from the oracle. We have yet no publication of General Scott's opinions. We are left to infer what those opinions are from private conversations." No man, he declared, could receive his support who occupied that position.[25] Stanly replied lamely that Scott might have been "more fastidious than was prudent had he regarded policy," although his motives were honorable. As a personal friend of Fillmore, Scott might have been loath to announce as a candidate; but, when the convention called upon him, he would answer. "If he does not,...consenting to be a mum candidate, he will not get my support."[26]

Stanly had earlier stated that Scott would make known his opinions before the Whig convention met at Baltimore; now, apparently, the declaration was not to come until the nomination was safely his. However, Meredith Gentry declared that Scott's nomination could not save the Whig Party, even if he *now* put himself distinctly on a finality platform. The South did not trust him, and he would not carry a single southern state. Gentry warned that Scott's nomination would elevate Seward to the leadership of the party, in the South as well as the North; and by destroying the southern wing of the party, would sectionalize and abolitionize the northern wing. Seward wanted to be president and in 1856 he would use this northern anti-slavery party to accomplish that object.[27] Stanly scoffed at the idea that Seward controlled Scott—"There is not a particle of evidence of it"—but there was nothing he said, or could have said, that would have eradicated the fears in the southern mind to which Gentry gave forceful expression in his House speech.[28]

To the dismay of the radical anti-slavery men, the Whig convention in Baltimore adopted a platform, 227 to 66, declaring that all the compromise measures were accepted as a final settlement in principle and substance of the dangerous questions they embraced. Scott's southern managers showed letters from him proving his soundness on the Compromise to the southern delegates. This opened the way for his nomination on the fifty-third ballot with 159 votes, as against Fillmore's 112 and Webster's 21. Virginia gave Scott eight votes, and Tennessee and Missouri three each. On June 29, the General formally accepted the nomination "with the resolutions annexed."[29]

William A. Graham received the nomination for Vice-President. Mangum declared that he might have been second on the ticket but declined: "The ill temper of No. Caro. is such that I thought it might hazard the vote." Stanly's first choice for Vice-President had been John J. Crittenden of Kentucky rather than Graham, who he thought would "add no strength out of No: Ca:"[30]

There was widespread dissatisfaction in North Carolina at Scott's nomination, but the Raleigh *Register* assured the Whigs that he was sound on the Compromise and promised to sustain him. Graham's name strengthened the Scott ticket in the state and helped to soothe injured feelings.[31] Nevertheless, disaffection soon appeared in the Whig ranks. Many Whigs considered Scott to be personally unfit for the Presidency—"a vain Coxcomb, whose silly acts would be the ridicule of the whole world," was the evaluation of one aged party member.[32] Local Whig leaders throughout the state either refused to support Scott or did so in the expectation of defeat. On October 8, Clingman in a public letter announced that he could not accept Scott, and that he would support Franklin Pierce of New Hampshire, the Democratic candidate.[33] David Outlaw was still cool toward Scott, and Kenneth Rayner declared publicly that "he would not walk forty yards to cast his vote for General Scott."[34]

The loyal Whig press, aided by Graham, tried with only limited success to convince the "doubting Whigs" that Scott was sound on the Compromise. Graham wrote a public letter stating that he had lodged in the same Washington hotel with Scott in 1850, and that when the fate of the compromise measures were in doubt, no man had been more their advocate, none had exerted himself more actively to procure votes in Congress in their favor, or rejoiced more heartily over the final settlement. He assured the voters that if elected, Scott would carry on the Government on the same principles as Fillmore. "He is too national, too enlarged a Statesman to yield to any factious, or sectional views."[35]

The Whigs also argued that it was Pierce, rather than Scott, who was unsound on the Compromise. They produced an affidavit from the Reverend Andrew J. Foss of New Hampshire swearing that at New Boston Centre on January 2, 1852, Pierce had expressed loathing for the fugitive slave law and had declared that it was "opposed to humanity and moral right." The Raleigh *Register* placed Pierce's reported opinion of the fugitive slave law at its masthead along with an italicized quote from a Pierce speech in the Senate: "I have no *hesitation* in saying that I consider *Slavery* a SOCIAL and POLITICAL EVIL, and MOST SINCERELY WISH *it had no existence on the face of the earth!*"[36]

Stanly, who was working for Scott in Washington while Congress
was in session, wrote a New Hampshire Whig that Foss's affidavit,
and affidavits bearing witness to the accuracy of his report, would be
of great service to the Whigs in the southern states. "You can have
no idea of the trouble caused among the Locos, by this report," he
noted with satisfaction. "It affords a good excuse for the discontented Fillmore men to come back: it justifies the moderate
democrats for supporting Scott, & annoys inconceivably the democratic orators." He hoped that the members of Foss's congregation
would support him, as to his standing in the church, even if they
should say nothing of the correctness of Pierce's speech. This should
be done if practicable. "Let us have whatever you can obtain
showing Pierce's duplicity & *'dough-face-ism.'*"[37]

In August, the state elections in North Carolina dealt the Whigs a
severe and unexpected blow. David Reid was reelected governor over
John Kerr of Caswell County by an increased majority of 5,564
votes, although the Whigs captured the House of Commons and had
a majority of two on joint ballot. The result encouraged the
Democrats and alarmed the Whigs in Washington. Stanly warned
Graham that something must be done to produce a systematic effort
by the North Carolina Whigs. "If we do so, we can beat them. If we
make no effort, they will carry the State."[38]

After the state election, the Whigs and Democrats intensified
their presidential campaigning. The Whigs blamed Kerr's defeat by
Reid on the free suffrage issue and predicted that North Carolina
would give an "old fashioned majority" for Scott and Graham.[39]
Stanly hoped that the Whigs would have sense enough to vote for
free suffrage and take it out of the contest thereafter.[40] Graham
wrote new letters vouching for Scott's soundness on the Compromise. The Democrats, on their part, insisted that the "*safety of
Southern rights* and *the salvation of the Union* depend on the
election of Pierce and King."[41] Both parties appealed to religious
prejudice during the campaign. The Whigs charged (falsely) that
Pierce had acquiesced in a clause of the New Hampshire constitution
disqualifying Catholics from office, while Scott was assailed by some
Democrats as a Catholic, because his daughter had become a nun![42]

Stanly's congressional duties kept him from the stump until the end of August. After adjournment, he campaigned for Scott and Graham in New York and in Pennsylvania, where his own vote for the Whig tariff of 1842 assured him a cordial welcome. "The burthen [*sic*] of my song in Pa: was the Tariff," he informed Graham, "& I denounced the Nullifiers & Secessionists by whom Pierce was nominated for their opposition to it. I think my remarks had some effect, among those who supported Jackson as a Tariff man, & wish an excuse to vote for Scott."[43]

Stanly returned to North Carolina in October to stump his district for the Whig ticket. Stopping briefly in Raleigh to "cheer" the Whigs, he addressed the Scott and Graham Club of that city on October 11. The Raleigh *Register* bestowed the usual encomiums on his speech, but the Raleigh *North Carolina Standard* pronounced his effort "tame," in that he appeared to labor under a feeling of despondency which he could not shake off. "The signs are all against Mr. Stanly, and he felt it."[44]

If Stanly was despondent, his schedule of speeches gave no evidence of any slackening of activity. Between October 12 and 28, he was to give eight speeches in his district; and the Raleigh *Register* promised that if his friends at other points desired to hear him, he would meet them, if in his power to do so.[45] On October 23, he went out of the district to appear with Outlaw and other Whig dignitaries at a mass meeting in Gatesville. According to one observer, Stanly spoke for two hours and made "by far the best speech I have heard during this campaign."[46]

Pierce carried North Carolina in November by the narrow margin of 686 votes, while Taylor had carried the state four years before by a 8,552 majority. Clingman's defection to the Democrats was partially responsible for the result, but many Whigs stayed away from the polls because they distrusted Scott, yet could not bring themselves to vote for Pierce.[47] The election confirmed what had been demonstrated previously—that the people of North Carolina accepted the Compromise as a final settlement of the slavery question. Stanly, Mangum, Graham, and the Raleigh *Register* might assure them that Scott was sound on the Compromise and could not be made the tool of faction; North Carolina Whigs still feared he would be controlled by Seward and the anti-slavery wing of the Whig Party.

Nationwide, Pierce scored a smashing victory, carrying every state except Massachusetts and Vermont in New England and Kentucky and Tennessee on the border. Leaders of both parties were astounded at the completeness of his victory. "The late election has surprised all—Whigs & Democrats," Stanly confided to Graham. "God save our Country!"[48] He admitted later that the Whig Party "had been as badly beaten as any party on earth."[49] Many Whigs thought it could not recover. Both the New York *Times* and the New York *Tribune* declared that Whiggism had received its death blow. Robert Toombs rejoiced at the party's downfall, writing John J. Crittenden:

> We can never have peace and security with Seward, Greeley & Co. in the ascendency in our national councils, and we can better purchase them by the destruction of the Whig Party than of the Union. If the Whig Party is incapable of rising to the same standard of nationality as the motley crew which offers it under the name of Democracy it is entitled to no ressurrection—It will have none.[50]

It is apparent in retrospect that the Whig nomination in 1852 should have gone to Fillmore, who had earned it. If Seward and Weed had permitted the President's renomination, the party might still have lost the election, but its strength in the South would have been preserved. But the northern anti-slavery wing refused to accept either the Compromise or Fillmore, who had faithfully executed the fugitive slave law. The result was the disruption of the Whig Party—a disaster from which it was never to recover.

Why did Stanly not join with the overwhelming majority of the southern Whigs in urging Fillmore's nomination? Certainly, the President's views on the Compromise were identical with his own. The answer is simply that he believed Scott was "the only man the whigs can elect."[51] To Stanly, victory over the despised Locofocos was of paramount importance. Moreover, he considered Scott (correctly) to be both a staunch nationalist and a supporter of the Compromise.[52] As a personal friend of both Seward and Weed, he did not share southern fears that they would dominate Scott. And he was not alone in this view. John A. Quitman, who had served under the General in Mexico, pronounced the idea that he would be controlled by Seward "stuff."[53] Yet the southern Whig revolt was none the less real for being ill founded, and Stanly might have done his party and his country a significant service by arguing more forcefully, as he did in his letter to Schouler, for an explicit endorsement of the compromise measures by Scott in the spring of 1852. Respected as he was by northern Whig leaders, he might have persuaded them to reconsider their determination to keep Scott "mum" on the Compromise.

The Whig defeat strengthened Stanly's often expressed desire to retire from public life. In January, 1853, both the Raleigh *Register* and the Raleigh *North Carolina Standard* reported a rumor that he intended to remove to California to practice law. The *Register* expressed the hope that the rumor would prove unfounded, since "North Carolina cannot afford to lose Edward Stanly." Less charitably, the *Standard* predicted from experience that he would "stir things up out there; but, fortunately, he will be in the minority, so that, politically, he will not be able to do any harm."[54]

Stanly did intend to move to California. His district had been gerrymandered after the Census of 1850 and now had a normal Democratic majority of about three thousand votes. He could not expect to win reelection. "Were I to remain in No: Ca:" he wrote Schuyler Colfax, an Indiana Whig, "I might be a candidate again, for the pleasure of defending good principles against numbers. But I cannot. There is little business doing in the Old North State & I am weary of public life." Perhaps remembering his own family's poverty after John Stanly's sudden illness, he added that it was "a terrible thing" to be old and poor. "I do not covet wealth, but any man is bound to provide a competence while health and youth attend him."[55]

Whig journals throughout the nation expressed their regret that financial considerations had forced "this noble-hearted Whig of the Old North State" to retire from public life and move to California. The Washington *North State Whig*, recalling the many evidences in the district of his "watchful care," predicted that "it will be long . . . before the people for whom Mr. Stanly has been so long toiling, will find another such representative."[56]

Among Stanly's last acts in Washington was a speech in support of a proposal to name a western territory after the President he most admired, George Washington. On February 8, 1853, a bill to organize a new territory called "Columbia" in northern Oregon was before the House. Stanly spoke in favor of an amendment offered by Richard Stanton of Kentucky changing the name of the territory to "Washington." "There has been but one Washington upon earth," he remarked, "and there is not likely to be another; and, as Providence has sent but one, for all time, let us have one State named after that one man, and let the name be Washington. I hope there will be no objection to the amendment."[57] The name change was adopted; and two days later, the bill passed the House, 128 to 29. On March 2, 1853, the Senate accepted the bill and Fillmore signed the measure the same day. The people of northern Oregon wholeheartedly accepted the name Washington.[58]

In March, 1853, the citizens of Beaufort County "without distinction of party" tendered Stanly a public dinner in Washington, which he declined because of the short time remaining before his departure for California. "The Old North State has many a worthier son, but none more proud of her glory, more anxious for her prosperity, or more grateful for the kindness of her people, than I am," he told the citizens of Beaufort. "What ever errors I have committed—and they have been numerous—the wish to keep untarnished her character, to advance the interests of her people, has ever been nearest my heart."[59]

Stanly was supposed to leave New York City for California aboard the steamer *Illinois* on April 23, 1853; but on that day, the railroad car in which he was riding was thrown into Rancorus Creek, between Philadelphia and New York, "by the drawbridge being up." Stanly was not injured, although his baggage was lost in the creek. He continued on to New York and sailed on May 5, aboard the steamer *Georgia.*[60]

Even before Stanly's departure, the Whigs in his district sought "some unselfish and daring spirit" to bear the Whig banner in the coming congressional election. "What other gallant Whig," asked the Raleigh *Register*, would take Stanly's place "in leading—what he has never failed to lead, when called to the field of action,—(what seems,) *'a forlorn hope?'*" No "gallant Whig" was forthcoming, but an independent Democrat, William C. Loften, contested the district with Thomas Ruffin, the regular Democratic nominee. Those Whigs who bothered to vote generally cast their ballots for Loften; but he was crushed, losing by a margin of some 3,159 votes.[61]

Although the Whigs did not yet realize it, their party supremacy was over in North Carolina. The Whig Party had lost much of the vigor and progressive outlook which had given it superiority over the Democratic Party in the state. Its opposition to "free suffrage," an issue used so effectively by David Reid, was an indication of this change in attitude. Moreover, the party's organization was rent with internal personal rivalries. Thomas L. Clingman left the Whigs in 1852 and carried his mountain district with him. The feud between Stanly and Kenneth Rayner continued, and when Rayner was nominated by the Whig caucus for Mangum's senate seat, Stanly's friends refused to support him. "It was a sin to vote for Rayner," Stanly wrote James Bryan at the time. "I hope I contributed something to his defeat. He is mean personally, he indulged in pitiful electioneering, [and] he opposed Scott's election."[62] It was perhaps well for the "Conqueror" that he left North Carolina when he did, for the Democratic supremacy would have been gall and wormwood to his fiery spirit.

9

IN THE LAND OF GOLD

IN JANUARY, 1848, shortly before the end of the Mexican War, gold was discovered at Sutter's Mill on the American River in the Sacramento Valley of California. The news spread rapidly, and by the end of 1849 thousands of men from every part of the globe were prospecting in the fabled "land of gold." California society after 1848 was a melting pot—"a gathering without parallel in history." It was, moreover, a community of young men, with few oldsters to be seen.[1] The miners were a hardy lot who scorned, or professed to scorn, refinement and lived in camps with such bizarre names as "Git-up-and-Git," "Gouge-Eye," "Skunk Gulch," and "Hell's Delight." Where there was great wealth, there was also vice and violent death to an extraordinary degree. According to one contemporary, there were forty-two hundred murders committed in California from 1849 to 1854, with twelve hundred in San Francisco alone.[2] That city on the Golden Gate grew overnight from a sleepy village to an El Dorado of twenty-five thousand people, despite frequent fires which leveled large areas of the city, "the houses being as inflammable as the temper of the inhabitants."[3]

Stanly arrived in San Francisco in June, 1853, to try his fortune at the Bar, not in the gold fields. His reputation as an honest and able lawyer had preceded him, and once he had mastered the complexities of California law he soon had a lucrative practice. In 1856, the San Francisco *Evening Bulletin* singled him out as "one of those honest lawyers who by their morality and social standing have preserved the profession of law from the disgrace a majority of the bar have brought upon it." After a brief association with William W. Hawks, Stanly formed a lasting partnership with William Hayes (Stanly & Hayes), and the two men took offices first in Naglee's Building, at the corner of Merchant and Montgomery, and then at 604 Clay at Montgomery.[4]

The local bar comprised an unusual number of able men, rivaling in that respect the New Bern of Stanly's youth. Among those practicing were Henry Stuart Foote, who had been governor of Mississippi and United States senator; Peter H. Burnett, the first governor of California; Serranus C. Hastings, a former Iowa congressman; Joseph G. Baldwin, the Virginia-Alabama author and lawyer; James A. McDougall, later United States senator; and Colonel Edward D. Baker, a hero of the Mexican War and Whig member of the House of Representatives from Illinois. Stanly had known Baker in Washington, and he had the melancholy duty of pronouncing his friend's funeral oration in San Francisco after Baker fell in battle at Balls Bluff, Virginia, in the fall of 1861.[5]

A devout Christian, Stanly was active in the Episcopal Church's affairs in San Francisco, serving at various times as Senior Warden of Grace Church, a member of the Standing Committee of the Diocese, parish delegate to the Diocesan Convention, and delegate to the General Convention. In October, 1855, Stanly was one of a small party that accompanied Episcopal Bishop William Ingraham Kip on a month's visit to Los Angeles and Forts Tejon and Miller in southern California to hold the first Episcopal services and explore the Church's future prospects in the area.[6]

Stanly announced after his arrival in California that he did not desire to "mingle" in politics, but intended to devote himself entirely to the law.[7] In fact, the Whig Party in the state did not offer much hope of political advancement to an ambitious man. Although President Taylor had hoped to make California "free and Whig," the Democratic Party controlled its political fortunes almost from the beginning. The Whigs, as long as their party existed, made a little noise at election time, but without result. The cities of San Francisco and Sacramento were Whig in 1852, but the state gave a majority for Pierce over Scott of 9,669, in a total vote of 71,189. [8]

Stanly said in 1855 that when he arrived in the state, "I found the Whigs were dead here; and I therefore pursued the even tenor of my way, voting for a Democrat here and there, voting for a Whig here and there, according as I thought them to be capable and honest."[9]

Within the dominant Democratic Party, the rivalry for leadership of two remarkable men, William McKendree Gwin and David C. Broderick, dominated California's political history from 1852 to 1859. The suave and polished Gwin, a native of Tennessee, serving his first term in the United States Senate, led the pro-southern or "chivalry" wing of the Democratic Party in the state, while Broderick, a likable Irishman and graduate of New York City's Tammany Hall, became the leader of its northern wing, made up largely of naturalized Irish and Germans. The feud between the two men began in 1852 when Broderick was defeated for the Senate by Gwin's candidate, John B. Weller. In 1855, Broderick gained his revenge by blocking Gwin's bid for reelection, leaving his seat vacant for two years.[10]

In 1854, a new political party, the Know Nothings, appeared in California, replacing the Whigs as the chief opposition to the Democracy. Growing out of a secret nativist organization, the Order of the Star Spangled Banner, the party advocated more rigorous naturalization laws and the exclusion of foreigners and Catholics from public office. Members, when asked about the Order, replied, "I know nothing." The party developed surprising strength in New England, New York, and elsewhere in 1854 as homeless Whigs in search of new moorings entered its ranks.

The first organization of Know Nothings in California took place in San Francisco in May, 1854. Adopting the role of a reform party, its leaders were able within three months to elect the entire city administration. By the end of September, 1854, the Order had a network of secret councils throughout California. The Know Nothings, or Americans, as they now styled themselves, met in Sacramento on August 7, 1855, and nominated a state ticket headed by John Neely Johnson for governor. Johnson had been president of the Whig convention in 1854. The Whig Party made no state nominations, and party leaders were rumored to have sent out a secret circular endorsing the Know Nothing ticket. The party also enjoyed the support of many Democratic Anti-Broderickites, who wanted to retaliate against Broderick by defeating his candidate for governor, incumbent John Bigler.[11]

The Know Nothings tried to enlist Stanly's services, paying him several visits and offering to elect him judge of the superior court in San Francisco if he would join the party. He refused, although the office paid $7,500 a year. He told them that he could not consent to any proscription for religion's sake; that he did not like their secret meetings and oaths, and could not support a repeal of the naturalization laws or the proscription of foreigners. "I am a zealous Protestant, trying to be a Christian," he confided to William A. Graham, "but wish to allow every man the privilege of worshipping God as he pleases, and free from proscription, because his opinions differ from mine."[12]

Other prominent San Francisco Whigs felt as Stanly did about Know Nothing principles. On the evening of August 18, 1855, they met to discuss the propriety of reorganizing the Whig Party in the city to demonstrate that it was not defunct, and to make war upon the Know Nothing Party. It was decided "to spread again the Whig banner to the breeze," and a twenty-seven man committee was elected to draft a party platform and to arrange the nomination of a county Whig ticket for the elections on September 5.[13] By polling a large vote the Whigs could insure a Democratic victory in the county races. The Sacramento *Daily Union*, which was advocating the Know Nothing cause, complained that hundreds of old-line Whigs in San Francisco would vote a clean Whig ticket who would not under any circumstances vote for an "out-in-out Broderick, Democratic, shoulder-striking ballot-box stuffing ticket."[14]

Stanly was asked to take part in the Whig movement, but at first declined: "If there be any offices or emolument or reward, I want none of these; I desire only permission to keep along in my private station, and want none of the rewards of office." He attended a mass meeting of the Young Men's Whig Club at the Union Hotel on the evening of August 27, and expressed doubt about the propriety of the reorganization. There were worse men than the Know Nothings in San Francisco—ballot-box stuffers "who take away the rights of us all." He thought that in the present canvass the Whigs ought to be allowed to vote for honest Democrats or Know Nothings; that would be the best thing for the community and the best course to pursue. The men who had joined the Know Nothings would on sober second thought repent of it, and he wanted to give them time for repentance—to come back to the Whigs and be forgiven. When his arguments were not heeded, Stanly agreed to run with Edward Baker for the state senate from San Francisco County, remarking that "he was ready to follow where Ned Baker would lead, he would stand at his shoulder and put him on the track and encourage him on; there could not be much danger, as the broad shape of the Colonel would protect him from all chance of being hit."[15]

The Whigs held a mass meeting in the hall of the Polka Saloon on the evening of August 29, with Stanly and Baker as the main speakers. Stanly reviewed Know Nothing principles and handled them "in a severe and cutting manner." He warned that while South Carolina would take one star from the flag, Know Nothingism would blot out every star. Did men think less of Charles Carroll, of Carrollton, or of Chief Justice Roger B. Taney, because they were Catholics? Did they think less of Alexander Hamilton because he was foreign born? It was the United States' mission to show that every man, whatever his creed, who worshipped God should be tolerated. That was the doctrine of the Declaration of Independence and the Constitution of the United States, and he could not be a Know Nothing as long as those documents stood. He "was intently listened to throughout, and at the conclusion of his stirring appeal was saluted with a tremendous round of applause," the band striking up the Star-Spangled Banner.[16]

On election eve, September 4, Stanly addressed a second Whig mass meeting in the Polka Saloon, and again was very severe on Know Nothingism, reading from the party's Philadelphia and Sacramento platforms and ridiculing their warnings of Catholic encroachments. He said the Whig Party was needed to oppose the iniquity of the Kansas-Nebraska Bill, to protect navigation, oppose filibusters, and advocate the Pacific Railroad. "To meet these issues the Whig Party has life yet, and must have life." However, he wanted no man to vote for him tomorrow—on the contrary, he would be thankful to any man who scratched his name from the ticket—he would be favoring him to do so. He had received enough honors in his native state. The crowd responded good-naturedly with six "deafening" cheers for Stanly and Baker and nine cheers for North Carolina![17]

The Know Nothings elected their entire state ticket on September 5, as Johnson received 50,948 votes to Governor Bigler's 45,937; the Order also secured a majority in both houses of the state legislature. However, in San Francisco County, the Democrats swept the senate and assembly seats and elected most of the other county and city officials. The Democratic candidates for state senator, Frank Tilford and William Shaw, polled 6,485 and 6,488 votes respectively; the Know Nothings, Harvey Brown and Louis Lull, 4,232 and 4,224; the Whigs, Stanly and Baker, 1,435 and 1,245. The San Francisco *Daily Herald*, in giving the official county returns, attributed the favorable result to the Whigs: "We warned the Whigs, from the first, that if they did not poll a large vote they would assist instead of defeating the Know Nothings. They polled a large vote, and in consequence have defeated the Secret Order."[18] However, the reorganized Whig Party in San Francisco did not long survive the election.

Despite their setback in San Francisco, the Know Nothings were now the dominant party in California, with every prospect of electing a senator to succeed Gwin at the next meeting of the state legislature. The party caucus selected Henry Stuart Foote, but friends of Gwin and Broderick in the Know Nothing camp prevented his election. Made up of the discontented fragments of the two older parties, the Know Nothings lacked any real cohesion and began to disintegrate almost in their hour of victory.[19]

In national politics, the slavery extension issue had slumbered since the Compromise of 1850. It was unexpectedly reopened in the spring of 1854 when the Administration forces in Congress, led by Stephen A. Douglas, passed the Kansas-Nebraska bill, repealing the venerable Missouri Compromise line of 1820 and opening the territory north of 36°30' to slavery. This ill-advised action aroused a tremendous storm of protest in the North, where it was viewed as the breaking of a sacred sectional compact, and led directly to the formation of a new political party. A meeting in a schoolhouse in Ripon, Wisconsin on February 28, 1854, resolved to oppose the extension of slavery and recommended the formation of a new

"Republican party" to do it. On July 6, 1854, a convention held at Jackson, Michigan, "under the oaks," adopted the name Republican and resolved to oppose the extension of slavery until the contest was terminated. The party grew slowly at first outside the Northwest, but picked up momentum when violence flared in Kansas between pro- and anti-slavery factions. Seward joined, as did most of the Free Soilers, northern Whigs, and "Anti-Nebraska" Democrats.

The Republican Party in California was not organized until 1856, and membership was extremely limited at first. In Sacramento the party numbered barely a dozen, including Cornelius Cole, Colis P. Huntington, Mark Hopkins, Leland Stanford, Edwin B. and Charles Crocker, and George C. Bates. "While our party, in Sacramento, was slow of growth, there were no deserters," Cole later recalled. "Those who came with us enlisted for the war, so to speak."[20] John Carr, who organized the Republican Party in Weaverville, Trinity County, wrote that the Republicans "had to take more scoffs and jeers than the Salvation Army of the present day" (1891). "When speaking of the Republicans, the rough element would generally call them thieving, black Republican s.o.b.'s; but the more refined would often say: 'John, I like you as a man, but d—n your politics!'"[21]

The first Republican mass meeting in California was held in Sacramento on April 19, 1856, with Edwin B. Crocker presiding. It was broken up by a mob that overturned the speaker's stand. On April 30, after a series of conferences, a Republican state convention met in Sacramento. The Sacramento *State Journal* briefly referred to the "convention of nigger-worshipers" as dangerous fanatics who had heretofore skulked in dark corners, hidden their identity, and kept in the background. Only thirteen counties were represented, several by but one delegate. Of 125 delegates, 66 were from Sacramento and San Francisco. The convention adopted the prohibition of slavery in all the national territories "as the cardinal principle of our organization," favored preventing the increase of the political power of slavery in the federal government, and unanimously accepted the platform of the party's recent Pittsburgh convention. It mentioned the San Jose *Telegraph* as the pioneer Republican paper on the Pacific coast, urged Republican support for the San Francisco *Evening Journal*, and asked that a Republican journal be started in

Sacramento. Cornelius Cole and James McClatchy responded by starting the Sacramento *Daily Times.* [22]

The Sacramento Republicans made an immediate effort to enlist Stanly in their cause, writing him on April 4, 1856, that a Republican Party had been formed in the city on the basis of the Pittsburgh Address and requesting him to address them on April 12, if his political views and engagements would permit. Stanly replied that his professional duties required all his time, but went on to say that he had neither the inclination nor the time to keep up with the progress of parties in the country. He had never read the Pittsburgh Address and could not take part in any party meeting in which its merits would be discussed, but insofar as it opposed the Kansas-Nebraska Bill, he was in thorough agreement, "and with all my heart. I fear it has brought nothing but trouble upon our country, without any good to justify the enormous wrong perpetrated by its enactment." Thus far he was a "Republican," but he feared that party held other views which he had always opposed. He had never regarded slavery as a blessing that should be extended over free territory—"very far from it"—yet as a native Southerner, he could not stand upon a platform from which "declarations of hostility" were made against a portion of the country which he still loved.

Stanly added that he could not be a Democrat, since he could not subscribe to the Kansas-Nebraska Bill; nor could he be a Know Nothing: "for their secrecies, grips and passwords I have an instinctive abhorrence." There was, then, but one course to follow:

> I have been, I am, and I shall be a Whig, and am now nothing but a Whig—a national Whig, supporting a tariff when necessary for the protection of American labor, securing National Independence, advocating internal improvements by the General Government; above all, the National Railroad, without which California is a giant with his limbs asunder; and though I know some of these opinions are regarded as obsolete, I do not entertain them with any less sincerity on that account. [23]

For Stanly, there was but one road to Heaven, and that was the Whig road; he would not stray from the path.

In 1856, Stanly, for the first time in twenty years, took no part in a presidential election. He favored the Republican nominee, John

C. Frémont, over Democrat James Buchanan and Millard Fillmore, the American candidate, but was in North Carolina on a visit during the election and did not vote. "Indeed," said the San Francisco *Daily Alta California* later, "his feelings were not such as to enable him to take an active part. His personal preferences were for Fillmore, but he disliked Americanism; he disliked Buchanan's Ostend Circular, and Nebraskaism still more; and therefore he preferred Fremont."[24]

The Republicans met in Sacramento on August 27, 1856, to nominate presidential electors and congressmen, and were called to order by Edwin Crocker, the chairman of the state committee. Ira P. Rankin was nominated for congressman from the southern district and Thomas Cox from the northern district. Cornelius Cole reluctantly consented to be a candidate for clerk of the supreme court, although he was "[not] disturbed by fear of an election." The convention endorsed the national ticket and platform and adopted the slogan "Freedom, Frémont and the Railroad." In an effort to arouse enthusiasm for Frémont over the state, a Bear Club, suggestive of his role in the Bear Flag Revolt, was organized, and the Republicans took over the San Francisco *Chronicle*. However, "The Pathfinder" was hurt by the disclosure that he was the eastern agent of Palmer, Cook & Company, a California banking house, that had defaulted on its bonds through fraudulent speculation. Frémont was entirely innocent, but the opposition made the most of the issue.[25]

In the November election, Buchanan carried California by a plurality, with 53,365 votes to Fillmore's 36,165 and Frémont's 20,339. Nationally, he won five free states and every slave state except Maryland, which voted for Fillmore. He received 174 electoral votes to Frémont's 114 and Fillmore's 8. California Democrats elected their state ticket and regained control of the legislature. The Sacramento *Daily Union* declared that four-fifths of the Republicans were from the American and old Whig parties—men who would have voted for Fillmore and the American state candidates had there been no Frémont ticket in the field. The people of the state should hold the leaders of the Republican movement responsible for again placing the "old fogy spoils Democratic party" in power in California.[26] A year later the Republicans would make a similar charge against the Americans.

The state legislature, which convened on January 5, 1857, had to elect two United States senators to fill the seats of William Gwin and John Weller. Stanly, although still absent from the state, was the Republican candidate to succeed Weller, whose term expired on March 3. Entirely unsolicited, it was a nominal honor since the Republicans were a distinct minority in the legislature. On January 9, David C. Broderick was elected to Weller's seat for the long term, receiving seventy-nine votes to James W. Coffroth's seventeen and Stanly's fourteen. Broderick then allowed the reelection of Gwin for the short term after the latter pledged him the federal patronage.[27]

However, in the Democratic state convention, the anti-Broderick faction nominated John B. Weller for governor over Judge Joseph McCorkle, Broderick's choice, by a vote of 254-61. Weller, a native of Ohio and former congressman from that state, had risen from private to colonel in the Mexican War, and had been appointed by President Polk to head a commission to survey the boundary between the United States and Mexico under the Treaty of Guadalupe Hidalgo. Upon his recall by President Taylor in 1850, he moved to California and opened a law office in San Francisco. The next year he was elected to the Senate to replace Frémont. In the Senate he had advocated the Pacific Railroad and homestead legislation and warmly supported the Kansas-Nebraska bill. He was a talented debater, had an easy command of language, a good presence, and an agreeable voice.[28]

The Republican state convention met on July 8, 1857, "in the Rev. Mr. Benton's Church" in Sacramento, with three hundred delegates present from twenty counties. The convention organized for business by selecting Frederick P. Tracy of San Francisco as Chairman *pro tem* and appointed a committee on resolutions. In adopting a platform at the evening session, the delegates did not express any opinions on questions of state policy, but cordially endorsed the resolutions adopted earlier by the National Republican Convention. The Sacramento convention declared that while the prohibition of slavery in the territories was "properly within the control of Congress, and all the people of the Union are therefore directly responsible should it be permitted to extend over such

Territories," slavery in the slave states depended solely upon state laws for existence and Congress had no power to modify, change, or repeal such laws. The platform endorsed the construction with federal aid of a transcontinental railroad by "the most central and eligble [*sic*] route," the speedy settlement of land titles in the state, and a free grant to actual settlers of reasonable portions of the public domain; welcomed "honest and industrious immigrants who seek our shores to escape from European despotism" and deprecated political persecution because of their foreign birth; denounced the Supreme Court's Dred Scott decision as "a palpable violation of the principles of the Declaration of Independence;" and, finally, extended to the free men of Oregon "an earnest desire for their success in the establishment of free principles as the basis of their State government."

The next order of business was the nomination of candidates for the office of governor and the delegates were asked to suggest names. Those nominated were Edward Stanly, Frederick P. Tracy, Joseph A. Nunes, Treanor W. Park, and Edward D. Baker of San Francisco; Samuel Bell of Mariposa; Edwin B. Crocker of Sacramento; J. M. Turner of Nevada; and D. R. Ashley of Monterrey. Joseph A. Nunes withdrew his name. Since Stanly had never affiliated with the Republican Party, several members asked whether he would accept the nomination if offered. A delegate stated that about ten days previously Stanly had told him that he had come to California to get rid of politics, and he would not accept the nomination for governor under any circumstances. However, Ira Rankin thought Stanly would be a very strong man and that he would not feel at liberty to decline. He was convinced of his "thorough Republicanism." Treanor Park admitted that he had pledged Stanly his word to vote against him, that in many conversations with him he had refused to run, and begged his friends not to nominate him. Still, Park believed his Republicanism, ability, and honesty to be unquestionable and that no man would be of more advantage to the party. He was confident he would run if nominated.

These assurances satisfied the delegates, and on the first ballot Stanly received 163 votes to 9 for Baker, 6 for Ashley, and 1 each for Park, Rankin, and R. Chenery. His nomination was made unanimous. Park, Edwin Crocker, and Aaron A. Sargent were appointed to inform Stanly of his nomination and to request a reply by wire.[29]

Stanly had purposely gone to Petaluma in Sonoma County on business to place himself beyond the reach of Park and the telegraph. Immediately after the convention adjourned on the first day, Park sent a telegram to San Francisco notifying Stanly of his nomination. His law partner, William Hayes, was requested to answer if Stanly was not at home. The next day, while the delegates were voting on the lesser state candidates, Park read a telegram from Hayes, stating that he had no doubt Stanly would be highly honored with the nomination, but that he had not heard definitely from him. He would return by two o'clock, when an answer would be given. The convention recessed until two o'clock to await Stanly's reply; but when it reassembled, Park reported that while the Petaluma boat had arrived in San Francisco, Stanly was not on board. The convention then adjourned *sine die* after appointing a committee to fill vacancies in the state ticket if any nominee declined.[30]

Stanly accepted the nomination upon his return to San Francisco, sending a telegram which was not received before the convention adjourned. It said in part: "If you cannot prevail, as I hope you may, upon a better man to be your standard-bearer, and can trust a North Carolinian upon faith in his past life and expressed opinions, my name as at your service."[31]

Despite his earlier disclaimers, Stanly, according to Cornelius Cole, accepted the nomination "without much reluctance, though he well knew there was not the slightest chance of his election." The Republicans on their part wanted to make "as good a showing as possible in point of numbers," and Stanly's nomination was deemed a fortunate one. "From his prominence in the affairs of his time, and on account of his great ability, sterling integrity and independence of character, he was well known throughout the whole country."[32]

Some of the San Francisco Republicans, dubbed by the *Daily Alta California* the "Simon Pures," who had favored Baker's nomination, grumbled that Stanly had never identified himself in any way with the party. However, the *Daily Alta California* thought no

Republican could be elected governor "under present circumstances," and predicted Stanly would poll a larger vote than any
other man the party could have nominated. Personally, he was
unobjectionable—"a man of high morality and honor, and one who
would well grace the gubernatorial chair." The Sacramento *Daily
Union* declared that few such men had been nominated for office in
California and predicted that he would make "a first rate Governor"
if elected.[33]

The "Simon Pures" could not have been reassured of Stanly's
"Republicanism" by his first remarks in the campaign, made to the
San Francisco Republican delegation, with many from the interior,
who marched to his residence upon arriving in the city to cheer the
Republican standard-bearer. Stanly did not bind himself to support
the Republican platform; on the contrary, he repudiated all platforms—"the platform of a man's past conduct and known opinions is
the best one for any party"—and went simply for a reformation of
government affairs in the state. In saying that he was "the first
Southern man who advocated the right of the people of California to
enter the Union with such a Constitution as she pleased to form," he
seemed to endorse the Democratic doctrine of popular sovereignty,
or letting the people of the territories decide the matter of slavery to
suit themselves. The Sacramento *Daily Bee*, after a careful perusal
of the speech, remarked that "we cannot find any strictly Republican doctrine in the whole of it, and for anything avowed in that
speech, he can as well be supported by the Democrats and Americans as any other party."[34]

In a letter to a committee of San Francisco Republicans, written
five days after his nomination, Stanly spelled out his political
opinions in more detail, assuring them they had not been recently
formed. During his public career, in common with all southern men,
he had condemned abolitionist attempts to interfere with southern
rights, but he had never hesitated to say, publicly as well as
privately, that slavery was an evil; nor had he been guilty of the
"folly" of denying that Congress had the power to prohibit the
extension of slavery to a free territory. The repeal of the Missouri
Compromise he thought an "enormous outrage," a "violation of
faith; a scheme of politicians to obtain Southern favor, at the risk of

creating sectional divisions, with the hope of securing their own personal aggrandisement." It had produced nothing but discord and sectional strife.

On matters of state policy, Stanly said it was the Republican Party's duty to impress upon the people the necessity of reform in state politics, economy in government, and a lessening of the oppressive tax burden. He promised to support the construction of a "National Railroad" uniting California with the East.[35]

All parties in the state generally assumed that Stanly could not win unless he received the support of the old line Whigs and the Americans, many of whom were former Whigs, who might be expected to cherish Stanly as one of their own. The Sacramento *Daily Union* thought that with their support he could give Weller a close race and might even defeat him; however, if they did not unite on him, his chances of being elected governor were "just as good as they are that he will be elected Emperor of France."[36]

Those who had known Stanly as a gallant North Carolina Whig in Congress and who remembered his speeches in San Francisco in 1855 as a Whig candidate for state senator were "pretty confident" that he would campaign as an old line Henry Clay Whig, and an opponent of the Democrats generally, and not as a Republican.[37] His first public remarks after his nomination tended to strengthen this idea. When it was announced that he would speak in Sacramento on the night of July 17, 1857, an old line Whig, David Meeker, was selected to preside over the meeting, assisted by several vice-presidents, not one of whom according to the Sacramento *Daily Union*, had ever voted with the Republicans. The *Daily Union* later said of this meeting:

> It was not organized as a Republican meeting, but as one opposed to the Democracy, and the large majority present expected to hear an old fashioned Whig speech, in which he would hold the Democratic party responsible for its sins of omission and commission, both State and national.[38]

However, in a two hour speech, Stanly took what the Whigs and Americans considered to be strong Republican ground. He spoke of himself as one of the "Black Republicans," denounced the "awful, odious, abominable Nebraska bill," argued against the Dred Scott decision, and upheld Congress' power to legislate on territorial matters. Said he:

> The validity of the Missouri Compromise was never doubted for thirty years. Congress passed laws fourteen times acknowledging it, but now we have a new and overturning principle. We have some new territories about to become States. The little giant Douglas wants to be President, and a new story, a fresh humbug is started. We are told that Congress must let the territories alone. The object is to thrust slaves into these new territories. That is what I am opposed to—that is what I have been opposed to all my life.

Stanly went on to say that while free labor was honorable, slave labor was degrading, because southern youth were brought up to look upon labor as beneath their dignity and never learned to put their necks to the yoke. He trusted he would never see the day that slavery would exist in California in competition with the labor of honest white men.

As for Oregon's impending statehood application, "he considered that she had a right to come in as she pleased, and he believed the Union would be just as safe with a majority of ten free states as a majority of one."[39]

The Americans and Whigs were dissatisfied with Stanly's remarks. The conservative Sacramento *Daily Union*, which had formerly spoken highly of his character and talent, now expressed itself as "a good deal disappointed" with his speech. His voice was feeble, his presence and manner not particularly impressive, his language not at all forcible, and the matter was such as had been put into ordinary Republican speeches since 1854. His total neglect of state matters was inexcusable, and the *Union* predicted that his "Republican argument" had put him beyond the reach of the American Party as a candidate for governor; the Americans would not support a candidate who confined himself solely to a discussion of a single sectional issue while ignoring questions of state policy.[40]

The Sacramento *Daily Bee* found fault with Stanly for his "considerable inconsistency" in his present course on the slavery question when his past career was examined. He seemed afraid to speak in favor of allowing the people of the territories to settle the question of slavery for themselves when they came to form a state constitution, and yet he had committed himself fully to that doctrine as late as 1850 during the debate on the Texas boundary bill. He had voted in favor of an amendment by Linn Boyd of Kentucky which provided for the organization of the New Mexico territory without the Wilmot Proviso and authorized the people of New Mexico, when forming a state constitution, to allow or prohibit slavery as they might see fit. He had later told Joshua Giddings of Ohio that if that gentleman did not try to tack on the Wilmot Proviso to territorial bills, Congress could get through its business, admit California, and adjourn in three weeks. To the *Daily Bee*, "this kind of conduct in the national legislature does not look much like Republicanism."[41]

Stanly was also vulnerable because of his four-year absence from national politics and his public admission at the beginning of the campaign that in that period he had not read four political speeches or a political platform of any party. The Democratic San Francisco *Herald* ridiculed his candidacy on this account. Calling him "this political fossil, this Rip Van Winkle, this modern mummy of politics," the paper queried sarcastically: "What Witch of Endor has scared this political bunch of dry bones from their charnelhouse?"[42]

Following his Sacramento address, Stanly made the usual stumping tour, visiting Marysville, Camptonville, Grass Valley, and other mining camps north and east of Sacramento.[43] One of the themes of his speeches was that he had never sought office, but had always been importuned by the people to *take* office, much to his annoyance.[44] This naturally exposed him to Democratic barbs. The San Francisco *Herald* gibed at this desire on the part of "the great resurrected" to keep out of public life in California and elsewhere:

> Unfortunate possessor of great talent! Extraordinary example of modest and retiring worth! Great disciple of Cincinnatus! Wonderful imitator of Moses, how we honor thee![45]

The *Herald* published a letter from Joseph G. Baldwin, the author of *The Flush Times of Alabama and Mississippi* (1853), in which Baldwin, writing anonymously as "Jack Cade, Jr.," drew a humorous picture of Stanly being chased out of several states and two territories by people who wanted him to take office. Wrote "Cade," mocking Stanly: "I swore I never would go into office when I left the Choctaw Nation; and afterwards when I left the Sandwich Islands; but politicians' oaths, like lovers' prejudices, the gods forget."[46]

During the campaign, Stanly, when in Sacramento, made his headquarters in the office of Cornelius Cole, where he prepared his speeches. Cole was struck as others had been earlier with Stanly's physical resemblance to William H. Seward. Also, like Seward, "he was extremely particular about everything that emanated from his tongue or pen. In style it had to be as near perfect as human ingenuity could make it." And Cole paid tribute as well to other character traits. "As a gentleman his approach to perfection was as near as that of any man I ever knew."[47]

Stanly returned to Sacramento on July 26 from his tour of the mining camps. John Weller had left that morning on the Marysville boat for a canvass of the northern section of the state.[48] The American Party was meeting in the city on July 28 to consider the nomination of a state ticket, and Stanly's friends in the party still had some hope of securing its endorsement for him, despite the unfavorable reception given his remarks at Sacramento on July 17. A group of Sacramento citizens submitted four questions to Stanly for the purpose of having his candidacy considered by the convention. The questions were:

> 1st. Do you believe that the people of a Territory have a right to organize a State Government with or without slavery, as they may elect?
> 2nd. If the people of such a Territory should form a State Government, authorizing Slavery, would you, if in Congress, vote for the admission of said State into the Union?
> 3rd. Do you believe that the decision of the Supreme Court of the United States, in the Dred Scott case, determines, finally, all the questions adjudicated by the Court in said case?
> 4th. Are you in favor of the thorough reform of all the abuses existing in our State Government, . . . and the introduction of rigid economy, strict accountability and unswerving integrity in all the departments of the State Government?[49]

To the first question, Stanly answered simply, "Yes." The second he also answered in the affirmative, adding that he would not have opposed California's admission had her constitution tolerated slavery, although he rejoiced, as one of her citizens, that it was excluded. While he differed with a majority of the Supreme Court on the Dred Scott decision, he regarded it "as finally determining the points properly before the Court, and to be acquiesced in by all good citizens until overruled." He went for a thorough reform in state affairs—reforms which could not be accomplished by the party that had perpetrated the abuses—"the promise-making, promise-breaking Democracy of California." Lastly, he wanted it distinctly understood that he was avowing no new principles but stood only upon the platform of his past life and expressed opinions.[50]

Stanly's affirmative answers did not bring him the American nomination as they were intended to do. His friends in the convention, seeing that they could not carry the delegates for him, favored adjournment without any nominations; but the convention rejected this suggestion and went on to nominate a state ticket headed by George W. Bowie, a Sacramento lawyer, for governor.[51] Bowie was a Whig and in 1854 had represented Colusi County in the state assembly. He was not a member of the American Party. The Sacramento *Daily Bee* described him as "an affable and honorable man, a pleasing speaker, of fair ability, but not of much force in a warmly contested canvass."[52] Bowie had been "favorably disposed" toward Stanly before the latter's Sacramento speech had changed his opinion of him.[53]

The Republican press bitterly denounced the proceedings of the American Convention. The Sacramento *Daily State Sentinel* declared that it had been emphatically a "Know Nothing *Sacramento County* Convention," called without authority by a half dozen insignificant "wire-pullers" in Sacramento and made up, in the main, of residents, office-holders, and hangers-on about the city and county. Moreover, the American ticket had been nominated by pro-southern "Chivalry Know Nothings" with the express purpose of deceiving the northern wing into its support while the southern wing would vote for Weller by the hundreds.[54]

To the charge that the American Convention had been controlled by the Weller, southern influence, the Sacramento *Daily Union* replied that "all this is very unreasonable, as well as totally unfounded." Stanly's emphasis on Republicanism had made it impossible for Americans to support him as an old line Whig without repudiating their state and national organizations and identifying themselves with the Republicans. In accordance with the wishes of the 36,000 Fillmore Americans in the state, they had nominated a full ticket. Finally, the Republican accusation that the Americans were giving the state to the Democrats by nominating a straight ticket came with bad grace from the men who had given the state to the same party the previous year by nominating a separate Republican ticket. "But circumstances do alter cases."[55]

Before leaving Sacramento for a brief visit to his home, Stanly spoke in the Forrest Theatre on July 30, sharing the platform with Colonel James Zabriskie, one of the best public speakers in California, who, although not a Republican, intended to stump the state for "Stanly and Reform." The Democratic press was charging Stanly with inconsistency because he had opposed the Wilmot Proviso in Congress, now endorsed popular sovereignty, and yet denounced the repeal of the Missouri Compromise. He replied that there was a difference between a total prohibition of slavery in the territories hereafter acquired by the United States and the enactment of a law restricting slave territory to a certain line. The Proviso had been regarded in the southern states as a "declaration of war," while the Compromise was "an adjustment," consecrating a certain portion to freedom forever and allowing states south of a certain line, if the citizens therein wished, to enter the Union with slavery. To enact the Proviso would be an "act of gross injustice and wrong." Said Stanly defiantly: "I denounced this Proviso [in 1850], and I would do it again under the same circumstances. A declaration by Congress that the South should never have any more slave States, I could not support."[56]

This bold avowal must have irritated the "Simon Pures" among the Republicans, who were pledged to the Proviso, but Stanly would not trim his sails. As the San Francisco *Daily Alta California* rightly observed, he had been given the Republican nomination without solicitation and without a request for any declaration that he approved the principles of the party.[57]

A fourth party—the "Settlers and Miners"—held a state convention in Sacramento on August 4, with about forty delegates present. The "Settlers and Miners" claimed to have 25,000 votes in California, although this figure was certainly too high. Bowie addressed the convention, after which a letter from Stanly to F. B. Austin, the secretary of the Settler's General Committee, was read to the delegates. Stanly endorsed the party's demand that actual settlers ought to be considered the legal owners of disputed property until the contrary was proved. Bowie's name was then withdrawn and Stanly was nominated for governor by acclamation.[58]

It was now the turn of the Weller and Bowie press to cry foul. The Sacramento *Daily Union* complained that the Settlers and Miners Convention had been emphatically a "city Settler Convention" of delegates from San Francisco and Sacramento with only a few "real Settlers" present from the country, and nearly all of them had withdrawn. The *Daily Union* suggested that the real Settlers set up a genuine convention in Sacramento about August 20, from which city delegates would be excluded.[59] The San Francisco *Herald* said the convention had represented the Settlers "just as much as it did the Royal Antiquarian Society, or the Philanthropic Association of Marriageable Spinsters for supplying the subjects of the King of Dahomey with flannel shirts and red night-shirts, and that the result arrived at will not have the effect of changing one single vote."[60] In fact, the nomination added little to Stanly's strength.

Among the party press in California, seven dailies and twenty-one weeklies supported the Democratic ticket; two dailies and two weeklies the American ticket; and four dailies and two weeklies the Republican ticket. The Republican press included the San Francisco *Chronicle*, the *State Sentinel* (Sacramento), Marysville *Herald, North Californian* (Oroville), San Jose *Telegraph*, and *El Clamor Público* (printed in Spanish) in Los Angeles. The Spanish paper in Los Angeles repudiated Stanly after the publication of his Settler letter.[61]

The Republicans ran local candidates in fourteen out of forty-three counties: El Dorado, Placer, Yuba, Nevada, Sacramento,

Sutter, Yolo, Butte, Amador, San Joaquin, Santa Clara, Alameda, San Francisco, and San Mateo. The Sacramento Republicans offered to meet the Americans halfway and make a county union ticket of respectable and substantial citizens to insure the defeat of the Democratic ticket, but their overtures were rejected. The Sacramento *Daily Union* reported no evidence in the papers of any Republican organizations in the strongly Democratic southern counties.[62]

Stanly, accompanied by James Zabriskie, made a second stumping tour of the mining camps, beginning in Stockton on August 7 and speaking in San Joaquin, Tuolumne, Amador, Calaveras, El Dorado, Placer, Nevada, Plumas, Colusi, Shasta, Siskiyou, and Trinity Counties.[63] The "knowing ones" in the Republican Party conceded privately that they could not elect their state ticket without American support; but Stanly gibed at the Know Nothing Order in his speeches, likening it to a June-bug, "bigger the first day he comes out than he ever is afterwards." He humorously advised the Know Nothings to lay aside their follies and help the Republicans in their effort at state reform, assuring them that "these Republicans are not such bad people as you suppose."[64] Speaking again in Sacramento on August 26, Stanly, in what the Sacramento *State Sentinel* termed "one of the most effective, as well as sarcastic speeches of the campaign," sharply attacked Know Nothing secrecy and proscription and claimed that Bowie had been nominated solely to insure Weller's election.[65]

The Democrats regarded their ticket's success as a fixed fact and did not make much effort in the canvass. Stanly's Democratic opponent, John Weller, concentrated his attacks on the Republicans and had little to say about the American Party. John Carr, who heard him speak at Petaluma, wrote later that "for nearly two hours he poured into the Republican ranks such a tirade of abuse as I think has never been excelled in the State." Weller advised the Americans, if they were true Americans, to come over to the Democratic Party and save their county; he appealed to all Democrats to stick to their ticket and not scratch a single name. He remarked that "no good Democrat ever scratched his ticket," and when someone in the crowd asked if he was going to vote for himself, he replied: "Yes, sir,

I am; I always vote for the best man, and when I vote the whole of the Democratic ticket I know I am voting for the best man."[66]

The Republicans in the counties north and east of Sacramento tried to arouse the prejudices of the Irish miners against Weller by charging that he had defended in the Senate the nativists who with "mob violence and outrage" had assailed the Papal Nuncio, Monsignor Gaetano Bedini, during his visit to Cincinnati, Ohio, in December, 1853. Weller had thereby disgraced his own government, "and so far as he was able, insulted that of the Pope."[67] For this and unspecified "other causes," the Sacramento *Daily Union* predicted that Weller's name would be stricken from a great many tickets.[68]

Stanly made his final speeches of the campaign in and around San Francisco, addressing a "Grand Rally of the Settlers" in the Music Hall on August 28 and a Republican meeting in the same hall on August 31.[69] With three major tickets in the field, the final issue was not in doubt. The Sacramento *Daily Bee* declared that it was "almost beyond a peradventure that the entire Democratic ticket will be elected by a sweeping majority." The election took place on September 2, 1857, and as the first returns came in it was apparent that Weller would win easily. He rolled up enormous majorities in the southern counties and ran well elsewhere in the state.[70]

With Weller's victory assured, interest centered on the Stanly and Bowie race for second place, with the backers of each in suspense as many bets depended on the result. The "first dash" from the mountains badly frightened Stanly's friends, but his large vote in San Francisco, Alameda, and Santa Clara counties checked the Bowie tide.[71] The Sacramento *Daily Bee* reported on September 8 that Stanly was ahead by some 2,800 votes, and it would require a good many "thirties and fifties" on the Bowie side to overcome this majority. On September 14, the *Daily Bee* noted cheerfully that Stanly was keeping ahead of Bowie in the southern "Cow Counties"—in Santa Barbara, for example, Stanly received three votes and Bowie two! Weller got the remainder. In San Diego, Stanly had one vote and Bowie none!"[72]

Complete returns gave Weller 53,122 votes to Stanly's 21,040 and Bowie's 19,481. This vote was 16,630 less than in the presidential election of 1856, as the American vote fell off sharply. Weller received 246 votes less than Buchanan; Stanly 345 more than Frémont; and Bowie some 16,729 less than Fillmore. Weller's majority over Stanly and Bowie was 12,601; while Stanly led Bowie by 1,559. Stanly carried only San Francisco and Alameda, polling about half his total state vote in these two counties.[73] The Republicans, it was humorously said, intended to give a public dinner to the lone man in Fresno who voted for Stanly, "if they can find him"; and the Americans were about to do the same thing to the Bowie man in Tulare.[74]

Stanly's showing disappointed the Republicans, since they had hoped for large gains over the previous year; but they put the best face they could on the returns and declared they had "rolled back the united foe without discomfiture or loss." Republican leaders were bitter against the Americans, saying they "did not turn out, and most of those that did, voted for Weller."[75] In a letter to the editor of the Sacramento *Daily Union*, written after the election, Stanly charged that the "chivalry Know Nothings" had nominated an American ticket "with the express purpose, among the leaders, of securing the election of the Democratic nominee."[76] The editor replied that the delegates to the American Convention were "not chivalry men and never had been, but they were and are ardent Americans, who would vote the ticket if it did not receive five thousand votes in the State." It was therefore incorrect to say that these men had nominated a ticket for the express purpose of electing Weller.

> It would be more correct to say that they nominated a candidate to prevent three-fourths of the Americans in the State from voting for Weller, if the contest were narrowed down to a choice between a Democrat and a Republican. Would it not be equally fair and as true to assert that the leaders in the Republican convention nominated a candidate 'with the express purpose of electing the Democratic nominee.' With their own strength they knew there was not the slightest chance for electing their candidate.[77]

In fact, neither the Republicans nor the Americans were willing to yield to the principles or candidates of the other and thus could not unite to defeat the Democracy. Old line Whigs, who made up the bulk of the American Party in California, would not vote for a Republican nominee, even though a former Whig congressman, and a Southerner, once he had expressed what the Sacramento *Daily Union* called the "Republican argument." Although Stanly differed from the Republicans on several points, notably his refusal to endorse the Wilmot Proviso or to disavow the admission of any future slave states, these differences did not commend him to his former political friends, to whom the very word Republican was anathema.

Moreover, the Democrats, while themselves divided between the supporters of William Gwin and David Broderick, were in substantial unity behind Weller's candidacy. John Carr asked a friend, a prominent Democrat: "Colonel, how is it you democrats are always fighting and quarreling and ready to cut each other's throats before [the] election, and yet when you come to the polls you all vote the straight Democratic ticket?" His friend replied, laughing, "Why John, we are like cats—the more we fight and quarrel, the more we propagate our species."[78]

California Democrats did divide in 1858 over Kansas' admission into the Union under the pro-slavery Lecompton constitution. The quarrel was the bitterest in the state's history. In 1859, the pro-Lecompton Gwin "chivalry" supported Milton S. Latham for governor, while the anti-Lecompton Broderick men, who were aligned nationally with Stephen A. Douglas against the Buchanan administration, nominated John Currey. The Republicans, spurning a proffered alliance with Broderick, nominated Leland Stanford, but were again badly beaten. Stanford polled only 10,110 votes, about half Stanly's total in 1857. Latham was elected with 62,255 votes to Currey's 31,298. On September 13, 1859, Broderick was mortally wounded in a duel with a chivalry Democrat, Judge David S. Terry of the State Supreme Court; the two men had exchanged heated words at the beginning of the campaign. His death left the "chivalry" supreme in the state; and their rule was not successfully challenged until 1861, when Stanford was elected governor with the support of many Douglas (Union) Democrats.[79]

As for Stanly, after his defeat he again retired from politics. His wife, Julia, had died in December 1854—"the severest sorrow" of his life. On May 10, 1859, in Sacramento, he married thirty-year old Cornelia Baldwin of Staunton, Virginia. Cornelia's father, Joseph Clarke Baldwin, had moved from Connecticut to the Shenandoah Valley early in the nineteenth century and established cotton and woolen mills at Friendly Grove Factory and Front Royal. The Baldwins were Episcopalians and Whigs, although Cornelia's lawyer-author brother, Joseph Glover Baldwin, joined the Democratic Party in California and in 1858 was its successful candidate to fill a state supreme court vacancy. After the wedding, the couple left on a tour of the Atlantic states and Europe.[80]

In 1860, the national Republican convention, meeting in the "Wigwam" in Chicago, passed over Stanly's friend William Seward and nominated Abraham Lincoln of Illinois for President, with Hannibal Hamlin of Maine as his running mate. The Democratic Party split on the southern demand for a federal slave code in the territories, the northern wing nominating Stephen A. Douglas of Illinois and Herschel V. Johnson of Georgia, and the Southern Rights men, John C. Breckinridge of Kentucky and Joseph Lane of Oregon. This division virtually assured a Republican victory in November. Former Whigs and moderates from both sections organized a Constitutional Union Party, and nominated John Bell of Tennessee and Edward Everett of Massachusetts on a simple platform of the Constitution, the Union, and the enforcement of the laws.

The California delegation in Washington, headed by Gwin, supported Breckinridge, while the martyred Broderick's followers favored Douglas. California Republicans had expected and desired Seward's nomination, and they were disappointed when Lincoln was chosen. Little was said of Lincoln in the state, since little was known. The Sacramento *Daily Union* was the first to announce two unknown details about the nominee: the correct spelling of his first name, Abraham not Abram, and that he was homely![81] On June 20, 1860, the Republican state convention met in Sacramento to nominate a slate of presidential electors. Stanly was one of those nominated, but was not elected. His private preference was for his old Whig friends Bell and Everett, although he did not campaign for them.[82]

Lincoln carried California by a seven hundred vote plurality over Douglas, although his three opponents' combined votes dwarfed his own.[83] Nationally, he carried every free state with thirty-nine percent of the popular vote and rolled up a large majority in the electoral college. Douglas was second in the popular vote, but carried only Missouri and three electoral votes in New Jersey. Virginia, Kentucky, and Tennessee, the last two traditionally Whig states, went for Bell, while Breckinridge carried the lower South, and North Carolina, Delaware, and Maryland.

Lincoln's victory gave California Republicans their first opportunity to secure the federal offices in the state which had been monopolized by the "chivalry" Democrats during the Pierce and Buchanan administrations. A furious patronage battle took place between a faction headed by Edward D. Baker and an anti-Baker faction led by James W. Simonton, one of the editors of the San Francisco *Bulletin*. On December 10, 1860, Stanly wrote Thurlow Weed recommending Ira P. Rankin, an anti-Baker leader, for the collectorship of San Francisco, the most coveted federal job on the Pacific coast. Rankin, he said, had the strongest recommendations from almost all the local merchants, bankers, and businessmen; and nine out of ten of them would prefer him to any other man. Stanly was especially anxious that Lincoln should have "a fair start, & make no unpopular appointments, while good men & true" were to be had. Some Whig Presidents had squandered the government patronage, and Lincoln should be saved from a similar error. He added that he wished the President's administration to be successful, "& shall support him in opposition to all democratic mischiefmakers shall attempt."[84] He wanted Lincoln to make Republicanism strong enough on the coast "to put down the infernal spirit of democracy, which has brought upon our country all the evils that now threaten our peace."[85] He was speaking, of course, of the *Democratic Party*, and not the American system of government.

The "democratic mischief-makers" were about to attempt the dissolution of the Union. It was a foregone conclusion that South Carolina would secede if Lincoln was elected. On December 20, 1860, a state convention met in Charleston and unanimously declared "that the Union now subsisting between South Carolina and other states under the name of 'The United States of America' is hereby dissolved." Elsewhere in the lower South, Unionist sentiment was stronger, but one by one the cotton states followed South Carolina's lead. Mississippi, Florida, Alabama, Georgia, Louisiana, and Texas were out of the Union by February 1, 1861. On February 4, the seceded states met in Convention at Montgomery, Alabama, and formed the Confederate States of America. Jefferson Davis of Mississippi was elected Provisional President, and Alexander H. Stephens of Georgia, Vice-President.

After Lincoln's election, some persons and newspapers in California spoke openly of a Pacific Republic if the Union should be dissolved. Both of California's representatives in the House, John C. Burch and C. L. Scott, favored such a course. Scott wrote the chairman of the Democratic state committee on December 21, 1860: "If this Union is divided and two separate confederacies are formed, I will strenuously advocate the secession of California and the establishment of a separate republic on the Pacific slope." However, the advocates of a republic, while vocal, were confined to the extreme secession sympathizers of the Breckinridge party, or its supporters.[86]

The Union men of San Francisco chose Washington's birthday, February 22, 1861, to express "in thunder tones" their devotion to the Union. Fourteen thousand persons assembled at the junction of Market, Montgomery, and Post streets, in the heart of the city, to hear Union speeches by Stanly, Eugene Casserly, Colonel J. B. Crockett, and Judge Delos Lake. Stanly made a fervent plea for mutual understanding and compromise for the sake of the Union, and expressed his confidence that with such men as Lincoln, Douglas, Bell, Breckinridge, Crittenden, and Seward in Washington, the Republic would yet be saved. He predicted that Seward would show the country that the politician could be lost in the patriot.

> He 'will not give up to party what was meant for mankind.' He will not take half of this Union, to be divided by the sword, nor allow his great abilities to be exerted against the interests of his country. He will prove to the world that his patriotism is as exalted and pure as his genius is great and 'irrepressible.'

[Applause]

As for California, from what he knew of her politicians, he thought there were few wicked or foolish enough to desire the Union's dissolution. He urged the people of the state to send a "cheerful message" to the patriots in the East, who would be animated to renewed hope by their example: "Let us tell them we entered into the Union to remain in it FOREVER; that we would as soon think of taking a constellation from the firmament, and bringing about universal ruin,...as to think of snatching California from the constellation that adorns our...flag." The meeting responded with strongly Unionist resolutions, denying the right of secession, and decrying the idea of a Pacific Republic as "visionary, mischievous, and impossible."[87] The San Francisco *Daily Alta California* said of the gathering: "If the Union-loving sentiments of this people ever admitted of question, the last shadow of doubt is now dispelled."[88]

In North Carolina, the overwhelming majority of the people did not consider Lincoln's election sufficient cause for secession; although by the time South Carolina withdrew, a small but very active secession party had arisen and was rapidly gaining momentum.[89] Senator Reverdy Johnson of Maryland, on his way to the East from San Francisco in November, 1860, wrote Stanly from Acapulco, Mexico, urging him to return to North Carolina, and to do what he could to prevent the secessionists from entangling the state in their disunion scheme.[90] Stanly did not go, but his friends there—William A. Graham, David L. Swain, George E. Badger, and John H. Bryan, among others—campaigned actively against secession, aided by Stanly's long-time foe, William W. Holden of the Raleigh *North Carolina Standard*, who now led the Union press in the state.[91]

While North Carolina did not approve of secession, Unionists and secessionists alike denied the federal government's right to coerce a state into remaining in the Union. The secession of the lower South, the failure of compromise at Washington, and Lincoln's inaugural address weakened Union sentiment in the state. The attack on Fort Sumter, in Charleston Harbor, on April 12, 1861, followed by Lincoln's call for volunteers to put down combinations "too powerful to be suppressed by the ordinary course of judicial proceedings," and the secession of Virginia, completed the revolution of opinion. "All are unanimous," wrote Charles Manly. "Even those who were loudest in denouncing Secession are now hottest & loudest the other way." Such leading Unionists as Graham, Badger, and Zebulon B. Vance resigned themselves to a separation, for as Graham sadly admitted: "Blood is thicker than water."[92]

A state convention met in Raleigh on May 20, to take the state out of the Union. Pathetically, the former Union Whigs, led by Badger, continued to deny the right of secession and argued that a separation could only be justified by a resort to revolution. Badger introduced a resolution of separation based upon the right of revolution, but it was defeated, seventy-two to forty. Badger then left the convention but returned later and asked to be recorded in favor of separation, adding, however, that he repudiated "all belief in any right of secession."[93]

On the West Coast, California Unionists were concerned lest southern sympathizers make some attempt to dislodge that state and Oregon from the Union. Edward Baker, recently elected United States senator from Oregon, insisted that the commander of the army forces on the Coast, Brevet-Brigadier Albert S. Johnston, be replaced by a man unquestionably loyal. A fortnight after the inauguration, General Edwin Vose Sumner was secretly sent to relieve Johnston, arriving in San Francisco on April 24, 1861. That evening, the *Alta California* and the *Bulletin* published the news of the firing on Fort Sumter.[94]

In his first report to Washington, Sumner stated that a majority of the people of California were Unionists but warned that the Secessionists were the more active and zealous party and were scheming to establish a Pacific Republic, with the intention of later joining the Confederacy. He at once concentrated his troops to guard the more important cities, forts, and army posts.[95]

Sumner's opportune arrival gave the Union men confidence; inspired by the eloquence of Thomas Starr King, Thomas Fitch, Henry Edgerton, Stanly, and others, they soon were "organized, alert, and determined."[96] Mass Union meetings were held in San Francisco, Oakland, San Jose, and at other points throughout the state. King lectured to large audiences on such themes as "Washington and the Union," "Lexington and the New Struggle for Liberty," and "The New Nation to Issue from the War." The Douglas Democrats met on May 8, and adopted a resolution demanding suppression of the rebellion and pledging their full support to the Lincoln administration. In September, 1861, the Republicans elected Leland Stanford governor over the candidate of the Breckinridge party; and when he took office in January, 1862, the state government at last lent hearty support to the war effort.[97]

10

MISSION OF LOVE

THE OCCUPATION BY UNION ARMIES of western Tennessee, northwestern Arkansas, the Albemarle and Pamlico Sounds region of North Carolina, and the area around New Orleans, Louisiana, in the winter and spring of 1862, compelled the Lincoln administration to consider the problems of political reconstruction. Denying the right of secession, the President held that the so-called "rebel" states remained in the Union, although out of their proper relationship to the federal government. He decided that once the rebellion had been suppressed in any state, or portion of a state, loyal citizens therein could organize new governments, and resume normal relations with the federal government. The removal by force of a disloyal Confederate governor, Claiborne F. Jackson, in Missouri, and the establishment of the Union Pierpont government in Virginia, in the spring and summer of 1861, had set the pattern. Lincoln viewed this reconstruction process as primarily an executive rather than a congressional function, to be implemented under his vaguely defined "war powers." On March 3, 1862, he appointed Senator Andrew Johnson of Tennessee as military governor of that state, with the rank of brigadier-general of volunteers. The task of Johnson and the men who were later appointed in North Carolina, Louisiana, and Arkansas, was to inaugurate reconstruction by encouraging and organizing Union sentiment in their states looking toward the formation of loyal state governments.[1]

In February and March, 1862, a Union expedition commanded

by General Ambrose E. Burnside occupied Roanoke Island and the coast of North Carolina from Fort Macon to the Virginia line. Only the port of Wilmington remained open to Confederate blockade-runners. Burnside established his headquarters at New Bern, and Union garrisons held the towns of Washington, Plymouth, Elizabeth City, and Beaufort City. The Administration hoped this conquered territory would be a more substantial base than the isolated Outer Banks (occupied in August, 1861) for the spread of Union propaganda into the interior of the state. On November 18, 1861, a convention at Cape Hatteras, with six or eight members, had repudiated secession, proclaimed Marble Nash Taylor, a Methodist minister of Virginia birth, provisional governor of North Carolina, and instructed him to call a congressional election. Charles Henry Foster, a native of Maine and former editor of the Murfreesboro (N.C.) *Citizen*, was elected with 268 votes; but Congress refused to seat him. The whole movement was farcical from the very beginning.[2] The *Weekly Raleigh Register* jeeringly predicted that the jurisdiction of his government would not give Taylor much trouble, "as his territory consists of a barren sand bank between the Ocean and the Sounds, and his constituents are some two hundred web-footed wreckers and fisherman, who, as long as they can decoy vessels with false signal lights . . . to their inhospitable shore, and catch plenty of fish, will not trouble the Governor much about the administration of the affairs of his *State*."[3]

Despite the ludicrous nature of the Hatteras Island government, there was a general belief in the North that a strong Union feeling existed in North Carolina which a leader more capable than Taylor could utilize to reclaim the state to the Union. As early as September, 1861, Colonel Rush C. Hawkins, commander of the Union troops at Fort Clark, Hatteras Inlet, had reported that "one-third of the State of North Carolina would be back in the Union within two weeks" if the United States forces were near enough to protect the people against the violence of the secessionists.[4] At the suggestion of Senator Reverdy Johnson and Secretary Seward, Lincoln decided to offer the military governorship of North Carolina to Stanly.[5]

Stanly said later that his appointment had been "entirely unexpected and unsolicited," but he had written Seward in February, 1862, that if the Administration could send him to North Carolina with authority to extend the olive branch—"some honorable terms of peace," he believed some good would result. If such a service was thought advisable, "I should like to undertake it, without expecting any compensation or reward."[6] From the Administration's point of view, Stanly was an admirable choice to foster Union sentiment in North Carolina; a staunch Unionist of known ability and integrity, he was intimately acquainted with the people and leaders of his native state. A large portion of his former congressional district, including his former home, Washington, was within the Union lines.

In early April, 1862, Stanly received a telegram from Secretary of War Edwin M. Stanton announcing his appointment as military governor of North Carolina and asking him to come to Washington as soon as possible.[7] He had just accepted an appointment from Governor Leland Stanford as City and County Attorney of San Francisco, but immediately resigned and prepared to leave for the East. He believed that he was about to go on a "most noble—yes, a heavenly mission—to aid in establishing peace in our beloved country."[8] Although Stanly had not seen a newspaper or letter from North Carolina for nearly eleven months, he was convinced in his own mind that the state had been forced into secession against the wishes of a large majority of her people. He told a group of San Francisco citizens that North Carolinians had always hated secession and loved the Union, until made to believe "by wicked stratagem" that their government had declared war against them. His own mission, a "mission of love," was to hold out the "olive branch of peace" on terms such as a brave people could honorably accept.[9]

Stanly left San Francisco on April 21, aboard the steamer *Orizaba*, and reached New York City via Panama on May 14.[10] Proceeding immediately to Washington, he arrived at the capital just as unofficial word was received there that General David Hunter, with headquarters at Port Royal, South Carolina, had issued a proclamation declaring "forever free" slaves in Georgia, Florida, and South Carolina. Stanly, "greatly grieved" at Hunter's action, called on Lincoln and told him that if sweeping emancipation was to be the Administration's policy, he could not go to North Carolina. He would return to California unless Hunter's proclamation was repudiated by the government. Lincoln had submitted his own plan of compensated emancipation by state authority to Congress in March, and he was still hoping for an affirmative response from the loyal border states. He would not then entertain favorably any proclamation which jeopardized his own conciliatory proposal. According to Stanly, the President assured him that sweeping emancipation was not his policy and, furthermore, that he had no such power.[11]

Lincoln repudiated and revoked Hunter's unauthorized proclamation on May 19; and Stanly, mollified, accepted his appointment the next day.[12] His commission, dated May 19, authorized him to "exercise and perform" within the limits of North Carolina,

> all and singular the powers, duties, and functions pertaining to the office of Military Governor (including the power to establish all necessary offices and tribunals and suspend the writ of habaes corpus) during the pleasure of the President or until the loyal inhabitants of that State shall organize a civil government in conformity with the Constitution of the United States.[13]

According to Stanton, the "great purpose" of Stanly's appointment was to reestablish federal authority in North Carolina, and "to provide the means of maintaining peace and security to the loyal inhabitants of that State until they shall be able to establish a civil government." General Burnside had been instructed to aid Stanly in the performance of his duties and to detail a governor's guard to act under his direction. No specific instructions were deemed necessary, reliance being placed on Stanly's "sound discretion" to adopt such measures as circumstances demanded. However, specific instructions would be furnished upon request; and he was assured of the "perfect confidence and full support" of the War Department in the performance of his duties.[14]

Stanly's instructions were dangerously vague, but Stanton assured him that he was "dictator" and "could do what I pleased."[15] Stanly then went to Lincoln, who referred him to Seward, who also said, "in complimentary terms," that no specific orders were necessary.[16] The Administration was clearly unwilling to commit itself to any definite reconstruction plan at this early day, preferring instead to rely upon the "sound discretion" of its military governors to avoid error. Still, the appointment of Johnson and Stanly pleased northern conservatives and angered abolitionists in Congress who were not consulted. The conservative New York *Herald* hailed the appointments as clear evidence that Lincoln was fighting the war for the integrity of the Union and not the extirpation of slavery. "His object is to give every possible encouragement and assurance to our revolted States that in returning to the Union they will return to its constitutional landmarks of protection and safety." The *Herald* pointed out that every southern state restored to the Union would diminish abolitionist power in Congress.[17]

On May 23, Stanly left New York City by steamer for his headquarters at New Bern. As a conciliatory gesture, he was accompanied by sixteen North Carolina prisoners of war, released at his request from Washington's Old Capitol Prison.[18] Rumors of his appointment had reached North Carolina, but friends there at first refused to credit the report, branding it a lie and libel on his character. The Raleigh *Weekly Standard* suggested the rumor had been made up by the Yankees in the East to make capital for the Union cause in a section where Stanly was known and popular. Stanly was thought to be under arrest in California because of his southern feelings and sentiments.[19] When confirmation came, the *Standard* expressed surprise that a man of Stanly's character and previous position would come back to his native state to aid Lincoln in his "wicked attempt to subjugate our people."[20]

The *Standard* was the spokesman of those North Carolinians who were hostile to the state and Confederate administrations. Since this group was largely former Whigs—many of them Stanly's pre-war friends and political allies—the paper was disposed to treat his apostasy "more in sorrow than in anger." The *Weekly Raleigh Register*, the organ of the state administration, sneered that the *Standard* "roars him as gently as a sucking dove." It declared that if Stanly came to North Carolina to become the instrument of enslaving or holding in slavery his kindred and friends, "we shall be rejoiced . . . to hear that he has received some patriot's bullet in his brains, or that his life has been chocked [*sic*] out of him by some patriot's rope of grapevine."[21] No less ungenerous was the reaction of Alfred Stanly to the news of his brother's appointment. Arrested by a Union cavalry patrol at Washington for secessionist activities, he was quoted as expressing "a fervent desire that North Carolina would open and swallow up his brother" if he should set foot upon her soil as military governor.[22]

Those who knew Stanly from before the war realized that he would prove no easy antagonist. Writing Nicholas Woodfin, a western North Carolina Whig, about possible candidates for the gubernatorial election on August 6, President David L. Swain of the University of North Carolina gave the following warning:

> If it be true, as I trust it is not, that Mr. Stanly is to be provisional governor of N.C. you have no ordinary domestic enemy to encounter, and will be fortunate if you shall [*sic*] be able to command the services of his superior. He is not merely a speech maker, but a man of tact, address and resources, knows how to manage men, and possesses the energy and courage requisite to the execution of his designs.

Who would be called upon to counteract him? asked Swain. His own first choice was William A. Graham, if he could be persuaded to accept a nomination. Thomas Clingman had decided ability, and if he had Woodfin's energy would be "altogether acceptable." "Ability [,] integrity and energy are indispensable requisites," Swain advised, "and wherever you find them united call them forth, without reference to past or present party affinities."[23]

Stanly arrived in New Bern aboard the *Jersey Blue* on the evening of May 26, in a pouring rain storm; and immediately met with General Burnside, who was sick in bed but got up to talk with him. The next morning, Stanly visited Burnside's headquarters where he was to mess and again talked at length with the General.[24] Burnside reported to Stanton after this second meeting that he had "consulted fully" with the Governor and had found their views of the course that should be adopted in the state "remarkably coincident." He promised to report more definitely in a few days the arrangements made to carry out the Administration's instructions.[25] Daniel Reed Larned, Burnside's private secretary, described Stanly as "a very slight diminutive man and not one that shows much energy of character in his manners or speech—but the General is much pleased with him, and thinks he is the right man for the position he occupies."[26]

On the evening of May 27, Stanly was serenaded at his lodgings at the Union Hotel by the band of the Twenty-fourth Massachusetts Regiment, after which he made a brief conciliatory speech, stating that his mission was one of peace and that he was hopeful North Carolina would soon return to the Union. Larned thought it "very short & to the point—though some consider it milk & water because he did not go into detail and *slash* right & left."[27] On June 3, Stanly and Burnside reviewed Foster's division. Stanly was mounted on a "splendid charger," and the correspondent of the Philadelphia *Inquirer* reported somewhat prematurely that "Gov. Stanly [is] about to proceed to Raleigh."[28]

Among Stanly's first visitors in New Bern was Vincent Colyer, Burnside's "Superintendent of the Poor," who was in charge of the Negro refugees and poor whites in the neighborhood. Coming to New Bern from Washington, where he had worked in the hospitals as an agent of the New York City YMCA, Colyer established a day school for white children and two evening schools for Negroes. They had been open about six weeks when Stanly arrived.[29] Although he approved all that Colyer had done in feeding and clothing the destitute, both white and black, Stanly objected to the Negro schools. "I . . . told him I had been sent to restore the old order of things," he explained to Stanton. "I thought his negro school, if approved by me, would do harm to the Union cause." The result of the war would be known in a few months. If emancipation should come by southern folly, the Negroes' spiritual welfare would not suffer by the delay, for he desired Colyer to give such oral religious instructions as he thought best. Stanly also told Colyer that North Carolina law forbade teaching slaves to read or write, and that he would be "most unsuccessful" in efforts at reconciliation if he encouraged the violation of her laws.[30] At the same time, he didn't want anything done abruptly. "As a man, I might do, perhaps, as you have done," Colyer quoted him as saying, "but as a Governor I must act in my official capacity according to my instructions, and administer the laws as I find them."[31]

Ignoring Stanly's request that he not act abruptly, Colyer immediately closed the Negro schools; still, when he informed the Governor what he had done, Stanly thanked him and told Burnside that he was pleased with the way Colyer had done his duty.[32] Had he approved the Negro schools, Stanly later declared, it would have enabled "secession-traitors to excite prejudice against me."[33]

Stanly also tried to avoid offending the people of North Carolina where fugitive slaves were concerned. Thousands of Negroes—men, women, and children—had fled into the Union lines after the occupation of New Bern; and Burnside, in the absence of any definite instructions from Washington, had allowed them to stay and had given them employment whenever possible. On May 19, he informed Stanton that he would deliver none to their masters under any circumstances, nor allow any of them to leave the Department, until he received definite instructions.[34]

On May 30, several persons applied to Stanly for the return of fugitive slaves. One owner, Nicholas Bray, who lived two miles from town on the Falmouth road, complained that one of his female slaves had been enticed away by soldiers and was being held against her will. After securing Bray's promise to take the oath of allegiance, Stanly authorized him to look for his property, using "mildness and persuasion" to secure her voluntary return. The girl was found and Stanly had an opportunity to question her, which he unwisely did not use, thinking the matter settled.[35] Masters also complained that ship captains were taking slaves north as stewards, cooks, and deck hands; to stop this traffic, Stanly ordered the harbor authorities to allow no person, white or black, to go north without a pass.[36] He hoped to assure the residents of New Bern by these actions that the Union army in their midst was waging a war of restoration and not one of abolition and destruction; without such assurance, he told Stanton, peace could not be restored in North Carolina for many years to come.[37]

The "Bray Affair," as it came to be called, created a panic among the fugitive slaves in New Bern, some of whom "like a flock of frightened birds" took to the swamps or hid in out-of-the-way places in anticipation of a general round up by irate masters. Elias Smith, the correspondent of the New York *Times*, in a highly colored letter to his paper, reported that the Negroes expressed "the greatest horror" at the prospect of being returned to their old homes and said they would be unmercifully "cut up" for having absconded. "One old man of sixty told me to-day that he would rather be placed before a cannon and blown to pieces than go back. Multitudes say they would rather die."[38]

New England soldiers in New Bern, most of whom were anti-slavery, denounced Stanly for the closing of Colyer's Negro schools and the "forced" return of Bray's female slave to her master. His administration was said to have fallen upon the Union army like "a wet blanket"; both officers and men spoke indignantly of his course.[39] Daniel Reed Larned wrote his sister that she could not imagine the depressing effect the closing of the Negro schools had had on them all. "It seems as if all we had accomplished was being undone. What the effect will be on the blacks I cannot tell."[40] Feelings ran high; and after one white officer tried to incite the Negroes against Stanly, Burnside ordered an armed guard to his home to protect him from possible harm.[41] Stanly assured the General that he would trust his life in the hands of the Negroes who had known his father, and knew him; it was only because many of them had come from a distance, that there was any apprehension on his part.[42]

Still another unpleasant incident added to the tension. Hardie Hogan Helper, a brother of the famous Hinton Rowan Helper, author of the *Impending Crisis*, wrote Stanly a letter offering him advice on how to run his office. The Governor resented it and imperiously ordered Helper to leave New Bern at once. As he reported the incident to Stanton: "One person ventured to give me advice. I gave him at once permission to go to New York. The person whose impertinent meddling I rebuked is H. H. Helper."[43]

Stanly's *supposed* activities in New Bern, as related in Elias Smith's letter to the New York *Times*, created a stir in Washington where Colyer's work in the Union hospitals was favorably known. A *Times* correspondent in the capital reported that "the account therein given of Gov. Stanly's summary closing of the colored schools, and the returning of slaves to rebel masters, no less than the harsh treatment of Mr. Helper, has been read with inexpressible surprise and indignation."[44] Stanton was said to have openly asserted that "he could not remain for five minutes in connection with a Government which sent anyone to North Carolina to enforce a black code."[45]

Colyer came north to Washington without delay, arrived in the evening, and reported immediately to Senator Charles Sumner, who hurried to the Executive Mansion, and, not finding the President there, followed him to the War Department. Sumner related what had occurred at New Bern, when Lincoln, "with an impatience which Mr. Sumner never encountered from him on any other occasion," exclaimed: "Do you take me for a School-Committee-man?" Sumner replied: "Not at all; I take you for the President of the United States; and I come with a case of wrong, in attending to which your predecessor, George Washington, if alive, might add to his renown." According to Sumner, Lincoln then "changed his tone, and with perfect kindness proceeded to consider the case."[46]

Colyer had an interview with Lincoln, who assured him that Stanly had no instructions to enforce the local laws of North Carolina and that fugitive slaves would not be returned to their masters. "For my part," the President was quoted as saying, "I have hated slavery from my childhood." A "thank the Lord for that" slipped from Colyer's lips. As he left the Executive Mansion with Sumner, who had been present during the interview, the latter remarked: "You have seen more of the real character of the President, and have heard a more important declaration than is usually seen or heard in a hundred ordinary interviews."[47] Sumner assured a friend in Massachusetts that Lincoln had no sympathy with Stanly "in his absurd wickedness, closing the schools, nor again in his other act of turning our camps into a hunting grounds for slaves. He repudiates both—positively."[48]

Northern abolitionists raised the "hue and cry" against Stanly, denouncing him as a tool of the "slavocracy," and calling for his resignation. Stanly later recalled that:

> I had not been in North Carolina a week, before I was made the subject of most unjust vituperation. Letter-writers reported to newspapers not what they knew, but all the 'it is said' reports to my discredit. Editors dealt in terms of abuse, and clergymen, thirsting for the applause of mobs, tired of

preaching peace on earth and good will to men, wearied with
the celestial truths of Holy Writ, turned aside to prey on the
garbage of abolition slanders.[49]

One instance of "unjust vituperation" was a speech by General
James Lane of Kansas to an antislavery meeting in New York
attended by Colyer and Helper. Lane declared, amidst laughter and
great applause, that "it would have been well after Stanly had put
his hand to that order [for the return of Bray's slave] the earth had
opened and he [had] been sent-down."[50]

Actually, no one in the North, except Colyer and Helper, had any
reliable information about Stanly's policies, and they were hardly
impartial witnesses. Only one slave had been returned, and she had
been freed again by Union soldiers that same day.[51] Contrary to
published reports, Colyer, not Stanly, had abruptly closed the Negro
schools. Even papers friendly to the Governor had no clear picture
of what had really happened; thus the New York *Herald* declared
that he had "very properly shut up a nigger school opened by some
Northern fanatics."[52]

Radical Republicans in Congress, still smarting from Lincoln's
repudiation of Hunter's proclamation, seized on the Colyer incident
to again affirm that reconstruction was the prerogative of Congress,
and not the President. Sumner secured passage of a Senate resolution
(June 2) requesting the Secretary of War "to communicate to the
Senate copies of any commissions or orders from his Department
undertaking to appoint provisional Governors in Tennessee and
North Carolina, with the instructions given to the Governors." The
House of Representatives passed by voice vote a resolution (June 2)
introduced by John Hickman, a Pennsylvania Republican, asking the
President what powers had been conferred on Stanly as military
governor; whether Stanly had "interfered to prevent the education
of children, white or black," and if so, by what authority and to
what extent and for what purpose.[53]

On June 6, Sumner introduced a resolution requesting the
President to cancel Stanly's letter of appointment from Stanton.
This letter, said the Senator, in assuming to create any person
military governor of a state, was "without sanction in the Constitution and laws; and . . . its effect is to subordinate the civil to the

military authority, contrary to the spirit of our institutions and in derogation of the powers of Congress, which, where a State government falls into the hands of traitors, can be the only legitimate authority, except martial law." Sumner asked the Senate to act immediately on his resolution, but it was objected to and delayed.[54]

Stanton sent copies of Stanly's letter of appointment and instructions (such as they were) to Congress, with a disavowal of any order to the Governor to prevent the education of North Carolina children, white or black. Stanly was furnished with a copy of the House resolution along with a sharp request for "a full and immediate answer to the same."[55] On June 9, Stanton telegraphed Burnside, then at Fortress Monroe, Virginia, on an official visit, asking for a confidential appraisal of Stanly's operations "and what the facts really are."[56] Burnside replied that Stanly's policy was evidently misunderstood by the northern people: "Mr. Colyer has misrepresented the matter, if newspapers are correct. Governor Stanley [sic] is as sound on the Union question as you or I."[57]

Stanly had related his side of the controversy in a letter to Stanton on May 31, which apparently had been lost. He now cited his instructions from the Secretary as authority for "the suggestion relative to the negro's school." Not a word had been said, nor any intimidation given, of any intention to "enforce" the laws of North Carolina. "No such thought was in my mind nor ever can be." He wished, however, to know what protection or compensation loyal masters could expect from the Government for their slave property. He reminded Stanton that he had been promised the "perfect confidence and full support" of the War Department, so quickly withdrawn; and if this pledge was not to be honored, he wished to know it.

> The loss of my humble abilities will not be felt by this great country. If I am to act without instructions and not to be supported when I pursue the deliberate dictates of my judgment and conscience, then I ask . . . to be allowed to tender my 'immediate' resignation, and to be restored as early as possible to the honor of a private station.[58]

Lincoln summoned Burnside to Washington where he explained Stanly's actions to the President, Stanton, and "other distinguished gentlemen"; upon his return to New Bern, he had a lengthy interview with Stanly (June 23), in which he repeated the substance of his Washington conversations. Stanly thanked Lincoln for the "kind confidence you reposed in me as reported . . . by Genl. Burnside," but complained that his influence in North Carolina had been weakened by reports that he lacked the Administration's confidence. He repeated his offer to resign if Lincoln deemed it advisable to appoint another in whom he had confidence: "I should be very unhappy, if I thought any consideration of personal kindness, kept me as a stumbling block, in the path of our country's prosperity—an object near and dear to the hearts of both of us."[59]

Stanly might rightly feel that he had been made a scapegoat by an administration reluctant to formulate a national policy for dealing with fugitive slaves that would offend either the abolitionists or the loyalists in the crucial border states. The Governor's dilemma was sympathetically and preceptively described by the New Bern correspondent of the antislavery New York *Tribune*: "If Mr. Stanly returns slaves he is denounced by the North and its army; if he fails to enforce the brutal Mason's law [Fugitive Slave Law of 1850], he is hated by the very people he is sent to conciliate. He may try to trim his sails to either breeze, but in vain. . . . He is a Governor, but only in name; and neither he nor any other of his rank will be more than mere puppets until the Government shapes a policy for itself, and orders them to adhere closely to it."[60]

On June 24, Colyer returned to New Bern to reopen his Negro schools and was kindly received by Stanly. The Governor's course was so mild that Burnside changed his mind about ordering Colyer out of the department, if he should return. At Stanly's request, Colyer published a letter in the northern press stating that he had misunderstood the Governor; that he had never intended to enforce the laws of North Carolina, and would neither return fugitive slaves nor interfere with the Negro schools until he received explicit instructions from Washington. Army opinion at New Bern now swung away from support for Colyer. "There is an impression that he committed a mistake in closing his schools as hastily as he did," reported the Boston *Journal* correspondent. "He received no peremptory order from Governor Stanly to close the negro schools, but was informed that it was in violation of the laws of the State, and as such, he was told that it would be prudent to close them."[61]

Despite the abolitionist furor over the return of fugitive slaves at New Bern, only Nicholas Bray had actually succeeded in taking away a slave and she had been quickly freed again. Other masters searched for their slaves, sometimes invading private homes, but the fugitives were adept at remaining concealed. Stanly told the New York *Tribune* correspondent that he had not and never expected to enforce the fugitive slave law. When Bray had tried to recover his slave woman a second time, Stanly had been powerless to assist him. Since he had no civil *posse comitatus*, and was forbidden to employ the military or naval force, the fugitive slave law was a dead letter. Stanly told one slaveholder that no slaves could be returned unless they chose to go of their own free will. The master found his slave and tried to hire her to return, but she refused and Stanly upheld her. There was said to be "a general sense of relief" at his new course.[62]

Although Congress dropped its investigation of Stanly, critics of military government returned to the larger issue raised by the Colyer incident: What kind of loyal government should be established in the rebel states, and who should have control of it? Toward the end of June, 1862, two Republican senators, James Dixon of Connecticut and Lyman Trumbull of Illinois, debated the legality of military governors. Dixon defended the President's policy in Tennessee, North Carolina, and Louisiana, although he conceded it was an error to refer to military governors *of* the states—"They are military governors *in* those States, not of or over them—placed in authority over subjugated public enemies, and not in any sense over the States." Referring to military government, Dixon insisted: "All this is no interference with State authority. That may exist or it may be in abeyance; but the authority of military governors appointed by the President as Commander-in-Chief of the Army, in time of war, over a conquered enemy, is wholly aside from and irrespective of, and may be in entire harmony with the authority of the State government."

Trumbull, in reply, complained that Lincoln, in appointing

Stanly, had not sought Senate confirmation, as he had in Andrew Johnson's case. According to the Constitution, the President appointed all officers with the Senate's advice and consent. Yet "what do we hear?" he asked. "We hear of a military Governor in North Carolina? Has his name been sent to the Senate? Was he appointed by the advice and consent of the Senate? No, sir. Is there any law of Congress vesting the power in the President to appoint a military Governor in North Carolina?" Said Trumbull: "Sir, the President can no more make a Governor of North Carolina than the Senator from Connecticut; no more than the most obscure citizen in the State of Connecticut. It is wholly without constitutional authority." Trumbull admitted that Johnson might act as governor in his capacity as a brigadier general, but he pointed out that Stanly had no such military appointment, so held no lawful office.[63]

On July 7, 1862, the Senate in committee of the whole took up a bill by Senator Ira Harris of New York authorizing the President to establish provisional civil governments in the rebel states by appointing governors, judges, and other necessary officials. Basically a moderate proposal as amended by Trumbull's Judiciary Committee, Harris' bill seemed to have a fair chance of passing, although state rights men disliked it. The most important change made by the Judiciary Committee was to limit the provisional government's legislative power by adding to the phrase, "all subjects of rightful legislation not inconsistent with the Constitution and laws of the United States," the words, "and not interfering with the laws and institutions existing in such State at the time its authorities assumed to array the same against the government of the United States further than shall be necessary to carry into effect the provisions and purposes of this act."

Charles Sumner attacked this amendment as in effect requiring the provisional governor to enforce existing state laws relating to slavery and the Negro, such as those prohibiting the teaching of slaves to read or write. With Stanly's recent conduct in mind, Sumner proposed an amendment leaving the provisional governor free to disregard laws such as the North Carolina Negro code, which he called "abhorent to civilization." The chair ruled this amendment out of order. Trumbull then said he thought it best not to adopt the

Committee's amendment in its present shape, although he had agreed to it earlier. He explained:

> Since I have seen the operation of these laws in the southern
> States, and the manner in which persons acting in behalf of the
> United States undertake to execute them, I have changed my
> opinion in regard to the propriety of such a clause as this, and
> I agree with the Senator from Massachusetts. . . . We know
> that recently in the State of North Carolina schools have been
> suppressed. . . . I am not for interfering with the general laws
> in the southern States; but in adopting this provisional govern-
> ment . . . I do not wish to be made a party to the enforcement
> of any laws of the character indicated by the Senator from
> Massachusetts.

Harris conceded the validity of Sumner's argument, but said that there was nothing in the bill "that requires the executive power conferred by this bill upon the Governor to execute these obnoxious laws." In a slap at Stanly, he remarked: "He may execute them, perhaps, as it is said the military Governor of North Carolina is doing, but if a proper man be appointed, he will not execute them. So far as this bill is concerned, it leaves that an open question."[64]

The Senate debate revealed that the bill's supporters could not agree on the precise limits of the provisional government's powers and Harris was unable to bring the Senate to a direct vote on it. It was set aside informally and was not taken up again during the session, which ended nine days later. Stanly's reported closing of the Negro schools had caused senators friendly to Harris' bill to have second thoughts about its wisdom and thus contributed significantly to the defeat of a moderate measure that might have prevented the later conflicts between the President and Congress over reconstruction. Lincoln was left free to proceed with the establishment of military governments in the rebel states; at the same time, the Radicals could claim this debate had shown that the Senate would not accept the new Unionist governments' enforcement of pre-war slave codes.

Meanwhile in North Carolina, Stanly had begun his efforts to secure her voluntary return to the Union. His "suggestion relative to the negro school," and the policy of "persuasion" in the return of fugitive slaves, were both intended to convince North Carolinians that restoration and not abolition was the sole purpose of the war. He tried to induce Union men to come and talk with him at New Bern. "I feel I shall be successful [*sic*] in a few weeks," he wrote Stanton on May 31.[65] He also sought to initiate a discreet correspondence with his kinsman, George E. Badger, who was living in Raleigh. John S. Ely of New York had written Stanly that he (Stanly) was a most suitable person to "foster Union sentiment" in North Carolina. Stanly sent this letter to Badger in an unsealed envelope, directed to the latter's wife.[66]

Badger replied about June 1 in a letter ostensibly to Ely, but actually for Stanly. He denied the existence of any serious Union sentiment in North Carolina since Lincoln's call for troops after Fort Sumter, although he admitted the existence of a very strong Union feeling in the state before that time. Stanly's mission was useless since North Carolinians would never voluntarily accept reunion on any terms, and revival of Union sentiment was "a mere impossibility." He asked Ely to give Stanly the following message:

> Say this to him. If he wishes the honorable name of Stanly to become a by-word and a reproach, and to be spoken with scorn and hatred by North Carolinians henceforth and forever, let him prosecute his present mission. If he does not wish this—let him return whence he came, and leave us to fight out this contest as best we may, without his interference.[67]

Badger at first refused permission to publish this letter, despite the opinion of Governor Henry T. Clark that "it was written in the strongest manner, and must have done great good to certain persons and parts."[68] But it was soon known in the state that Badger had written a letter declining to cooperate in any movement to bring North Carolina back into the Union.[69]

On the morning after his arrival in New Bern, Stanly learned that Colonel Henry A. Gilliam of Plymouth, a pre-war friend, was in the local jail on a charge of violating his parole by advocating the Confederate cause. Hoping to enlist Gilliam's aid, Stanly secured his release, explained to him his purpose in coming to North Carolina, and spoke of his hopes for her peaceful return to the Union. Gilliam suggested that nothing could be done until the impending conflict near Richmond had been resolved. General George B. McClellan had led the Union Army of the Potomac to the very gates of the Confederate capital; and it was expected that a climactic battle would soon decide the city's fate, and that of the Confederacy. Stanly felt the force of Gilliam's argument, but remarked: "After this is over, why cannot honorable terms be proposed and listened to?" He pointed out that under the Confederate Constitution, each state was sovereign and independent, and reserved the right to secede; North Carolina need not be bound by her sister states, but could inform them what she intended to do.[70]

Gilliam left New Bern and went to Williamston, where he wrote to Governor Clark that he had seen the "rival sovereign, Mr. Stanley [*sic*] & had a great deal of conversation with him as to his plans & purposes." He promised to give Clark this information as soon as he had his family settled.[71]

The policy of the state and Confederate governments was to ignore Stanly and to communicate only with Union officers. Governor Clark wrote Adjutant General James G. Martin that Stanly's appointment was "a clear usurpation of power which we cannot recognize in fact or form." Contact with New Bern should be kept at a minimum.

> The return of persons to Newbern must be under your discretion, and the privilege should be granted with much caution, not *entirely* prohibited; and all letters from there received, speaking favourably of the Lincoln Government should be suppressed, all attempts to sustain or praise Stanly should be treated as insiduous attacks on our Government—to be satisfied with one would necessarily create dissatisfaction with the other government.[72]

Martin was advised to ignore Stanly's position and title and also to restrict his dealing with General Burnside.[73]

On June 15, Stanly left New Bern on board the steamer *Massasoit* for Washington, North Carolina, where he had been invited to give an address. The people were told he would speak on June 17 and anyone wishing to hear him would be allowed to enter the Union lines. Upon his arrival, he was "besieged" in his quarters by friends and the curious. The correspondent of the Boston *Journal* reported that to some of the gentry, his "plain, wholesome truths about this wicked rebellion" had been as oracles to the untutored.

> He told them, decidedly, that they had blindly rushed into a
> suicidal course; that they were opposing one of the strongest
> and best governments the world ever saw, and *all* the vast
> power of that government would be used, and all its loyal
> people would sacrifice themselves ere there could be such a
> fact as the permanent dissolution of the Union.[74]

Stanly's remarks at the Court House on the afternoon of the 17th
were even more unpalatable to his audience. He blamed the war on
the politicians who had broken up the Charleston Democratic
Convention to nominate their own candidate, denied that North
Carolina had had any grievances justifying secession, and defended
Lincoln's call for troops to suppress the rebellion. The Administration did not wish to destroy the South, but to restore good
government and secure to the southern people blessings which had
not been equaled "since the time when God expelled the first
secessionist from Heaven." He urged North Carolina to take the
proffered olive branch of peace: "Give back your forts, arsenals, and
lighthouses, and send members of Congress from North Carolina to
Washington, and in thirty days every [Union] soldier will be
withdrawn from your state." If the North Carolina legislature asked
for peace it would be granted; the people should tell their delegates
to discontinue the rebel alliance: "that you want the Government at
Washington." He concluded his speech with an ominous but pro-
phetic warning.

> I come to serve and save you. Listen to me ere it is too late.
> The march of this army cannot continue with the same policy.
> Tell your secession brethren so. *In twelve months more there
> won't be room in North Carolina for a slave's foot.* In the
> name of reason, stop it. Lincoln's rebuke of Hunter is
> significant. Heed the warning he gives. Why not have peace?
> Your patriotism and interest are involved in it. The result of
> this war must be emancipation or Union—evils unnumbered, or
> blessings such as no nation ever had.[75]

Reaction to Stanly's eloquent plea varied with the viewpoint of
the listener. The New Bern *Progress*, the Union paper in that city,
thought it a great speech, "the most eloquent and profound of the

hour," and predicted it would "revolutionize the Old North State, and be the means of bringing her back into the Union at once."[76] A Confederate sympathizer in Washington declared that "no pen save that of a Wendell Phillips or a Wm. Lloyd Garrison could do justice to the speech as delivered. In truth it is without parallel, unless one could be found at a meeting presided over by Fred Douglas [*sic*]."[77] However, some northern observers did not think Stanly's views were "advanced" enough.[78]

Whatever the effect of Stanly's remarks on his audience, he accurately reflected the President's views. "This government cannot much longer play a game in which it stakes all, and its enemies stake nothing," Lincoln wrote August Belmont on July 31. "Those enemies must understand that they cannot experiment for ten years trying to destroy the government, and if they fail still come back into the Union unhurt. If they expect in any contingency to ever have the Union as it was, I . . . [say], Now is the time."[79]

Stanly remained in Washington until June 23, and then returned on the *Massasoit* to New Bern where he learned the result of Burnside's interview with Lincoln and Stanton. On June 28, he again left New Bern to visit Roanoke Island and the principal towns on Albemarle Sound, where it was hoped his presence would encourage Union sentiment.[80] He spoke at Edenton on July 1 and at Plymouth on the following day, largely repeating his Washington remarks. At Plymouth he also urged the Union men to organize themselves into companies of one or two hundred men, as a home guard, and promised that if they would do so, he would arm them and afford them the protection of the army.[81]

Hezekiah G. Spruill, one of the Plymouth town commissioners, inferred from Stanly's remarks that the Union force in the town might be withdrawn, leaving the loyal men to protect themselves. If this was the case, he told the Governor that evening, the "strong southern men" would be compelled to flee for safety "for if these [loyal] men were turned loose on us we should be ravaged." Stanly assured him that the soldiers would not be removed and that southern sympathizers would be protected, as long as they remained quiet. He added that while he could not order the army to surrender fugitive slaves, if the loyal men would organize themselves into companies, they could go to New Bern, Washington, and Roanoke, and "take their negroes by force," without interruption by the army.[82]

After returning to New Bern, Stanly reported to Lincoln that in Carteret, Beaufort, and Washington counties he had been received with more than cordiality—in fact even with enthusiasm. The Secessionists of property—"all except young scape-graces, of no business, or hope of profit by peace"—were heartily sick of the war; but they repressed "decided and open manifestations" of their opinions in the fear that the Union forces would be withdrawn to be followed by the return of those Stanly called "Secession ruffians." This fear would continue to exercise its influence over them while the contest at Richmond was uncertain. However, he believed that a majority of the people in the state, if allowed to vote peaceably, would express a preference for the President's plan of gradual emancipation, and return to the Union.[83] When Stanly wrote this letter, he did not know that in the so-called "Seven Days Battle" (June 26-July 1), McClellan had been driven away from the environs of Richmond by the Army of Northern Virginia under its new commander, Robert E. Lee. This victory gave a tremendous lift to Confederate morale, and made Stanly's own task even more difficult.

An observer on the scene had predicted shortly after Stanly's arrival in North Carolina that while he was shut up within the narrow limits of the Union lines, the "whole state under the rule of the Rebels will be educated to despise his authority & hate the man."[84] This was an astute observation and was borne out by events. The Confederate press early represented the "Governor" as greatly disappointed at the slight extent of the Union sentiment in the state and "quite sick" of his mission; he was said to be trying the "Bribe Game," holding out the strongest inducements to true southern men to take the oath of allegiance to Lincoln, although without effect.[85] The *Weekly Raleigh Register* declared that his vanity had led him to believe he could persuade the people of his native state "to swallow the gilded pill of slavery, and that *his* name would go down to posterity as the great 'Pacificator'—as the man who restored North Carolina to the Union and laid the foundation of its entire reconstruction." Having failed in this mission, he had but two alternatives—to return to California, or remain as the "supple tool of a despicable tyrant" and get "a ball, fired by some patriot hand, through the place where his brains ought to be." Perhaps Governor Clark could offer a handsome reward for Stanly's delivery, dead or alive, at Raleigh.[86]

In a lighter vein, the Wilmington *Daily Journal* published what purported to be a "Proclamation" from Governor Marble Nash Taylor to his loyal subjects in North Carolina, asserting his authority as *"the* Governor of Hatteras, New Bern, and Beaufort," and rebuking the presumptions of the bogus Governor Stanly. He called upon his loyal subjects, the "Bankers and Beachers," to rally at once to his flag. A reasonable price would be paid for Stanly's carcass brought dead or crippled to Hatteras, "payment to be in fish, or New York censation money." This proclamation was signed "Marble Nash Taylor, Governor *de facto*, and Minister Plenipotentiary to Hatteras."[87]

Mrs. Catherine Ann Edmondston of "Looking Glass" plantation in Halifax County confided the following lines about Stanly to her journal on June 22, "that it at least may see how I loath the Traitor!"

Lines

Richard Dobbs Speight [*sic*]—Gov of N.C.—was killed in a duel—by Edward Stanley's [*sic*] father—many years ago—His grave was violated by the Yankees when they had possession of New Berne—and his skull stuck upon a pole was one of the first objects which met Stanley's eyes when he landed in New Berne as Lincoln's Governor—appointed—to subjugate his native State

Room for the Traitor! room! Lo thy father's
    Sins—rise from the grave to greet thee!
Look on me thou false Stanley! look on me and
    shuddering hear thy welcome!
By thy father's hand—untimely nipped my
    days were ended—my budding fame cut down—
And to dust—my name was given! Yet revenge
    like this—I had not dared to picture!

Thanks! to the impious hand—which rudely burst
　　My coffined cerements—and brought me forth
To greet thee! Thanks! tho unwilling all! for
　　that base act of sacrilegious violence
Has filled my cup of Vengeance!—

I see that name—that name of Stanley which
　　thy father bore—proudly and purely!
('Een tho' I hated him—yet this he forced
　　me to accord him)
I see that once revered name I say—discrowned!
　　dishonoured, a by word! and a hissing!
Babes shall lisp it out with scorn! Woman
　　shall forget her gentleness and learn
To curse it!—And Stanley the Statesman!
　　Stanley the patriot shall be by men—
Forgot—in Stanley—the Traitor!—

Thy foul presence doth eclipse his greatness!
　　doth blot out his nobleness!
And with the noisome stench of Treason!
　　thou has drowned the perfume of his memory!
Welcome thou traitor! welcome here to infamy!
　　hug thou the chains of Life—
Until thou loathest them—and then thou
　　false one—doubly dyed in Treason!
Welcome to the feast—where Arnold's self
　　awaits thee!—[88]

On July 23, the Raleigh *Weekly Standard* published Badger's letter of early June to John Ely of New York, noting that he had consented to make it public "at the request of a friend in whose judgment he has every confidence." Stanly had not taken public notice of Badger's letter, but had commented upon his charges in the Washington speech. Badger then wrote Henry A. Gilliam that in the winter of 1860-1861 Stanly had informed him that he would stand by North Carolina in the event of a sectional contest. A copy of Badger's letter was sent to Stanly under a flag of truce. Stanly wrote Gilliam denying Badger's allegation and challenging his kinsman to produce the letter. It was well known that he had "ever held Secession and Nullification as treason." Having answered Badger's "insinuations," Stanly then went on to reaffirm his belief that an

extensive Union sentiment existed in North Carolina and again
warned that if the war lasted another year, emancipation would be
inevitable under the war power.[89]

Stanly's letter to Gilliam was published in the New Bern *Progress*
on August 4 and was also printed in pamphlet form. Copies of this
pamphlet were sent under cover to Badger and Charles Manly by flag
of truce via Kinston in the care of a Confederate officer. When
Governor Clark learned these pamphlets were circulating in Raleigh,
he wrote Colonel John Windish at Kinston ordering him to confis-
cate any copies there and to have them "promptly destroyed or sent
back whence they came." The utmost vigilance should be maintained in the future to see "that nothing spoken—written—or
printed, of an improper or foreign character should be permitted."[90] Clark considered Stanly's letter to be an insidious attack
on the Confederacy and an attempt to foster discontent and
disloyalty among the people of North Carolina, and it "should be
treated like other vile incendiary missiles that are thrown in our
midst."[91]

Stanly's frequent assertion that a "large majority" of North
Carolina's citizens desired to return to the old flag, although sincere,
was undoubtedly an exaggeration; still, there were many North
Carolinians who would have welcomed peace and reunion on the
basis of the *status quo ante bellum*. Union sentiment appeared in the
eastern part of the state at the time of the federal occupation,
particularly among the non-slaveholding whites. As the months
passed, cases of "disloyalty" became more frequent elsewhere.
Extreme disloyalty was said to exist among the Quakers in Davidson,
Forsyth, Randolph, and Guilford counties. State elections were to
be held in August, 1862, and Thomas Bragg noted in his diary on
July 31 that "here & there" candidates for the legislature "as in
Forsythe Co. are shewing [*sic*] the cloven foot, & coming out for
closing the War by a Compromise &&. In other words for submission."[92] In the western counties of Wilkes, Madison, and Yadkin,
where there were few slaveholders, matters were even more serious.
Troops had to be sent to these counties to keep Confederate
deserters from interfering at the polls. General E. Kirby Smith wrote
Governor Clark that the whole population of Laurel Valley was

hostile to the Confederacy and all the males were under arms.[93] In light of this situation, it is understandable why Clark was so concerned about the effect of Stanly's "vile incendiary missiles" on the people of the state.

As the state elections of 1862 approached, the discontented element was slowly and quietly organized into a "Conservative" Party by William W. Holden, editor of the Raleigh *Standard*, who had shifted in 1860 from a militant advocate of secession to a Unionist position. Most of the old line Whigs, including William A. Graham, George E. Badger, John M. Morehead, and Jonathan Worth were Conservatives. Forced out of the Union in 1861 against their better judgment and wishes, they now opposed reunion with the North, but were critical of the Davis administration's "destructive" policies. While favoring southern independence, they were unwilling to discard constitutional government for a military dictatorship or surrender individual and state rights and liberties to the Confederate government. Nationalists in the old Union; in the Confederacy, they were champions of state rights.[94]

The Conservative Party nominated Zebulon Baird Vance of Buncombe County, a Unionist prior to Lincoln's call for troops, as its gubernatorial candidate for 1862. The Confederate Party, then in office, was composed chiefly of original secessionists. It advocated the election of William Johnston, an obscure Charlotte railroad president, Whig, and secessionist, on a platform pledging "An unremitting prosecution of the war; the war to the last extremity; complete independence; eternal separation from the North; no abridgement of Southern territory; no alteration of Southern boundaries; no compromise with enemies, traitors, or tories. Jeff. Davis, Our Army and the South." Neither candidate campaigned actively. The thirty-two year old Vance was on duty in Virginia as colonel of the Twenty-sixth North Carolina Regiment, issued no platform, and made only a few amiable speeches in the army. However, the campaign among the eleven newspapers supporting Johnston and the ten backing Vance was extremely bitter. Holden blamed the Richmond authorities for high prices, the unpopular conscription act, military defeats, the suffering of the soldiers, and the suspension of the writ of habeas corpus. He was outspoken in his hostility to the war. "All those who, with South Carolina, preferred to break up the government, and who have not repented for so doing, will vote for Colonel Johnston." Privately, Holden felt it would be better to negotiate an honorable peace now, while still possible, instead of being forced to accept unconditional surrender later.[95] How ironic that this astute politician, who had opposed Stanly in so many hard fought contests as an enemy to "southern rights," should now share his views as to the desirability of immediate reunion!

Holden's avowed hostility to the war, although not shared by most of the Conservatives, was seized upon by the Confederate Party as an election issue. The Raleigh *Weekly State Journal* declared that since Vance was supported by those newspapers which had opposed secession until Lincoln's call for troops the issue in the campaign was between Union and Secession.[96] The *Weekly Raleigh Register* warned that Vance's election would be hailed by the Yankees as an "indubitable sign that Yankee sentiment is in the ascendancy in the heart of the Southern Confederacy."[97]

Stanly's government in eastern North Carolina was injected into the campaign when the Washington (N.C.) *New Era*, a Union paper, announced that an election for state senator and representatives would be held in Beaufort County in the Washington precinct on August 7. In allowing this election to be held, said the *New Era*, the military authorities had in view the good that might result from the election of "conservative men, who have yielded for a time, from the pressure of necessity, to rebel force, but who still look forward to the restoration of the Union."[98]

A correspondent of the Wilmington *Daily Journal* in Washington, who forwarded the clipping from the *New Era*, declared that it was self-explanatory: "Stanly's work is deep. He has an underground railroad, and *corresponds with persons in the interior*. I can call no names, but know what I write to be true." It was thought in Washington that he was trying to secure the election of certain men from the East through whom he could operate when the legislature met. However, the Stanly candidates would be spotted when the result was announced at the Court House.[99]

The *Weekly Raleigh Register* took note of the *New Era* announcement with the charge that "Conservatism," whether on the seacoast, in the centre, or the mountains, was *"destruction"* to southern liberties and "re-union" with Yankee tyrants. The voters could no longer doubt that the "Conservatives" of Stanly's department and the "Conservatives" in the rest of the state were united by the common ties of "reconstruction." The *Register* pleaded with the people to see the gulf that was yawning at their feet and to crush out a party that would force them into a Union "with those who are waging against you the most brutal war that the malice of the devil ever instigated."[100]

Actually, there is no firm evidence that Stanly was fostering what Weldon Edwards called "a federal scheme" to elect twenty-five or thirty peace men to the legislature from the occupied eastern counties, although he may have considered it.[101] Both the Raleigh *Weekly Standard* and the Fayetteville *Observer* objected to the *Register*'s interpretation of the Conservative Party's motives, the latter sincerely, and called upon the voters to "resent this monstrous calumny." The *Standard* published Badger's letter to John Ely, which reassured many voters as to the loyalty of the leading Conservatives.[102]

Vance scored a smashing victory in the election, receiving a stupendous 54,423 votes out of a total vote of 74,871. Johnston carried only twelve of eighty counties. Nothing like it had ever happened before in a state election.[103] As the Confederate press had predicted, the northern press hailed Vance's election as a repudiation of secession and a vote for the Union. "The issue in North Carolina was squarely secession against anti-secession," declared the Philadelphia *Inquirer*. "The result is a Union victory." The New Bern *Progress* agreed. The New York *Times*, which refused to place any "undue value" on the election, still contended that while North Carolina had not voted to return to the Union, "it has very nearly, if not quite, voted *to quit the Southern Confederacy*."[104] Events were to demonstrate that the election was not a vote for reunion, but it is understandable why northern papers were misled since the Confederate press in the state had waged the campaign on the issue of secession or Union.

Stanly, meanwhile, had heard nothing from the War Department concerning the protection and compensation loyal masters could expect from the federal government. He therefore wrote Stanton on July 20, asking a short leave of absence to attend to important business and to confer with the Secretary on the future regulation of his official conduct in the Department of North Carolina. Permission was readily granted, but Stanly did not leave for the North until August 27, when he sailed from Beaufort City aboard the steamer *Baltimore.*[105] He told John A. Hedrick, Collector at Beaufort, that he wished to see the Administration personally to find out what its policy was on the slavery question "and could learn more by talking with the President two hours than by writing a week."[106]

Stanly could not know that events in the North were rapidly carrying Lincoln toward a shift of policy on the slavery question. In April, 1862, Congress had abolished slavery in the District of Columbia, with compensation to loyal masters; and in June, disregarding the Dred Scott decision, it extended the prohibition to the territories. In July, the radicals in Congress passed a sweeping confiscation act, which freed the fugitive slaves of rebel masters and provided for the immediate forfeiture of the property of Confederate officers, and after sixty day's warning, the property of all other persons supporting the rebellion. "By this time," James G. Randall has written, "the increasing radicalism of the war mind, the presence of thousands of slaves attending the armies in the field, and the growing recognition of foreign antislavery sentiment in its bearing upon the war, had produced their effect in overcoming the President's conservatism and caution."[107] On July 13, Lincoln told both Seward and Secretary of the Navy Gideon Welles that he had about reached the conclusion that an emancipation proclamation was absolutely essential for the preservation of the Union. At a Cabinet meeting on July 22, he announced his intention to issue an order freeing all slaves in those states still in insurrection on January 1, 1863.[108]

At Seward's suggestion, Lincoln laid his proclamation aside, while waiting for a Union victory. Meanwhile, he continued to issue public statements based upon his previous policy of gradual and compensated emancipation. As late as September 13, he told a religious delegation from Chicago that a proclamation at the present time "must necessarily be inoperative, like the Pope's bull against the comet." When Horace Greeley reproached Lincoln for not striking out more boldly at slavery, he replied candidly:

> My paramount object in this struggle is to save the Union, and is *not* either to save or destroy slavery. If I could save the Union without freeing *any* slaves I would do it; and if I could save it by freeing all the slaves I would do it; and if I could save it by freeing some and leaving others alone I would also do that. What I do about slavery and the colored race, I do because I believe it helps to save the Union; and what I forbear, I forbear because I do not believe it would help to save the Union.

Lincoln added that "the sooner the national authority can be restored; the nearer the Union will be 'the Union as it was.'"[109]

Stanly had long since reached this conclusion, and had made it the basis of his appeals for a speedy peace and reunion between North Carolina and the federal government. More clearly than most, he realized that if the war continued much longer (his own estimate was a year), emancipation would be inevitable under the President's war powers. He had told the people of North Carolina so; but his warnings had been ignored by the state authorities; and the Confederate press had reviled him as "Lincoln's Satrap." Now as he went north to learn the President's policy on the slavery question, Lincoln's public statements gave him no inkling that a decisive change in that policy had already been decided upon and awaited only the proper moment.

11

A BARREN SCEPTRE

BEFORE GOING TO WASHINGTON to see Lincoln, Stanly went to New York City to visit his wife, who was staying with friends in the country. From the Astor House, he wrote the President that he had been "so constantly engaged" during the hot weather in North Carolina, "and so much excited and distressed" by the scenes around him, that his health was suffering, making some rest indispensable. The Union army under General John Pope had just suffered a crushing defeat at Second Bull Run and was retiring in confusion on the Washington defenses. Stanly understood that in view of the great excitement prevailing in the capital, he could not talk with Lincoln as he desired, without distracting the President from more important matters. However, if Stanton would telegraph that Lincoln had the leisure now, he would come at once; if not, he would wait until next week and recruit his exhausted strength in the meantime.[1]

Stanly did not in fact go to Washington until the latter part of September. By that time, Lee's invasion of the North had been thrown back at Antietam, Maryland, giving Lincoln the desired opportunity to issue the preliminary emancipation proclamation on September 22, 1862. After reiterating that the purpose of the war was the restoration of the Union and reaffirming his intention to labor for compensated emancipation, the President declared that on January 1, 1863, slaves in rebellious states or parts of states should be "then, thenceforward, and forever free."[2]

Surprised and disturbed by the sudden appearance of the Proclamation, Stanly called on the President for an explanation of his action; and had several interviews with him on the subject. Stanly related the substance of these meetings to James C. Welling, editor of the Washington *National Intelligencer*, who recorded the information in his diary. According to Stanly, the President had stated to him:

> that the proclamation had become a civil necessity to prevent the Radicals from openly embarrassing the government in the conduct of the war. The President expressed the belief that, without the proclamation for which they had been clamoring, the Radicals would take the extreme step in Congress of withholding supplies for carrying on the war—leaving the whole land in anarchy. Mr. Lincoln said that he had prayed to the Almighty to save him from this necessity, adopting the very language of our Savior, 'If it be possible, let this cup pass from me,' but the prayer had not been answered.[3]

Most significant human actions are taken from a complex of motives, and there is no reason to believe that Lincoln's emancipation decision was an exception. Having made it, it would be understandable if he gave each of those who inquired the explanation most likely to mollify his objection. Still, these interviews alone would not have prevented Stanly from giving up his commission and returning to California. The President must have pointed out to him that the Proclamation would not take effect for three months, thus affording North Carolina ample opportunity to escape emancipation by making peace with the federal government. Verbal balm was also applied to Stanly's irritation. Lincoln and Stanton expressed approval of his conduct as military governor, with the Secretary once more assuring him "of the cordial confidence and co-operation of the department."[4] As an added inducement, he was authorized to enlist independent volunteer companies of loyal citizens to serve within the state or their respective counties and districts; these companies were to be organized, officered, armed, equipped, paid (while in actual service), and subsisted as other volunteers, and were to be commanded by the military commandant of the department when on active service. Officers were to be commissioned by the military governor.[5] Stanly had urged the formation of such loyal guard companies in his speech at Plymouth the previous July.

Mollified, Stanly agreed to continue as military governor. On September 29, he wrote Lincoln that he had completed his business with the War Department and was ready to return to North Carolina. He expressed his "deep gratification" for the Administration's approval since his influence at New Bern had been "palsied" by the public's impression that he did not possess the President's confidence. Without that confidence, he added, "I should be powerless to do anything, and should not be guilty of the folly, of attempting to discharge the responsible trust, which I was invited to accept."[6]

Lincoln replied with renewed assurances of his "entire approbation" for Stanly's conduct as military governor, "as reported to me by General Burnside, and as I have heard it personally from yourself, . . . and it is with great satisfaction that I learn you are now to return in the same capacity, with the approbation of the War Department." He asked Stanly to hold congressional elections in North Carolina before January, "if you can find it practical," and expressed "a sincere wish that North Carolina may again govern herself conformably to the constitution of the United States."[7]

At the suggestion of the President, Stanly, back in New Bern, sought an interview with Zebulon Vance. On October 21, 1862, he wrote the new governor a courteous letter requesting a meeting, either personally or with "one or more good citizens, natives of, or residing in *North* Carolina," to see "whether some measures cannot be adopted which may lead to an honorable peace." Nations, like individuals, sometimes quarreled because they misunderstood each other. This, he said, was now the case between the Government of the United States and the State of North Carolina. He confidently believed he was in a position to confer blessings upon the people of North Carolina if the state officials would lend him their assistance. If, unfortunately, this "consummation so 'devoutly wished'" could not be obtained, the two men could still do much to alleviate the inevitable sufferings attending the war, since Stanly had authority to negotiate for an exchange of political prisoners. He concluded humbly:

> I desire to do nothing in secret, will not stand on any question
> of etiquette, wishing only to be instrumental in doing good to

my country, and to that brave and. noble hearted people who hitherto have conferred honor upon both of us, whose glory and welfare I am solicitous to protect as any other son of North Carolina can be.[8]

Correctly assuming that Stanly had in mind a separate peace between the United States and North Carolina, Vance replied that his proposal was "inadmissible." North Carolina had left the Union with great unanimity, and would fulfill her obligations to the Confederacy with the last dollar and the last drop of her blood. Vance was surprised that Stanly would have thought North Carolinians base enough to desert their confederates in an hour of trial to secure terms for themselves. He declined either to have a personal interview with Stanly or to send others for that purpose.[9]

The correspondence ended with an exchange of sharp letters. Stanly complained about the unbecoming tone of Vance's letter and promised to make every effort consistent with duty and patriotism to protect the "unfortunate misguided," as well as the loyal people of his native state, from the "disastrous tyranny of your new government."[10] Vance, in turn, informed Stanly that his mission was a failure, "miserable and complete," and that "your name is execrated, and only pronounced with curses in North Carolina." In a supreme burst of rhetoric, he advised him:

Dismiss therefore your hopes of the subjugation of North Carolina through the weakness and baseness of her people. She *may* be subjugated, you *may* reach her Capitol and take possession of her government, the fortunes of war are fickle. But I assure you upon the honor of a Son, who will follow as he has followed and maintained her, *whether right or wrong*, who has every means of knowing the sentiments of her people, that you can only do so over the dead bodies of the men who once respected you, through the smoking ashes of the homes which once greeted you with hospital welcome, and through fields desolated, which once gladdened your eye, rich with the glorious harvest of peace.[11]

Stanly forwarded copies of his correspondence with Vance to Stanton with the laconic comment that at an early day, he hoped to give information of a "more pleasing character." He still believed, despite his failure to obtain an interview with Vance, that if the people of the state "could be allowed free expression of their wishes and opinions they would decide to separate themselves from any association with the rebel States." After the President had read the correspondence, Stanly asked to be informed if he had any further wishes to communicate.[12]

Union papers accepted Vance's reply as conclusive on the question of North Carolina's voluntary resumption of her normal relationship to the federal government. The New York *Times*, in an editorial, "The Futility of Peace Advances," declared that while it had no means of determining to what extent Vance spoke the sentiments of his people, it saw no reason to believe that he had materially misrepresented them. "We may as well accept it as settled, that in old staid North Carolina, as in every other state under the Confederate dominion, the order of the day is war, and will so remain until that dominion is either accepted or exterminated."[13] The New Bern *Progress* stated flatly that a voluntary resumption by any Confederate state of its constitutional relations with the federal government was "the most baseless of visions," and that the war must go on, "and the sword must precede the olive-branch."[14]

Was Stanly then guilty of mere wishful thinking in his constant avowals that North Carolinians would prefer their old allegiance? Not entirely. He undoubtedly exaggerated the extent of *Union* sentiment in North Carolina, but feeling *against* the Confederate government at Richmond was still very strong. Vance warned President Davis that without the warm, ardent, and constant support of the "old Union men," the "present status could not be maintained forty-eight hours. *These are facts.*" If they were not heeded with regard to the government of the state's affairs, the worst consequences might ensue. "I believe, sir, most sincerely," he continued, "that the conscript law could not have been executed by a man of different antecedents from myself, without outbreaks among our people."[15]

Just at this time the Conservative majority in the new General Assembly was purging state officials, replacing them with old Union men. Some observers believed that Vance alone kept the Assembly from declaring for reunion. "Letters from North Carolina are distressing enough," the "Rebel War Clerk," John B. Jones, noted in his diary on November 27, 1862. "They say, but for the influence of Gov. Vance, the *legislature* would favor reconstruction!"[16] Kenneth Rayner said privately that "the leading and controlling spirits" in the state were shaping their course to meet contingencies.

> If we succeed in achieving our freedom and independence, the world will never know and history will never write their intentions. They will shout louder, and boast more valiantly of their sacrifices and achievements, than all the others. But if disasters come, and the spirit of our people succumbs; then they intend to have it in their power to say that they were first and foremost, in raising the flag of *reconstruction*.[17]

It is not surprising then that Stanly, shut up within the Union lines, should have interpreted rumblings of discontent as evidence of a strong Union feeling.

During the months he spent in North Carolina, Stanly did all in his power to relieve the sufferings of loyal citizens (and those nominally loyal) within the Union lines. Cut off from both the interior of the state and the outside world by the Union blockade, they could neither ship commodities out nor buy necessities not produced at home. Precious salt, used for the preservation of meat and fish in the hot summer months, was scarce.[18]

In June, 1862, Stanly gave several New Bern and Washington residents permission to take cargoes of pine lumber to the West Indies. At the same time northern shipowners were authorized to trade in the sounds and rivers of North Carolina within the Union lines and to buy products from loyal citizens. No trade in contraband was permitted and all trading had to be done in accordance with military regulations.[19] The Boston *Journal* correspondent, noting that New Bern residents were hurrying to repair their coastal schooners, thought that Stanly's trade permits gave the people "still greater confidence, and encourages a better feeling."[20]

Stanly, in some instances, extended aid even to those who refused to swear an oath of allegiance to the Union. With his permission, one Captain Bowen, a Union sympathizer, sold a load of groceries and shoes in Plymouth for "N. C. money" without discrimination. However, the Governor refused to allow anyone to purchase salt unless they first took either the oath of allegiance or an oath of neutrality drafted by Stanly himself. "The instruction (to exact an oath of allegiance) which was forced on us, I have no power to dispense with," he explained to Hezekiah G. Spruill, who had received permission to purchase salt if he would take the oath of neutrality. "I have done all I could, & hope it may be of service to you." However, Spruill refused the salt on Stanly's terms.[21]

The Governor was hampered in his conciliation efforts by the depredations of the Union troops in the occupied area of the state. Accusing the soldiers of insult, unauthorized search, theft, and house-burning (but not murder or rape), Stanly declared that thousands and thousands of dollars' worth of property—pianos, libraries, carpets, family portraits, mirrors, "everything, in short, that could be removed"—was sent north, forty thousand dollars' worth by one regiment alone. Nor were the Negroes spared. "There was scarcely a day in which I was not called upon to interpose in behalf of some poor negro, treated inhumanly by some abolition soldier....Again and again have I forbidden soldiers to remove their garden fences to build stables, or for firewood."[22] A New Bern residence, C. C. Howard, recorded one of Stanly's interventions to protect the town's citizens.

> A negro *fellow* from the North got a squad of ten soldiers, went up town and said he had the authority and orders to search houses. [He] went into several houses of our poor citizens, searching from the cellar to the garret. E. [Stanly] got intelligence of it about sunset, got in his buggy and in a few moments was at the scence [*sic*] of action, had the fellow put in jail and has since sent him out of the state.[23]

Stanly repeatedly complained to General John Foster, Burnside's successor in the Department, about the depredations, but with little success. The "numerous instances of pillage frequently complained of, require some remedy at your hands," he advised the General in November, 1862. "Loyal people, as well as the infirm and aged are not spared. I most earnestly invoke the interposition of your authority, to prevent these barbarous outrages in the future."[24]

Stanly gave loyal citizens outside New Bern signed "protections" to prevent their molestation by Union soldiers, as well as passes authorizing them to take goods for their own use through the Union lines. Federal officers soon complained that these protections and passes were falling into rebel hands, where they were used to obtain "immense quantities" of supplies from Union posts for the Confederate army.[25] Confederate guerrillas were reported to have been captured with passes and protections signed by Stanly in their possession. The New Bern *Progress* branded one such "yarn" printed in the New York *Express* to be "an unmitigated falsehood," adding that it was apparently the design of some "evil disposed person or persons in this Department, to cast a slur upon the integrity of our worthy Governor, [at] every opportunity, that some base hireling press will afford."[26]

The Union commandant at Washington, Colonel Simon S. Mix, refused to recognize Stanly's passes because he said they allowed known secessionists to come and go at will. He complained to headquarters and Foster ordered that no one should be admitted within the lines unless he was known to be good for the Union's interest. A correspondent of the New York *Herald* reported such cases were scarce, and "very, very few pass." He observed smugly that "of course our pickets have a better chance than a civilian in town [Stanly] to know who is truly loyal and who not."[27] The Union soldiers generally ignored the Governor's protections thereafter, and the Wilmington *Daily Journal* said they were worth a little less than the paper they were printed on.[28]

One observer in New Bern thought that Stanly's leniency with "rebels" would never bring them back to their old allegiance; and that on the contrary, "a pacific policy only gives the enemy more courage, and suffices to help them, while it too often cripples our officials, and disheartens our soldiers."[29] This view was widely shared by the officers and men of the Union army. But however unpopular Stanly's policies made him with the military, they did win him the respect and esteem of New Bern's residents. C. C. Howard testified that:

> Edward . . . is a real blessing to the citizens here he has it in his power to protect and defend them and see that justice is done and he discharges his duty faithfully, he is good and kind to every body, he is a friend to the humblest individual, notwithstanding he differs in politicks [*sic*] from the people here they

all respect and love him and look up to him for advice &
councils as children to a parent, were he to leave there would
be weeping & wailing here.[30]

In December, 1862, Stanly became involved in a dispute with
officers of the North Atlantic blockading squadron over his licensing
of coastal trade by loyal citizens. Naval officers in North Carolina
admitted that his licenses had relieved much suffering among the
Union people, but objected to the traffic because it might afford an
opportunity for traders to sell to Confederate buyers.[31] Admiral
Samuel P. Lee, commander of the North Atlantic squadron, asked
the Navy Department if Stanly's permits to enter by Hatteras Inlet
or Core Sound, and also his permits to trade, were proper in respect
to the Union blockade. Secretary of the Navy Gideon Welles replied
they were not, and Lee issued orders on December 2 that no vessels
other than those with cargoes for the Union army could enter the
sounds through Hatteras Inlet, without authorization from the War,
Navy, or Treasury departments.[32]

Stanly chose to interpret Lee's order as not prohibiting *internal*
trade within North Carolina from one point to another, and
continued to issue permits for such trade. On December 4, he
authorized Captain William Williams of the schooner *Mary Jane
Kennedy*, of Elizabeth City, to trade in any of the navigable waters
of North Carolina. He was neither to deal in contraband nor trade
with the enemy, and upon arriving at a port where Union troops
were stationed, was to report to the officer in command. The permit
was valid until February 4, 1863.[33]

Commander H. K. Davenport of the U.S.S. *Hetzel*, then off New
Bern, refused to allow the *Mary Jane Kennedy* to depart. He wrote
Stanly that his permit to trade was in direct opposition to Admiral
Lee's orders, in accordance with which it would be impossible to
allow the vessel to proceed on her voyage.[34] Stanly then modified
his permit, limiting the schooner to a sealed voyage to Plymouth and
back. "This permission I hope you will respect," he wrote Davenport, adding a warning that he would regard the Commander's
"further interference in this case as a disregard of my order, which it
will be my duty to sustain."[35]

Davenport allowed the *Mary Jane Kennedy* to proceed, but

sought an interview with Stanly and called his attention to the latitude of his first permit. Stanly admitted there was "something in that"; but in the course of a "frank and friendly conversation," he insisted that the loyal people must have salt, sold under military supervision; that no officer had the right to decline to obey his permit; and that any officer pursuing such a course would make himself liable to arrest. Davenport, in reporting this conversation to Lee, admitted that the salt question was "a delicate one to touch" and requested instructions. In the meantime, his immediate superior, Commander Alexander Murray, out of respect for Stanly's high position, ordered that his permits be honored between United States posts in the state.[36]

Admiral Lee refused to concede Stanly's authority to issue permits, however limited, and lectured Murray on his duties. *All* trade was to be prohibited with the insurrectionary region, and Stanly's passes were therefore unauthorized and could not be regarded. "Your instructions come from the Navy Department through me, and it is not competent for Governor Stanly to give you orders or instructions in regard to the blockade or any portion of your naval duties."[37]

Stanly also appealed to higher authority, laying the whole controversy before the War Department with a request for instructions. Receiving none, he asked his friend Seward to consult with Stanton and Welles to relieve his embarrassment. He reviewed his license policy and made it clear that he regarded the Navy's prohibition on trade as a serious infringement on his authority as military governor. He pointedly reminded the Secretary that Stanton "said I was 'dictator,' could do what I pleased," while Seward himself had said that no instructions were necessary. He concluded by again threatening to resign:

> I am here doing my best, to protect and encourage loyal people, but if I am controlled by Navy orders, & Treasury regulations, I hold a 'barren sceptre' and shall soon be Sancho Panza the Second. I do not wish to exercise any power, except for the public good. I do not wish to remain here an hour longer than I can be useful & every day increases the time to be away. . . . Are the Treasury officials & Navy officers to command or obey me? Can loyal people look to me for

protection of property, or must I act as a clerk merely &
trouble the Department with each little care?—When this
becomes the order, please have me recalled.[38]

The War Department ignored Stanly's threat to resign and refused
to sustain him in his fight with the Navy. He was told that with the
exception of Beaufort City, all the ports and navigable waters of
North Carolina remained subject to the blockade; and this rule was
decisive against his authority to issue trade licenses of however
limited a character.[39] But Stanly refused to accept this ruling as
final. On January 10, 1863, he called Stanton's attention to the
necessity of relieving the business people of New Bern, as well as the
citizens, from the onerous restraints put upon them by the Navy and
Treasury regulations. There was no uniformity, no system, no
intelligent rule to serve as a guide. Sometimes a Navy officer "in
good humor" would allow a boat with Stanly's pass to proceed,
while the next in command would refuse. Stanly did not wish the
power to grant trade permits—"far from it"; but he entreated that
the power be confined to the Navy alone or to the Navy officers in
command jointly with the military commander of the post—anything but the present disorder.[40] General John G. Foster, probably
at Stanly's instigation, suggested to Stanton that New Bern be made
a port of entry for the inland trade of the state and that the
Governor be empowered to authorize vessels to trade in "lawful &
needful articles."[41]

In the absence of any reply from Stanton, the Governor continued to issue trade permits in violation of the explicit instructions
of the War Department and the orders of the Navy. On January 19,
1863, he authorized Isaiah Respass to take a load of lumber to
Beaufort City via Core Sound and to return to Washington (N.C.)
with three hundred sacks of salt.[42] In February, Commander
Murray complained to Admiral Lee that Stanly had inaugurated a
commerce within the sounds that was altogether wrong. But despite
a desire to see these passes put down, he did not wish to make an
issue of them with the Governor at present, and usually allowed
vessels with Stanly's passes to proceed unmolested to their destina-
tions.[43] Admiral Lee informed Welles that Murray had allowed six
violations of the blockading instructions in the sounds of North

Carolina between February 1 and 25, 1863.[44] He and the Secretary continued to insist that Stanly had no authority to issue trade permits. "Governor Stanly's pass is not to be recognized," Welles endorsed on a letter from Lee (February 22, 1863), "and naval officers will give no passes for trafficking."[45] On March 30, Murray was relieved of his command in the Sounds, possibly because he had failed to stop Stanly's passes.[46]

A temporary victor in his controversy with Murray, Stanly was less successful in his efforts to secure the election of a loyal North Carolinian to Congress. In the preliminary proclamation of emancipation, Lincoln had stated that representation in Congress would be taken as proof of renewed allegiance to the Union, and that states, or parts of states, so represented would be exempted from the final emancipation proclamation. Eager to make it easy for the rebel states to return, he advised his military governors and other Union officers in the South to aid the people in holding congressional elections, if they desired them, following forms of law as far as convenient. The largest number of qualified voters should be urged to cast ballots; and the men elected should be "gentlemen of character, willing to swear support to the constitution, as of old, & known to be above reasonable suspicion of duplicity."[47]

On August 21, 1862, the Washington correspondent of the New York *Times* reported that Lincoln had authorized Stanly to order the election of representatives in Congress for the First and Second Districts of North Carolina.[48] This news pleased northern conservatives, who wanted the Union restored, "as it was," with slavery and state rights intact. The New York *Herald* saw in Lincoln's authorization a significance beyond the mere addition of two members to the House. By permitting the loyal citizens in a seceded state to elect representatives to Congress as soon as they had returned to their allegiance, the President had "emphatically and explicitly" recognized the *"unimpaired State character,"* not only of North Carolina but of all the seceded states. He had thereby rebuked and disavowed Sumner's theory that they had lost their character as states and should be regarded as territories until they had organized loyal state governments acceptable to Congress. The President's action in North Carolina would be a precedent for similar cases in the future.[49]

When Stanly talked with Lincoln in September, the President again asked him to hold congressional elections, if practicable, before January, 1863; but the Governor took no action after returning to New Bern. "It is surmised that he fears undesirable persons would be elevated to office," reported the New York *Times* correspondent in New Bern, after several weeks had passed without an order for an election. "But this can hardly be true, because of the assumption of power it would imply."[50] However, this surmise was substantially correct. The "undesirable" person whose election Stanly feared was that Charles Henry Foster who had been "elected" to Congress under the short lived regime of Marble Nash Taylor at Hatteras. He had appeared before the House Committee of Elections as a claimant on four separate occasions, the last as recently as June, 1862. The Committee reported his final claim, based on an election held at Hatteras on January 30, 1862, as fraudulent and utterly without basis, and found it difficult to understand "how anyone can, seriously and in good faith, claim this to be an election of a representative to the Thirty-seventh Congress."[51] Foster was now known to Unionist North Carolinians in exile as "humbug Foster."[52] Yet despite this unsavory reputation, Lincoln appointed him a recruiting officer for North Carolina troops with the rank of Captain, and gave him a pass to New Bern.[53] On September 9, the New Bern *Progress* announced that Foster had arrived in town ready to run for a seat in Congress at the ensuing election. Without apparent irony, the *Progress* added that he was "a persevering, energetic man, and will win, if these qualities will insure success."[54]

To oppose Foster in the event of an election, Stanly, while in Washington, D.C., hired Jennings Pigott as his private secretary to return with him to New Bern. A native of Carteret County, Pigott had served as a Whig member of the North Carolina House of Commons from 1846 to 1850, before moving to the national capital where he spent the next ten or eleven years as a claims agent.[55] When John A. Hedrick learned from his brother Benjamin in Washington that Pigott was coming to North Carolina, he replied: "If Mr. Pigott comes, you need have no fears about Foster."[56]

Following Pigott's arrival in New Bern, Stanly was reported ready to order an election if any considerable number of people should petition for it. The New Bern *Progress* urged the people to at once circulate petitions, asking Stanly to order an election for the remainder of the Thirty-Seventh Congress; it warned that they would have only themselves to blame if they failed to escape the penalties of the confiscation and emancipation acts by being represented in Congress on January 1, 1863.[57] This warning had some effect. On November 28, the New York *Times* correspondent reported election petitions were circulating in the eastern part of the state.[58] A Unionist in Plymouth wrote General Foster that from all he had seen and heard "the people are daily becoming more reconciled and express generally a wish for the Governor to call an election for Congress, which I hope he will see the importance of doing at an early a day as practical."[59]

On December 10, 1862, Stanly ordered an election in the Second District on January 1, 1863, to fill the district's vacancy in the Thirty-Seventh Congress. All loyal free white men twenty-one years or older who had been inhabitants of any county in the district for twelve months preceding the election would be qualified to vote. Elections would be held in the other congressional districts when the loyal men therein petitioned for them, and when the condition of the country would permit.[60] Poll inspectors at Beaufort City were advised in holding the election to follow as nearly as they could the state requirements in force before the rebellion. No test oath was to be required of any North Carolina citizen wishing to vote, since many loyal men, for what Stanly vaguely termed "good and sufficient reasons," had been excused from taking the oath of allegiance. His justification of this action was that "a citizen offering to vote manifests a desire to do his duty to his country in that respect, and ought to be encouraged."[61] No doubt Stanly wished to swell the meager voting rolls as large as possible, hence his leniency with regard to the oath of allegiance; still its omission would open the Governor to the charge of sympathy with "rebels."

Stanly sought to hold the election in accordance with state law and precedent; but conditions in eastern North Carolina precluded all but a fraction of the normal electorate from voting, even if they had wished to do so, which was by no means the case. The Union army on the mainland exercised effective control in only a few coastal towns; the rest of the nominally Union territory was subject to incursions by Confederate guerrillas and regular forces; and men openly professed Unionism only at peril of their lives and property. In Bay River, Craven County, there were said to be some two or three hundred Unionists who could not vote because of guerrillas. Seven counties in the Second District—Pitt, Lenoir, Greene, Wayne, Onslow, Edgecombe, and Jones—were still under Confederate control. In the remaining four—Beaufort, Hyde, Craven, and Carteret—polls could be opened only in New Bern (Craven), Washington (Beaufort), Beaufort City (Carteret), and in some Hyde County precincts, chiefly on the Outer Banks.[62] The anticipated small vote, even without the requirement of an oath of allegiance, may have been the reason why Stanly scheduled the election *on* and not *before* the President's January 1, 1863 deadline. Perhaps he hoped that the mere fact of the election would lead Lincoln to exempt North Carolina, or at least that portion of it within the Second District, from the Emancipation Proclamation.

Stanly's favorite, Jennings Pigott, and Stephen F. Willis of Beaufort City, "a good Union man," and popular, announced as candidates on December 20 in cards published in the New Bern *Progress*. Pigott declared in favor of "the Constitution and the Union" and promised if elected to leave "no effort untried to advance your interest, to secure the blessings of peace, and to obtain compensation for losses occasioned by the war." Willis simply announced that if sent to Washington the Constitution would be his guide and "the Union . . . my motto." Both men declined to canvass the district: Pigott, because of sickness in his family—Willis, because the election was too near.[63]

Foster did not formally announce as a candidate, but was the favorite of the so-called "Free Labor Associations," which had recently been organized in Carteret, Craven, and Hyde counties in support of the Emancipation Proclamation. They were composed almost entirely of non-slaveholding whites, many of whom were serving in the First North Carolina Union Regiment. The New York *Tribune* correspondent said these non-slaveholders, or "white trash" as the Negro drivers called them, were easily made into Free Labor men; one speech was sufficient to convert a whole community. He gave the following analysis of the movement: "They are generally down on the negro as well as his master, and desire his deportation out of the country; but they heartily wish the slaves were all free as the first necessary step in getting rid of them." They disliked Stanly and his policy of leniency and loudly demanded the harshest measures against the "rebels" and their sympathizers, including the vigorous and prompt enforcement of the confiscation and emancipation acts passed by the previous Congress. Stanly, in turn, viewed the Free Labor movement as a serious threat to his conciliation policy, and denounced Free Labor sentiments as "wicked" and their followers as "bad men."[64]

Foster was the champion of this Free Labor movement in eastern North Carolina; and the New Bern *Progress* quoted him as saying at a Union and Free Labor meeting in Beaufort City (December 2) that he "was pledged, and his oath registered in Heaven, to the extirpation of the accursed negro-driving aristocracy, and to the establishment of Free Labor in North Carolina."[65] The *Progress* criticized these remarks. It insisted that the Union army had come to the state to extirpate the wicked doctrine of secession, to restore the constitutional rights of southern loyalists, and to prevent the destruction of the Union, even if the emancipation of slavery should follow. But, said the *Progress*:

> we did not come here 'to establish free labor in North Carolina.' Nor is this the avowed policy of the Administration. For if North Carolina will cut loose from secession, all her constitutional rights are at once restored, and among them the right to retain her property of all descriptions.[66]

According to the New York *Tribune* correspondent, this editorial was written at Stanly's instigation and reflected his viewpoint.[67]

The Free Labor Associations strongly opposed any election for the remainder of the Thirty-Seventh Congress, because they feared it would afford Lincoln a pretext to exempt the rich lands and slaves within the district from confiscation and emancipation. They claimed that the petitions which they had signed had been for the next Congress and charged Stanly with bad faith, alleging that they had been told only a few days before the appearance of the Governor's proclamation directing an election, that none would be ordered at present.[68]

On December 10, the presidents of the three Free Labor Associations protested to Lincoln that Stanly was denying them the free expression of their views in the New Bern *Progress*, and had either written or instigated the paper's declaration that Free Labor was not the "avowed policy" of the Administration. They wished to know whether this discouragement of the Free Labor cause was in accordance with Lincoln's policy.

> If it be so, then we have most *deplorably misinterpreted* your executive utterances & acts. If it be *not* so, & if, as we yet believe, you are inclined favorably to the expression & promulgation of Free Labor doctrine, we respectfully request that you will either *thus instruct* your representative here, or give the people of North Carolina *a more correct exponent of your policy.*[69]

If Lincoln bothered to answer this letter, forwarded to him, by Senator Samuel Pomeroy of Kansas, a Radical, his reply has not been found.

As election day neared, the contest narrowed down to Pigott and Foster, with Willis a distant third. Foster declined the Free Labor nomination for Congress, since he had applied to the Federal authorities for permission to raise a second North Carolina Union regiment. Still, his name remained before the people, with the North Carolina troops pledged to his support as a token of friendship. It was said that if Pigott was elected, Foster would contest the seat on the ground that he was not an inhabitant of North Carolina as required by the Federal Constitution.[70] The New Bern *Progress* did not endorse a candidate by name, but probably had "humbug Foster" in mind when it warned the people in casting their ballots to avoid "political adventurers and charlatans" as they would a viper. Since it would be the representative's duty to press the indemnity claims of loyal citizens, he should be capable and honest and, like Caesar's wife, above suspicion.[71]

On Christmas day, political speeches caused considerable excitement in Beaufort City; and in the evening Stanly was hung in effigy in front of the city markethouse. The New Bern *Progress* said hotly that not a dozen persons in Beaufort knew of it, or approved it. It had been the act of "some worthless contemptible fellow, that is not worth salt enough to keep his body sweet and clean."[72]

The election itself passed off quietly, with polls open in nineteen precincts in three counties—Carteret, Craven, and Hyde.[73] The whole number of votes cast was 864; of these Pigott had 595 votes; "all others" (Foster and Willis) 259 votes. In New Bern, Pigott had 78 votes and Foster 21. The heaviest vote was polled at the court houses in Beaufort City where Pigott received 95 votes, Foster 61, and Willis 57, with 1 blank, a total of 214. Foster received the solid vote of all the North Carolina Union soldiers qualified to vote. Many could not, because they were not from the district. On January 8, 1863, Stanly certified that Jennings Pigott had been duly elected to represent the Second District in the Thirty-Seventh Congress.[74] The New Bern *Progress* put the best face it could on the election, and declared that the large vote cast was "gratifying to every earnest lover of the Union...as reflecting the fact that the Unionism of North Carolina is not a myth, but a sober, well established fact."[75]

Foster's friends in the First North Carolina Regiment contested the validity of Pigott's election on the grounds that he had received secessionist support at the polls. Abraham Congleton, sixty-four years of age, a private in Company F, and president of the Free Labor Association of Carteret County, declared in a sworn statement that in the voting at Beaufort City on January 1, he had openly challenged more than forty voters "known to me personally as secessionists and . . . open enemies to the government of the United States," who had been allowed to vote by Stanly's order without any evidence of loyalty. He testified that "the majority, if not all, of these disloyal votes were cast for Mr. Pigott, the difference in the appearance of the tickets being sufficiently obvious as to fully establish this fact."[76] Forty-five "loyal Union citizens of Carteret County," members of Company F, and thirty-six members of Company G at New Bern, petitioned Congress not to seat Pigott because he had received secessionist support.[77]

On January 5, the New York *Herald* correspondent wrote from New Bern that the impression was general there that Congress would refuse to recognize the validity of the election "in consequence of the reception of many disloyal votes, which were received in accordance with the express instructions of the Military Governor."[78] The next evening, the "Union and free labor men of eastern North Carolina" held a public meeting in Beaufort City, with Congleton presiding, to renew their protests against Pigott's election. The meeting, said by Stanly to number barely a dozen persons, unanimously resolved that the North Carolina Unionists regarded "with unqualified indignation the admission of traitors and rebels to an equality at the ballot-box with loyal men; and that we [will] not submit to be trampled down under the cloven hoof of treason shown in the recent sham election for a representative to Congress from this district." The meeting requested Congress to send a commission to North Carolina to investigate grave charges against Stanly, with a view to his immediate removal if they were substantiated.[79]

Foster sent this petition and other documents pertaining to the election to Henry L. Dawes, chairman of the House Committee of Elections, with the request that he make such use of them as he saw fit. Foster denied any interest in claiming a seat on the basis of the recent election; and said he had not yet decided whether to come to Washington to dispute Pigott's admission, since "It is a matter of no particular personal concern to me." However, he had just learned that no voting was done in Beaufort County—"two hundred native Union soldiers being disfranchised in consequence of the secesh magistrate and inspectors refusing to open the polls in the town of Washington, in that county." Dawes could draw the inference that these votes would have been cast for Foster.[80]

The House Committee of Elections held hearings on the Second District election, at which both Pigott and Foster testified, and then decided that Pigott could not be deemed the choice of the loyal voters in a district in which more than one-half had been unable to express a choice. The Committee also ruled that at the time of his election he was a sojourner rather than an inhabitant as required by the Federal Constitution. It recommended that he be denied a seat and the House of Representatives concurred on February 23, 1863.[81]

While Pigott's case was pending before Congress, "Free Labor" feeling continued very bitter against Stanly at New Bern. The New York *Times* correspondent reported on January 21 that the President was to be memorialized for Stanly's removal and for the abolition of his office, which he had made so odious with the army, navy, and Union men generally that no one could acceptably hold it thereafter. General Foster was quoted as saying that a military governor was no longer a military necessity in the Department.[82]

At Washington, a distinguished delegation headed by Wendell Phillips, representing the antislavery men of Boston, had an interview with Lincoln on January 25, and submitted a complaint against Stanly, "urging the necessity of having in such positions men who were heart and soul in favor of his (the President's) declared policy of emancipation." One delegate suggested General Frémont as Stanly's successor; but the President was unenthusiastic, and the men returned sadly home convinced that Lincoln "was not competent to grapple with the tremendous combination of issues before him."[83]

Stanly himself believed it would be futile to continue as military governor after Lincoln issued the final Emancipation Proclamation on January 1, 1863. He wrote Stanton that it had "put to flight all hope of peace by any measure of conciliation."[84] Moreover, Stanly was out of sympathy with the Administration's announced intention to receive Negroes "of suitable condition" into the Union army. He protested to Foster against the enlistment and drilling of Negroes at Elizabeth City, and elsewhere, on the grounds that subordinate military officers were unfit to judge when their condition was suitable in the meaning of the President's proclamation, and because it raised the danger of a servile war.[85]

On January 15, Stanly submitted his resignation to the President and briefly exclaimed the reasons for his action. He noted that he had assured the people of North Carolina in public addresses and in conversation that the Administration in its military movements was only trying to restore the Union and to secure to the people their rights and privileges under the Constitution. But since the Emancipation Proclamation, he could no longer give such assurance. As for the Proclamation itself, he feared it would do infinite mischief.

> It crushes all hope of making peace by any conciliatory measures. It will fill the hearts of Union men with despair, and strengthen the hands of the detestable traitors whose mad

ambition has spread desolation and sorrow over our country. To the negroes themselves it will bring the most direful calamities.

Stanly offered to remain until his successor could be appointed, and as long as his experience could be of use to the new governor. He expressed his gratitude for Lincoln's confidence and support: "Though I cannot approve of the measures you adopt, I know your motives are good and your purposes patriotic."[86]

Stanly sent his resignation to Stanton to be handed to the President, and asked to be informed at "an early day" when he could be relieved without inconvenience to the public service. However, the War Department did not officially acknowledge his resignation until March 4, 1863, when he was told that it had been accepted by the President, to take effect on March 1.[87] One unnamed observer reported that everyone in New Bern except the secessionists were glad he had resigned. "I hear loud complaints—that he is a secessionist, aids the rebels, prevents the administration of justice, opposes the President's policy, that he is a block to all onward movements."[88]

In his last months as military governor, Stanly found it necessary to protest repeatedly against the destruction or theft of loyalist property by both Confederate and Union soldiers. In March, he carried on an acrimonious correspondence with Confederate General Daniel Harvey Hill over Stanly's charge that the forces under Hill's command had made a premeditated attempt to burn Plymouth. Hill admitted that some houses in the town had been burnt to oust some "Yankee thieves and marauders" who had taken shelter in them, but quickly shifted his defense by blaming the "brutal invaders of a peaceful and peace-loving people" for war damages. He expressed the hope that Stanly, having rebuked Confederate "atrocities," would now devote some time to preventing Yankee excesses. Becoming more personal in his abuse, Hill contrasted the courage of Governor Vance who had "often bared his bosom to the deadly bullet in defence of his native state" with that of Stanly who had not exposed *his* person in battle. "It is to be hoped, however, that when he [Stanly] has organized his negro brigade, his Excellency the military Governor will (having laid in an abundant supply of attar of roses and eau de cologne) put himself at its head, and strike for his own, his native land." Hill concluded by reminding Stanly that there was a Yankee general named Arnold, who turned Tory, and a southern general named Washington, who was a rebel. "The British honored the rebel and despised the tory. North-Carolina has a civil Governor and a military Governor—a rebel and a tory. Mean as the Yankees are, they respect the former and loathe the latter."

Stanly's reply to this "insolent falsehood and blackguard abuse" was equally biting. He renewed his charge that the burning of Plymouth had been "a premeditated attempt to destroy the whole town." Said he: "The houses of widows, of Union men, and of secessionists . . . were indiscriminately burned, without regard to the entreaties and tears of their wives and daughters." Stanly denied any connection with organizing Negro troops, but declared that if compelled to choose between fighting "with such secessionists and town-burners as you, attempting to destroy the government, and with 'a negro brigade' to prevent its destruction, I should prefer the negro brigade." Dismissing Hill's invocation of Arnold as "beneath contempt" and of Washington as "the height of hypocritical audacity," Stanly taunted the General with Confederate losses in eastern North Carolina since Hill had come to protect the state. "You had possession of Roanoke Island, Fort Macon, Newbern, Washington, and Hatteras. How are they now?" His parting shot was a word of advice:

> You have committed a great crime in your part in this horrid war. You commenced with perjury, and are trying to sustain yourself with impudence and falsehood. As a State rights village politician you were simply ridiculous. Do not attempt, like the frog in the fable, to swell to the size of the ox, by parading your insolence under the name of a 'Major-General in the Confederate States Army.' You will soon be, in the eyes of all sensible people, utterly contemptible.[89]

It was a case of "Greek meeting Greek" when these two fiery spirits clashed; and the exchange had rapidly degenerated into a "scolding match," reflecting little credit on either man.

Before leaving New Bern for the North, Stanly complained to General Foster that loyal citizens in Hyde County had been robbed and insulted by Union troops, who had treated his protections with scorn. "I know you have uniformly rebuked these atrocities," he lamented, "but your words have been treated like my protections."[90] On this final note of futility, Stanly's career as military governor came to an end.

Stanly visited Washington before returning to California, and, despite his resignation, was said to be "on the best possible terms with all members of the Administration."[91] Stanton expressed the usual regrets that the Government was losing his "able and patriotic services" in a trying hour, and declared that his official duties, though often "onerous and vexatious," had been discharged with a "zeal and fidelity unsurpassed by any public servant."[92] On April 22, Stanly called at the Executive Mansion and asked Lincoln to have Foster's appointment as major general dated back to the time he assumed command of the Department from Burnside in July, 1862. The President endorsed the request with the comment that "Gen. F's conduct at Washington, N. C. I think, entitles him to additional consideration."[93] Stanly's relationship with Foster had been cordial enough, despite the opposition to the Governor's policies from Union army and navy officers.

Daniel Reeves Goodloe, a North Carolina abolitionist, and one of the commissioners to arrange emancipation in the District of Columbia, was mentioned in Washington as Stanly's successor; and forty-three congressmen joined in recommending his appointment to Lincoln.[94] John A. Hedrick advised his brother Benjamin that if Goodloe should come to North Carolina as governor he should have his powers defined as accurately as possible before he left Washington. If he was to be "Dictator of the State," he should have it so stated in his instructions from the Secretary of War. Thus, he could profit from Stanly's experience.

> I think that Gov. Stanley [sic] would have had much less trouble if his powers had been well defined. He had verbal instructions to consider himself absolute Dictator in the State, while his written instructions only gave him power to use such measures as would protect the loyal inhabitants. Loyalty is very different according to the notions of different individuals.[95]

On the morning of April 18, Stanly wrote Seward that he had enjoyed a "very pleasant interview" with Lincoln the previous evening; and the President had said he would appoint Goodloe military governor of North Carolina, if Stanton did not object. Stanly said it was "a matter of great importance to the loyal people of that State, within our lines," and asked Seward if he could, to please say a word to Stanton.[96] However, either Stanton objected or Lincoln changed his mind, for Goodloe was not appointed. Nor was any further effort made to "reconstruct" the state during the war. Stanly's failure had apparently convinced the President that any such attempt would be futile.

Unfortunately for the fulfillment of his peace hopes, Stanly's administration in North Carolina coincided in time with the high noon of Confederate military success. In the West, the Union advance begun auspiciously by General Ulysses S. Grant at Forts Henry and Donelson in February, 1862, slowed and then halted, and the Confederates rallied to invade Kentucky. In the East, Robert E. Lee and the Army of Northern Virginia drove McClellan away from Richmond in the Seven Days battle, defeated General John Pope in the second battle of Bull Run, and invaded Maryland. Forced to withdraw south of the Potomac River after the bloody battle of Antietam, Lee dealt hammer blows to the Union army at Fredericksburg and Chancellorsville, Virginia, and then invaded Pennsylvania in June, 1863. Few North Carolinians, particularly in the eastern counties, were willing to renew openly their allegiance to the old flag when the issue of the war was in doubt. Stanly left New Bern in March, 1863, before any decisive upswing in Union fortunes influenced public opinion in the state.

12

AN INVETERATE OLD LINE WHIG

IN JULY, 1863, the fall of Vicksburg to Grant after a lengthy siege and Lee's defeat at Gettysburg gave a tremendous lift to the peace movement in North Carolina. Within eight weeks, over a hundred peace meetings were held in the state at which either a white or United States flag was raised, speeches were made, and resolutions were passed, usually calling for a state convention to negotiate peace on the basis of the old Constitution.[1] In Surry County, a meeting openly endorsed reunion by resolving that "under the present circumstances, the best thing the people of North Carolina could do would be to go in for the 'Constitution as it is, and the Union as it was.'"[2] Two secret societies of "root-and-branch Unionists," the Peace Society and the Heroes of America, were organized to work for the Confederacy's defeat. Armed bands of Unionists, deserters, and draft dodgers denied the western North Carolina mountain counties to the Confederacy.[3] William W. Holden, editor of the Raleigh *North Carolina Standard*, organizer of the Conservative Party, and one of the ablest politicians in the state, was cautiously for peace and reunion. "Peace: When shall we have peace?" he cried in July, 1863, quoting with approval from the Raleigh *Progress*: "We favor peace because we believe that peace now would save slavery, while we very much fear that a prolongation of the war will obliterate the last vestige of it."[4] Stanly had given the same warning a year earlier; but, a prophet without honor in his own country, his words had gone unheeded. Jonathan Worth, an original Unionist, who had declared in December, 1861, that the state would "fight to extermination" before reuniting with the North,[5] had decided by February, 1864, that a "Union on the old basis" would be better for both sections than separate independence; and he was sure this was the opinion of a majority of the people in the state.[6] Governor Vance wrote Jefferson Davis that the discontent in North Carolina could only be removed by an attempt to negotiate with the enemy. Davis replied that the Washington authorities would not negotiate and urged greater firmness on Vance's part.[7]

Reports of the peace meetings reached the North and led to a belief there that North Carolina was about to withdraw from the Confederacy. "Very encouraging accounts from No: Car:" also came to Stanly's ears in California. "If she could have a fair expression of the wishes of her people, she would separate from the Confederacy," he wrote Secretary of the Treasury Salmon P. Chase in September, 1863. "Already, leading men are openly advocating a cessation of hostilities, & negotiation for an 'honorable peace.' Would to God something could be done to give the always loyal men there a chance to be heard without danger of death or imprisonment. Can no inducements be held out to them?" If anything conciliatory could be offered, he would gladly make the effort to begin negotiations, although he could not go as a United States officer, sought no office, and wanted no compensation.[8] In a December letter to Seward, he remarked that if the Administration would say to North Carolina, "Let the prodigal son return"—then "we shall have well founded hopes of peace"; otherwise, the war must continue for years.[9]

On January 27, 1864, Stanly wired the President that he had received the following telegraph message from a loyal, well-informed man: "New Berne, January 19, 1864. (Via New York, 25th.) Important movements on foot in interior. Your friends want you to come here. C. B. Dabble." Said Stanly: "When the country needs my services, not as Governor, I am ready to come."[10] Lincoln replied that he had rumors similar to the New Bern dispatch, but nothing specific. Knowing Stanly to be an able man, and not doubting his patriotism, he expressed a willingness to see him "with his old acquaintances South of Virginia"; but was unable to suggest anything definite on the subject.[11]

This tactful refusal of Stanly's services meant he would not be sent on a second "mission of love" to his native state; nor would a new effort to negotiate a peace have been more successful than before. In the summer of 1864, Governor Vance decisively defeated Holden, the peace candidate for governor, 58,065 to 14,471 after pledging, if reelected, to continue the struggle until independence was won. Only two counties returned small Holden majorities—Randolph and Johnston. The hope that North Carolina might hold a convention, withdraw from the Confederacy, and make a separate peace was totally dispelled. Vance said privately that the recent election had contradicted reports of much disaffection in the state. "My Competitor a bold and popular demagogue made the issue distinctly of peace on terms less than independence and I have beaten him worse than any man was ever beaten in North Carolina."[12]

Stanly's increasing dissatisfaction with the Administration's policies on slavery and the conduct of the war led him reluctantly to support the Democratic candidate for president in 1864, General George B. McClellan; he acted upon impulse and without the advice of any other old line Whig. "The thought of supporting a democrat for the Presidency was revolting to me," he later admitted, "but . . . I could not do otherwise."[13] The Democrats, meeting in Chicago in August, 1864, nominated McClellan to please the war Democrats, while the drafting of the platform was assigned to the peace faction headed by the notorious Copperhead, Clement L. Vallandigham of Ohio. The key plank in the platform spoke of "four years of failure" to restore the Union by war, called for cessation of hostilities, and an ultimate convention of all the states, or other peaceable means, to restore peace at the earliest practicable moment on the basis of the "Federal Union of the States."

Embarrassed by this peace plank, McClellan laid the strongest emphasis on the Union in his acceptance letter: "The re-establishment of the Union in all its integrity is, and must continue to be, the indispensable condition of any settlement." However, his personal predilections were no guarantee that the war would be pressed until the Union was restored. As president, he would be dependent upon a Congress and state authorities whose support for a continuation of the war seemed doubtful at best.[14]

Stanly played a modest role in the McClellan campaign in California. In a public letter to General David D. Colton, chairman of the McClellan Central Union Club of San Francisco, he declared that the same reasons which had induced him voluntarily to resign as military governor now compelled him to support that candidate whose doctrines would lead to peace, and to the country's salvation. McClellan had announced that any state might return to her allegiance, by laying down her arms, with possession of all her constitutional rights. Stanly had maintained this for years. He had believed in 1862, and believed now, that with proper conciliation, had not the Emancipation Proclamation of January 1, 1863, been issued, North Carolina would have called a convention and taken steps to cancel her secession ordinance, and to return to her allegiance to the General Government. But the Proclamation had brought a great and decided change in public opinion. "It seemed as if 'Hope for a season, bade the world farewell.' While good men mourned, secessionists in rebellion and devils in hell rejoiced, and war was accepted as the least of threatened evils." With the kindest feelings towards Lincoln and his Cabinet, he thought a war waged on the terms of the Proclamation, and with a refusal to negotiate for peace except upon submission to immediate uncompensated emancipation, would last fifty years. Even if Richmond was taken, Lee's army captured, and Charleston reduced to a pile of ashes, the "war is but begun." As now conducted, it would not be ended unless the North was determined to exterminate the Southern people. "The youngest man now living would not be in existence when that war ended."[15]

The Republican San Francisco *Bulletin*, in printing this letter, declared sarcastically that the "Democracy have captured the Hon. Edward Stanly" and defied the most careful reader of his letter to say whether he was a war or peace Democrat. He had swallowed the Democratic platform in its entirety, and McClellan's incongruous letter on top of it, and from the mass had digested a letter for publication full of the inconsistencies and incompatibilities of both. Any administration trying in good faith to follow the path he had marked would move in a circle and make as much progress "as a well-conditioned weathercock on a town-house steeple."[16]

Stanly immediately published a card in the *Bulletin* to prevent the paper's readers from being misled as to his position. He denied that he was a Democrat, or that he had "swallowed" the party's platform. He had paid no attention to it, disapproved of a portion, and regarded McClellan as the candidate representing his opinions expressed several years before. Stanly added that he was not a platform man. "They are ridiculous contrivances to procure the support of a weak-minded people, and generally fall into contempt before the election is over."[17] However, the *Bulletin* retorted sharply that a vote for McClellan was a vote for an armistice, a convention, and ultimate dissolution, "and no sophistry can make anything else of it."[18]

On October 29, Stanly spoke in McClellan's behalf at a rowdy Democratic mass meeting in Union Hall, San Francisco. He began by vigorously attacking General Irvin McDowell, commander of the Department of the Pacific, who had criticized McClellan in a recent speech. McDowell's motives, he declared, were "malignant," his attack "dastardly," his speech "insolent & full of misrepresentations." He taunted McDowell with his defeat at Bull Run in July, 1861, hinting strongly that this was his real motive for lashing out at McClellan, who had rallied the demoralized Union army after the battle. North Carolina, he said, wanted to return to the Union, but could not, and would not, so long as the Emancipation Proclamation stood. He denounced the pillaging by the Union soldiers in the state and warned that her citizens would fight a hundred years rather than submit to such men. Still, Stanly was too good a patriot to advocate defiance of the Lincoln administration. He concluded by advising his listeners "to stand by the Government in every event."[19]

Upon reflection, Stanly thought his Union Hall speech had been "too Southern, too much in the style & temper of my boyish days of 1837–& 1840." But he could not help it, as he explained to his old friend, Robert Winthrop of Massachusetts. "Genl McDowell had violated all propriety, in making stump speeches & dealing in falsehood & calumny, & I thought it right to attack him, and did it. I was in some danger, but that rather provoked me, and caused me to speak more freely."[20]

Until September, 1864, with Grant stalled before Richmond, and William T. Sherman not yet in Atlanta, events seemed to presage a Democratic victory. Some Republican editors spoke of discarding Lincoln for some other candidate. Horace Greeley of the New York *Tribune* warned the President on July 7 that a widespread conviction among the people that the government and its prominent supporters were not anxious for peace "is doing great harm now, and is morally certain, unless removed, to do far greater in the approaching election." Radical Republicans, led by B. Gratz Brown and Wendell Phillips, dissatisfied with Lincoln's conduct of the war, had met in Cleveland, Ohio, on May 31, 1864, and nominated General John C. Frémont for President, thus threatening to divide the Union vote.[21] Even Lincoln thought he would probably fail of reelection. At an August Cabinet meeting he asked the secretaries to endorse unopened a document he had prepared. After the election, he read it to them: "This morning," it said, "as for some days past, it seems exceeding probable that this Administration will not be re-elected Then it will be my duty to co-operate with the President-elect, as to save the Union between the election and the inauguration; as he will have secured his election on such ground that he cannot possibly save it afterwards."[22]

Union successes saved the Administration. Admiral David Farragut's victory at Mobile Bay in August, followed by Sherman's capture of Atlanta on September 2, and General Phil Sheridan's victories in the Shenandoah Valley in September and October, lifted northern hearts and gave the lie to the Democratic cry that the war was a failure. Frémont withdrew from the campaign in favor of Lincoln on September 22; and Radical Republicans, appeased by the retirement of Montgomery Blair from the Cabinet, closed ranks behind the President. On election day, Lincoln carried every Union state except Kentucky, Delaware, and New Jersey, an electoral victory of 212 to 21, and had a popular majority of 400,000 votes. In California, where Republicans made Lincoln's reelection a final test of the state's loyalty to the Union, he had a solid majority of 18,302 or 59.2 percent of the total votes cast.[23] But McClellan's large vote in New York, Pennsylvania, Ohio, Indiana, and Illinois, indicated what might have happened had the Union armies and navy failed to win important victories before the election. Had McClellan won, the South, weary unto death, might have been encouraged to carry on the war with renewed vigor.

Stanly placed much of the blame for McClellan's defeat not on Union victories but upon the Democratic platform. He wrote Winthrop after the election that if George Hillard's "most interesting and able" life of the General had been published six months earlier, "& had been allowed to be circulated, it would have elected him in spite of the foolish platform, which I unite with you in condemning." Still, he found some consolation in Lincoln's recent recall of General Benjamin F. Butler, a notorious Radical politician, from his command in Virginia. ("I felt like going to church and singing a Te Deum.") It gave him hope that the President would put aside the Falstaffs who had led him astray for four years, and that if the war must continue, the North would have "Military gentlemen" to conduct it, "& not politican [*sic*] civilians, who have always been brutes in the estimation of gentlemen."[24]

Stanly carried on his own private war in these months with his old antagonist, Senator Charles Sumner. In October, 1863, Sumner published an anonymous article in the *Atlantic Monthly* attacking Lincoln's appointment of military governors in the South as a step toward one-man power in Washington. The President had adopted a "Cromwellian policy," the prototype of which could be found in Oliver Cromwell's appointment of eleven major generals to supervise the eleven districts into which he had divided the realm. Noting that these generals or "bashaws" had acted arbitrarily, and, in the words of one Royalist, with "unheard-of-insolence in their several precincts," Sumner declared that the conduct of at least one of Lincoln's military magistrates seemed to have been a counterpart to that of Cromwell's bashaws: "and there is no argument against that early military despotism which may not be urged against any attempt to revive it in our day. Some of the acts of Governor Stanly in North Carolina are in themselves an argument against the whole system."[25]

Stanly, who had returned to San Francisco, understandably took offense at these remarks. Learning from the publishers, Ticknor & Fields, that Sumner was the author, he asked the senator to specify "'some of the acts' which you think deserve the condemnation you have given them."[26] Sumner replied after a lengthy delay that he had intended nothing personal by the brief allusion to Stanly, the remarks in question being simply for illustration. However, a pamphlet recently published in New York by Vincent Colyer—*"Brief Report of the Services Rendered by the Freed People"*—contained an enumeration of the acts referred to in the *Atlantic Monthly* article.[27] As listed by Colyer, these included the closing of the Negro schools at New Bern, Nicholas Bray's capture of his fugitive slave with Stanly's approval, the Governor's prohibition against taking slaves north, the expulsion of Helper, and "the promise to Mr. Perry, of $1,000 for the man Sam Williams, whom I had taken North with me; the demand upon General Burnside for that amount, because I had not returned Sam."[28]

After trying unsuccessfully to locate a copy of Colyer's pamphlet in San Francisco, Stanly came east in the winter of 1864-1865, to look after a California case before the Supreme Court, and to prepare for a year's absence in Europe, and with some difficulty found a copy in New York. He was thoroughly irritated by the charge of military despotism set forth in Sumner's article and documented by Colyer in his pamphlet. "I think I shall publish something in answer to these repeated assaults," he wrote Winthrop from New York. "Oh! for one hour, in Committee of the whole in the House of Reps! I would teach some persons, that when they assailed me, falsely, there would be 'blows to receive' as well as to give." The target of constant abuse in relation to his conduct as military governor, he was particularly hurt by hostility in Massachusetts. How often in Congress he had defended the state and her representatives, thereby incurring the "deadly hostility" of southern men! He recalled that "with most of the So: Ca: members, on account of my often expressed hatred of the treason of secession, & the absurdity of their State-rights, I had no social intercourse whatever: the aversion was mutual & so strong as sometimes, in the days of my wicked folly, to threaten a resort to the 'code of honor.'" And now, because he followed the teachings of Washington, Clay, and Webster, he was held up by cowardly, thieving abolitionists as a traitor! Well, his patience was nearly exhausted. "I

have tried to 'beware of entrance into a quarrel' but feel inclined
now to bear it, that my enemies may 'beware' of me."[29]

In February, 1865, Stanly struck back at his abolitionist critics,
publishing a pamphlet in New York entitled *A Military Governor
Among Abolitionists. A Letter from Edward Stanly to Charles
Sumner*. A biting refutation of attacks upon his conduct as military
governor, the pamphlet was directed mainly at Sumner and Colyer,
and included a written denial from General Burnside that Stanly had
ever demanded payment for Perry's slave; "nor," said Burnside, "did
I hear you promise payment to any one for slaves." Helper had been
sent off with Burnside's entire approval. The General added that his
personal intercourse with Stanly had been of a most friendly nature,
while their official relations had been marked by a cordial disposition on Stanly's part to cooperate with and assist him on all
occasions.[30]

Although excoriating both Sumner and Colyer, Stanly reserved
his most caustic comments for the depredations of the Union army
in North Carolina. Burnside, Foster, and other West Pointers had
never tarnished their fame by stealing or "trophy-finding"; but it
had been impossible for them to watch the enemy and the morals of
abolition officers at the same time. If the war in North Carolina had
been conducted by soldiers who were Christians and gentlemen, the
state would have long since rebelled against the rebellion. Instead
thousands and thousands of dollars of property—libraries, pianos,
carpets, mirrors, and family portraits—had been "conveyed north"
by abolitionist soldiers; and even family burial vaults had been
violated in the search for spoils. Stanly knew of one instance in
which a vault had been entered, a metallic coffin removed, and the
remains cast out, so that a dead Union soldier might be put in their
place. Against these brutal and beastly barbarities, who had ever
heard the voices of Sumner and Colyer raised? "'Bloodhounds,
Miscegenation, Liberty, Justice, and Civilization; give every negro-
child a spelling book and one of Colyer's illustrated reports,' would
be the song of these philantropists. 'That's in our line.'"[31]

Stanly had predicted that a war fought on the basis of the
Emancipation Proclamation would last fifty years or more; but
Confederate resistance steadily weakened in the winter of 1864-1865

as Union armies marched through the South. The fall of Richmond on April 2, 1865, followed by the surrender of Lee to Grant at Appomattox Courthouse on April 9, and that of Joe Johnston to Sherman in North Carolina, ended the war. Other Confederate forces followed their example. Hopes for a speedy reconciliation of the two sections suffered a crushing blow with Lincoln's assassination on April 14, 1865. The President's murder, in which the Davis government was mistakenly thought to be implicated, convinced many moderate Northerners that the South must be severely punished for its "sins."

Vice-President Andrew Johnson took office as the seventeenth President of the United States a few hours after Lincoln's death on April 15. Like Lincoln of humble origin, he possessed many of his predecessor's virtues, but lacked the martyred President's skill in handling men. Lincoln had always worked within the party harness, first as a Whig and then as a Republican, while Johnson was a political lone wolf. One biographer has written that the "only role whose attributes he fully understood was that of the maverick, operating on the fringe of things."[32] He played into the hands of his enemies by replying to unjust abuse with imprudent and tactless language.

Johnson's formal reconstruction plan rested fundamentally on Lincoln's war-time plan, although it incorporated certain features of the Radical Wade-Davis bill of 1864. On May 29, 1865, he granted amnesty to Confederates willing to take an oath of future allegiance, excepting certain classes (among them holders of taxable property exceeding $20,000) who could petition for special pardons. These he granted liberally. Johnson recognized the Lincoln governments in Tennessee, Virginia, Arkansas, and Louisiana, and appointed provisional governors for the other seven Confederate states, which would receive executive recognition and be readmitted to Congress when they had repudiated their war debts, abolished slavery, disavowed their ordinances of secession, and ratified the Thirteenth Amendment.

Significantly, Johnson, an orthodox state rights Democrat, left to the seceded states the task of defining the qualifications for voting and office-holding, since this was a power the states had "rightfully

exercised" from the origin of the Government. However, he privately suggested that a few substantial and intelligent Negroes be
given the ballot to disarm the Radicals. "I hope and trust," he wrote
Provisional Governor William Sharkey of Mississippi, "you consent
to grant a qualified suffrage, and as a consequence, the Radicals,
who are wild upon negro suffrage, will be completely foiled in their
attempt to keep the southern states from renewing their relation to
the Union by not accepting their senators and representatives."[33]
This well-intentioned advice was ignored by Mississippi and the other
southern states; and Johnson, true to his constitutional view of the
state's authority in suffrage matters, unwisely did not insist upon it.

When Congress met in December, 1865, all the seceded states
except Texas had largely complied with Johnson's minimal terms,
although sometimes grudgingly, and had sent representatives to
Washington to claim their House and Senate seats. But congressional
Republicans wanted some evidence of repentance, civil rights for the
Negro under federal protection, and the assurance that their own
control of the government would not be shaken by a postwar
coalition of northern and southern Democrats. They refused to seat
the southern representatives until a joint committee of fifteen from
both Houses had investigated the situation in the South and made its
report. Meanwhile, to protect the southern Negroes, who were being
subjected to rigorous "Black Codes" by the Johnson governments,
Congress sought to extend indefinitely the life of the Freedmen's
Bureau, a war-time relief agency, and to empower it to try by
military commission persons accused of depriving Negroes of their
civil rights. Johnson vetoed the bill on the grounds that Congress had
no power to legislate for the South while the former Confederate
states were unrepresented, and that the provision for military trials
in peace time violated the Fifth Amendment's procedural guarantees. An attempt by the Radicals to override this veto failed
narrowly in the Senate.

On April 9, 1866, Congress passed the Civil Rights Act, which
gave the Negro citizenship and granted him equality in civil rights
with white citizens. Johnson, against the advice of his Cabinet, also
vetoed this bill on constitutional grounds; but Congress passed it
over his veto, and went on to enact a new Freedmen's Bureau bill

over a second veto. The President's stubborn refusal to accept these two measures alienated many Republican moderates, and helped the Radicals to consolidate their control over the Republican Party.

The congressional substitute for the President's plan was embodied in the Fourteenth Amendment, passed on June 14, and sent to the states for ratification. The first section defined national citizenship to include Negroes and tried to insure that they would enjoy the same civil rights and equal protection of the laws as other citizens. The second section abrogated the 3/5's clause of the Constitution, the so-called "Federal Ratio," whereby five Negroes were counted as three whites in apportioning representation and direct taxes, but provided for proportionate reduction in representation when a state denied suffrage "except for participation in rebellion or other crime." The southern states would be forced to either enfranchise the Negro, thus establishing the Republican Party in the South, or suffer a reduction in representation in the House and electoral college that would insure Republican ascendency. Other sections of the amendment guaranteed the federal debt and repudiated the Confederate debt; and excluded certain classes of former Confederates from office until this disability was removed by two-thirds vote of both houses of Congress. Tennessee, under Radical control, quickly ratified the amendment; and her representatives were readmitted to Congress on July 24, 1866. The other southern states, with Johnson's encouragement, rejected the amendment, confident the northern people would repudiate the Radicals in the fall congressional elections.[34]

Stanly had been in Europe during this period and did not return to San Francisco until June, 1866. On his arrival in the United States, he read the newspapers to discover what the Administration had been doing. His sympathies were immediately enlisted with Johnson in the continuing struggle with the Republican majority in Congress, and he hurried to assure the President of his support. "President Johnson's conduct has excited my highest admiration & gratitude," he informed Seward, who had continued as Secretary of State:

> The people must & will sustain him. If his advice is taken we shall have peace; if the radical policy is pursued, we shall have

terrible trouble in less than five years. The issue then will not
be as it was—but those who sustain the President North &
South will be fighting for the Union.[35]

Seward replied in a brief, courteous note that Stanly's "complimentary approval of the proceedings of the President" had induced
the Secretary to show his letter to Johnson.[36]

Stanly thought Seward's own support of Johnson had been "most
noble, suitable and patriotic."[37] He asked Thurlow Weed if there
was any reasonable hope that Seward could be made President; and,
if so, when steps should be taken to bring about "that 'consumation,
so devoutly to be wished.' " He could not help but wonder at the
strange mutations in the world which had made Seward more
popular in the South than any northern man, "And I, an inveterate
old line Whig, as earnest a supporter of the old democrat, Andrew
Johnson, as there is in the Country!"[38]

Both the Radicals and friends of Johnson recognized the crucial
significance of the approaching congressional elections. If the Republicans retained control of Congress, Johnson's plan would be
finished; if the President's supporters won, or increased their
numbers sufficiently to prevent the overriding of his vetoes, then
Johnson could still triumph. A stumbling effort was made to unite
Democrats, old line Whigs, and moderate Republicans behind the
President and his program by a bipartisan movement which centered
in the National Union convention at Philadelphia in August, 1866.
Among the supporters of the convention were such eminent Northerners as Senator James Doolittle of Wisconsin, General John A. Dix,
O. H. Browning, and Henry J. Raymond, congressman and editor of
the New York *Times*; and in the South, Alexander H. Stephens of
Georgia and Governor James Orr of South Carolina. The movement
had Johnson's open approval and its object was to elect a Congress
that would uphold his policies against the Radicals.[39]

The President's friends in California met in a state convention in
San Francisco on August 3, 1866, and elected a ten-man delegation
to represent them at the National Union convention. The convention
resolutions praised Johnson and his Cabinet as "sterling patriots and
wise and comprehensive statesmen," approved Johnson's reconstruction policy, and recognized the right of the southern states to be

represented in Congress by loyal men who were qualified by existing laws of the United States to serve. Stanly was one of six men selected as a state central committee to coordinate the Johnson campaign in California. On September 26, the committee issued an address to the state's voters, urging the formation of Johnson clubs, and the appointment of county committees, so that the President's policy could be vigorously supported.[40] But the fatal weakness of this bipartisan movement, in California as elsewhere, was that the Democrats, numerically the strongest element, had been discredited by their lukewarm support of the war; and the requisite public support was not forthcoming. Nor could the California Democrats be weaned from obsolete state rights orthodoxies. Bret Harte, a special correspondent of the Springfield *Republican*, reported from San Francisco on September 9, 1866, that the "democracy here are terribly old-fogyish and at least six-years behind the age."[41]

Johnson took his case to the people in a "swing around the circle" to Chicago and back again to Washington, begun August 28, which did his cause more harm than good. His careless and irresponsible harangues and undignified exchanges with hecklers planted by the Radicals were embarrassing to his friends and revolting to his critics. Senator John Sherman of Ohio complained that Johnson had "sunk the Presidency to the level of the grog-house." Race riots in Memphis and New Orleans, in which Negroes were hunted like animals and killed without mercy, further injured the President's cause. The Fourteenth Amendment seemed more and more indispensable to the establishment of a just and lasting peace in the South.

The election resulted in an overwhelming victory for the Radicals. The next Congress would contain 42 Republicans and 11 Democrats in the Senate and 143 Republicans and only 49 Democrats in the House. The question of who would define and control Reconstruction had been decisively answered in favor of the Radicals. In March, 1867, the newly elected Congress divided the ten unreconstructed southern states into five military districts under a general of the army and decreed that no state could return to civilian rule until its voters, both white and colored, framed a constitution that guaranteed Negro suffrage and was acceptable to Congress and the people

of the state. Each state legislature must also ratify the Fourteenth
Amendment. Under this First Reconstruction Act, and later supple-
mentary acts, control of the ten southern states passed into the
hands of a triumvirate of Negroes and their white allies, the
"Carpetbaggers" and "Scalawags," whose regimes aroused bitter and
not altogether deserved resentment among southern whites.

Johnson served out his term, escaping removal from office by a
single vote in 1868, but isolated and largely ineffectual. Distance
added to the difficulties of his supporters on the West Coast in
opposing the Radical program. Stanly complained to Senator Reverdy Johnson of Maryland that the President's California friends
were so far off and had been so unsuccessful in their attempts to
hear from Washington, that they were doing nothing and could do
nothing. All the government patronage, with very few exceptions,
was against them, with Radicals holding the lucrative and influential
positions. The Democrats seemed to be paralyzed and more solicitous to preserve their party organization than to allow others to aid
them in saving the country from anarchy. "They do not heed the
advice of an old Whig like myself," Stanly lamented:

> But for the fear of doing harm & being regarded as Quixotic, I
> should, solitary & alone, if need be, have been making
> speeches, in defence of the President's policy. My fears of the
> future, & my anxiety to save suffering, in greater degree, if
> possible, than that now endured by the Southern people,
> tempt me sometimes to lay aside all considerations, of what
> the democrats wish & try to act independent of them. But I do
> not see how we can hope to succeed, without the cooperation
> of that party.

He predicted gloomily that "We [will] have terrible times in the
future, if Congress continues to treat the Constitution with contempt."[42]

Stanly maintained a close interest in the affairs of his native state
and felt "great anxiety" because of conditions there. Writing William
A. Graham in November, 1866, he declared that he wanted to see
her represented in Congress, but could not see how her people could
be expected to disfranchise "so many good and excellent patriots, as
is expected by one of the proposed constitutional amendments."

Would it not be better for the state voluntarily to allow Negroes to vote who could read and write, and had a fixed amount of property? They always voted with the best portion of society; and had a natural ambition to be with gentlemen. Could they ever do worse than to elect such men as "Beast Butler" and the "prize fighting gambler Morrissey" to office?[43] This was sensible advice, but it was ignored, and North Carolina also passed under Radical control.

In California, the politics of the state were settling back into their pre-war footing. The dominant Union Party was divided into two hostile factions; one, made up chiefly of war Democrats, was known as the "short-hair" party; the other, the "long-hair," was composed of old line Republicans. In 1867, the short-hair faction nominated a notorious railroad lobbyist, George C. Gorham, for governor. Crying corruption, the regular Republicans selected Caleb T. Fay as their candidate with the intention of insuring Gorham's defeat. The California Democrats, with victory in sight for the first time since 1860, nominated Henry H. Haight, a respected San Francisco lawyer, for governor. Both Union factions endorsed Radical Reconstruction, while the Democrats denounced it as "harsh, illiberal, and oppressive," and more likely to result in a "hollow truce than enduring peace."[44]

The three parties vigorously prosecuted the campaign, called by historian Hubert Howe Bancroft, "the most bitter and exciting of the many . . . witnessed by this politician-ridden state."[45] The long-hair press generally ignored the Democrats and kept up a hot fire on Gorham and the short-hair party. The Sacramento *Union* declared that he and his friends had followed the Union Party "like the camp followers of any army, with a greedy eye for loot." Stanly, after failing to win the Democratic nomination for Congress in the First District, took the stump in behalf of Haight's candidacy and against Gorham.[46] Speaking at Platt's Hall, San Francisco, on August 7, he defined Gorham's public character as uniformly black—"black in speech, black in principle, black all over." He urged the voters to go the polls and drive this "prince of lobbyists" and his "Short-hair Arabs" to the dens where they properly belonged. Turning to Reconstruction, he opposed Negro suffrage, except in cases of intelligent, property-owning Negroes, and argued the inferiority of the Negro when left uncontrolled.[47] Stanly repeated the substance of these remarks at Sacramento on August 17, 1867.[48]

The state election was held on September 4; and with most of the old line Republicans voting for Haight, the Union party suffered its first defeat since the beginning of the war. The entire Democratic state ticket was elected, and the party captured two of the three house seats. Haight received 49,905 votes to Gorham's 40,359, and Fay's 2,088.[49] This victory, followed by Radical setbacks in Ohio and Pennsylvania, led Stanly to hope "that the radicals & abolitionists will soon cease to rule our much afflicted country."[50]

To speed the hour of deliverance, Stanly campaigned actively in the presidential election of 1868 in support of the Democratic ticket of Horatio Seymour and Frank Blair, and against the Republican candidates, the popular Ulysses S. Grant and Schuyler Colfax. He denied being a party man, however, and said he was neither a Republican nor a Democrat, but one of the "old line Whigs." In his speeches, Stanly frequently quoted from Lincoln's works to support his contention that Negroes were inferior to white men and that the states and not the federal government should be responsible for their welfare. Speaking in the hall of the Mercantile Library in San Francisco, he declared that the reconstruction measures had been adopted to humiliate the white South and to elevate the Negroes. While 200,000 Negroes could vote in the South, in the North they were refused the ballot.[51]

In a letter to the Sacramento *Daily Union*, Stanly said once more that he did not object to intelligent and property owning Negroes being given the suffrage, but claimed the right to object because Congress had done it in gross violation of the Constitution. "In this respect," he declared, "I stand on the Lincoln platform, which you and the radical Congress have kicked scornfully from under your feet." Stanly charged that the Radicals did not dare at present to admit they were in favor of social equality, which must necessarily follow the political equality which they advocated. Said he:

> If a negro man is elected to the Senate of the United States—which Charles Sumner is in favor of—and takes his seat by the side of that Senator, must not the negro's wife be allowed to sit in the galleries in the place appropriated for the

wives of Senators, side by side, with the wives of white Senators? And if this equality is brought about by the radicals, what forbids 'social intercourse?' What forbids the negro Senator's son from aspiring to be the husband of a white man's daughter?[52]

Miscegenation—here was the specter that troubled the white South's dreams. In reply to Stanly's tortuous logic, the Sacramento *Union* denied that Negro citizenship and suffrage would lead to Negro social equality since social equality depended upon essentially different things. When Stanly pictured so graphically the social consternation to arise at Washington from the arrival of a colored Senator's wife, he revealed himself the very radical antipathies which would prevent any "*social mesalliances*." Moreover, any danger of social admixture in the future seemed more likely to come from the Democratic Party. The possession of the ballot by the Negroes would attract toward them a Democratic ardor of affection which could only be measured by that party's present fervor of animosity. It rested, then, with the Democrats themselves whether they would mix or not. "If it is his want of confidence in his present companions which raises these nightmare visions in Stanly's brain, let him talk to them, not to us. It is not our Desdemona."[53]

The Sacramento *Union* claimed to be an independent paper, and its reply was mild as compared with the reaction of the avowedly Republican press in California. One Radical journal, in language reminiscent of the San Francisco *Herald* in 1857, called Stanly a "superannuated political charlatan" who did not know what party he belonged to or where to go: "He is like one of old, of whom it is said his hand was against every man's hand, and every man's hand was against his hand. He can be summed up in these words—he is a perfect old conceited bilk." A Democratic paper in Sacramento, replying to this "contemptible attack," observed that Stanly did not claim to be a Democrat; but stood by Lincoln's teachings and policy on reconstruction and Negro equality, and had shown conclusively that the radical party had repudiated the advice and principles of the "Martyr President." "The deadly blows he is dealing the monster of radicalism cause the little minds of Nasby journalism to spit their venom at Edward Stanley [*sic*], but his reputation is such that he can laugh to scorn their puny efforts."[54]

Nationally, the Republican campaign involved much "waving of the bloody shirt," as blaming the South for the war was called, and denunciation of the Democratic Party for its "treasonous" conduct during the war. With so many southern states under Radical control, Grant won an easy victory in the electoral college, with 214 votes to 81 for Seymour, although his margin of victory in many northern states was surprisingly narrow. His popular majority of about 300,000 was made possible only because of some 450,000 Negro ballots; "a majority of the white men of the country favored the Democratic party in 1868."[55] In California, the Republicans re-gained enough ground after their 1867 debacle to give the state to Grant by a bare 506 vote majority.[56] Writing to California's Republican senator, Cornelius Cole, a few weeks after the election, Stanly asked if his party would now "'have peace'?" as Grant had urged during the campaign. "'A soft answer turneth away wrath,' from an individual and from a people. Try now the policy of kindness." Cole, and men like him, ought not to be following extreme men or measures. Stanly did not believe that Grant could follow radical counsels (he was mistaken), and promised the new president a fair trial and a liberal support. Perhaps he could act with Cole, Seward, and Weed in the next presidential election. "I shall hope it may be so."[57]

After 1862, when he went to North Carolina as military governor, Stanly, by his own statement, "paid very little attention to law."[58] In 1866, his nephew John A. Stanly, the son of Alexander Stanly, came to San Francisco from North Carolina with his family, and became a junior partner in the law firm of Stanly, Hayes & Stanly. Edward Stanly retired from the firm in 1868 and went to live on his 1,500 acre ranch in Napa County, just west of the village of St. Helena, in the center of the vineyard district. The Napa Valley railroad ran from Calistoga in the upper part of the county through St. Helena, Oakville, Yountville, and Napa City to Vallejo, and connected at that point with steamers for San Francisco. A resident of almost any part of the county could visit San Francisco and return in twenty-four hours, while from most parts of the central valley the same journey could be made in twelve hours.[59]

Stanly entered in a modest way into the social, economic, and political life of Napa County. One of the largest landholders in the county, he was a stockholder in the Napa Valley Railroad Company and one of the original trustees of the Bank of Napa, which first opened its doors on October 2, 1871.[60] He registered as a voter in the St. Helena Precinct on September 9, 1868.[61] From time to time, he would deliver a political address to his fellow citizens. The *Napa County Reporter* of October 3, 1868, proudly announced that "Governor Edward Stanly" would speak that evening in front of the Napa Hotel in Napa City on the political issues of the day. The paper lauded him as a fine speaker—"about the best on the Pacific Coast—able and argumentative; and being one of our own citizens we trust our people will give him a cheerful welcome and an attentive ear. We wouldn't miss hearing him for considerable, as his speech is sure to be a treat."[62]

In the fall of 1869, Stanly and his wife, Cornelia, planned a brief visit to the East to see her relatives in Virginia, Alabama, and Mississippi, whom she had not seen for more than ten years. But he could not go to North Carolina. As he explained to young Thomas Roulhac: "There is too much sorrow there, which I cannot alleviate, and no duty calls me there at present. When I think of visiting my own home, and friends ever dear to me I feel as if I were going to occupy a tent pitched in a grave-yard."[63] Perhaps, too, he dreaded a hostile welcome, because of his service as Union military governor. His failure in that office still weighed heavily on his mind. "While I had the power in 1862," he wrote the widow of a North Carolina friend, "I protected all whom I could protect in person & property, in N. C.: I mourned over their suffering & did all that I could to relieve them. Would to Heaven I could have done more!"[64]

Never physically strong, Stanly suffered in 1871 from what John A. Stanly called "dyspepsia & general debility."[65] In the winter of 1871-1872, he spent some weeks in the Sandwich (Hawaiian) Islands for his health, sailing from San Francisco on November 9, 1871, on the *Moses Taylor*, for Honolulu.[66] He wrote John A. Stanly that the island climate was delightful and he thought it would be beneficial.[67] However, there was no real improvement.

Upon his return to Napa County, Stanly received two honors

from his fellow citizens. He was selected as President of the County Fourth of July celebration at St. Helena and was elected a delegate to represent the County in the Democratic state convention at San Francisco on June 19, 1872.[68] He acknowledged the latter honor in a letter to F. E. Johnson, the secretary of the Democratic Central Committee of Napa County, suggesting wryly that he might not have the wedding garment proper for the occasion since he had never been recognized as a Democrat, nor ever claimed to be one. He repeated a now familiar refrain. "I was an old line Whig, am proud of having been so, and have the comfort of believing I never did anything to cast reproach on its glorious history." Still, if the Democratic national convention at Baltimore would endorse Horace Greeley, the Liberal Republican candidate for president, the party would have his "most cordial and whole-souled support." Stanly pledged to omit nothing to aid the cause. He had known Greeley for more than thirty years, and often differed with him on public questions; but his bitterest enemies could not question the New York editor's integrity nor doubt his great ability. "I believe we can elect him if we will," Stanly concluded. "But if the Convention at Baltimore should refuse to endorse the Cincinnati nominations, the result will be a repetition of the old fable of the four bulls and the lion: they were safe, until they quarreled and separated, when they did, they were easily destroyed."[69]

The Democratic Party did endorse Greeley, to little purpose as events proved; but Stanly had waged his last political campaign; and now faced that final opponent he could not hope to "conquer." On Wednesday afternoon, July 10, 1872, while talking in the parlor of the Grand Hotel in San Francisco with a friend, Dr. Hitchcock, he was stricken with paralysis, became unconscious, and died quietly on Friday, July 12, at 9:45 in the evening.[70] His funeral was held on July 14, in Grace Church (Episcopal), where he had been Senior Warden for many years. Members of the San Francisco bar and other friends served as pallbearers. The Reverend William Ingraham Kip, Episcopal Bishop of California, and a long-time friend of the deceased, officiated and pronounced an "eloquent eulogy" on his life and character. Bishop Kip aptly observed that Stanly had been "gifted with wonderful powers in debate, and a facility of caustic repartee which few possess." He was "an antagonist on the floor of Congress whom not many cared to meet." After the services, Stanly was buried in Mountain View Cemetery, Oakland.[71]

On July 15, members of the San Francisco bar met in the Fifteenth District Court and unanimously adopted a preamble and resolution "highly eulogistic of the deceased." The chair appointed a committee to present copies in the various federal and state courts in California.[72] The city papers paid the expected warm tributes to his memory. Said the San Francisco *Daily Alta California*:

> Governor Stanly was a ready debater, an earnest advocate, his fidelity and straight forwardness gaining for him even the good opinion of his opponents. Pure in his morals, firm in his religious belief, a true friend, upright in his dealings with his fellow man, affable in his manners, he leaves behind him an unblemished reputation.[73]

Stanly had no children, and the bulk of his estate ultimately passed into the hands of John A. Stanly and his heirs, who inherited the Napa Valley estate, and the Stanly family portraits and silver.[74] Even in death, Stanly did not forget his family obligations. Included among the bequests in his will was a house and lot in New Bern, for life, to his father's faithful Negro servant and companion, Moses Kennedy.[75] Stanly's wife, Cornelia, survived him by thirty-one years, dying in San Francisco on April 13, 1903.[76]

Stanly's death ended an eventful and often turbulent political career spanning thirty-five years. Throughout that period he had clung with undiminished fervor to three abiding loyalties—North Carolina, the Whig Party and, above all else, the Federal Union. He spent the last nineteen years of his life (with brief intervals) in California, but spiritually never left North Carolina, and remained to the end a devoted son of the Old North State. Although Stanly supported Republicans and Democrats for public office on merit after the demise of the Whig Party, he never regarded himself in any other light than as an "inveterate, old line Whig." The Whig Party died in 1852, but its memory remained green in the minds and hearts of men like Stanly, north and south, who had led it in victory and ultimate defeat. Finally, the preservation of the Federal Union was always uppermost in his mind; he never wavered from the nationalist creed of Washington, Marshall, and John Stanly. "From the beginning of my public life to this day," Stanly wrote in 1865, "no man has been more constant or earnest in denouncing Secession, or Nullification, as Treason."[77] If he had failed in North Carolina as military governor to accomplish a task beyond the powers of any man, he could find some comfort in knowing that his beloved Union had been preserved and the threat of disunion forever laid to rest.

Notes

Chapter 1

1. Charles Francis Adams (ed.), *The Memoirs of John Quincy Adams, Comprising Portions of His Diary from 1795-1848*, 12 volumes (Philadelphia: J. B. Lippincott and Company, 1874-1877), XI, 19, hereinafter cited as Adams, *Memoirs*.

2. Raleigh *Star*, September 15, 1841; Adams, *Memoirs*, XI, 11; *Congressional Globe*, 27 Cong., 1 Sess. (Washington: Globe Office, 1841), X, 445.

3. Arthur Charles Cole, *The Whig Party in the South* (Washington: American Historical Association, 1913), p. 81, hereinafter cited as Cole, *Whig Party in the South*.

4. William H. Bailey, Jr., "Reminiscences of North Carolinians: Edward Stanly," unidentified newspaper clipping in North Carolina Collection, University of North Carolina at Chapel Hill, hereinafter cited as Bailey, "Edward Stanly."

5. John H. Wheeler, *Reminiscences and Memoirs of North Carolina and Eminent North Carolinians* (Columbus, Ohio: Columbus Printing Works, 1884), p. 17, hereinafter cited as Wheeler, *Reminiscences*.

6. Bailey, "Edward Stanly."

7. Daniel Reed Larned to Henry ———, May 28, 1862, Daniel Reed Larned Papers, volume II, Manuscript Division, Library of Congress, hereinafter cited as Larned Papers.

8. Joshua R. Giddings, *History of the Rebellion: Its Authors and Causes* (New York: Follet, Foster & Co., 1864), p. 306, hereinafter cited as Giddings, *History of the Rebellion*.

9. Mary B. Pettigrew to ———, January 7, 1850, John Herritage Bryan Papers, State Department of Archives and History, Raleigh,

hereinafter cited as John H. Bryan Papers.

10. John D. Whitford, "The Home Story of a Walking Stick—
Early History of the Biblical Recorder and Baptist Church at New
Bern, N. C., Told in Every Day Talk," pp. 145-146. Typed copy in
John D. Whitford Collection, State Department of Archives and
History, Raleigh, hereinafter cited as Whitford, "Home Story of a
Walking Stick."

11. Edmund Ruffin Beckwith to George S. Godard, June 9, 1933,
Edmund Ruffin Beckwith Papers, Southern Historical Collection,
University of North Carolina at Chapel Hill, hereinafter cited as
Beckwith Papers; Memorandum of the Reverend Harvey Stanley,
undated, Beckwith Papers.

12. Genealogical data on William Stanley, Beckwith Papers; Louis
Dow Scisco, "Baltimore County Records of 1665-1667," *Maryland
Historical Magazine*, XXIV (December, 1929), 344, 346.

13. Genealogical data on John Stanley, Beckwith Papers. In 1689,
John Stanley was appointed to a commission to treat with the
Indians of the Eastern Shore, and if necessary to reduce them by
force. The Nanticoke Indians had been committing depredations
along the shore of Talbot County, on the Choptank, and the Saint
Michaels and Chester rivers. Oswald Tilghman, *History of Talbot
County Maryland, 1661-1861*, 2 volumes (Baltimore: William &
Wilkes Company, 1915), I, 32.

14. He dropped the *e* from Stanley before the American Revolution.

15. William Gaston's obituary of John Stanly, signed "A," New
Bern *Spectator*, August 9, 1833, hereinafter cited as Gaston, "John
Stanly Obituary."

16. Genealogical data on John Wright Stanly, Beckwith Papers;
Edmund Ruffin Beckwith to Jamaica Historical Society, March 14,
1949, typed copy in Beckwith Papers; Unfinished manuscript biography of John Wright Stanly, Beckwith Papers; John Wright Stanly
Prayer Book, State Department of Archives and History, Raleigh.

17. William Tisdale to North Carolina Council of Safety, August
31, 1776, William L. Saunders (ed.), *The Colonial Records of North
Carolina*, 10 volumes (Raleigh: P. M. Hale, State Printer, 1886-1890),
X, 788.

18. Alonzo Thomas Dill, Jr., "Eighteenth Century New Bern—A
History of the Town and Craven County, 1700-1800, Part VII, New
Bern During the Revolution," *The North Carolina Historical Review*,
XXIII (July, 1946), 348, hereinafter cited as Dill, "Eighteenth
Century New Bern"; Walter Clark (ed.), *The State Records of North
Carolina*, 16 volumes (Winston and Goldsboro, 1895-1905), XIV,
645, 650, 748; XV, 68-69, hereinafter cited as Clark, *State Records*.

19. Undated clipping, New Bern *Journal*, Beckwith Papers; John D. Whitford, "Notes on John Wright Stanly, of New Bern, North Carolina," *Publications of the Southern History Association*, IV (November, 1900), 472, hereinafter cited as Whitford, "Notes on John Wright Stanly"; Lida Tunstall Rodman (ed.), "Journal of a Tour to North Carolina by William Attmore, 1787," *The James Sprunt Historical Publications*, XVII (Chapel Hill: University of North Carolina, 1922), p. 17, hereinafter cited as Rodman, "Attmore Journal."

20. Quoted in Dill, "Eighteenth Century New Bern," 348.

21. Rodman, "Attmore Journal," p. 17.

22. Whitford, "Notes on John Wright Stanly," 471-473.

23. John Wright Stanly to ———, February 20, 1783, Miscellaneous Papers, series I, volume I, State Department of Archives and History, Raleigh.

24. Clark, *State Records*, XVII, 311; XVIII, 114; XIX, 466; XXIV, 607, 720, 821; John D. Moore, *History of North Carolina; From the Earliest Discoveries to the Present Time*, 2 volumes (Raleigh: Alfred Williams & Co., 1880), I, 366, hereinafter cited as Moore, *History of North Carolina*; Dill, "Eighteenth Century New Bern," 349.

25. Gertrude S. Carraway, *Crown of Life. History of Christ Church New Bern, N. C. 1715-1940* (New Bern: Owen G. Dunn, Publisher, 1940), p. 98, hereinafter cited as Carraway, *Crown of Life*; Edenton *State Gazette of North-Carolina*, June 18, 1789.

26. Family Record, Births and Deaths, Beckwith Papers.

27. Gaston, "John Stanly Obituary"; Whitford, "Home Story of a Walking Stick," p. 172; Craven County, North Carolina, Marriage Bonds, 3 volumes, State Department of Archives and History, Raleigh, III, 328; Stephen F. Miller, "Recollections of Newbern Fifty Years Ago; with an Appendix, Including Letters from Judges Gaston, Donnell, Manly and Gov. Swain," *Our Living and Our Dead*, I (November, 1874), 245, hereinafter cited as Miller, "Recollections of Newbern." "Miss Elizabeth Franks has lost her Brother and by that means has doubled her fortune and become the Belle of the town. It is expected she will be married very soon to Mr. John Stanly." Jane Gaston to William Gaston, June 6, 1795, William Gaston Papers, Southern Historical Collection, University of North Carolina at Chapel, Hill hereinafter cited as Gaston Papers.

28. Whitford, "Home Story of a Walking Stick," p. 172.

29. William Henry Hoyt (ed.), *The Papers of Archibald D. Murphey*, 2 volumes (Raleigh: Publications of the North Carolina Historical Commission, 1914), II, 354, hereinafter cited as Hoyt,

Murphey Papers. Murphey made this statement in an oration delivered at the University of North Carolina, June 27, 1827.

30. Miller, "Recollections of Newbern," 244.

31. Whitford, "Home Story of a Walking Stick," pp. 169-170.

32. John Marshall to Archibald Murphey, October 6, 1827, Hoyt, *Murphey Papers,* I, 365.

33. Hamilton C. Jones to Elisha Mitchell, February 2, 1819, Kemp P. Battle (ed.), "Letter of Hamilton C. Jones, the Elder," *North Carolina University Magazine,* New Series, XII (April, 1893), 213.

34. Gaston, "John Stanly Obituary."

35. John H. Wheeler, *Historical Sketches of North Carolina from 1584 to 1851.* Two volumes in one. Second Edition (New York: Frederick H. Hitchcock, 1925), II, 122, hereinafter cited as Wheeler, *Historical Sketches;* D. H. Gilpatrick, "North Carolina Congressional Elections, 1803-1810," *The North Carolina Historical Review,* X (July, 1933), 168, hereinafter cited as Gilpatrick, "North Carolina Elections"; Raleigh *Register, And North-Carolina Weekly Advertiser,* August 26, 1800, hereinafter cited as Raleigh *Register.*

36. Richard Dobbs Spaight to John Gray Blount, March 28, 1800, Alice Barnwell Keith and William H. Masterson (eds.), *The John Gray Blount Papers,* 3 volumes (Raleigh: State Department of Archives and History, 1952-1965), III, 356.

37. *Controversy Between Gen. Richard D. Spaight and John Stanly Esq. To Which Is Annexed an Extract from a Funeral Discourse, Intended to Have Been Delivered by the Rev. Thomas P. Irving on the Death of the Former* (New Bern: Printed by John S. Pasteur, 1802), pp. 1-10, hereinafter cited as *Controversy Between Spaight and Stanly.*

38. John Stanly to ———, n.d., Stanly Correspondence, 33, Francis Lister Hawks Papers, The Church Historical Society, Austin, Texas. The Hawks papers contain original letters and drafts of the Spaight-Stanly correspondence as well as letters written after the duel by Stanly and friends relating to the matter.

39. *Controversy Between Spaight and Stanly,* pp. 10-29.

40. Wheeler, *Historical Sketches,* II, 112-114; Whitford, "Home Story of a Walking Stick," p. 154; Moore, *History of North Carolina,* I, 436-437; Wheeler, *Reminiscences,* p. 136.

41. John Stanly to John Rutledge, April 25, 1803, John Rutledge Papers, Southern Historical Collection, University of North Carolina at Chapel Hill.

42. Henry McGilbert Wagstaff, "Federalism in North Carolina," *The James Sprunt Historical Publications,* IX (Chapel Hill: University of North Carolina, 1910), p. 39; Raleigh *Register,* August 29,

1803; William R. Davie to John Steele, August 20, 1803, Henry M. Wagstaff (ed.), *The Papers of John Steele*, 2 volumes (Raleigh: Publications of the North Carolina Historical Commission, 1924), I, 405; Gilpatrick, "North Carolina Elections," 178.

43. Quoted in Blackwell P. Robinson, *William R. Davie* (Chapel Hill: University of North Carolina Press, 1957), p. 386.

44. Gilpatrick, "North Carolina Elections," 179; Samuel A. Court Ashe, *History of North Carolina*, 2 volumes (Raleigh: Edwards & Broughton, 1925), II, 213, hereinafter cited as Ashe, *History of North Carolina*; William Tatham to Thomas Jefferson, May 6, 1808, Elizabeth Gregory McPherson (ed.), "Unpublished Letters from North Carolinians to Jefferson," *The North Carolina Historical Review*, XII (October, 1935), 362-363.

45. Raleigh *Minerva*, February 28, 1811.

46. *Ibid.*, February 7, 1811.

47. New Bern *Carolina Federal Republican*, June 30, 1810, quoting New York *Evening Post*, n.d. The Raleigh *Star* is quoted in Gilpatrick, "North Carolina Elections," 174. Footnote.

48. New Bern *Carolina Federal Republican*, August 18, 1810.

49. J. A. Cameron to Duncan Cameron, August 27, 1810, quoted in Joseph Herman Schauinger, *William Gaston Carolinian* (Milwaukee: The Bruce Publishing Company, 1949), p. 58.

50. Ashe, *History of North Carolina*, II, 218; New Bern *Carolina Federal Republican*, March 8, 27, 1813.

51. John Stanly to William Gaston, August 28, 1812, Gaston Papers.

52. New Bern *Carolina Federal Republican*, November 28, December 5, 1812.

53. Tombstone, Stanly plot, Mountain View Cemetary, Oakland, California.

54. Information sheet, New Bern Library, formerly John Wright Stanly home.

55. Genealogical data in Beckwith Papers; Miller, "Recollections of Newbern," 244-245; Thomas Marshall Spalding, "Lewis Addison Armistead," *Dictionary of American Biography*, 22 volumes and index. Edited by Allen Johnson, Dumas Malone, and others (New York: Charles Scribner's Sons, 1928-), I, 347, hereinafter cited as *DAB*. In 1920, John P. Green, a Negro attorney in Cleveland, Ohio, published an autobiography in which he claimed that his father, John Rice Green, was a "natural" son of John Stanly and a Negro slave, Sarah Rice. According to Green, John Stanly on his death bed handed John R. Green a steel engraved likeness of himself with acknowledgment of his paternity. John P. Green, *Fact Stranger Than Fiction. Seventy-Five Years of a Busy Life with Reminiscences of*

Many Great and Good Men and Women. (Cleveland, Ohio: Riehl Printing Company, 1920), pp. 3-4.

56. Miller, "Recollections of Newbern," 245.

57. Whitford, "Home Story of a Walking Stick," pp. 137-138; Moore, *History of North Carolina*, II, 22; Miller, "Recollections of Newbern," 454. In a 1813 circular, John Stanly speaks of his brother Richard "who has been five years in his grave!" New Bern *Carolina Federal Republican*, July 17, 1813.

58. Archibald Murphey to Thomas Ruffin, November 24, 1814, Hoyt, *Murphey Papers*, I, 76.

59. John Stanly to William Gaston, November 11, 1814, Gaston Papers.

60. Delbert H. Gilpatrick, *Jeffersonian Democracy in North Carolina, 1789-1816* (New York: Columbia University Press, 1931), pp. 215-216, 225-226; Raleigh *Minerva*, December 30, 1814; Whitford, "Home Story of a Walking Stick," p. 173.

61. Duncan Cameron to Archibald Murphey, November 27, 1816, Hoyt, *Murphey Papers*, I, 88.

62. Wheeler, *Historical Sketches*, II, 122; New Bern *Carolina Sentinel*, July 29, 1826.

63. Edward Stanly, *A Military Governor Among Abolitionists. A Letter from Edward Stanly to Charles Sumner* (New York: n.p., 1865), p. 16, hereinafter cited as Stanly, *Military Governor Among Abolitionists*.

64. John Stanly to General Samuel Simpson, July 30, 1818, Samuel Simpson Biddle Letters, 1764-1829, Flowers Collection, Duke University Library, Durham.

65. John West to John H. Bryan, August 11, 1818, John H. Bryan Papers; New Bern *Carolina Centinel*, August 15, 1818. The next year, in a letter to General James Iredell, Stanly complained: "As to myself, I am sick of elections & most heartily tired of Raleigh—Yet a foolish notion, that prevails among my friends, that I ought not to leave room for my opponents to say that I was beaten off or scared off the ground may bring me forward once more." John Stanly to General James Iredell, July 9, 1819, James Iredell, Sr. and Jr. Papers, Manuscript Department, Duke University Library, Durham. Stanly consented to be a candidate and was elected without opposition to the New Bern seat; however, he did not run in 1820 and his friend, Edward Graham, was chosen. New Bern *Carolina Centinel*, August 14, 1819, August 12, 1820.

66. Richard Benbury Creecy, *Grandfather's Tales of North Carolina History* (Raleigh: Edwards & Broughton, 1901), p. 82.

67. William Henry Haywood, Jr. to Willie Mangum, December 20, 1823, Henry Thomas Shanks (ed.), *The Papers of Willie Person*

Mangum, 5 volumes (Raleigh: State Department of Archives and History, 1950-1956), I, 94, hereinafter cited as Shanks, *Mangum Papers*.

68. Gaston, "John Stanly Obituary."

69. John H. Bryan to Mrs. John H. Bryan, November 25, 1825, John H. Bryan Papers; David F. Caldwell to Willie P. Mangum, December 4, 1825, Shanks, *Mangum Papers*, I, 207-208.

70. Raleigh *Register*, March 1, 8, 1822.

71. *Ibid.*, December 11, 1812; New Bern *Carolina Sentinel*, December 6, 1823.

72. Raleigh *Register*, December 19, 1817, January 25, 1818.

73. *Ibid.*, January 6, 1826; Bartlett Yancey to Willie P. Mangum, January 25, 1826, Shanks, *Mangum Papers*, I, 240.

74. Moore, *History of North Carolina*, I, 483, 487-488.

75. Whitford, "Home Story of a Walking Stick," pp. 174, 286.

76. *Ibid.*, pp. 284-285.

77. Miller, "Recollections of Newbern," 342; John Stanly, *To the Freeholders of Craven County* (New Bern, 1822); New Bern, *Carolina Centinel*, August 3, 1822; see also John Chalmers Vinson, "Electioneering in North Carolina, 1800-1835," *The North Carolina Historical Review*, XXIX (April, 1952), 174.

78. University of North Carolina Faculty Minutes, 1821-1841, August 4, 1826, Manuscript volume; Philanthropic Society Records 1821-1832, September 6, 1826, Manuscript volume; Student Records, April-December, 1826, Report of the Faculty to the Honourable Board of Trustees, Manuscript volume. All in North Carolina Collection, University of North Carolina at Chapel Hill.

79. Raleigh *Register*, January 19, 1827.

80. Isc. Croom to John H. Bryan, January 17, 1827, typed copy in Beckwith Papers.

81. William Gaston to ———, February 4, 1827, Gaston Papers. Stanly seems to have had a premonition that illness or death might cut short his career. The previous year he had written John H. Bryan: "I never have been more exhausted by the labors of my profession than I find myself at the close of the late circuit—my feelings press strongly upon me the necessity of more time 'to patch up my old carcass for heaven' if not for any other purpose—I must still further abridge my labors—" John Stanly to John H. Bryan, May 10, 1826, John H. Bryan Papers.

82. New Bern Carolina *Sentinel*, June 23, September 29, 1827; Matthias E. Manly to William A. Graham, August 31, 1827, Joseph Gregoire de Roulhac Hamilton (ed.), *The Papers of William Alexander Graham*, 4 volumes (Raleigh: State Department of Archives and History, 1957-1961), I, 154, hereinafter cited as Hamilton, *Graham*

Papers; William S. Hoffmann, *Andrew Jackson and North Carolina Politics*, volume XL, *The James Sprunt Studies in History and Political Science* (Chapel Hill: University of North Carolina Press, 1958), p. 17, hereinafter cited as Hoffmann, *Andrew Jackson and North Carolina Politics*; New Bern *Carolina Sentinel*, November 24, December 1, 1827.

83. Frederick Spaight Blount to John H. Bryan, January 12, 1828, John H. Bryan Papers.

84. Raleigh *Register*, December 7, 14, 1827, June 6, 1828; New Bern *North Carolina Sentinel*, December 1, 8, 1827.

85. Raleigh *Register*, December 7, 1827; New Bern *North Carolina Sentinel*, January 16, 1830.

86. William Gaston to Hannah M. Gaston, May 20, 1827, Gaston Papers; Grenville M. Dodge and William Arba Ellis, *Norwich University, 1819-1911: Her History, Her Graduates, Her Roll of Honor*, 3 volumes (Montpelier, Vermont: The Capital City Press, 1911), I, *passim*.

87. Victor H. Johnson, Librarian, Norwich University, to the author, April 6, 1962.

88. Joseph Gregoire de Roulhac Hamilton, "Edward Stanly," *DAB*, XVII, 515, hereinafter cited as Hamilton, "Edward Stanly."

89. John H. Bryan to Mary Shepard Bryan, March 6, 1828, John H. Bryan Papers.

90. Gaston, "John Stanly Obituary."

91. Miller, "Recollections of Newbern," 244-245; Carraway, *Crown of Life*, p. 142.

92. John Stanly to [John H. Bryan], March 4, 1829, Miscellaneous Papers, series one, volume II, State Department of Archives and History, Raleigh.

93. John H. Bryan to Ebenezer Pettigrew, May 7, 1830, Pettigrew Papers, volume III, State Department of Archives and History, Raleigh, hereinafter cited as Pettigrew Papers, SDAH; James W. Bryan to John H. Bryan, February 22, 1828, John H. Bryan Papers; New Bern *Spectator*, September 2, October 7, 1831, October 5, 1832.

94. Mary Shepard Bryan to John H. Bryan, May 2, 1828, John H. Bryan to [Mary Shepard Bryan], May 7, 1828, John H. Bryan Papers; William Gaston to Hannah M. Gaston, May 20, 1827, Gaston Papers.

95. New Bern *North Carolina Sentinel*, July 6, 13, 1831.

96. New Bern *Spectator*, November 25, December 2, 1831.

97. New Bern *North Carolina Sentinel*, December 7, 14, 1831.

98. John H. Bryan to Ebenezer Pettigrew, July 27, 1832, quoted in John Hope Franklin, *The Free Negro in North Carolina*,

1790-1860 (Chapel Hill: University of North Carolina Press, 1943), p. 100.

99. *Proceedings and Debates of the Convention of North Carolina, Called to Amend the Constitution of the State. Which Assembled at Raleigh, June 4, 1835* (Raleigh: Joseph Gales and Son, 1836), pp. 79-81.

100. Matthias E. Manly to William A. Graham, August 31, 1830, Hamilton, *Graham Papers*, I, 192; Hamilton, "Edward Stanly," 515; Whitford, "Home Story of a Walking Stick," pp. 152-153; New Bern *Spectator*, April 27, 1832.

101. Lindsay C. Warren, *Beaufort County's Contribution to a Notable Era of North Carolina History* (Washington: Government Printing Office, 1930), p. 5, hereinafter cited as Warren, *Beaufort County's Contribution*.

102. Ann Stanly Taylor to James Green Stanly, Jr., April 18, 1833, Beckwith Papers.

103. Miller, "Recollections of Newbern," 244; New Bern *Spectator*, August 9, 1833; William Gaston to Stephen F. Miller, February 25, 1834, typed copy in Gaston Papers. See also Jo. Seawell Jones, *A Defence of the Revolutionary History of the State of North Carolina from the Aspersions of Mr. Jefferson* (Boston: Charles Bowen, 1834), pp. 215-216.

104. Quoted in Whitford, "Home Story of a Walking Stick," p. 172.

105. A. R. Newsome, "Debate on the Fisher Resolution," *The North Carolina Historical Review*, V (April, 1928), 22, hereafter cited as Newsome, "Debate on the Fisher Resolution."

106. Edward Stanly to John Wright and others, October 1851, Raleigh *Register*, November 19, 1851.

107. Whitford, "Home Story of a Walking Stick," p. 147.

108. Newsome, "Debate on the Fisher Resolution," 204-205.

109. *Congressional Globe*, 26 Cong. 2 Sess. (Washington: Blair & Rives, 1841), IX, Appendix, 360.

110. Raleigh *Register*, March 27, 1850.

111. Edward Stanly to Leverett Saltonstall, January 16, 1844, Leverett Saltonstall Papers, Massachusetts Historical Society, Boston, hereinafter cited as Saltonstall Papers.

112. *Ibid*.

Chapter 2

1. Edward Stanly to Richard S. Donnell and others, March 25, 1853, *Semi-Weekly Raleigh Register*, April 20, 1853.

2. Wilson B. Hodges to Ebenezer Pettigrew, November 4, 1835, Pettigrew Papers, volume IV, SDAH.

3. Raleigh *Star*, December 3, 1835; William Gaston to Susan Gaston Donaldson, December 1, 1835, Gaston Papers.

4. Edward Stanly to William Gaston, December 4, 1835, Gaston Papers. Stanly asked Gaston's opinion as to what books on criminal law he should read, in what order, and what was the best book of forms. Said he: "If you will mark out a course for me, I can pursue it more cheerfully and confidently, than one of my own selection."

5. R. D. W. Connor, *William Gaston, A Southern Federalist of the Old School and His Yankee Friends—1778-1844* (Worcester, Massachusetts: American Antiquarian Society, 1934), pp. 3, 12-13.

6. William Gaston to Messrs. Fitzpatrick, Hooks, Robinson, and others, October 3, 1832, Gaston Papers; William Gaston to Robert Donaldson, September 3, 1831, in *ibid*.

7. Edward Stanly quoted Gaston's words in remarks on the floor of the House of Representatives, March 7, 1850, in reply to Henry Hilliard of Alabama.

8. Eber Malcolm Carroll, *Origins of the Whig Party* (Durham: Duke University Press, 1925), pp. 118-126; Clement Eaton, *Henry Clay and the Art of American Politics* (Boston: Little, Brown and Company, 1957), pp. 113-114; Frank Otto Gatell, "Money and Party in Jacksonian America: A Quantitative Look at New York City's Men of Quality," *Political Science Quarterly*, LXXXII (June, 1967), pp. 235-252; Edward Pessen, *Jacksonian America: Society, Personality, and Politics* (Homewood, Illinois: The Dorsey Press, 1969), pp. 211-274.

9. Charles Grier Sellers, Jr., "Who Were the Southern Whigs?" *The American Historical Review*, LIX (January, 1954), 335-346; Cole, *Whig Party in the South*, pp. 71-72; Paul Murray, *The Whig Party in Georgia, 1825-1853* (Chapel Hill: University of North Carolina Press, 1948); Herbert J. Doherty, *The Whigs of Florida, 1845-1854* (Gainesville: University of Florida Press, 1959); Grady McWhiney, "Were the Whigs a Class Party in Alabama?" *Journal of Southern History*, XXIII (November, 1957), 510-522.

10. Hugh T. Lefler and Albert Ray Newsome, *North Carolina: The History of a Southern State*. Revised Edition (Chapel Hill: University of North Carolina Press, 1963), p. 340, hereinafter cited as Lefler and Newsome, *North Carolina*.

11. Clarence C. Norton, *The Democratic Party in North Carolina, 1835-1861*, volume XXI, *The James Sprunt Historical Studies* (Chapel Hill: University of North Carolina Press, 1930), pp. 43-47.

12. For the formation of the Whig Party in North Carolina see William S. Hoffmann, "The Downfall of the Democrats: the Reaction of North Carolinians to Jacksonian Land Policy," *The North Carolina Historical Review*, XXXIII (April, 1956), 166-182, and

Hoffmann, "John Branch and the Origins of the Whig Party in North Carolina," *The North Carolina Historical Review*, XXV (July, 1958), 299-315; Max R. Williams, "The Foundations of the Whig Party in North Carolina: A Synthesis and a Modest Proposal," *The North Carolina Historical Review*, XLVII (April, 1970), 115-129.

13. Cole, *Whig Party in the South*, p. 63.

14. Edward Stanly to Ebenezer Pettigrew, April 16, 1836, Pettigrew Papers, volume VI, SDAH.

15. Edward Stanly to Ebenezer Pettigrew, January 16, 1837, *ibid.*, volume VII.

16. Edward Stanly to Ebenezer Pettigrew, April 16, 1836, *ibid.*, volume VI.

17. Raleigh *Register*, May 24, 1836.

18. Edward Stanly to Ebenezer Pettigrew, April 16, 1836, Pettigrew Papers, volume VI, SDAH.

19. Joseph Gregoire de Roulhac Hamilton, *Party Politics in North Carolina, 1835-1860*, volume XV, *The James Sprunt Historical Publications* (Chapel Hill: University of North Carolina, 1916), p. 41, hereinafter cited as Hamilton, *Party Politics in North Carolina*; see also William Hoffmann, "The Election of 1836 in North Carolina," *The North Carolina Historical Review*, XXXII (January, 1955), 31-51.

20. Ebenezer Pettigrew to James Johnston, May 29, 1836, Pettigrew Papers, Southern Historical Collection, University of North Carolina at Chapel Hill, hereinafter cited as Pettigrew Papers, SHC; Ebenezer Pettigrew to Mrs. John H. Bryan, January 22, 1837, *ibid.*

21. Edward Stanly to Ebenezer Pettigrew, January 16, 1837, Pettigrew Papers, volume VII, SDAH.

22. Raleigh *Register*, May 16, 23, 1837.

23. Edward Stanly to Richard Hines and others, May 6, 1837, *ibid.*, May 23, 1837.

24. New Bern *Spectator*, May 12, 1837. See also Raleigh *Register*, May 16, 1837.

25. J. Kelly Turner and John L. Bridges, Jr., *History of Edgecombe County, North Carolina* (Raleigh: Edwards & Broughton Printing Company, 1920), pp. 123-124; New Bern *Spectator*, May 19, 1837; Edward Stanly to Ebenezer Pettigrew, May 20, 1837, Pettigrew Papers, volume VIII, SDAH.

26. New Bern *Spectator*, July 28, 1837; *ibid.*, August 11, 1837, quoting Tarborough *Scaevola*, n.d.

27. Moore, *History of North Carolina*, II, 86; New Bern *Spectator*, August 28, 1835.

28. Raleigh *Register*, August 21, 1837.

29. Pettigrew had hoped that Stanly's vote in Tyrrell would match his own in 1835, "but I suppose it could not have been expected for there are some here who like Ephrain of old were so joined unto their idols that it was not possible to detach (them) in favour of a stranger." Ebenezer Pettigrew to George Daniel and others, July, 1837, rough draft in Pettigrew Papers, volume VIII, SDAH.

30. New Bern *Spectator*, August 4, 1837, quoting Washington *Whig*, n.d.

31. In the New Bern district, Charles Shepard defeated Jesse Speight, a Democrat. The other Whigs were Stanly, James Graham, Samuel T. Sawyer, Edmund Deberry, Augustine H. Shepperd, Abraham Rencher, and Lewis Williams. Democrats elected were: Jesse A. Bynum, James J. McKay, M. T. Hawkins, William Montgomery, and Henry W. Connor. Hamilton, *Party Politics in North Carolina*, pp. 31, 44-45.

32. Charles Grier Sellers, Jr., *James K. Polk: Jacksonian, 1795-1843* (Princeton: Princeton University Press, 1957), pp. 326-327, hereinafter cited as Sellers, *James K. Polk*.

33. *Ibid*.

34. Adams, *Memoirs*, IX, 369-370; Sellers, *James K. Polk*, p. 327.

35. *Congressional Globe*, 25 Cong., 1 Sess. (Washington: Globe Office, 1837), V, 18, hereinafter cited as *Congressional Globe* with appropriate numeration.

36. James D. Richardson (ed.), *A Compilation of the Messages and Papers of the Presidents, 1789-1897*, 10 volumes (Washington: Government Printing Office, 1896-1899), III, 324-346, hereinafter cited as Richardson, *Messages and Papers of the Presidents*.

37. Adams, *Memoirs*, IX, 376; Glyndon G. Van Deusen, *The Jacksonian Era, 1828-1848* (New York: Harper & Brothers, 1959), p. 124, hereinafter cited as Van Deusen, *Jacksonian Era*.

38. *Congressional Globe*, 25 Cong., 1 Sess., V, 81, 85, 93-94.

39. Van Deusen, *Jacksonian Era*, p. 126.

40. James Graham to William A. Graham, October 1, 1837, Hamilton, *Graham Papers*, I, 529.

41. Edward Stanly to Ebenezer Pettigrew, September 25, 1837, Pettigrew Papers, volume XVIII, SDAH.

42. *Congressional Globe*, 25 Cong., 1 Sess., V, 103-105, 141.

43. *Ibid*., 85, 89-91; James A. Graham to William A. Graham, October 1, 1837, Hamilton, *Graham Papers*, I, 528-529.

44. *Congressional Globe*, 25 Cong., 1 Sess., V, 120. The bill passed the Senate 35 to 6, and the House 127 to 98.

45. Edward Stanly to Ebenezer Pettigrew, September 25, 1837, Pettigrew Papers, volume XVIII, SDAH.

46. Edward Stanly to John H. Bryan, October 13, 1837, John H. Bryan Papers.

47. Sellers, *James K. Polk*, pp. 331-334; *Congressional Globe*, 25 Cong., 2 Sess. (Washington: Globe Office, 1838), VI, 478, hereinafter cited as *Congressional Globe* with appropriate numeration.

48. *Congressional Globe*, 24 Cong., 1 Sess. (Washington: Globe Office, 1836), III, 406.

49. Sellers, *James K. Polk*, pp. 337-338.

50. *Congressional Globe*, 25 Cong., 2 Sess., VI, 45; Adams, *Memoirs*, IX, 454-455.

51. Edward Stanly to Ebenezer Pettigrew, December 22, 1837, Pettigrew Papers, volume VIII, SDAH.

52. *Congressional Globe*, 25 Cong., 2 Sess., VI, 55.

53. Edward Stanly to Ebenezer Pettigrew, January 11, 1838, Pettigrew Papers, volume VIII, SDAH.

54. Van Deusen, *Jacksonian Era*, pp. 113-134.

55. Don C. Seitz, *Famous American Duels* (New York: Thomas Y. Crowell Company, 1929), pp. 251-266, hereinafter cited as Seitz, *American Duels*.

56. *Ibid.*, pp. 266-275; *Congressional Globe*, 25 Cong., 2 Sess., VI, 320.

57. *Congressional Globe*, 25 Cong., 1 Sess., VI, 323, 336.

58. *Ibid.*, 341.

59. Edward Stanly, *Remarks of Edward Stanly, of North Carolina, upon the Motion to Print the Report of the Committee Appointed to Investigate the Causes of the Late Duel. Delivered in the House of Representatives, April 28, 1838* (Washington: n.p., 1838), p. 6.

60. *Ibid.*, p. 7.

61. Tarborough *Tarboro' Press*, May 12, 1839, quoting Baltimore *Patriot*, n.d., hereinafter cited as *Tarboro' Press*.

62. New Bern *Spectator*, May 11, 1838.

63. Edward Stanly to Ebenezer Pettigrew, May 30, 1838, Pettigrew Papers, volume VIII, SDAH.

64. New Bern *Spectator*, May 11, 1838. The majority report of the duelling committee failed of acceptance, and Graves remained a member of the House until 1841. However, a censure resolution was passed, 102 to 76. Seitz, *American Duels*, pp. 277-278.

65. Nathan Sargent, *Public Men and Events from the Commencement of Mr. Monroe's Administration, in 1817, to the Close of Mr. Fillmore's Administration, in 1853,* 2 volumes (Philadelphia: J. B. Lippincott & Co., 1875), II, 47.

Chapter 3

1. Edward Stanly to Ebenezer Pettigrew, May 30, 1838, Pettigrew Papers, volume VIII, SDAH.

2. Edward Stanly to Ebenezer Pettigrew, March 20, 1838, *ibid*.

3. *Tarboro' Press*, October 6, 1838.

4. Sellers, *James K. Polk*, p. 338; *Congressional Globe*, 25 Cong., 3 Sess. (Washington: Globe Office, 1839), VII, 23, hereinafter cited as *Congressional Globe* with appropriate numeration.

5. *Congressional Globe*, 25 Cong., 3 Sess., VII, 23-24.

6. Edward Stanly to Ebenezer Pettigrew, December 29, 1838, Pettigrew Papers, volume VIII, SDAH.

7. *Ibid*.

8. *Congressional Globe*, 25 Cong., 3 Sess., VII, 87.

9. Edward Stanly to Gales and Seaton, December 14, 1838, *Niles' National Register*, LV (December 22, 1838), 258.

10. Raleigh *Register*, February 11, 1839.

11. Edward Stanly, *Speech of Edward Stanly, of North Carolina, in Reply to Dr. Duncan, of Ohio: the Defender of the Administration; the 'Dear Sir' of Levi Woodbury, and the Pet of the Globe; in Which the Anti-Slavery Letter of Dr. Duncan is Examined. Delivered in the House of Representatives, January 17, 1839* (n.p., n.d.), *passim*.

12. *Ibid*.

13. *Niles' National Register*, LVI (March 9, 1839), 19-22.

14. *Ibid*., 22.

15. *Congressional Globe*, 25 Cong., 3 Sess., VII, 209-214. See also Dallas C. Dickey, *Seargent S. Prentiss, Whig Orator of the Old South* (Baton Rouge: Louisiana State University Press, 1945), pp. 159-160.

16. Edward Stanly to Ebenezer Pettigrew, February 22, 1839, Pettigrew Papers, volume IX, SDAH.

17. Raleigh *Register*, February 11, 1839; Washington (N. C.) *Whig*, February 12, 1839, quoting Raleigh *Star*, n.d.; New Bern *Spectator*, March 1, 22, 1839.

18. Charles Shepard to John H. Bryan, July 9, 1838, John H. Bryan Papers.

19. Adams, *Memoirs*, X, 309.

20. Edward Stanly to Ebenezer Pettigrew, December 29, 1838, Pettigrew Papers, volume VIII, SDAH; Charles Shepard to John H. Bryan, July 9, 1838, John H. Bryan Papers.

21. *Congressional Globe*, 25 Cong., 3 Sess., VII, Appendix, 43.

22. *Tarboro' Press*, July 28, 1838, quoting Washington *Whig*, July 24, 1838; *Congressional Globe*, 25 Cong., 2 Sess., VI, 210, 310; Edward Stanly to Ebenezer Pettigrew, March 20, 1838, Pettigrew Papers, volume VIII, SDAH.

23. New Bern *Spectator*, May 24, 1839; *ibid.*, May 17, 1839, quoting Washington *Whig*, n.d.

24. Raleigh *Register*, April 27, 1839; *Tarboro' Press*, April 27, 1839; *Tarboro' Press*, June 1, 1839, quoting Washington (N. C.) *Republican*, n.d.

25. *Tarboro' Press*, June 1, 1839.

26. Edward Stanly to Ebenezer Pettigrew, June 25, 1839, Pettigrew Papers, volume IX, SDAH.

27. *Tarboro' Press*, May 4, 11, June 8, 29, July 6, 1839.

28. Edward Stanly to Ebenezer Pettigrew, June 25, 1839, Pettigrew Papers, volume IX, SDAH.

29. *Ibid.* Asa Biggs, a Democratic leader in Martin County, declared that if Stanly "could be defeated it would be the greatest triumph we could have." Asa Biggs to James R. Hoyle, June 11, 1839, Asa Biggs Letter Book, SDAH. See also Raleigh *Star*, June 19, 1839.

30. Ebenezer Pettigrew to James Johnston, July 30, 1839, Pettigrew Papers, SHC. See also Samuel Ralston and others to Ebenezer Pettigrew, July 15, 1839, Pettigrew Papers, volume IX, SDAH.

31. Wilson B. Hodges to Ebenezer Pettigrew, July 27, 1839, Pettigrew Papers, volume IX, SDAH. Writes historian Guion G. Johnson of Hodges' remarks: "Had the writer been impartial in relating the events of the day, he would have added that a goodly number of Whigs were also sleeping off too much 'ardent' or boisterously celebrating their victory in the village streets with 'three sheets in the wind' [a common term for drunkenness]." Guion Griffis Johnson, *Ante-Bellum North Carolina: A Social History* (Chapel Hill: University of North Carolina Press, 1937), p. 149.

32. William Pettigrew to Johnson Pettigrew, July 22, 1839, Pettigrew Papers, SHC.

33. *Tarboro' Press*, August 24, 1839.

34. Raleigh *Register*, August 3, 1839, quoting "Extra," July 31, 1839. See also New Bern *Spectator*, August 2, 1839.

35. New Bern *Spectator*, August 16, 1839, quoting Boston *Atlas*, n.d. See also Ebenezer Pettigrew to Levi Lincoln, August 12, 1839; Pettigrew Papers, volume IX, SDAH.

36. Raleigh *Register*, August 17, 1839, quoting New Bern *Spectator*, n.d.

37. Raleigh *Register*, August 17, 1839. Whigs elected: Lewis Williams, James Graham, Edmund Deberry, Edward Stanly, and Kenneth Rayner; Democrats, M. T. Hawkins, Jesse A. Bynum, William Montgomery, James J. McKay, Charles Shepard, Henry Connor, John Hill, and Charles Fisher.

38. Ebenezer Pettigrew to Levi Lincoln, August 12, 1839,

Pettigrew Papers, volume IX, SDAH.

Chapter 4

1. Horace Greeley, *Recollections of a Busy Life* (New York: J. B. Ford & Co., 1869), p. 130.

2. Henry W. Hilliard, *Politics and Pen Pictures at Home and Abroad* (New York: G. P. Putnam's Sons, 1892), pp. 10-11, hereinafter cited as Hilliard, *Politics and Pen Pictures.*

3. Harriet A. Weed (ed.), *The Autobiography of Thurlow Weed* (Boston: Houghton, Mifflin and Company, 1884), I, 482, hereinafter cited as Weed, *Autobiography of Thurlow Weed.*

4. Raleigh *Register*, December 14, 1839. The *Register* added that Tyler's nomination "meets with the cordial approbation of all."

5. Hilliard, *Politics and Pen Pictures*, p. 11.

6. *Congressional Globe*, 26 Cong., 1 Sess. (Washington: Globe Office, 1840), VIII, 79, hereinafter cited as *Congressional Globe* with appropriate numeration.

7. *Ibid.*, 52-53, 56, 58; Henry Harrison Simms, *Life of Robert M. T. Hunter: A Study in Sectionalism and Secession* (Richmond: William Byrd Press, 1935), pp. 45-46.

8. Henry Harrison Simms, *Emotion at High Tide: Abolition as a Controversial Factor, 1830-1845* (Richmond: William Byrd Press, 1960), pp. 137-138.

9. Adams, *Memoirs*, X, 196.

10. Edward Stanly, *Speech of Mr. Stanly, of North Carolina, on Abolition Petitions. Delivered in the House of Representatives January 16, 1840* (n.p., n.d.), *passim.* John Quincy Adams noted in his diary that Stanly "read the abolition letters of Governor Marcus Morton, of Parmenter, and of Henry Williams, the most thorough-going of all. Parmenter made a great distinction between anti-slavery and abolitionism. It was well for Henry Williams that he was not present." Adams, *Memoirs*, X, 196.

11. Hilliard, *Politics and Pen Pictures*, pp. 9-10.

12. Freeman Cleaves, *Old Tippecanoe: William Henry Harrison and His Time* (New York: Charles Scribner's Sons, 1939), p. 296.

13. Edward Stanly to Ebenezer Pettigrew, February 6, 1840, Pettigrew Papers, volume IX, SDAH.

14. Edward Stanly, *Speech of Edw. Stanly, of North Carolina, Establishing Proofs That the Abolitionists Are Opposed to Gen. Harrison, and That Gen. Harrison is Opposed to Their 'Unconstitutional Efforts.' Delivered in the House of Representatives, April 13, 1840* (Washington: n.p., 1840), *passim.*

15. Edward Stanly, *Sketch of the Remarks of Mr. Stanly, on the Branch Mint in North Carolina; Together with Extracts from the*

Speeches of Messrs. Everett, Morgan, and Reed, Exposing Various Abuses in the Expenditures of the Public Money (Washington: Gales and Seaton, 1840), *passim*.

16. Adams, *Memoirs*, X, 278-279. The motion was lost.

17. James Graham to William A. Graham, May 10, 1840, Hamilton, *Graham Papers*, II, 87-88; Raleigh *Star*, May 20, 1840.

18. *Tarboro' Press*, November 21, 1840, quoting Huntsville *Democrat*, n.d.

19. Edward Stanly to Ebenezer Pettigrew, June 8, 1840, Pettigrew Papers, volume IX, SDAH.

20. Edward Stanly, Lewis Williams, Edmund Deberry, and Kenneth Rayner, *To the People of the State of North Carolina* (Washington: n.p., 1840), pp. 1-2, hereinafter cited as Stanly, *To the People of North Carolina*; Herbert Dale Pegg, "The Whig Party in North Carolina, 1834-1861" (Unpublished doctoral dissertation, University of North Carolina at Chapel Hill, 1932), p. 162, hereinafter cited as Pegg, "Whig Party in North Carolina."

21. James Graham to William A. Graham, June 16, 1840, Hamilton, *Graham Papers*, II, 96; Stanly, *To the People of North Carolina*, pp. 6-7.

22. Van Deusen, *Jacksonian Era*, p. 128.

23. William H. Seward to ———, August 25, 1840, Frederick W. Seward, *William H. Seward: An Autobiography from 1801 to 1834. With a Memoir of His Life and Selections from His Letters, 1831-1846.* Second Edition (New York: Derby and Miller, 1891), p. 492, hereinafter cited as Seward, *Autobiography*.

24. *Ibid.*, p. 493.

25. William H. Seward to Thurlow Weed, January 1, 1846, *ibid.*, p. 769.

26. Hamilton, *Party Politics in North Carolina*, pp. 65-66.

27. *Ibid.*, p. 66; Raleigh *Star*, October 7, 14, 21, 1840.

28. New Bern *Spectator*, October 24, 31, 1840.

29. ——— to Edward Stanly, October 18, 1840, in *ibid.*, October 31, 1840.

30. Hamilton, *Party Politics in North Carolina*, p. 68; Van Deusen, *Jacksonian Era*, pp. 148-149.

31. Hamilton, *Party Politics in North Carolina*, p. 70.

32. Paul C. Cameron to Thomas Ruffin, [November 15, 1840], Joseph Gregoire de Roulhac Hamilton (ed.), *The Papers of Thomas Ruffin*, 4 volumes (Raleigh: Publications of the North Carolina Historical Commission), II, 188, hereinafter cited as Hamilton, *Ruffin Papers*.

33. Lawrence Foushee London, "The Public Career of George Edmund Badger" (Unpublished doctoral dissertation, University of

North Carolina at Chapel Hill, 1936), pp. 1-37, hereinafter cited as London, "George Edmund Badger."; William B. Shepard to Ebenezer Pettigrew, September 28, 1840, Pettigrew Papers, volume IX, SDAH.

34. Hamilton, *Party Politics in North Carolina*, pp. 70-71; William A. Graham to James W. Bryan, November 27, 1840, Hamilton, *Graham Papers*, II, 119.

35. Edward Stanly to David L. Swain, January 12, 1841, Miscellaneous Papers, Series One, volume III, SDAH.

36. Raleigh *Register*, January 29, 1841, quoting Harrisburg *Daily Telegraph*, n.d.

37. George Rawlings Poage, *Henry Clay and the Whig Party* (Chapel Hill: University of North Carolina Press, 1936), p. 20, hereinafter cited as Poage, *Clay and the Whig Party*.

38. William A. Graham to James W. Bryan, February 13, 1841, Hamilton, *Graham Papers*, II, 161-162; William A. Graham to Susan W. Graham, February 15, 1841, *ibid.*, II, 163.

39. George E. Badger to William A. Graham, February 16, 1841, *ibid.*, II, 164-166.

40. William A. Graham to James W. Bryan, June 13, 1841, *ibid.*, II, 199.

41. *Congressional Globe*, 26 Cong., 2 Sess. (Washington: Globe Office, 1841), IX, 11-12, hereinafter cited as *Congressional Globe* with appropriate numeration.

42. *Ibid.*, 113, 117-118, 150.

43. *Ibid.*, Appendix, 352-356.

44. *Ibid.*, 357-358.

45. *Ibid.*, 358-359.

46. *Ibid.*, 362.

47. American relations with England were precarious at this time because of the Maine boundary dispute and incidents on the New York-Canadian border growing out of Mackenzie's Rebellion. On February 25, Stanly wrote Ebenezer Pettigrew that while he hoped their fears of war were groundless, a "little war" might be of service. "A war would unite us thoroughly, and make us all feel, that we were brethren of one country." Edward Stanly to Ebenezer Pettigrew, February 25, 1841, Pettigrew Papers, volume X, SDAH.

48. Adams, *Memoirs*, X, 426.

49. Ben: Perley Poore, *Perley's Reminiscences of Sixty Years in the National Metropolis*, 2 volumes (Philadelphia: Hubbard Brothers, 1886), I, 263-264, hereinafter cited as Poore, *Perley's Reminiscences*.

50. Adams, *Memoirs*, X, 426-427.

51. Edward Stanly to Ebenezer Pettigrew, February 25, 1841,

Pettigrew Papers, volume X, SDAH.

52. William A. Graham to James W. Bryan, February 13, 1841, Hamilton, *Graham Papers*, II, 163.

53. Poage, *Clay and the Whig Party*, pp. 28-32.

54. Hamilton, *Party Politics in North Carolina*, p. 78.

55. Edward Stanly to Ebenezer Pettigrew, January 6, 1841, Pettigrew Papers, volume X, SDAH; Raleigh *Register*, April 16, 1841.

56. Edward Stanly to Ebenezer Pettigrew, April 12, 1841, Pettigrew Papers, volume X, SDAH.

57. Washington *Whig*, May 5, 1841.

58. *Tarboro' Press*, May 29, 1841; Hamilton, *Party Politics in North Carolina*, p. 79. Whigs elected, besides Stanly: Kenneth Rayner, William A. Washington, Edmund Deberry, A. H. Shepperd, Abraham Rencher, James Graham, and Lewis Williams; Democrats, J. R. J. Daniel, James J. McKay, Archibald H. Arrington, Romulus M. Saunders, and Green W. Caldwell.

59. Edward Stanly to Ebenezer Pettigrew, April 12, 1841, Pettigrew Papers, volume X, SDAH.

Chapter 5

1. Poage, *Clay and the Whig Party*, pp. 41, 43; *Congressional Globe*, 27 Cong., 1 Sess. (Washington: Globe Office, 1841), X, 1-3, 37, 44, hereinafter cited as *Congressional Globe* with appropriate numeration.

2. *Congressional Globe*, 27 Cong., 1 Sess., X, 3-4, 9, 15-18, 26-28, 42, 51, 55-56.

3. *Ibid.*, 22.

4. Poage, *Clay and the Whig Party*, p. 46.

5. Washington *Daily National Intelligencer*, June 15, 1841; Edward Stanly to Ebenezer Pettigrew, May 23, June 14, 1841, Pettigrew Papers, volume X, SDAH; Petition Draft, no date, Pettigrew Papers, volume XVIII, SDAH.

6. Edward Stanly to Ebenezer Pettigrew, June 23, 1841, Pettigrew Papers, volume X, SDAH.

7. Poage, *Clay and the Whig Party*, pp. 50-51, 64-66; *Congressional Globe*, 27 Cong., 1 Sess., X, 303.

8. William A. Graham to Susan W. Graham, August 8, 1841, Hamilton, *Graham Papers*, II, 225.

9. Seward, *Autobiography*, pp. 558-559.

10. William A. Graham to Susan W. Graham, August 16, 1841, Hamilton, *Graham Papers*, II, 228.

11. William A. Graham to Susan W. Graham, August 27, 1841, *ibid.*, II, 235.

12. Washington *Madisonian*, August 25, September 4, 1841.

13. Adams, *Memoirs*, X, 542.

14. Washington *Madisonian*, September 4, 1841.

15. *Ibid.*, August 25, 1841; Adams, *Memoirs*, X, 542; William A. Graham to Susan W. Graham, August 29, 1841, Hamilton, *Graham Papers*, II, 236.

16. William A. Graham to Susan W. Graham, August 29, 1841, Hamilton, *Graham Papers*, II, 236.

17. William A. Graham to James W. Bryan, September 13, 1841, *ibid.*, II, 241. For a more sympathetic view of Tyler's actions see Oliver Perry Chitwood, *John Tyler: Champion of the Old South*. Second Edition (New York: Russell & Russell, Inc., 1964), pp. 217-268.

18. William A. Graham to James W. Bryan, September 13, 1841, Hamilton, *Graham Papers*, II, 241.

19. Poage, *Clay and the Whig Party*, pp. 104-105.

20. *Congressional Globe*, 27 Cong., 1 Sess., X, 62.

21. Adams, *Memoirs*, XI, 14-16.

22. William A. Graham to Susan W. Graham, September 12, 1841, Hamilton, *Graham Papers*, II, 240; Adams, *Memoirs*, XI, 18.

23. Baynard Tuckerman (ed.), *The Diary of Philip Hone, 1828-1851*, 2 volumes (New York: Dodd, Mead and Company, 1889), II, 92-93, hereinafter cited as Tuckerman, *Diary of Philip Hone*.

24. *Congressional Globe*, 27 Cong., 1 Sess., 313; X, 155-156; Seward, *Autobiography*, p. 554.

25. Stanly voted for all three measures. Rencher, Graham, and Shepperd voted with the Democrats against the bankruptcy bill. Washington did not vote on the measure. *Congressional Globe*, 27 Cong., 1 Sess., X, 191, 274, 350.

26. Edward Stanly to William Gaston, July 29, 1841, Gaston Papers.

27. Raleigh *Register*, July 23, 1841.

28. *Ibid.*, September 28, 1841.

29. Adams, *Memoirs*, XI, 19.

30. Edward Stanly to Ebenezer Pettigrew, December 14, 1841, Pettigrew Papers, volume X, SDAH.

31. Thomas S. Hoskins to William A. Graham, May 9, 1842, Hamilton, *Graham Papers*, II, 307.

32. Edward Stanly to Ebenezer Pettigrew, January 8, 1842, Pettigrew Papers, volume X, SDAH.

33. Henry A. Wise to Edward Stanly, January 24, 1842; Stanly to Wise, January 26, 1842, Raleigh *Star*, February 9, 1842, quoting Washington *Daily National Intelligencer*, n.d.

34. Raleigh *Star*, May 17, 1842.

35. Willie P. Mangum's Memorandum of the Wise-Stanly Controversy [May 9, 1842], Henry T. Shanks (ed.), *The Papers of Willie Person Mangum*, 5 volumes (Raleigh: State Department of Archives and History, 1950-1956), V, 464-465, hereinafter cited as Shanks, *Mangum Papers*.

36. Washington *Daily National Intelligencer*, May 14, 1842; Edward Stanly to Willie P. Mangum, May 12, 1842, Shanks, *Mangum Papers*, III, 331.

37. Willie P. Mangum to ———, May 15, 1842, Shanks, *Mangum Papers*, V, 465-466; Edward Stanly to Willie P. Mangum, [May 16, 1842], *ibid.*, III, 339-340; Poore, *Perley's Reminiscences*, I, 295; Edward Stanly to Willie P. Mangum, May 12, 1842, Shanks, *Mangum Papers*, III, 331.

38. The correspondence appears in the *Tarboro' Press*, June 25, 1842. Information concerning McCarty is from Ben C. Truman, *The Field of Honor: Being a Complete and Comprehensive History of Duelling in All Countries* (New York: Fords, Howard, & Hubert, 1884), pp. 428-429, hereinafter cited as Truman, *Field of Honor*.

39. Edward Stanly to Ebenezer Pettigrew, May 22, 1842, Pettigrew Papers, SHC.

40. Edward Stanly to John M. McCarty, May 23, 1842, Shanks, *Mangum Papers*, III, 342.

41. Jesse Turner to William A. Graham, June 15, 1842, Hamilton, *Graham Papers*, II, 343.

42. Edward Stanly to John M. McCarty, May 23, 1842, Shanks, *Mangum Papers*, III, 343; Ebenezer Pettigrew to Edward Stanly, June 20, 1842, copy in Pettigrew Papers, SHC.

43. Raleigh *North Carolina Standard*, August 31, 1842.

44. Eliza Gaston to William Gaston, August 28, 1842, Gaston Papers.

45. Raleigh *North Carolina Standard*, August 31, 1842.

46. *Congressional Globe*, 27 Cong., 2 Sess. (Washington: Globe Office, 1842), XI, Appendix, 831-832.

47. *Tarboro' Press*, November 12, 1842, quoting Washington (N. C.) *Republican*, n.d.; Washington *Whig*, November 16, December 21, 1842.

48. Raleigh *Register*, February 28, 1843. See also Joseph B. Hinton to William A. Graham, December 14, 1842, Hamilton, *Graham Papers*, II, 400.

49. Raleigh *Register*, February 28, 1843.

50. Edward Stanly to Ebenezer Pettigrew, March 10, 1843, Pettigrew Papers, volume X, SDAH.

51. Edward Stanly to Ebenezer Pettigrew, [March 11, 1843], *ibid.*

52. Joseph Beasley to William S. Pettigrew, March 28, 1843, Pettigrew Papers, SHC. Pettigrew replied that it would be no easy matter to move the Whigs to action behind any candidate, however suitable. "Their failure in accomplishing the end proposed by General Harrison's election, the treachery of John Tyler [,] has tended to dampen their ardour, a desire to shrink from exertion is too prevalent." William S. Pettigrew to Joseph Beasley, April 4, 1843, Pettigrew Papers, SHC.

53. Raleigh *Star*, April 6, 1843; Edward Stanly to Robert G. Moore and others, April 19, 1843, Raleigh *Register*, May 5, 1843; *ibid.*, April 21, 1843.

54. *Tarboro' Press*, April 15, 1843; *ibid.*, quoting Washington *Republican*, n.d.

55. *Ibid.*, April 1, May 20, 1843, quoting Washington *Republican*, n.d.

56. *Ibid.*, May 6, 1843; Raleigh *Register*, May 23, 1843.

57. Hamilton, *Party Politics in North Carolina*, pp. 90-91. See also Raleigh *Register*, July 18, 1843.

58. Raleigh *Democratic Signal*, July 14, 1843. See also the *Tarboro' Press*, July 8, 1843, and Raleigh *North Carolina Standard*, July 12, 1843.

59. *Tarboro' Press*, July 15, 1843. See also Raleigh *North Carolina Standard*, June 7, 1843.

60. Raleigh *Democratic Signal*, July 21, 1843. Stanly denied the charge that he had exceeded his mileage allowance in a letter to Weston Gales, editor of the Raleigh *Register*. See the *Register*, July 18, 1843.

61. Chester, *The Campaigns of a "Conqueror"; Or, the Man "Who Bragged High for a Fight"* (Raleigh: n.p., 1843), *passim*.

62. Raleigh *Register*, July 28, 1843.

63. Edward Stanly to James W. Bryan, May 13, 1843, Bryan Papers, Southern Historical Collection, University of North Carolina at Chapel Hill, hereinafter cited as Bryan Papers; Edward Stanly to Ebenezer Pettigrew, May 15, 1843, Pettigrew Papers, volume X, SDAH.

64. *Tarboro' Press*, August 12, 1843.

65. *Ibid.*

66. Raleigh *Register*, August 18, 1843, quoting Washington (N. C.) *North State Whig*, n.d. The *North State Whig*, edited by Henry Dimock, replaced the Washington *Whig* in the spring of 1843. Henceforth, it spoke for Stanly. Unfortunately, only scattered issues have been preserved.

67. Edward Stanly to Leverett Saltonstall, January 16, 1844, Saltonstall Papers.

68. Doctrine P. Davenport to Ebenezer Pettigrew, August 10, 1843, Pettigrew Papers, SHC.

69. Edward Stanly to Leverett Saltonstall, January 16, 1844, Saltonstall Papers.

70. Rufus Barringer, *History of the North Carolina Railroad* (Raleigh: News and Observer Press, 1894), p. 19, hereinafter cited as Barringer, *History of the North Carolina Railroad.* Hinton Rowan Helper placed Stanly in the group of southern men who entertained "sentiments similar to those that were entertained by the immortal Fathers of the Republic—that slavery is a great moral, social, civil, and political evil, to be got rid of at the earliest practical period." Hinton Rowan Helper, *The Impending Crisis of the South: How to Meet It* (New York, 1857), pp. 167-168.

71. Edward Stanly to Leverett Saltonstall, January 16, 1844, Saltonstall Papers.

72. Edward Stanly to Robert C. Winthrop, January 13, 1865, Robert C. Winthrop Papers, Massachusetts Historical Society, Boston, hereinafter cited as Winthrop Papers.

73. Joel H. Silbey, *The Shrine of Party: Congressional Voting Behavior, 1841-1852* (Pittsburgh: University of Pittsburgh Press, 1967), pp. 51-58, 161, hereinafter cited as Silbey, *Shrine of Party.*

74. Edward Stanly to Leverett Saltonstall, January 16, 1844, Saltonstall Papers.

Chapter 6

1. Charles L. Hinton to William A. Graham, January 20, 1843, Hamilton, *Graham Papers*, II, 416; Charles L. Hinton to William A. Graham, February 1, 1843, *ibid.*, II, 417. See also Max R. Williams, "William A. Graham and the Election of 1844: A Study in North Carolina Politics," *The North Carolina Historical Review*, XLV (January, 1968), 23-46.

2. Raleigh *Star*, September 20, 1843, quoting New Bern *Newbernian*, n.d.; Raleigh *Register*, September 15, 1843.

3. James W. Bryan to John H. Bryan, September 25, 1843, John H. Bryan Papers; James W. Bryan to William A. Graham, October 13, 1843, Hamilton, *Graham Papers*, II, 446.

4. Richard Hines to Willie P. Mangum, October 18, 1843, Shanks, *Mangum Papers*, III, 469.

5. Raleigh *Register*, October-November, 1843.

6. Hamilton, *Party Politics in North Carolina*, p. 92.

7. Edward Stanly to Willie P. Mangum, December 15, 1843, Shanks, *Mangum Papers*, III, 484.

8. Washington *North State Whig*, March 28, 1844; Raleigh *Register*, March 12, 1844; Edward Stanly to Willie P. Mangum,

December 15, 1843, Shanks, *Mangum Papers*, III, 484.

9. Raleigh *Register*, April 12, 16, 1844.

10. Henry Clay to John J. Crittenden, April 17, 1844, Letters to Crittenden, typed copies in State Department of Archives and History, Raleigh, hereinafter cited as Letters to Crittenden.

11. Poage, *Clay and the Whig Party*, pp. 136-138.

12. *Ibid.*, p. 138.

13. Raleigh *Star*, May 15, 1844.

14. Tuckerman, *Diary of Philip Hone*, II, 219-220.

15. Raleigh *Register*, May 21, 1844; Hamilton, *Party Politics in North Carolina*, pp. 96-97.

16. Hamilton, *Party Politics in North Carolina*, p. 97; Raleigh *Register*, August 16, 1844.

17. Washington *North State Whig*, July 4, 1844. See also Raleigh *Register*, July 4, 1844.

18. Washington *North State Whig*, July 4, 1844. Letter from "J," Greenville, June 28, 1844.

19. *Ibid.*

20. *Ibid.* Richard Hines informed Mangum that "Saunders was met by Stanly at Greenville as we are informed greatly to the advantage of the Whigs. He failed to meet his appointment at Beaufort and Williamston, Cherry and Stanly attending and addressing the different meetings." Richard Hines to Willie P. Mangum, July 4, 1844, Shanks, *Mangum Papers*, IV, 151.

21. Hamilton, *Party Politics in North Carolina*, p. 99; Washington *North State Whig*, August 3, 1844.

22. Hamilton, *Party Politics in North Carolina*, p. 99; Nathan Sargent to Willie P. Mangum, August 21, 1844, Shanks, *Mangum Papers*, IV, 179.

23. Edward Stanly to Willie P. Mangum, December 2, 1844, Shanks, *Mangum Papers*, IV, 225.

24. *Journals of the Senate and House of Commons of the General Assembly of the State of North Carolina, At Its Session in 1844-'45* (Raleigh: Register Office, 1845), pp. 359-362; Raleigh *Register*, November 22, 1844.

25. Edward Stanly to Willie P. Mangum, December 10, 1844, Shanks, *Mangum Papers*, IV, 229.

26. Hamilton, *Party Politics in North Carolina*, p. 100; Edward Stanly to Willie P. Mangum, February 10, 1845, Shanks, *Mangum Papers*, IV, 261.

27. Raleigh *Register*, January 14, 1845.

28. *Ibid*; Raleigh *North Carolina Standard*, January 15, 1845; Charles R. Kinney to Harvey Stanley, January 10, 1845, Beckwith Papers.

29. Edward Stanly to Ebenezer Pettigrew, June 9, 1845, Pettigrew Papers, SHC.

30. Raleigh *Register*, April 18, July 29, 1845; Raleigh *North Carolina Standard*, August 27, 1845.

31. Raleigh *Register*, January 16, 1846.

32. Raleigh *North Carolina Standard*, January 21, 1846.

33. Edward Stanly to Willie P. Mangum, January 27, 1846, Shanks, *Mangum Papers*, IV, 374.

34. Hamilton, *Party Politics in North Carolina*, pp. 105-107; Raleigh *North Carolina Standard*, May 6, 1846.

35. Edward Stanly to William A. Graham, June 3, 1846, Hamilton, *Graham Papers*, III, 128.

36. Hamilton, *Party Politics in North Carolina*, p. 107-109.

37. Raleigh *Register*, August 14, 1846; Raleigh *North Carolina Standard*, August 12, 1846.

38. *Journals of the Senate and House of Commons of the General Assembly of the State of North Carolina, At Its Session in 1846-47* (Raleigh: Star Office, 1847), p. 251.

39. Hamilton, *Party Politics in North Carolina*, p. 110; John H. Bryan to James W. Bryan, August 13, 1846, Bryan Papers; Raleigh *North Carolina Standard*, November 11, 1846.

40. Thomas Clingman to Willie P. Mangum, August 25, 1846, Shanks, *Mangum Papers*, IV, 478.

41. Raleigh *North Carolina Standard*, November 25, 1846.

42. John H. Bryan to ———, August 22, 1846, Pettigrew Papers, SHC.

43. Raleigh *Register*, December 8, 15, 1846. On the decisive ballot, Stanly received 92 votes in both houses, to 18 for Moore, and 26 for John Kerr, with 21 votes scattered.

44. Hamilton, *Party Politics in North Carolina*, p. 100; Raleigh *North Carolina Standard*, December 2, 1846; Raleigh *Register*, January 29, 1847.

45. Raleigh *North Carolina Standard*, August 25, 1847.

46. Hamilton, *Party Politics in North Carolina*, p. 114; James W. Bryan to William A. Graham, January 21, 1843, Bryan Papers; Kenneth Rayner to Charles Moore, November 15, 1847, Raleigh *Register* November 27, 1847. See also Raleigh *North Carolina Standard*, December 1, 1847.

47. William A. Graham to James W. Bryan, January 11, 1848, Hamilton, *Graham Papers*, III, 212-213.

48. Edward Stanly to Fenner B. Satterthwaite, January 15, 1848, Raleigh *Register*, March 22, 1848, quoting Washington *North State Whig*, n.d.

49. Raleigh *Register*, February 26, 1848.

50. Raleigh *North Carolina Standard*, March 8, 1848, quoting Washington *North State Whig*, March 1, 1848.

51. Fenner B. Satterthwaite to Henry Dimock, March 8, 1848, Raleigh *Register*, March 22, 1848, quoting Washington *North State Whig*, n.d.

52. Raleigh *North Carolina Standard*, April 19, 1848.

53. David Outlaw to Emily B. Outlaw, February 10, 1848, David Outlaw Papers, Southern Historical Collection, University of North Carolina at Chapel Hill, hereinafter cited as Outlaw Papers.

54. David Outlaw to Emily B. Outlaw, March 3, 1848, *ibid*.

55. Washington *North State Whig*, January 26, 1853; Kenneth Rayner to Richard I. Wynne, May 23, 1853, *Semi-Weekly Raleigh Register*, July 13, 1853.

56. William A. Graham to James Graham, April 5, 1848, Hamilton, *Graham Papers*, III, 217.

57. David Outlaw to Emily B. Outlaw, March 3, 1848, Outlaw Papers.

58. Edward Stanly to Thomas Sparrow, April 10, 1855, Thomas Sparrow Papers, East Carolina Manuscript Collection, East Carolina University, Greenville, North Carolina.

59. William A. Graham to James Graham, April 5, 1848, Hamilton, *Graham Papers*, III, 217; Raleigh *North Carolina Standard*, May 17, 1848.

60. Frederick W. Seward, *Seward at Washington as Senator and Secretary of State. A Memoir of His Life, With Selections from His Letters, 1846-1861* (New York: Derby and Miller, 1891), p. 78, hereinafter cited as Seward, *Seward at Washington*.

61. Hamilton, *Party Politics in North Carolina* pp. 114, 123; Joseph Gregoire de Roulhac Hamilton, "Kenneth Rayner," *DAB*, XV, 417.

62. William A. Graham to James Graham, April 5, 1848, Hamilton, *Graham Papers*, III, 238.

63. Hamilton, *Party Politics in North Carolina*, pp. 118-119; James W. Bryan to William A. Graham, July 18, 1848, Hamilton, *Graham Papers*, III, 238.

64. Raleigh *Register*, June 10, 1848.

65. Hamilton, *Party Politics in North Carolina*, pp. 120, 124; Raleigh *Register*, June 28, 1848.

66. Raleigh *Register*, July 12, 1848; Raleigh *North Carolina Standard*, June-October, 1848.

67. Asa Biggs to B. B. French, September 15, 1848, Miscellaneous Papers, Series one, volume III, State Department of Archives and History, Raleigh.

68. Hamilton, *Party Politics in North Carolina*, p. 124.

69. Raleigh *Register*, February 26, 1847.

70. Lawrence F. London, "George Edmund Badger in the United States Senate, 1846-1849," *The North Carolina Historical Review*, XV (January, 1938), 18-19.

71. Joseph Carlyle Sitterson, *The Secession Movement in North Carolina*, volume XXIII, *The James Sprunt Studies in History and Political Science* (Chapel Hill: University of North Carolina Press, 1939), p. 41. Footnote, hereinafter cited as Sitterson, *Secession Movement in North Carolina*; Hamilton, *Party Politics in North Carolina*, p. 123.

72. William H. Washington to James W. Bryan, November 26, 1848, quoted in London, "George Edmund Badger," p. 26.

73. George E. Badger to John J. Crittenden, October 12, 1848, Letters to Crittenden.

74. Thomas Clingman to Willie P. Mangum, September 1, 1848, Shanks, *Mangum Papers*, V, 110.

75. *Journals of the Senate and House of Commons, of the General Assembly of the State of North Carolina, At Its Session in 1848-49* (Raleigh: Wesley Whitaker, Jr., Printer, 1849), pp. 90, 109-110, 476-477, 505-506, hereinafter cited as *House Journal, 1848-1849* or *Senate Journal, 1848-1849*; David L. Swain to William H. Battle, December 16, 1848, Battle Family Papers, Series A, Southern Historical Collection, University of North Carolina at Chapel Hill, hereinafter cited as Battle Family Papers, A.

76. The correspondence may be found in Thomas L. Clingman, *Address of T. L. Clingman on the Recent Senatorial Election* (Washington, 1849), pp. 4-5, hereinafter cited as Clingman, *Address*.

77. Raleigh *Register*, December 27, 1848.

78. *Senate Journal, 1848-1849*, pp. 125-126; *House Journal, 1848-1849*, pp. 521-525; George E. Badger to John J. Crittenden, January 13, 1849, Letters to Crittenden. According to London: "On the third ballot Clingman, who was in Raleigh looking after his interest, advised Farmer, who had voted for him throughout, to change his vote to Badger. He did so on the fifth ballot." London, "George Edmund Badger," p. 128.

79. Clingman, *Address, passim*.

80. *House Journal, 1848-1849*, p. 365.

81. Raleigh *Register*, December 13, 23, 1848; Raleigh *North Carolina Standard*, December 13, 20, 1848.

82. *Senate Journal, 1848-1849*, pp. 211-212.

83. Raleigh *Register*, February 17, 1849.

84. *Ibid*.

85. *House Journal, 1848-1849*, pp. 732-736, 749-750.

86. Raleigh *Register*, February 17, March 7, 28, April 14, May 2,

1849. Edward J. Hale, editor of the Fayetteville *Observer*, also accused Shepard of voting against Badger for personal reasons. London, "George Edmund Badger," pp. 130-131. See also William Bryan to J. Johnston Pettigrew, April 29, 1849, Pettigrew Papers, SHC.

87. Hamilton, *Graham Papers*, III, 255-259.

88. Barringer, *History of the North Carolina Railroad*, pp. 15-19; Hamilton, *Party Politics in North Carolina*, p. 133; Raleigh *Register*, January 20, 1849.

89. Charles L. Hinton to William A. Graham, January 26, 1849, Hamilton, *Graham Papers*, III, 273.

90. Raleigh *Register*, April 11, 1849; George E. Badger to John J. Crittenden, January 13, 1849, Letters to Crittenden.

91. Willie P. Mangum to William A. Graham, March 1, 1849, Shanks, *Mangum Papers*, V, 135-136.

92. Willie P. Mangum to William A. Graham, May 25, 1849, *ibid.*, V, 149-150; Raleigh *Register*, June 6, 27, 1849; Robert T. Paine to William A. Graham, June 1, 1849, Hamilton, *Graham Papers*, III, 287-288.

93. Raleigh *North Carolina Standard*, May 30, 1849.

94. Raleigh *Register*, December 13, 1848.

95. Sitterson, *Secession Movement in North Carolina*, p. 48. See also Asa Biggs to James K. Polk, December 27, 1848, Asa Biggs Letter Book, SDAH.

96. George E. Badger to John J. Crittenden, January 13, 1849, Letters to Crittenden.

97. Raleigh *Register*, April 4, June 6, 1849; James W. Bryan to John H. Bryan, May 31, 1849, John H. Bryan Papers.

98. Washington *North State Whig*, June 27, 1849; Raleigh *Register*, July 7, 1849, quoting Washington *North State Whig*, n.d.

99. Raleigh *Register*, July 7, 1849, quoting Philadelphia *North American*, n.d.; Raleigh *Register*, June 27, 1849; *ibid.*, June 30, 1849, quoting Washington *Republic*, n.d.

100. Raleigh *North Carolina Standard*, July 4, 1849.

101. New Bern *Republican*, August 1, 1849. See also the *Republican* of June 27 and July 11, 1849.

102. New Bern *Newbernian*, July 24, 1849.

103. Edward Stanly to S. P. Allen and others, July 23, 1849, Raleigh *Register*, August 1, 1849.

104. William H. Washington to ———, August 11, 1849, Bryan Papers.

105. Raleigh *North Carolina Standard*, August 22, 1849.

106. New Bern *Republican*, August 15, 1849.

107. New Bern *Newbernian*, November 13, 1849.

108. Edward Stanly to James W. Bryan, August 20, 1849, Bryan Papers.

109. Sitterson, *Secession Movement in North Carolina*, p. 52. The Whig members were: Thomas L. Clingman, Joseph P. Caldwell, A. H. Shepperd, Edmund Deberry, David Outlaw, and Edward Stanly; Democrats: A. W. Venable, J. R. J. Daniel, and W. S. Ashe. Hamilton, *Party Politics in North Carolina*, p. 136.

110. Sitterson, *Secession Movement in North Carolina*, p. 52.

Chapter 7

1. Myrta Lockett Avary (ed.), *Recollections of Alexander H. Stephens His Diary Kept When a Prisoner at Fort Warren, Boston Harbour, 1865; Giving Incidents and Reflections of His Prison Life and Some Letters and Reminiscences* (New York: Doubleday, Page & Company, 1910), p. 25, hereinafter cited as Avary, *Recollections of Alexander H. Stephens*.

2. Holman Hamilton, "'The Cave of the Winds' and the Compromise of 1850," *The Journal of Southern History*, XXIII (August, 1957), 334, hereinafter cited as Hamilton, "Cave of the Winds"; Edward M. Steel, Jr., *T. Butler King of Georgia* (Athens: University of Georgia Press, 1964), pp. 72-83.

3. Avary, *Recollections of Alexander H. Stephens*, pp. 25-26; Cole, *Whig Party in the South*, pp. 152-153; Raleigh *North Carolina Standard*, December 12, 1849.

4. Cole, *Whig Party in the South*, p. 154.

5. David Outlaw to Emily B. Outlaw, December 2, 1849, Outlaw Papers.

6. David Outlaw to Emily B. Outlaw, December 9, 1849, *ibid*.

7. Robert C. Winthrop, Jr., *A Memoir of Robert C. Winthrop* (Boston: Little, Brown, and Company, 1897), p. 96, hereinafter cited as Winthrop, *Memoir of Robert C. Winthrop*; Holman Hamilton, *Zachary Taylor: Soldier in the White House* (Indianapolis: The Bobbs-Merrill Company, Inc., 1951), pp. 245-246, hereinafter cited as Hamilton, *Zachary Taylor*; George W. Julian, *The Life of Joshua R. Giddings* (Chicago: A. C. McClurg and Company, 1892), p. 271.

8. Hamilton, *Zachary Taylor*, p. 249; Giddings, *History of the Rebellion*, pp. 302-304.

9. *Congressional Globe*, 31 Cong., 1 Sess. (Washington: John C. Rives, 1850), XXI, part 1, 19, hereinafter cited as *Congressional Globe* with appropriate numeration; David Outlaw to Emily B. Outlaw, December 12, 1849, Outlaw Papers.

10. *Congressional Globe*, 31 Cong., 1 Sess., XXI, part 1, 37-38, 51; David Outlaw to Emily B. Outlaw, December 15, 1849, Outlaw Papers.

11. Hamilton, *Zachary Taylor*, pp. 251-252; *Congressional Globe*, 31 Cong., 1 Sess., XXI, part 1, 65.

12. Winthrop, *Memoir of Robert C. Winthrop*, pp. 98-99.

13. *Congressional Globe*, 31 Cong., 1 Sess., XXI, part 1, 66.

14. Hamilton, *Zachary Taylor*, p. 257.

15. Richardson, *Messages and Papers of the Presidents*, V, 19, 24.

16. Edward Stanly to John H. Bryan, January 11, 1850, John H. Bryan Papers.

17. Hamilton, *Zachary Taylor*, pp. 270-271. Outlaw wrote his wife concerning Clingman's speech: "I see that Clingman's speech creates some excitement at the North, and he thus succeeds in accomplishing one object dear to his heart, notoriety." David Outlaw to Emily B. Outlaw, January 30, 1850, Outlaw Papers.

18. David Outlaw to Emily B. Outlaw, January 11, 1850, *ibid*.

19. Edward Stanly to John H. Bryan, January 11, 1850, John H. Bryan Papers.

20. Sitterson, *Secession Movement in North Carolina*, p. 55.

21. Raleigh *North Carolina Standard*, February 6, 27, 1850.

22. Washington *National Intelligencer*, February 23, 1850, quoting Hillsborough *Recorder*, n.d.; Washington *North State Whig*, February 6, 1850; Raleigh *Register*, February 23, 1850.

23. *Congressional Globe*, 31 Cong., 1 Sess., XXII, Appendix, 115-127.

24. Cole, *Whig Party in the South*, pp. 165-166.

25. Edward Stanly, *Remarks of Hon. E. Stanly, of North Carolina, in the House of Representatives, February 11, 1852, in Reply to Mr. Giddings, of Ohio* (Washington: Congressional Globe Office, 1852), p. 4.

26. *Congressional Globe*, 31 Cong., 1 Sess., XXI, part 1, 276. Root's resolution was laid on the table by a vote of 105 to 75. Eighteen northern Democrats and fourteen northern Whigs voted against the resolution. Hamilton, "Cave of the Winds," 339.

27. Cole, *Whig Party in the South*, p. 166.

28. Winthrop, *Memoir of Robert C. Winthrop*, pp. 109-110.

29. *Ibid*., p. 110. Many years later, Winthrop told George P. Fisher that "the larger part of that Speech, was, I think, prepared before he had decided precisely to what conclusions he would come, & would have served as well for one side of the question as for the other. And, even after the Speech was made, I think, I have reason for thinking that he intended to fall in to the support of Genl. Taylor's policy, as I had done. But the violence with which he was denounced at the North, & the ferocious assaults of the Abolitionists in the West, made him angry, & impelled him to stand at bay & defy them." Robert C. Winthrop to George P. Fisher, March 12, 1884,

quoted in George P. Fisher, "Webster and Calhoun in the Compromise Debate of 1850," *Scribner's Magazine*, XXXVII (May, 1905), 582.

30. Cole, *Whig Party in the South*, p. 165, footnote, quoting New York *Herald*, April 13, 1852.

31. Augustine H. Shepperd to William A. Graham, April 26, 1852, Hamilton, *Graham Papers*, IV, 295.

32. Edward Stanly, *Speech of Edward Stanly, of N. Carolina, Exposing the Causes of the Slavery Agitation. Delivered in the House of Representatives, March 6, 1850* (Washington: Gideon & Co., 1850), *passim*.

33. Washington *Republic*, March 7, 1850; Washington *Daily Union*, March 7, 1850.

34. David Outlaw to Emily B. Outlaw, March 8, 1850, Outlaw Papers.

35. Raleigh *North Carolina Standard*, March 20, 1850; New Bern *Eastern Carolina Republican*, March 13, 27, April 17, 1850.

36. William A. Graham to James Graham, March 24, 1850, Hamilton, *Graham Papers*, III, 319.

37. New Bern *Newbernian*, March 26, 1850; Raleigh *Register*, March 27, 1850; Washington *North State Whig*, April 3, 10, 1850. See also Raleigh *Register*, April 24, 1850.

38. Sitterson, *Secession Movement in North Carolina*, p. 62.

39. Edward Stanly to James W. Bryan, April 6, 1850, Bryan Papers.

40. James W. Bryan to Edward Stanly, April 13, 1850, *ibid*.

41. Raleigh *North Carolina Standard*, April 3, 1850.

42. Sitterson, *Secession Movement in North Carolina*, pp. 62-63. See also Raleigh *North Carolina Star*, May 15, 1850.

43. Hamilton, "Cave of the Winds," 340, 345.

44. For a good analysis of the slavery provisions of the New Mexico and Utah acts, see Robert R. Russel, "What Was the Compromise of 1850?" *The Journal of Southern History*, XXII (August, 1956), 292-309.

45. David Outlaw to Emily B. Outlaw, May 13, 1850, Outlaw Papers.

46. Edward Stanly to James W. Bryan, May 13, 1850, Bryan Papers.

47. David Outlaw to Emily B. Outlaw, May 13, 1850, Outlaw Papers.

48. Hamilton, *Zachary Taylor*, pp. 336-337.

49. William W. Holden to David Reid, June 1, 1850, David S. Reid Papers, II, State Department of Archives and History, Raleigh.

50. Sitterson, *Secession Movement in North Carolina*, p. 69;

Raleigh *North Carolina Star*, June 26, 1850. See also New Bern *Newbernian*, May 28, 1850.

51. David Outlaw to Emily B. Outlaw, June 24, 1850, Outlaw Papers.

52. Edward Stanly to James W. Bryan, April 6, 1850, Bryan Papers.

53. Orlando Brown to John J. Crittenden, April 18, 1850, Hamilton, *Zachary Taylor*, p. 342.

54. *Ibid.*, pp. 346-352.

55. *Ibid.*, p. 352. Stanly's remarks during the debate may be found in Edward Stanly, *The Galphin Claim. Speech of Mr. E. Stanly, of North Carolina, in the House of Representatives, Saturday, July 6, 1850* (Washington: n.p., 1850).

56. Hamilton, *Zachary Taylor*, p. 382.

57. Weed, *Autobiography of Thurlow Weed*, pp. 590-592.

58. David Outlaw to Emily B. Outlaw, May 13, June 14, 1850, Outlaw Papers.

59. Hamilton, *Zachary Taylor*, p. 379; David Outlaw to Emily B. Outlaw, June 29, 1850, Outlaw Papers.

60. David Outlaw to Emily B. Outlaw, June 25, 1850, Outlaw Papers; Avary, *Recollections of Alexander H. Stephens*, p. 26.

61. Hamilton, *Zachary Taylor*, pp. 401-402; Holman Hamilton, *Prologue to Conflict: The Crisis and Compromise of 1850* (Lexington: University of Kentucky Press, 1964), pp. 118-132, hereinafter cited as Hamilton, *Prologue to Conflict*.

62. Augustine H. Shepperd to William A. Graham, April 26, 1852, Hamilton, *Graham Papers*, IV, 295.

63. Hamilton, *Zachary Taylor*, p. 402.

64. George Badger, Willie P. Mangum, and others to Millard Fillmore, July 16, 1850, Millard Fillmore Papers, Buffalo Historical Society, Buffalo, New York, hereinafter cited as Fillmore Papers.

65. *Congressional Globe*, 31 Cong., 1 Sess., XXII, 1509.

66. See Holman Hamilton, "Democratic Senate Leadership and the Compromise of 1850," *The Mississippi Valley Historical Review*, XLI (December, 1954), 405-418.

67. Hamilton, "Cave of the Winds," 348.

68. Sitterson, *Secession Movement in North Carolina*, p. 70.

69. Pegg, "Whig Party in North Carolina," pp. 70-71.

70. New Bern *Eastern Carolina Republican*, September 18, 1850; Pegg, "Whig Party in North Carolina," pp. 317-318; Sitterson, *Secession Movement in North Carolina*, pp. 70-71.

71. Hamilton, *Prologue to Conflict*, p. 165.

72. *Congressional Globe*, 31 Cong., 1 Sess., part 1, 787-792, 818, 909-910, 923, 995-996.

73. Washington *Daily Union*, May 10, 1850, quoting Philadelphia *Spirit of the Times*, n.d.

74. Washington *Republic*, May 13, 1850.

75. David Outlaw to Emily B. Outlaw, May 6, 1850, Outlaw Papers.

76. Washington *Daily Union*, April 27, May 11, 1850.

77. *Ibid.*, August 29, 1850, Washington *Republic*, October 3, 1850.

78. *Congressional Globe*, 31 Cong., 1 Sess., part 1, 1679-1680, 1692-1695, 1714-1716, 1724-1725; committee report in part 2, Appendix, 1319-1320. Stanly's remarks on the committee's investigation are printed in the appendix to the *Congressional Globe*, 31 Cong., 1 Sess., part 2, 1255-1258.

79. New Bern *Eastern Carolina Republican*, September 18, 1850.

80. Sitterson, *Secession Movement in North Carolina*, p. 72; Washington *North State Whig*, September 18, 1850.

81. Richard Hines to William A. Graham, September 16, 1850, Hamilton, *Graham Papers*, III, 392; James W. Osborne to William A. Graham, October 19, 1850, *ibid.*, III, 460.

82. Raleigh *Register*, November 13, 1850; Richard Hines to William A. Graham, October 14, 1850, *ibid.*, III, 452-453; Daniel M. Barringer to Edmund Deberry, December 13, 1850, Edmund Deberry Papers, Southern Historical Collection, University of North Carolina at Chapel Hill.

83. William A. Graham to James Graham, January 6, 1851, Hamilton, *Graham Papers*, IV, 3.

84. Edward Stanly to Henry Dimock, January 24, 1851, Washington *North State Whig*, February 5, 1851.

85. *Congressional Globe*, 31 Cong., 2 Sess. (Washington: John C. Rives, 1851), XXIII, 586-587.

86. Edward Stanly to William A. Graham, February 25, 1851, Hamilton, *Graham Papers*, IV, 47.

87. Truman, *Field of Honor*, pp. 430-431; Lorenzo Sabine, *Notes on Duels and Duelling, Alphabetically Arranged, With a Preliminary Historical Essay* (Boston: Crosby, Nichols, and Company, 1855), pp. 284-285; Stephen B. Weeks, "The Code in North Carolina, Contributions to the History of the Duello," *The Magazine of American History* (December, 1891), 450; Raleigh *Weekly North Carolina Standard*, March 5, 1851.

88. Edward Stanly to William A. Graham, February 25, 1851, Hamilton, *Graham Papers*, IV, 47. See also Edward Stanly to John Beckwith, February 24, 1851, John Beckwith Letters and Papers, Manuscript Department, Duke University Library, Durham, North Carolina.

89. Raleigh *Register*, March 8, 1851.

90. *Ibid.*

91. *Ibid.*, July 16, 1851.

92. *Ibid.*, July 9, 1851.

93. Edward Stanly to Henry Dimock, February 17, 1851, Washington *North State Whig*, February 26, 1851.

94. Hezekiah G. Spruill to William A. Graham, July 4, 1851, Hamilton, *Graham Papers*, IV, 140.

95. William S. Pettigrew to [James C. Johnston], June 24, 1851, Pettigrew Papers, SHC; Washington *North State Whig*, July 2, 1851.

96. Raleigh *Weekly North Carolina Standard*, June 11, 1851; *ibid.*, July 2, 1851, quoting Goldsborough *Republican and Patriot*, n.d.; Raleigh *Register*, July 2, 1851, quoting Plymouth *Villager*, n.d.

97. Edward Stanly to Millard Fillmore, June 18, 1851, Fillmore Papers.

98. A. S. Chesson to Colonel J. B. G. Roulhac, September 17, 1851, Ruffin-Roulhac-Hamilton Papers, Southern Historical Collection, University of North Carolina at Chapel Hill; Hezekiah G. Spruill to William A. Graham, July 4, 1851, *Graham Papers*, IV, 141.

99. James W. Bryan to William A. Graham, July 7, 1851, Hamilton, *Graham Papers*, IV, 142-143; Hezekiah G. Spruill to William A. Graham, July 4, 1851, *ibid.*, IV, 141. See also Raleigh *Register*, July 2, 1851.

100. Warren, *Beaufort County's Contribution*, p. 7.

101. Raleigh *Register*, June 25, 1851, quoting Goldsborough *Telegraph*, n.d.; Washington *North State Whig*, July 2, 1851.

102. Goldsborough *Republican and Patriot*, July 17, 1851. The *Republican and Patriot* denied that Ruffin was a disunionist, terming it an "INFAMOUS FALSEHOOD."

103. Raleigh *Register*, July 19, 1851, quoting Goldsborough *Telegraph*, n.d.

104. Raleigh *Weekly North Carolina Standard*, July 16, 1851, quoting Goldsborough *Republican and Patriot*, n.d.

105. Washington *North State Whig*, August 6, 1851; L. D. Battle to Kemp P. Battle, August 5, 1851, Battle Family Papers, A.

106. Washington *North State Whig*, July 30, 1851; Raleigh *Weekly North Carolina Standard*, July 30, August 6, 1851. See also Raleigh *Register*, August 2, 1851.

107. Raleigh *Weekly North Carolina Standard*, August 20, 1851; Washington *North State Whig*, August 13, 20, 1851; Hezekiah G. Spruill to William A. Graham, August 8, 1851, Hamilton, *Graham Papers*, IV, 184.

108. Edward Stanly to John Blackwell, H. T. Guion, W. H. Washington, J. W. Bryan, and others, August 16, 1851, Raleigh

Register, September 3, 1851. The Raleigh *North Carolina Standard* found Stanly's letter "in perfect keeping with his past political conduct." Raleigh *Weekly North Carolina Standard*, September 17, 1851.

109. Raleigh *Weekly North Carolina Standard*, August 20, 1851; Goldsborough *Republican and Patriot*, August 21, 1851.

110. Sitterson, *Secession Movement in North Carolina*, p. 93.

111. *Ibid.*, pp. 88-90.

112. Raleigh *Register*, August 16, 1851.

Chapter 8

1. *Congressional Globe*, 32 Cong., 1 Sess. (Washington: John C. Rives, 1852), XXIV, part 1, 9. See also Washington *National Intelligencer*, December 3, 1851.

2. Washington *National Intelligencer*, December 2, 1851.

3. Alexander H. Stephen to Howell Cobb, December 5, 1851, Ulrich B. Phillips (ed.), *The Correspondence of Robert Toombs, Alexander H. Stephens, and Howell Cobb*, volume II of the *Annual Report of the American Historical Association for 1911* (Washington, 1913), 268-269.

4. Alexander H. Stephens to Linton Stephens, December 10, 1851, *ibid.*, 273.

5. Robert Toombs to Absalom H. Chappell and others, February 15, 1851, *ibid.*, 227.

6. Edward Stanly to Robert C. Winthrop, November 24, 1851, Winthrop Papers.

7. Edward C. Cabell to William A. Graham, July 3, 1851, Hamilton, *Graham Papers*, IV, 137.

8. Allan Nevins, *Ordeal of the Union*, 2 volumes (New York: Charles Scribner's Sons, 1947), II, 28, hereinafter cited as Nevins, *Ordeal of the Union*.

9. Sitterson, *Secession Movement in North Carolina*, p. 95.

10. Quoted in Nevins, *Ordeal of the Union*, II, 27.

11. William A. Graham to James W. Bryan, March 22, 1852, Hamilton, *Graham Papers*, IV, 263.

12. Cole, *Whig Party in the South*, p. 231.

13. Raleigh *Register*, April 14, 1852.

14. *Ibid.*, April 21, 28, 1852.

15. William A. Graham to James W. Bryan, April 17, 1852, Hamilton, *Graham Papers*, IV, 290.

16. Edward J. Hale to William A. Graham, April 21, 1852, *ibid.*, 292.

17. Raleigh *Register*, May 19, 1852; Henry W. Miller to Willie P. Mangum, April 17, 1852, Shanks, *Mangum Papers*, V, 225; Dennis

Heartt to ———, March 31, 1852, *ibid.*, V, 223.

18. Cole, *Whig Party in the South*, pp. 234-236.

19. Outlaw declared in the House that "finding I was mistaken in the position which the Whig Party of the North occupied, as disclosed by their votes . . . upon the resolution of . . . Mr. Jackson, I wished to know, and understand, distinctly, what that position was." David Outlaw, *Whig Congressional Caucus—Fugitive Slave Law—The Presidency. Speech of Hon. David Outlaw, of North Carolina, in the House of Representatives, June 10, 1852* (Washington: Gideon, 1852), p. 5.

20. Cole, *Whig Party in the South*, pp. 236-238; Raleigh *Register*, April 28, May 22, 1852; Goldsborough *Republican and Patriot*, April 27, 1852.

21. Raleigh *Register*, April 28, 1852.

22. *Ibid.* On April 23, Outlaw wrote Colonel J. B. G. Roulhac that the only reason he could imagine for Scott's silence was "a desire to conciliate the abolitionists and free soilers, and that makes me more solicitous he should speak out." David Outlaw to Colonel J. B. G. Roulhac, April 23, 1852, Ruffin-Roulhac-Hamilton Papers.

23. Edward Stanly to William Schouler, May 10, 1852, William Schouler Papers, Massachusetts Historical Society, Boston, hereinafter cited as Schouler Papers.

24. Nevins, *Ordeal of the Union*, II, 27.

25. Outlaw, *Whig Caucus*, p. 7.

26. Edward Stanly, *Speech of Hon. Edward Stanly, of North Carolina, on the Indian Appropriation Bill, Delivered in the House of Representatives of the U.S., June 12, 1852* (Washington: Gideon and Co., 1852), *passim*.

27. Meredith P. Gentry, *Speech of Hon. M. P. Gentry, of Tennessee. Delivered in the House of Representatives, June 14, 1852* (Washington: Gideon and Co., 1852), *passim*.

28. *Congressional Globe*, 32 Cong., 1 Sess., XXV, 704-708.

29. Cole, *Whig Party in the South*, pp. 245-259; Nevins, *Ordeal of the Union*, II, 28-29.

30. Willie P. Mangum to Martha P. Mangum, June 23, 1852, Shanks, *Mangum Papers*, V, 234; Edward Stanly to William Schouler, May 18, 1852, Schouler Papers.

31. *Semi-Weekly Raleigh Register*, June 23, 1852; Frederick Nash to William A. Graham, [June, 1852], Hamilton, *Graham Papers*, IV, 334; George Little to William A. Graham, June 22, 1852, *ibid.*, 314.

32. Joseph B. Hinton to William A. Graham, June 23, 1852, *ibid.*, 322.

33. Raleigh *Weekly North Carolina Standard*, October 13, 1852.

34. S. J. Webb to Colonel J. B. G. Roulhac, June 28, 1852,

Ruffin-Roulhac-Hamilton Papers.

35. *Semi-Weekly Raleigh Register*, July 17, 1852; William A. Graham to John Barnett, July 6, 1852, Hamilton, *Graham Papers*, IV, 340-341.

36. *Semi-Weekly Raleigh Register*, July 21, 23, August 4, 1852.

37. Edward Stanly to Aaron P. Hughes, August 4, 1852, Miscellaneous Papers, series one, volume III, State Department of Archives and History, Raleigh.

38. Edward Stanly to William A. Graham, August 17, 1852, Hamilton, *Graham Papers*, IV, 373.

39. Thomas M. Blount to William A. Graham, August 16, 1852, *ibid.*, IV, 376.

40. Edward Stanly to James W. Bryan, August 25, 1852, Bryan Papers.

41. William A. Graham to Thomas Loring, August 24, 1852, Hamilton, *Graham Papers*, IV, 377-379; William A. Graham to W. P. Caldwell and others, September 4, 1852, *ibid.*, IV, 389-392; Raleigh *Weekly North Carolina Standard*, October 20, 1852.

42. Edward Stanly to James W. Bryan, August 25, 1852, Bryan Papers.

43. Edward Stanly to William A. Graham, October 4, 1852, Hamilton, *Graham Papers*, IV, 416.

44. *Semi-Weekly Raleigh Register*, October 13, 16, 1852; Raleigh *Weekly North Carolina Standard*, October 20, 1852.

45. *Semi-Weekly Raleigh Register*, October 13, 1852.

46. William D. Valentine Diaries, volume 12, Southern Historical Collection, University of North Carolina at Chapel Hill.

47. Raleigh *Weekly North Carolina Standard*, November 17, 1852; James C. Johnston to William S. Pettigrew, November 10, 1852, Pettigrew Papers, SHC; William S. Pettigrew to James C. Johnston, November 18, 1852, *ibid.* See also James R. Morrill, "The Presidential Election of 1852: Death Knell of the Whig Party of North Carolina," *The North Carolina Historical Review*, XLIV (October, 1967), 342-359.

48. Edward Stanly to William A. Graham, November 8, 1852, Hamilton, *Graham Papers*, IV, 430.

49. *Semi-Weekly Raleigh Register*, January 5, 1853.

50. Quoted in Nevins, *Ordeal of the Union*, II, 36-37.

51. Edward Stanly to William Schouler, May 18, 1852, Schouler Papers.

52. Edward Stanly to James W. Bryan, January 12, 1852, Bryan Papers.

53. Nevins, *Ordeal of the Union*, II, 34. Nevins contends that Scott was "far too independent to be controlled by Seward."

54. *Semi-Weekly Raleigh Register*, January 1, 1853; Raleigh *Weekly North Carolina Standard*, January 5, 1853.

55. Edward Stanly to Schuyler Colfax, February 4, 1853, Schuyler Colfax Letters, Manuscript Division, Library of Congress.

56. *Semi-Weekly Raleigh Register*, January 26, 1853, quoting Springfield (Mass.) *Republican*, n.d.; *ibid.*, February 23, 1853, quoting Norfolk (Va.) *Beacon*, n.d.; *ibid.*, February 23, 1853, quoting Washington *North State Whig*, n.d.

57. *Congressional Globe*, 32 Cong., 2 Sess. (Washington: John C. Rives, 1853), XXVI, 541-542. "It was but a moment ago," Stanly remarked, "that, without having any conference with the gentleman from Kentucky, I made the suggestion to a gentleman upon my right, that if this Territory was to be organized, it ought not to be done under the name of Columbia, but under that of Washington."

58. Warren J. Brier, "How Washington Territory Got Its Name," *Pacific Northwest Quarterly*, LI (January, 1960), 13-15.

59. Edward Stanly to Richard S. Donnell and others, March 25, 1853, *Semi-Weekly Raleigh Register*, April 20, 1853, quoting Washington *North State Whig*, n.d.

60. Washington *North State Whig*, May 4, 1853; Raleigh *Semi-Weekly North Carolina Standard*, May 11, 1853.

61. *Semi-Weekly Raleigh Register*, March 30, April 23, August 17, 1853. Ruffin polled 5,812 votes to 2,653 for Loften.

62. Edward Stanly to James W. Bryan, December 12, 1852, Bryan Papers.

Chapter 9

1. Hubert Howe Bancroft, *History of California*, 7 volumes (San Francisco: The History Company, 1884-1890), VI, 221-222, hereinafter cited as Bancroft, *California*.

2. Elijah R. Kennedy, *The Contest for California in 1861* (Boston: Houghton Mifflin Company, 1912), p. 19, hereinafter cited as Kennedy, *Contest for California*.

3. Bancroft, *California*, VI, 202.

4. San Francisco *Evening Bulletin*, June 14, 1856; San Francisco city directories for the years 1854 to 1862, in California State Library, Sacramento.

5. Kennedy, *Contest for California*, pp. 115-117, 288-289.

6. William Ingraham Kip, *Address Delivered in Grace Church, San Francisco, Sunday, July 14, 1872, at the Funeral of the Hon. Edward Stanly* (San Francisco: Edward Bosqui & Co., 1872), p. 5, hereinafter cited as Kip, *Address*; William Ingraham Kip, *The Early Days of My Episcopate* (New York: Thomas Whittaker, 1892), pp. 203-241.

7. San Francisco *Daily Alta California*, August 5, 1857.

8. Kennedy, *Contest for California*, p. 70; Bancroft, *California*, VI, 672-673.

9. San Francisco *Daily Herald*, August 28, 1855.

10. William Henry Ellison, *A Self-governing Dominion: California, 1849-1860* (Berkeley: University of California Press, 1950), pp. 276-287, hereinafter cited as Ellison, *A Self-governing Dominion*.

11. Peyton Hurt, "The Rise and Fall of the 'Know-Nothings' in California," *California Historical Society Quarterly*, IX (March-June, 1930), 24-44; Ellison, *A Self-governing Dominion*, p. 287.

12. San Francisco *Evening Bulletin*, August 11, 1857; Edward Stanly to William A. Graham, March 15, 1855, Hamilton, *Graham Papers*, IV, 594.

13. Sacramento *Daily Union*, August 20, 1855.

14. *Ibid.*, August 30, 1855.

15. San Francisco *Daily Herald*, August 28, 1855.

16. San Francisco *Daily Alta California*, August 30, 1855; San Francisco *Daily Herald*, August 30, 1855.

17. San Francisco *Daily Herald*, September 5, 1855; Sacramento *Daily Union*, September 5, 1855.

18. San Francisco *Daily Herald*, September 20, 1855.

19. Bancroft, *California*, VI, 697-698.

20. Cornelius Cole, *Memoirs of Cornelius Cole* (New York: McLaughlin Brothers, 1908), pp. 112-113, hereinafter cited as Cole, *Memoirs*.

21. John Carr, *Pioneer Days in California: Historical and Personal Sketches* (Eureka, California: Times Publishing Company, 1891), pp. 328-329, hereinafter cited as Carr, *Pioneer Days in California*.

22. Winfield J. Davis, *History of Political Conventions in California, 1849-1892* (Sacramento, 1893), pp. 59-61, hereinafter cited as Davis, *Political Conventions in California*; Edward A. Dickson, "How the Republican Party was Organized in California," *Historical Society of Southern California Quarterly*, XXX (September, 1948), 198, hereinafter cited as Dickson, "Republican Party in California"; Milton H. Shutes, *Lincoln and California* (Stanford University, California: Stanford University Press, 1943), pp. 15-16, hereinafter cited as Shutes, *Lincoln and California*.

23. Edward Stanly to E. B. Crocker, April 7, 1856, San Francisco *Evening Bulletin*, April 29, 1856.

24. San Francisco *Daily Alta California*, August 5, 1857. While in the East, Stanly visited in Washington, D. C. and had dinner with Senator William Seward, who wrote a friend: "Edward Stanley [*sic*] is here from San Francisco, the same true, loyal friend that he

always was, and improved moreover by his emancipation from serfdom in [a] slave State." William Seward to — — —, July 19, 1856, Seward, *Seward at Washington*, p. 283.

25. Dickson, "Republican Party in California," 199; Cole, *Memoirs*, p. 113; Shutes, *Lincoln and California*, p. 20.

26. Sacramento *Daily Union*, November 6, 1856. California's vote in the presidential election of 1856 is taken from Walter Dean Burnham, *Presidential Ballots 1836-1892* (Baltimore: Johns Hopkins Press, 1955), p. 292.

27. Theodore Hittell, *History of California*, 4 volumes (San Francisco: N. J. Stone & Company, 1885-1898), IV, 202.

28. Ellison, *A Self-governing Dominion*, p. 296; P. Orman Ray, "John B. Weller," *DAB*, XIX, 628-629.

29. Sacramento *Daily Union*, July 9, 1857.

30. *Ibid*. See also San Francisco *Daily Alta California*, July 10, 1857.

31. San Francisco *Evening Bulletin*, August 11, 1857.

32. Cole, *Memoirs*, p. 130.

33. San Francisco *Daily Alta California*, July 10, 1857; Sacramento *Daily Union*, July 11, 1857.

34. San Francisco *Daily California Chronicle*, July 10, 1857; Sacramento *Daily Bee*, July 11, 1857.

35. Edward Stanly to F. M. Haight and others, July 13, 1857, San Francisco *Evening Bulletin*, July 14, 1857.

36. Sacramento *Daily Union*, July 11, 1857.

37. *Ibid*., August 18, 1857.

38. *Ibid*.

39. *Ibid*., July 18, 1857.

40. *Ibid*.

41. Sacramento *Daily Bee*, July 20, 1857.

42. San Francisco *Herald*, July 18, 1857.

43. Sacramento *Daily Union*, July 20, 27, 1857. Charles E. De Long, a local Democratic leader, who heard Stanly speak at Camptonville, thought he made "a might poor break of it"; but refrained from a reply because of the lateness of the hour. Carl I. Wheat (ed.), "'California's Bantam Cock' The Journals of Charles E. De Long, 1854-1863," *California Historical Society Quarterly*, IX (June, 1930), 153.

44. Oscar T. Shuck, *Bench and Bar in California: History, Anecdotes, Reminiscences* (San Francisco: The Occidental Printing House, 1889), p. 280.

45. San Francisco *Herald*, July 20, 1857.

46. *Ibid*., August 10, 1857.

47. Cole, *Memoirs*, p. 131.

48. Sacramento *Daily Union*, July 27, 1857.

49. David Meeker and others to Edward Stanly, July 27, 1857, San Francisco *Evening Bulletin*, July 28, 1857.

50. Edward Stanly to David Meeker and others, July 27, 1857, *ibid*.

51. Davis, *Political Conventions in California*, p. 81.

52. Sacramento *Daily Bee*, July 30, 1857.

53. G. W. Bowie to Editor of the Union, August 16, 1857, Sacramento *Daily Union*, August 18, 1857.

54. Sacramento *Daily State Sentinel*, July 30, August 7, 1857; San Francisco *Evening Bulletin*, August 4, 1857.

55. Sacramento *Daily Union*, August 3, 4, 1857.

56. San Francisco *Evening Bulletin*, August 11, 1857.

57. San Francisco *Daily Alta California*, August 5, 1857. The *Alta* noted that Stanly's published letters plainly indicated "that he differs with the party on several important points."

58. Davis, *Political Conventions in California*, p. 83; San Francisco *Daily Alta California*, August 6, 1857; Edward Stanly to F. B. Austin, August 2, 1857, San Francisco *Evening Bulletin*, August 4, 1857.

59. Sacramento *Daily Union*, August 4, 5, 6, 1857.

60. San Francisco *Herald*, August 6, 1857.

61. Sacramento *Daily Bee*, August 19, 1857; Sacramento *Daily Union*, August 28, 1857.

62. Sacramento *Daily Bee*, July 13, 1857; Sacramento *Daily Union*, August 28, 1857.

63. Sacramento *Daily Bee*, August 3, 5, 1857.

64. San Francisco *Evening Bulletin*, August 11, 1857.

65. Sacramento *Daily State Sentinel*, August 27, 1857; Sacramento *Daily Bee*, August 27, 1857.

66. Carr, *Pioneer Days in California*, p. 343.

67. San Francisco *Daily California Chronicle*, July 29, 1857.

68. Sacramento *Daily Union*, September 1, 1857.

69. San Francisco *Daily California Chronicle*, August 29, September 1, 1857.

70. Sacramento *Daily Bee*, August 19, 1857; San Francisco *Daily California Chronicle*, October 7, 1857. Examples: San Bernadino, Weller 414, Stanly 7, and Bowie 0; Fresno, Weller 276, Stanly 1, and Bowie 0; Los Angeles, Weller 1,304 and Stanly 82.

71. Sacramento *Daily Bee*, September 8, 1857.

72. *Ibid*., September 8, 14, 1857.

73. San Francisco *Daily California Chronicle*, October 7, 1857.

74. Sacramento *Daily Bee*, September 29, 1857.

75. Quoted in Hurt, "Know Nothings in California," 116.

76. Edward Stanly to Editor of the Union, September 7, 1857, Sacramento *Daily Union*, September 9, 1857.

77. *Ibid.*

78. Carr, *Pioneer Days in California*, p. 345.

79. Dickson, "Republican Party in California," 200; Ellison, *A Self-governing Dominion*, pp. 297-307.

80. San Francisco *Daily Alta California*, May 12, 1859; Charles Candee Baldwin, *The Baldwin Genealogy: From 1500 to 1881* (Cleveland, Ohio, 1881), p. 468; Joseph Glover Baldwin, *The Flush Times of California*. Edited by Richard E. Amacher and George W. Polhemus (Athens: University of Georgia Press, 1966), pp. 65, 76.

81. Kennedy, *Contest in California*, p. 145; Shutes, *Lincoln and California*, p. 35.

82. Davis, *Political Conventions in California*, p. 116; Edward Stanly to Thurlow Weed, December 10, 1860, Thurlow Weed Collection, Rush Rhees Library, University of Rochester, hereinafter cited as Weed Collection.

83. The vote: Lincoln, 38,733; Douglas, 37,999; Breckinridge, 33,969; Bell, 9,111. See also Kennedy, *Contest for California*, p. 161, and Ellison, *A Self-governing Dominion*, p. 309.

84. Harry J. Carman and Reinhard H. Luthin, *Lincoln and the Patronage* (Gloucester, Massachusetts: Peter Smith, 1964), pp. 68-69; Edward Stanly to Thurlow Weed, December 10, 1860, Weed Collection. The White House chose Rankin for the collectorship over F. B. Folger, Baker's choice.

85. Edward Stanly to Thurlow Weed, January 10, 1861, Weed Collection.

86. Ellison, *A Self-governing Dominion*, pp. 310-311.

87. San Francisco *Daily Alta California*, February 24, 1861.

88. *Ibid.*

89. Sitterson, *Secession Movement in North Carolina*, pp. 180, 188.

90. Edward Stanly, *Letter from Hon. Edward Stanly, Military Governor of North Carolina, to Col. Henry A. Gilliam, Refuting Certain Charges and Insinuations Made by Hon. George E. Badger, in Behalf of the Southern Confederacy* (New Bern?, 1862), p. 2, hereinafter cited as Stanly, *Letter to Col. Henry A. Gilliam*.

91. Sitterson, *Secession Movement in North Carolina*, p. 197.

92. *Ibid.*, pp. 196-242; Glenn Tucker, *Zeb Vance Champion of Personal Freedom* (Indianapolis: The Bobbs-Merrill Company, 1965), pp. 96-106, hereinafter cited as Tucker, *Zeb Vance*.

93. Sitterson, *Secession Movement in North Carolina*, pp. 245-249.

94. Kennedy, *Contest for California*, pp. 202, 206-209.

95. *Ibid.*, p. 210.

96. *Ibid.*, p. 251.

97. Ellison, *A Self-governing Dominion*, pp. 313-314; Kennedy, *Contest for California*, p. 251. See also William Day Simonds, *Starr King in California* (San Francisco: Paul Elder and Company, 1917). Stanly's oration at the funeral of E. D. Baker, killed at Balls Bluff, Virginia, was strongly Unionist in tone. He urged the parents of "unnumbered generations" yet unborn to "encourage their children to love that country for which Baker died—to cherish our Government and its institutions, which can thus advance the humblest of her sons." San Francisco *Evening Bulletin*, December 11, 1861.

Chapter 10

1. Charles H. McCarthy, *Lincoln's Plan of Reconstruction* (New York: McClure, Phillips & Co., 1901), p. 11. For a more recent treatment of Presidential Reconstruction see William B. Hesseltine, *Lincoln's Plan of Reconstruction* (number XIII, Wm. Stanley Hoole, ed., *Confederate Centennial Studies*), Tuscaloosa, Alabama: Confederate Publishing Company, Inc., 1960.

2. Ben Dixon MacNeill, *The Hatterasman* (Winston-Salem: John F. Blair, 1958), pp. 166-167; Norman C. Delaney, "Charles Henry Foster and the Unionists of Eastern North Carolina," *The North Carolina Historical Review*, XXXVII (July, 1960), 358-359, hereinafter cited as Delaney, "Charles Henry Foster"; Thomas C. Parramore, "In the Days of Charles Henry Foster," Chapter 13 of *The Roanoke-Chowan Story* (Murfreesboro, North Carolina: Daily Roanoke-Chowan News, n.d.), pp. 146-156.

3. *Weekly Raleigh Register*, December 18, 1861.

4. Rush C. Hawkins to John E. Wool, September 7, 1861, R. N. Scott and others (eds.), *War of the Rebellion: A Compilation of the Official Records of the Union and Confederate Armies*, 130 volumes (Washington: Government Printing Office, 1880-1901), series I, volume IX, 608, hereinafter cited as *Official Records Armies*. In his first annual message to Congress (December 3, 1861), Lincoln noted that the Union had obtained a footing at isolated points on the southern coast; "and we likewise have some general account of popular movements, in behalf of the Union, in North Carolina and Tennessee. These things demonstrate that the cause of the Union is advancing steadily and certainly southward." Roy P. Basler and others (eds.), *The Collected Works of Abraham Lincoln*, 8 volumes (New Brunswick: Rutgers University Press, 1953), V, 50, hereinafter cited as Basler, *Collected Works of Lincoln*.

5. Joseph Gregoire de Roulhac Hamilton, *Reconstruction in North Carolina*, volume LVIII, *Studies in History, Economics and Public Law* (New York, Columbia University: Longmans, Green &

Company, 1914), p. 88, hereinafter cited as Hamilton, *Reconstruction in North Carolina*; Edward Stanly to William Seward, December 18, 1862, Edwin M. Stanton Papers, volume IX, Manuscript Division, Library of Congress, hereinafter cited as Stanton Papers.

6. Edward Stanly to William H. Seward, February 6, 1862, William H. Seward Collection, Rush Rhees Library, University of Rochester, hereinafter cited as Seward Collection.

7. Edward Stanly, *A Military Governor Among Abolitionists. A Letter from Edward Stanly to Charles Sumner* (New York, 1865), p. 4, hereinafter cited as Stanly, *A Military Governor Among Abolitionists*.

8. Edward Stanly to Leland Stanford, April 9, 1862, San Francisco *Daily Alta California*, April 11, 1862.

9. Edward Stanly to William H. Seward, February 6, 1862, Seward Collection; Edward Stanly to Stephen J. Field and others, April 17, 1862, New York *Times*, May 15, 1862.

10. New York *Herald*, April 23, 1862; New York *Times*, May 15, 1862.

11. New York *Herald*, May 20, 1862; New Bern *Daily Progress*, June 20, 1862.

12. New York *Times*, May 21, 1862.

13. Edwin M. Stanton to Edward Stanly, May 19, 1862, *Official Records Armies*, series I, volume IX, 396-397.

14. Edwin M. Stanton to Edward Stanly, May 20, 1862, *ibid.*, 397. Unlike Johnson and the other military governors, Stanly was not nominated to the Senate as a brigadier-general of volunteers. The most reasonable explanation is that he did not wish to appear in North Carolina in the guise of a military conqueror.

15. Edward Stanly to William H. Seward, December 18, 1862, Stanton Papers, volume IX.

16. Stanly, *A Military Governor Among Abolitionists*, p. 32.

17. New York *Herald*, May 22, 1862.

18. *Ibid.*, May 28, 1862.

19. Raleigh *Weekly Standard*, May 7, 1862.

20. *Ibid.*

21. *Weekly Raleigh Register*, May 28, June 4, 1862.

22. New York *Times*, May 23, 1862.

23. David L. Swain to Nicholas W. Woodfin, May 11, 1862, Nicholas Woodfin Papers, Southern Historical Collection, University of North Carolina at Chapel Hill.

24. New York *Times*, May 31, 1862; Boston *Daily Journal*, June 4, 1862; Daniel Reed Larned to Mrs. Ambrose E. Burnside, May 27, 1862, Larned Papers.

25. Ambrose E. Burnside to Edwin M. Stanton, May 28, 1862,

Official Records Armies, series I, volume IX, 393-394.

26. Daniel Reed Larned to Henry ———, May 28, 1862, Larned Papers.

27. Philadelphia *Inquirer,* June 2, 1862; Daniel Reed Larned to Henry ———, May 28, 1862, Larned Papers.

28. Philadelphia *Inquirer,* June 11, 1862.

29. Vincent Colyer, *Report of the Services Rendered by the Freed People to the United States Army, in North Carolina, in the Spring of 1862, After the Battle of Newbern, by Vincent Colyer, Superintendent of the Poor under General Burnside* (New York: Vincent Colyer, 1864), pp. 43-49, hereinafter cited as Colyer, *Report of the Services Rendered by the Freed People.*

30. Edward Stanly to Edwin M. Stanton, May 31, 1862, quoted in Stanly to Stanton, June 12, 1862, *Official Records Armies,* series I, volume IX, 400.

31. Statement of Vincent Colyer as dictated to his clerk, C. H. Mendell, New Bern, May 28, 1862, *Congressional Globe,* 37 Cong., 2 Sess. (Washington: Congressional Globe Office, 1862), part 3, 2477-2478, hereinafter cited as *Congressional Globe* with appropriate numeration.

32. New York *Times,* June 10, 1862.

33. Stanly, *A Military Governor Among Abolitionists,* p. 32.

34. Ambrose E. Burnside to Edwin M. Stanton, May 19, 1862, *Official Records Armies,* series I, volume IX, 390.

35. New York *Semi-Weekly Tribune,* June 20, 1862.

36. *Ibid.*

37. Edward Stanly to Edwin M. Stanton, May 31, 1862, quoted in Stanly to Stanton, June 12, 1862, *Official Records Armies,* series I, volume IX, 400.

38. New York *Times,* June 4, 1862.

39. *Ibid.*

40. Daniel Reed Larned to his sister, May 28, 1862, Larned Papers.

41. Stanly, *A Military Governor Among Abolitionists,* pp. 21-22.

42. *Ibid.,* p. 19.

43. Edward Stanly to Edwin M. Stanton, May 31, 1862, quoted in Stanly to Stanton, June 12, 1862, *Official Records Armies,* series I, volume IX, 400.

44. New York *Times,* June 5, 1862.

45. *Ibid.*

46. Charles Sumner and others, *The Works of Charles Sumner,* 15 volumes (Boston: Lee and Shepard, 1870-1883), VII, 112.

47. Colyer, *Report of the Services Rendered by the Freed People,* pp. 51-52.

48. Boston *Daily Journal*, June 13, 1862.

49. Stanly, *A Military Governor Among Abolitionists*, p. 4.

50. New York *Times*, June 6, 1862.

51. *Ibid.*, June 4, 1862.

52. New York *Herald*, June 3, 1862.

53. *Congressional Globe*, 37 Cong., 2 Sess., part 3, 2477-2478, 2495.

54. *Ibid.*, 2596.

55. Edwin M. Stanton to Edward Stanly, June 3, 1862, *Official Records Armies*, series I, volume IX, 395-396.

56. Edwin M. Stanton to Ambrose E. Burnside, June 9, 1862, *ibid.*, 398.

57. Ambrose E. Burnside to Edwin M. Stanton, June 9, 1862, *ibid.*

58. Edward Stanly to Edwin M. Stanton, June 12, 1862, *ibid.*, 399-402.

59. Ambrose E. Burnside to Edwin M. Stanton, June 24, 1862, *ibid.*, 403; Edward Stanly to Abraham Lincoln, July 7, 1862, Robert Todd Lincoln Collection of the Papers of Abraham Lincoln, volume 80, Manuscript Division, Library of Congress, hereinafter cited as Lincoln Papers.

60. New York *Semi-Weekly Tribune*, June 20, 1862.

61. New York *Times*, July 1, 1862; Boston *Daily Journal*, June 30, 1862.

62. New York *Semi-Weekly Tribune*, June 20, 1862; Boston *Daily Journal*, June 30, 1862.

63. *Congressional Globe*, 37 Cong., 2 Sess., part 4, 2927, 2973-2974. According to Edward L. Pierce, Sumner's protest against Stanly's appointment caused Stanton to withdraw the offer of a similar appointment for South Carolina to Pierce made through Secretary of the Treasury Salmon P. Chase, "who desired this appointment to be made as an offset to that of Stanly, and hoped by means of it to secure in the reorganized State a recognition of the negroes as citizens and voters." Edward L. Pierce, *Memoir and Letters of Charles Sumner*, 4 volumes (Boston: Roberts Brothers, 1877-1893), IV, 78, Footnote. See also Herman Belz, *Reconstructing the Union: Theory and Policy during the Civil War* (Ithaca: Cornell University Press, 1969), pp. 85-88, hereinafter cited as Belz, *Reconstructing the Union*.

64. *Congressional Globe*, 37 Cong., 2 Sess., part 4, 3138-3140; Belz, *Reconstructing the Union*, pp. 88-99.

65. Edward Stanly to Edwin M. Stanton, May 31, 1862, quoted in Stanly to Stanton, June 12, 1862, *Official Record Armies*, series I, volume IX, 400.

66. Hamilton, *Reconstruction in North Carolina*, p. 88.

67. Raleigh *Weekly Standard*, July 23, 1862.

68. Henry T. Clark to James G. Martin, June 11, 1862, Henry T. Clark Letter Book, 1861-1862, State Department of Archives and History, Raleigh, hereinafter cited as Clark Letter Book.

69. Wilmington *Daily Journal*, June 12, 1862.

70. Stanly, *Letter to Col. Henry A. Gilliam*, p. 3.

71. Henry A. Gilliam to Henry T. Clark, June 10, 1862, Governor Papers, Henry T. Clark, 1862, State Department of Archives and History, Raleigh.

72. Henry T. Clark to James G. Martin, June 3, 1862, Clark Letter Book.

73. Henry T. Clark to James G. Martin, June 11, 1862, *ibid*.

74. New Bern *Daily Progress*, June 20, 1862; Boston *Morning Journal*, June 26, 1862.

75. Boston *Morning Journal*, June 26, 1862.

76. New Bern *Daily Progress*, June 20, 1862.

77. Wilmington *Daily Journal*, July 25, 1862.

78. Alfred S. Roe, *The Twenty-Fourth Regiment Massachusetts Volunteers 1861-1866 "New England Guard Regiment"* (Worcester: Massachusetts: Twenty-Fourth Veteran Association, 1907), p. 129.

79. Abraham Lincoln to August Belmont, July 31, 1862, Basler, *Collected Works of Lincoln*, V, 350.

80. Washington (N. C.) *New Era*, June 25, 1862; New Bern *Weekly Progress*, July 5, 1862; Boston *Daily Journal*, July 9, 1862.

81. Memorandum of interviews between Hezekiah G. Spruill and the officers of the federal fleet, typed copy in Pettigrew Papers, volume 57, SHC, p. 40, hereinafter cited as Spruill Memorandum.

82. *Ibid.*, pp. 40-43.

83. Edward Stanly to Abraham Lincoln, July 7, 1862, Lincoln Papers, volume 80.

84. J. W. Page to Benjamin Hedrick, June 7, 1862, Benjamin Sherwood Hedrick Papers, Manuscript Department, Duke University, Durham, hereinafter cited as Hedrick Papers.

85. Wilmington *Daily Journal*, June 7, 12, 1862.

86. *Weekly Raleigh Register*, June 11, 17, 1862.

87. Wilmington *Daily Journal*, July 21, 1862.

88. Edmondston Diary, 1861-1865-66, typed copy in State Department of Archives and History, Raleigh.

89. Raleigh *Weekly Standard*, July 23, 1862; Stanly, *Letter to Col. Henry A. Gilliam, passim*.

90. Henry T. Clark to John Windish, August 13, 1862, Clark Letter Book.

91. Henry T. Clark to Thomas Clingman, August 13, 1862, *ibid*.

92. Diary of Thomas Bragg, 2 volumes, typed copy in Southern Historical Collection, University of North Carolina at Chapel Hill, II, 63.

93. Hamilton, *Reconstruction in North Carolina*, p. 45.

94. Lefler and Newsome, *North Carolina*, p. 438.

95. Hamilton, *Reconstruction in North Carolina*, p. 41; Tucker, *Zeb Vance*, pp. 145-158; Raleigh *Weekly Standard*, June 21, 1862; Horace W. Raper, "William W. Holden and the Peace Movement in North Carolina," *The North Carolina Historical Review*, XXXI (October, 1954), 493-495.

96. Quoted in Richard E. Yates, "Zebulon B. Vance as War Governor of North Carolina, 1862-1865," *The Journal of Southern History*, III (February, 1937), 48.

97. *Weekly Raleigh Register*, August 6, 1862.

98. Wilmington *Daily Journal*, July 31, 1862, quoting Washington *New Era*, July 24, 1862.

99. *Ibid.*

100. *Weekly Raleigh Register*, August 6, 1862.

101. Weldon N. Edwards to Thomas Ruffin, July 30, 1862, Hamilton, *Ruffin Papers*, III, 257.

102. Hamilton, *Reconstruction in North Carolina*, p. 42.

103. *Ibid.*, p. 43.

104. *Ibid.*, p. 42, quoting Philadelphia *Inquirer*, n.d.; New Bern *Daily Progress*, August 12, 1862; New York *Times*, July 30, August 20, 1862.

105. C. P. Wolcott to Edward Stanly, July 24, 1862, *Report of Committees of the House of Representatives*, 40 Cong., 1 Sess. (Washington: Government Printing Office, 1868), Report No. 7, p. 729, hereinafter cited as *Reports of Committees* with appropriate numeration.

106. John A. Hedrick to Benjamin S. Hedrick, September 25, 1862, Hedrick Papers.

107. James G. Randall, *The Civil War and Reconstruction*, Second Edition (Boston: D. C. Heath and Company, 1953), p. 371.

108. *Ibid.*, pp. 486-487.

109. Abraham Lincoln to Horace Greeley, August 22, 1862, Basler, *Collected Works of Lincoln*, V, 388-389.

Chapter 11

1. Edward Stanly to Abraham Lincoln, September 2, 1862, Lincoln Papers, volume 86.

2. The "Preliminary Emancipation Proclamation" is in Basler, *Collected Works of Lincoln*, V, 433-436.

3. James C. Welling, "Reminiscences of Abraham Lincoln by

James C. Welling," *Reminiscences of Abraham Lincoln by Distinguished Men of His Time*, Seventh Edition. Edited by Allen Thorndike Rice (New York: North American Review, 1888), XXX, 531-533.

4. Edwin M. Stanton to Edward Stanly, September 29, 1862, *Report of Committees*, 40 Cong., 1 Sess., Report No. 7, p. 729.

5. War Department Order, signed Edwin M. Stanton, September 29, 1862, *ibid.*, p. 730.

6. Edward Stanly to Abraham Lincoln, September 29, 1862, Lincoln Papers, volume 89.

7. Abraham Lincoln to Edward Stanly, September 29, 1862, Basler, *Collected Works of Lincoln*, V, 445.

8. Edward Stanly to Zebulon B. Vance, October 21, 1862, *Official Records Armies*, series III, volume II, 845-846.

9. Zebulon B. Vance to Edward Stanly, October 29, 1862, *ibid.*, 846-847.

10. Edward Stanly to Zebulon B. Vance, November 7, 1862, *ibid.*, series III, volume II, 847-849.

11. Zebulon B. Vance to Edward Stanly, November 24, 1862, copy in Zebulon B. Vance Papers, volume I, State Department of Archives and History, Raleigh. See also Tucker, *Zeb Vance*, pp. 199-201.

12. Edward Stanly to Edwin M. Stanton, November 19, 1862. *Official Records Armies*, series III, volume II, 845.

13. New York *Times*, November 19, 1862.

14. New Bern *Weekly Progress*, October 25, 1862.

15. Zebulon B. Vance to Jefferson Davis, October 25, 1862, quoted in Clement Dowd, *Life of Zebulon B. Vance* (Charlotte, 1897), p. 74.

16. John B. Jones, *A Rebel War Clerk's Diary at the Confederate States Capital*, 2 volumes (Philadelphia: J. B. Lippincott & Co., 1866), I, 197.

17. Kenneth Rayner to Thomas Ruffin, November 23, 1862, Hamilton, *Ruffin Papers*, III, 271-272.

18. New York *Herald*, July 22, 1862.

19. *Ibid.*, June 28, 1862.

20. Boston *Daily Journal*, July 1, 1862.

21. Spruill Memorandum, pp. 70-71, 84-85. The oath of neutrality was as follows: "I solemnly swear that I will not bear arms against the U States or give any information which can be used to their prejudice or do anything to aid or abet their enemies: so help me God."

22. Stanly, *A Military Governor Among Abolitionists*, pp. 39-40.

23. C. C. Howard to Harvey Stanley, August 21, 1862, Beckwith

Papers.

24. Edward Stanly to John G. Foster, November 13, 1862, Letters Received S, Department of North Carolina, National Archives, Washington, D. C.

25. W. P. Derby, *Bearing Arms in the Twenty-Seventh Massachusetts Regiment of Volunteer Infantry During the Civil War, 1861-1865* (Boston: Wright & Potter, 1883), p. 111, hereinafter cited as Derby, *Bearing Arms*.

26. New Bern *Daily Progress*, November 12, 1862.

27. New York *Herald*, August 25, 1862.

28. Wilmington *Daily Journal*, July 2, 1862.

29. Derby, *Bearing Arms*, p. 159.

30. C. C. Howard to Harvey Stanley, August 21, 1862, Beckwith Papers.

31. C. W. Flusser to S. P. Lee, December 2, 1862, R. Rush and others (eds.), *Official Records of the Union and Confederate Navies in the War of the Rebellion*, 30 volumes (Washington: Government Printing Office, 1880-1901), series I, volume VIII, 247, hereinafter cited as *Official Records Navies*.

32. S. P. Lee to Gideon Welles, November 17, 1862, *ibid.*, 213-214; H. K. Davenport to S. P. Lee, December 8, 1862, *ibid.*, 306.

33. *Ibid.*, series I, volume VIII, 306-307.

34. H. K. Davenport to Edward Stanly, December 6, 1862, *ibid.*, 307.

35. Edward Stanly to H. K. Davenport, December 6, 1862, *ibid.*, 307-308.

36. H. K. Davenport to S. P. Lee, December 8, 1862, *ibid.*, 306; Alexander Murray to S. P. Lee, December 9, 1862, *ibid.*, 305.

37. S. P. Lee to Alexander Murray, December 16, 1862, *ibid.*, 308-309.

38. Edward Stanly to William Seward, December 18, 1862, Stanton Papers, volume IX.

39. C. P. Wolcott to Edward Stanly, December 15, 1862, *Report of Committees*, 40 Cong., 1 Sess., Report No. 7, p. 731.

40. Edward Stanly to Edwin M. Stanton, January 10, 1863, Stanton Papers, volume X.

41. John G. Foster to Edwin M. Stanton, January 16, 1863, Letters and Discharges, Department of North Carolina, volume 32, National Archives, Washington, D. C.

42. Stanly's permit is in the Isaiah Respass Papers, Manuscript Department, Duke University Library, Durham.

43. Alexander H. Murray to S. P. Lee, February 7, 1863, *Official Records Navies*, series I, volume VIII, 556; Murray to R. T.

Renshaw, February 9, 1863, *ibid.*, 516-517.

44. S. P. Lee to Gideon Welles, March 25, 1863, *ibid.*, 628.

45. S. P. Lee to Alexander Murray, February 22, 1863, *ibid.*, 556-557; S. P. Lee to Gideon Welles, February 22, 1863, *ibid.*, 550.

46. Alexander Murray to H. K. Davenport, March 30, 1863, *ibid.*, 637.

47. Abraham Lincoln to Benjamin F. Butler, George F. Shepley, and others, October 14, 1862, Basler, *Collected Works of Lincoln*, V, 462-463.

48. New York *Times*, August 22, 1862.

49. New York *Herald*, August 28, 1862.

50. New York *Times*, November 14, 1862.

51. Delaney, "Charles Henry Foster," 362.

52. John A. Hedrick to Benjamin S. Hedrick, October 13, 1862, Hedrick Papers.

53. Delaney, "Charles Henry Foster," 362.

54. New Bern *Daily Progress*, September 9, 1862.

55. *House Reports Committees and Court of Claims*, 37 Cong., 3 Sess. (Washington: Government Printing Office, 1863), Report No. 41, p. 2, hereinafter cited as *House Reports* with appropriate numeration.

56. John A. Hedrick to Benjamin S. Hedrick, October 13, 1862, Hedrick Papers.

57. New York *Times*, November 14, 1862; New Bern *Daily Progress*, November 28, 1862.

58. New York *Times*, December 5, 1862.

59. M. Bowen to John G. Foster, November 30, 1862, *Official Records Armies*, series II, volume IV, 772.

60. *House Miscellaneous*, 37 Cong., 3 Sess. (Washington: Government Printing Office, 1863), volume I, Mis. Document 13, pp. 1-3, hereinafter cited as *House Miscellaneous* with appropriate numeration.

61. Edward Stanly to James Ward, Robert Chadwick, and Cicero Bell, December 21, 1862, *ibid.*, p. 3.

62. New York *Herald*, December 25, 1862.

63. New Bern *Daily Progress*, December 20, 1862.

64. New York *Daily Tribune*, December 9, 25, 1862.

65. New Bern *Weekly Progress*, December 4, 1862. In a letter to the *Progress*, Foster said he was not pledged to the extirpation of individuals who belonged to the "negro-driving aristocracy," but of the "'aristocracy' itself, as a system and a political power, by which a small minority keep down the great masses of poor white men, and deny to them education and equality." However, this and other reforms would be accomplished not by revolutionary violence, but

"by the writ of the majority expressed at the ballot box." *ibid.*,
December 13, 1862.

66. *Ibid.*, December 4, 1862.

67. New York *Daily Tribune*, December 25, 1862.

68. *Ibid.*

69. Abraham Congleton (Carteret), E. M. Carpenter (Craven), and
J. F. Millen (Hyde), to Abraham Lincoln, December 10, 1862,
Lincoln Papers, volume 94.

70. New York *Daily Tribune*, December 24, 1862; New York
Herald, December 29, 1862.

71. New Bern *Weekly Progress*, December 13, 1862.

72. New Bern *Daily Progress*, January 12, 1863.

73. New Bern *Weekly Progress*, January 10, 1863. The nineteen
precincts were: New Bern, Portsmouth, Newport, Smyrna, Beaufort
City, Cape Lookout Banks, Morehead City, Kinnakeet, Trent, Lake
Landing, Chicamacomico, Ocracoke, Hunting Quarters, Cedar Island,
Straits, Davis Shore, Harlow's Creek, Currituck, and Swan Quarter.

74. *House Reports*, 37 Cong., 3 Sess., Report No. 41, p. 1; New
Bern *Weekly Progress*, January 10, 1863; New York *Herald*,
January 10, 1863; *House Miscellaneous*, 37 Cong., 3 Sess., I, Misc.
Document 13, p. 1.

75. New Bern *Weekly Progress*, January 10, 1863.

76. *House Miscellaneous*, 37 Cong., 3 Sess., I, Misc. Document
14, p. 9.

77. *Ibid.*, p. 7.

78. New York *Herald*, January 10, 1863.

79. *House Miscellaneous*, 37 Cong., 3 Sess., I, Misc. Document
14, pp. 1-2; Stanly, *A Military Governor Among Abolitionists*, p. 43.
Stanly charged that several of the men at this meeting "made oath
that the resolutions had been changed by an unprincipled 'soldier of
fortune' [Foster], to whose hands they had been entrusted to be
forwarded to Washington. Thus forgery was joined to falsehood in
the work of detraction."

80. Charles Henry Foster to Henry L. Dawes, January 9, 1863,
House Miscellaneous, 37 Cong., 3 Sess., I, Misc. Document 14, p. 1.

81. *House Reports*, 37 Cong., 3 Sess., Report No. 41, pp. 1-2;
Congressional Globe, 37 Cong., 3 Sess., pp. 1208-1212.

82. New York *Times*, January 27, 29, 1863.

83. Moncure Daniel Conway, *Autobiography Memories and Experiences of Moncure Daniel Conway*, 2 volumes (Boston: Houghton, Mifflin and Company, 1904), I, 376-383.

84. Edward Stanly to Edwin M. Stanton, January 10, 1863,
Stanton Papers, volume X.

85. Edward Stanly to John G. Foster, January 20, 1863, *Official*

Records Armies, series I, volume XVIII, 525.

86. Edward Stanly to Abraham Lincoln, January 15, 1863, *Report of Committees*, 40 Cong., 1 Sess., Report No. 7, 731-732.

87. Edward Stanly to Edwin M. Stanton, January 15, 1863, *ibid.*, 731; Lorenzo Thomas to Edward Stanly, March 4, 1863, *ibid.*, 732.

88. Boston *Daily Journal*, February 18, 1863.

89. Edward Stanly to John G. Foster, December 29, 1862, *Official Records Armies*, series I, volume XVIII, 498; Stanly to Foster, January 20, 1863, *ibid.*, 525-526; Frank Moore (ed.), *Rebellion Record: A Diary of American Events, with Documents, Narratives, Illustrative Incidents, Poetry, etc.*, 11 volumes (New York: Putnam, 1861-1868), VI, 474-476.

90. Edward Stanly to John G. Foster, March 28, 1863, *Official Records Armies*, series I, volume XVIII, 182.

91. New York *Times*, April 25, 1863.

92. Edwin M. Stanton to Edward Stanly, May 12, 1863, quoted in Stanly, *A Military Governor Among Abolitionists*, p. 48.

93. Basler, *Collected Works of Lincoln*, VI, 184. On April 19, Foster had driven General Hill's Confederate forces out of Washington, North Carolina, which they had taken on March 30, 1863. Foster's appointment as Major-General, dated from July 18, 1862, was confirmed by the Senate on March 10, 1863. Stanly's request therefore seems to have been unnecessary.

94. New York *Times*, March 13, 1863; Petition, dated Washington, D. C., February 23, 1863, Lincoln Papers, volume 103.

95. John A. Hedrick to Benjamin S. Hedrick, March 13, 1863, Hedrick Papers.

96. Edward Stanly to William H. Seward, April 18, 1863, Seward Collection.

Chapter 12

1. A. Sellew Roberts, "The Peace Movement in North Carolina," *The Mississippi Valley Historical Review*, XI (September, 1924), 195, hereinafter cited as Roberts, "Peace Movement." See also Georgia Lee Tatum, *Disloyalty in the Confederacy* (Chapel Hill: University of North Carolina Press, 1934), pp. 118-127.

2. Richard Yates, *The Confederacy and Zeb Vance* (Tuscaloosa: Confederate Publishing Company, 1958), p. 87, hereinafter cited as Yates, *Confederacy and Vance*.

3. Roberts, "Peace Movement," 196-198; John L. Black to Captain Feilden, May 10, 1864, *Official Records Armies*, series I, volume LIII, 332.

4. Hamilton, *Reconstruction in North Carolina*, p. 50.

5. Jonathan Worth to H. B. Elliott, December 7, 1861, Joseph

Gregoire de Roulhac Hamilton (ed.), *The Correspondence of Jonathan Worth*, 2 volumes (Raleigh: Broughton Printing Company, 1909), I, 159.

6. Jonathan Worth to John Pool, February 6, 1864, *ibid.*, I, 289.

7. Hamilton, *Reconstruction in North Carolina*, pp. 55-56.

8. Edward Stanly to Salmon P. Chase, September 11, 1863, Papers of Salmon P. Chase, volume 80, Library of Congress.

9. Edward Stanly to William H. Seward, December 18, 1863, Seward Collection.

10. Edward Stanly to Abraham Lincoln, January 27, 1864, *Official Records Armies*, series I, volume XXXIII, 430.

11. Abraham Lincoln to Edward Stanly, January 28, 1864, Basler, *Collected Works of Lincoln*, VII, 158.

12. Quoted in Yates, *Confederacy and Vance*, p. 106.

13. Edward Stanly to Robert C. Winthrop, January 15, 1865, Winthrop Papers.

14. Edward Chase Kirkland, *The Peacemakers of 1864* (New York: Macmillan Company, 1927), pp. 132-136, hereinafter cited as Kirkland, *Peacemakers of 1864*.

15. Edward Stanly to David D. Colton, October 7, 1864, in Edward Stanly, *Letter from the Hon. Edward Stanly. His reasons for Supporting Gen. George B. McClellan* (San Francisco, 1864), *passim*.

16. San Francisco *Bulletin*, October 10, 1864.

17. *Ibid.*, October 12, 1864.

18. *Ibid.*

19. San Francisco *Daily Alta California*, October 30, 1864.

20. Edward Stanly to Robert C. Winthrop, January 15, 1865, Winthrop Papers.

21. Kirkland, *Peacemakers of 1864*, p. 76.

22. Basler, *Works of Lincoln*, VII, 514.

23. Shutes, *Lincoln and California*, pp. 167-168.

24. Edward Stanly to Robert C. Winthrop, January 15, 1865, Winthrop Papers.

25. [Charles Sumner], "Our Domestic Relations; Or, How to Treat the Rebel States," *The Atlantic Monthly*, XII (October, 1863), 507-509.

26. Edward Stanly to Charles Sumner, February 18, 1864, Stanly, *A Military Governor Among Abolitionists*, p. 10.

27. Charles Sumner to Edward Stanly, May 18, 1864, *ibid.*, pp. 10-11.

28. Colyer, *Report of the Services Rendered by the Freed People*, p. 5.

29. Edward Stanly to Robert C. Winthrop, January 15, 1865, Winthrop Papers.

30. Ambrose E. Burnside to Edward Stanly, January 16, 1865, Stanly, *A Military Governor Among Abolitionists*, pp. 12-13.

31. *Ibid., passim*.

32. Eric McKitrick, *Andrew Johnson and Reconstruction* (Chicago: University of Chicago Press, 1960), p. 85, hereinafter cited as McKitrick, *Johnson and Reconstruction.*

33. Quoted in *ibid.*, p. 190.

34. Two excellent studies of Johnson, Congress, and Reconstruction are La Wanda and John H. Cox, *Politics, Principle, & Prejudice, 1865-66: Dilemma of Reconstruction America* (New York: Free Press of Glencoe, 1963), and W. R. Brock, *An American Crisis: Congress and Reconstruction, 1865-67* (London: Macmillan and Co., 1963).

35. Edward Stanly to William H. Seward, July 9, 1866, Seward Collection.

36. William Seward to Edward Stanly, August 2, 1866, copy in *ibid*.

37. Edward Stanly to William H. Seward, July 9, 1866, *ibid*.

38. Edward Stanly to Thurlow Weed, July 9, 1866, Weed Collection.

39. McKitrick, *Johnson and Reconstruction*, pp. 394-420.

40. Davis, *Political Conventions in California*, pp. 237-239.

41. George R. Stewart and Edwin S. Fussell (eds.), *San Francisco in 1866 by Bret Harte. Being Letters to the Springfield Republican* (San Francisco: The Book Club of California, 1951), p. 55.

42. Edward Stanly to Reverdy Johnson, January 30, 1867, Reverdy Johnson Papers, Manuscript Division, Library of Congress.

43. Edward Stanly to William A. Graham, November 23, 1866, typed copy in William Alexander Graham Papers, Southern Historical Collection, University of North Carolina at Chapel Hill.

44. Davis, *Political Conventions in California*, pp. 242-254, 263-265.

45. Bancroft, *California*, VI, 327.

46. Davis, *Political Conventions in California*, p. 267.

47. San Francisco *Bulletin*, August 8, 1867.

48. Sacramento *Daily Union*, August 19, 1867.

49. Davis, *Political Conventions in California*, p. 267.

50. Edward Stanly to Eliza A. Ellison, October 16, 1867, Edward Stanly Letter–1867, Southern Historical Collection, University of North Carolina at Chapel Hill, hereinafter cited as Stanly Letter.

51. San Francisco *Daily Alta California*, October 11, 1868.

52. Sacramento *Daily Union*, October 21, 1868.

53. *Ibid.*, October 21, 1868.

54. Both quotes are from an unidentified newspaper clipping

from a Sacramento newspaper, dated October, 1868, in a Bancroft scrapbook, "Educated Men of California," in the Bancroft Library, University of California, Berkeley.

55. Charles H. Coleman, *The Election of 1868: The Democratic Effort to Regain Control* (New York: Columbia University Press, 1933), p. 369.

56. Davis, *Political Conventions in California*, p. 288.

57. Edward Stanly to Cornelius Cole, November 23, 1868, Cornelius Cole Papers, University of California Library, Los Angeles.

58. Edward Stanly to Thomas R. Roulhac, September 18, 1869, Ruffin-Roulhac-Hamilton Papers.

59. Campbell A. Menefee, *Historical and Descriptive Sketch Book of Napa, Sonoma, Lake and Mendocino, Comprising Sketches of Their Topography, Productions, History, Scenery, and Peculiar Attractions* (Napa City: Reporter Publishing House, 1873), p. 60.

60. *Ibid.*, p. 106.

61. *Great Register of the Election Precincts of the County of Napa, California, For 1872*, No. 2031 (Napa County Reporter Job Printing Office, 1872). Bound in *Napa Great Register, 1867-1890*, California State Library, Sacramento.

62. *The Napa County Reporter* (Napa City), October 3, 1868.

63. Edward Stanly to Thomas R. Roulhac, September 18, 1869, Ruffin-Roulhac-Hamilton Papers.

64. Edward Stanly to Eliza A. Ellison, October 16, 1867, Stanly Letter.

65. John A. Stanly to David M. Carter, December 16, 1871, David M. Carter Papers, Southern Historical Collection, University of North Carolina at Chapel Hill, hereinafter cited as Carter Papers.

66. *The Napa County Reporter*, November 11, 1871.

67. John A. Stanly to David M. Carter, December 16, 1871, Carter Papers.

68. *The Napa County Reporter*, June 8, 1872.

69. Edward Stanly to F. E. Johnson, June 16, 1872, *ibid.*, June 22, 1872.

70. *Ibid.*, July 20, 1872; San Francisco *Daily Alta California*, July 13, 1872.

71. San Francisco *Daily Alta California*, July 15, 1872; Kip, *Address*, p. 3.

72. San Francisco *Daily Alta California*, July 17, 1872.

73. *Ibid.*, July 13, 1872.

74. Margaret S. Beckwith to Edmund R. Beckwith, November 30, 1924, Beckwith Papers.

75. Whitford, "Home Story of a Walking Stick," p. 142.

76. San Francisco *Chronicle*, April 14, 1903.

77. Stanly, *A Military Governor Among Abolitionists*, p. 46.

Bibliography

I. PRIMARY SOURCES

A. Manuscripts

Battle Family Papers, 1765-1919. Series A. 7 boxes and oversized papers. Approximately 3,000 items. Papers of William H. Battle and his family including Kemp P. Battle. One letter on the Stanly-Ruffin congressional campaign of 1851. Southern Historical Collection, University of North Carolina at Chapel Hill.

Battle Family Papers, 1876-1955. Series B. 6,000 items, 5 volumes. Of little value for this study. Southern Historical Collection, University of North Carolina at Chapel Hill.

B. C. Beckwith Papers, 1808-1906 and n.d. 3 manuscript boxes. Of little value for this study. State Department of Archives and History, Raleigh.

Edmund Ruffin Beckwith Papers, 1753-1949. 3 boxes containing 45 folders of papers and 7 inches of 4 x 6 note cards. Correspondence of Edmund Ruffin Beckwith, New York lawyer, who was collecting material for a biography of his maternal great-great grandfather, John Wright Stanly, New Bern merchant. The collection contains very little material on Edward Stanly, but is invaluable for genealogical and background information on the Stanly family. Southern Historical Collection, University of North Carolina at Chapel Hill.

John Beckwith Letters and Papers, 1810-1882. 51 pieces. One letter from Stanly to Beckwith concerning the former's duel with Representative Samuel Inge of Alabama. Manuscript Department, Duke University Library, Durham.

Asa Biggs Papers, 1830-1849. I manuscript box. Letterbook of Asa Biggs, Democratic leader of Martin County, North Carolina. Almost entirely concerned with private business matters. Of little value for this study. State Department of Archives and History, Raleigh.

Thomas Bragg Diary, 1861-1862. 2 typed volumes. Civil War diary of Confederate Attorney-General Thomas Bragg. Several references to Stanly as military governor. Southern Historical Collection, University of North Carolina at Chapel Hill.

Bryan Papers, 1704-1929. 23,000 items including 111 volumes. For this study the most important letters are those to or from James W. Bryan, Whig of New Bern. Southern Historical Collection, University of North Carolina at Chapel Hill.

John Herritage Bryan Collection, 1773-1906. 5 volumes of mounted papers and 16 manuscript boxes. Bryan was a Union Whig from Wake County. The collection contains a number of interesting comments on the Stanly family. State Department of Archives and History, Raleigh.

David M. Carter Papers, 1713-1917. 5,625 items. A number of letters to Carter from John A. Stanly in California. Of little value for this study. Southern Historical Collection, University of North Carolina at Chapel Hill.

Henry T. Clark Letter Book, 1861-1862. Copies of letters to or from the governor's office. Several letters reveal Clark's concern over the influx of Stanly propaganda into the interior of North Carolina. State Department of Archives and History, Raleigh.

Cornelius Cole Papers, 1840-1940. 36 linear feet. Papers of Senator Cornelius Cole, one of the early Republican leaders in California. Of little value for this study. University of California Library, Los Angeles.

Schuyler Colfax Letters and Papers, 1839-1880. 3 manuscript boxes. A small collection of letters and other papers of Vice-President Schuyler Colfax of Indiana. One letter from Stanly giving his reasons for retiring from politics and moving to California. Manuscript Division, Library of Congress.

Craven County, North Carolina, Marriage Bonds, 3 volumes, State Department of Archives and History, Raleigh.

Edmondston Diary, 1861-1865-66. Typed copy in State Department of Archives and History, Raleigh.

Millard Fillmore Papers. 44 volumes. Consists of letters received by Fillmore as President and Vice-President, and 200 pieces of earlier and later material relating to him. One valuable Stanly letter to Fillmore giving his views on his impending contest with Thomas Ruffin (1851). Buffalo Historical Society, Buffalo.

William Gaston Papers, 1744-1814, 1,407 items. Business, personal, and political correspondence of William Gaston, North Carolina Federalist and leading jurist. A useful collection. Southern Historical Collection, University of North Carolina at Chapel Hill.

Governors Papers, Henry T. Clark, 1862. Of some value for this study. State Department of Archives and History, Raleigh.

William Alexander Graham Papers, 1750-1927. 14,614 items including 7 volumes. Letters and papers of William A. Graham, prominent North Carolina Whig. Typewritten copies of Graham's correspondence after 1856 in the Southern Historical Collection were used in place of the original documents. Southern Historical Collection, University of North Carolina at Chapel Hill.

Benjamin Sherwood Hedrick Papers, 1848-1893. 6,033 items and 4 volumes. Several letters from John Hedrick, Collector at Beaufort, North Carolina, commenting upon Stanly as military governor. Manuscript Department, Duke University Library, Durham.

Reverdy Johnson Papers, 1826-1876. 1 manuscript box. A small collection of the papers of Senator Reverdy Johnson of Maryland. One Stanly letter. Manuscript Division, Library of Congress.

Daniel Reed Larned Papers, 1861-1865. About 350 pieces in 3 manuscript boxes. Larned was General Ambrose E. Burnside's private secretary in North Carolina. His letters to his sister and friends contain several references to Stanly and to the closing of the Negro schools. Manuscript Division, Library of Congress.

Letters Received S. Department of North Carolina. Of little value for this study. National Archives, Washington.

Robert Todd Lincoln Collection of the Papers of Abraham Lincoln. 194 volumes, 2 manuscript boxes, 99 microfilm boxes. Several letters from Stanly to Lincoln. Manuscript Division, Library of Congress.

Miscellaneous Papers, 1697-1912. Approximately 1,500 items mounted in 5 volumes. State Department of Archives and History, Raleigh.

North Carolina Letters from the John J. Crittenden Papers, 1827-1863. 29 letters mounted in 1 volume. Typewritten copies from the Crittenden papers in the Library of Congress of letters to Crittenden from or relating to North Carolinians. Of some value for this study. State Department of Archives and History, Raleigh.

David Outlaw Papers, 1847-1853. 326 items. The papers consist almost entirely of Outlaw's letters to his wife while he was a member of Congress. A valuable collection. Southern Historical Collection, University of North Carolina at Chapel Hill.

Pettigrew Papers, 1772-1900. Approximately 3,500 items in 18 volumes of mounted papers and 7 manuscript boxes. This collection contains the papers of three generations of the Pettigrew family, Whig planters of Tyrrell and Washington counties. There are many letters from Stanly to Ebenezer Pettigrew, chiefly on political affairs, written from Washington, D. C., 1837-1841. The most important manuscript collection for this study. State Department of Archives and History, Raleigh.

Pettigrew Family Papers, 1684-1926. 14,000 items including 46 volumes. The correspondence of William S. Pettigrew contains considerable information on political affairs in Stanly's congressional district from 1849-1852. Very valuable for this study. Southern Historical Collection, University of North Carolina at Chapel Hill.

David Reid Papers, 1803-1880. 6 volumes of mounted papers and 17 extra pieces. Chiefly letters to Reid as Democratic governor and senator from North Carolina. Of little value for this study. State Department of Archives and History, Raleigh.

Isaiah Respass Papers, 1787-1887. 1,000 pieces. Mainly the business papers of Isaiah Respass, Mayor and merchant of Washington, North Carolina. Of little value for this study. Manuscript Department, Duke University Library, Durham.

Ruffin-Roulhac-Hamilton Papers, 1785 (1810-1900) 1935. 6,887 items including 8 volumes. Chiefly letters of the related Ruffin, Roulhac, and Hamilton families, with the bulk of the collection falling in the period 1810-1900. Southern Historical Collection, University of North Carolina at Chapel Hill.

John Rutledge Papers, 1782-1877. 633 items. Chiefly the papers of John Rutledge, a prominent South Carolina Federalist. One John Stanly letter. Of little value for this study. Southern Historical Collection, University of North Carolina at Chapel Hill.

Leverett Saltonstall Papers. One important Stanly letter. Massachusetts Historical Society, Boston.

William Schouler Papers. Several Stanly letters bearing on the election of 1852. Massachusetts Historical Society, Boston.

William Henry Seward Collection, 1776 (1840-1872) 1900. 100,000 unbound letters. Chiefly the correspondence of William H. Seward, governor and senator of New York, and Secretary of State under Lincoln and Johnson. Several letters from Stanly to Seward, who was a close personal friend. Rush Rhees Library, University of Rochester.

Thomas Sparrow Papers. Four Stanly letters. East Carolina Manuscript Collection, East Carolina University, Greenville, North Carolina.

Edward Stanly Letter, 1867. 1 item. Southern Historical Collection, University of North Carolina at Chapel Hill.

Edwin M. Stanton Papers, 1831-1870. 38 volumes, 1 envelope, 1 folder, 7 letterbooks, 4 manuscript boxes, 1 portfolio. Correspondence of Secretary of War Stanton, chiefly of the war period. There are two letters from Stanly (one addressed to Seward) complaining about his difficulties with the Union navy in North Carolina and one letter (also to Seward) requesting Stanton's approval of Daniel Reeves Goodloe as Stanly's successor in North Carolina. Manuscript Division, Library of Congress.

University of North Carolina Faculty Minutes, 1821-1841. Student Records, 1826-1827. Philanthropic Society Library Register, 1826-1829. North Carolina Collection, University of North Carolina Library, Chapel Hill.

William D. Valentine Diaries, 1837-1855. 15 unbound volumes filed in 2 boxes. Valentine was a Whig leader in Bertie County. Valuable chiefly for an account of an 1852 Whig mass meeting in Gatesville, North Carolina, addressed by Stanly. Southern Historical Collection, University of North Carolina at Chapel Hill.

Zebulon Baird Vance Papers, 1827-1903. 18 volumes of mounted papers and 6 manuscript boxes. Correspondence of North Carolina's "war governor" and later Democratic senator. A useful collection. State Department of Archives and History, Raleigh.

Thurlow Weed Collection, 1816-1882. 14,000 pieces. The papers of a New York Whig leader. Of some value for this study. Rush Rhees Library, University of Rochester.

John D. Whitford Collection, 1770-1899. 13 manuscript boxes and 2 volumes. Chiefly valuable for Whitford's lengthy reminiscence of early New Bern and its citizens. State Department of Archives and History, Raleigh.

Robert C. Winthrop Papers, 1498-1894. 38 volumes. The papers of Robert C. Winthrop, Massachusetts Whig representative and senator. Several Stanly letters to Winthrop. Massachusetts Historical Society, Boston.

Nicholas Woodfin Papers, 1795-1919. 150 items. One letter commenting upon Stanly's appointment as military governor. Southern Historical Collection, University of North Carolina at Chapel Hill.

B. National Government Documents

Congressional Globe, 1837-1843, 1849-1853, 1862-1863.

House Reports, 40 Cong., 1 Sess., 1868.

House Reports Committees and Court of Claims, 37 Cong., 3 Sess., 1863.

House Miscellaneous, 37 Cong., 3 Sess., 1863.

Richardson, James D., *A Compilation of the Messages and Papers of the Presidents, 1789-1897,* 10 volumes. Washington: Government

Printing Office, 1896-1899.

Rush, R. and others (eds.), *Official Records of the Union and Confederate Navies in the War of the Rebellion*, 30 volumes. Washington: Government Printing Office, 1894-1922.

Scott, R. N. and others (eds.), *War of the Rebellion: A Compilation of the Official Records of the Union and Confederate Armies*, 130 volumes. Washington: Government Printing Office, 1880-1901.

C. State and County Government Documents

Clark, Walter (ed.), *The State Records of North Carolina*, 16 volumes. Winston and Goldsboro, North Carolina, 1895-1905.

Great Register of the Election Precincts of the County of Napa, California. For 1872, No. 2031 (Napa County Job Printing Office, 1872). Bound in *Napa Great Register, 1867-1890*, California State Library, Sacramento.

Journals of the Senate and House of Commons of the General Assembly of the State of North Carolina, 1844-1849.

Saunders, William L. (ed.), *The Colonial Records of North Carolina*, 10 volumes. Raleigh: P. M. Hale, State Printer, 1886-1890.

D. Newspapers and Periodicals

Boston *Daily Journal*
Goldsborough *Republican and Patriot*
Napa County Reporter
New Bern *Carolina Federal Republican*
New Bern *Carolina Sentinel*
New Bern *Daily Progress*
New Bern *Eastern Carolina Republican*
New Bern *Newbernian*
New Bern *Spectator*
New Bern *Weekly Progress*
New York *Daily Tribune*
New York *Herald*
New York *Semi-Weekly Tribune*
New York *Times*
Niles' Weekly Register
Philadelphia *Inquirer*
Raleigh *Minerva*
Raleigh *North Carolina Standard*
Raleigh *North Carolina Star*
Raleigh *Register*
Raleigh *Semi-Weekly Register*

Raleigh *Star*
Raleigh *Weekly North Carolina Standard*
Raleigh *Weekly Register*
Raleigh *Weekly Standard*
Sacramento *Daily Bee*
Sacramento *Daily State Sentinel*
Sacramento *Daily Union*
Sacramento *Democratic State Journal*
San Francisco *Daily Alta California*
San Francisco *Daily California Chronicle*
San Francisco *Daily Herald*
San Francisco *Evening Bulletin*
Tarboro' Press
Tarboro' Southerner
Washington *Daily National Intelligencer*
Washington *Madisonian*
Washington *Republic*
Washington *Daily Union*
Washington *North State Whig.*
Washington (N.C.) *Whig.*

E. Contemporary Pamphlets

Chester, *The Campaigns of a "Conqueror"; Or, the Man "Who Bragged High for a Fight."* Raleigh: n.p., 1843.

Clingman, Thomas L., *Address of T. L. Clingman on the Recent Senatorial Election.* Washington: Gideon, 1849.

Colyer, Vincent, *Report of the Services Rendered by the Freed People to the United States Army, in North Carolina, in the Spring of 1862, After the Battle of Newbern, by Vincent Colyer, Superintendent of the Poor Under General Burnside.* New York: Vincent Colyer, 1864.

Gentry, Meredith P., *Speech of Hon. M. P. Gentry, of Tennessee. Delivered in the House of Representatives, June 14, 1852.* Washington: Gideon & Co., 1852.

Kip, William Ingraham, *Address Delivered in Grace Church, San Francisco, Sunday, July 14, 1872, at the Funeral of the Hon. Edward Stanly.* San Francisco: Edward Bosqui & Co., 1872.

Outlaw, David, *Whig Congressional Caucus–Fugitive Slave Law– The Presidency. Speech of Hon. David Outlaw, of North Carolina, in the House of Representatives, June 10, 1852.* Washington: Gideon, 1852.

Stanly, Edward, *Remarks of Edward Stanly, of North Carolina, Upon the Motion to Print the Report of the Committee Appointed to Investigate the Causes of the Late Duel. Delivered in the House of Representatives, April 28, 1838.* Washington: Gales & Seaton, 1838.

———, *Speech of Edward Stanly, of North Carolina, in Reply to Dr. Duncan, of Ohio: the Defender of the Administration; the 'Dear Sir' of Levi Woodbury, and the Pet of the Globe; in Which the Anti-Slavery Letter of Dr. Duncan is Examined. Delivered in the House of Representatives, January 17, 1839.* n.p., 1839.

———, *Speech of Mr. Stanly, of North Carolina, on Abolition Petitions. Delivered in the House of Representatives, January 16, 1840.* n.p., 1840.

———, *Speech of Edw. Stanly, of North Carolina, Establishing Proofs That the Abolitionists Are Opposed to Gen. Harrison, and That Gen. Harrison is Opposed to Their "unconstitutional effort." Delivered in the House of Representatives, April 13, 1840.* Washington (?): n.p., 1840.

———, *Sketch of the Remarks of Mr. Stanly, on the Branch Mint in North Carolina; Together with Extracts from the Speeches of Messrs. Everett, Morgan, and Reed, Exposing Various Abuses in the Expenditures of the Public Money.* Washington: Gales and Seaton, 1840.

———, *To the People of the State of North Carolina.* Washington: n.p., 1840.

———, *Speech of Edward Stanly, of N. Carolina, Exposing the Causes of the Slavery Agitation. Delivered in the House of Representatives, March 6, 1850.* Washington: Gideon & Co., 1850.

———, *The Galphin Claim. Speech of Mr. E. Stanly, of North Carolina, in the House of Representatives, Saturday, July 6, 1850.* Washington: n.p., 1850.

———, *Remarks of Hon. E. Stanly, of North Carolina, in the House of Representatives, February 11, 1852, in Reply to Mr. Giddings, of Ohio.* Washington: Congressional Globe Office, 1852.

———, *Speech of Hon. Edward Stanly, of North Carolina, on the Indian Appropriation Bill, Delivered in the House of Representatives of the U. S., June 12th, 1852.* Washington: Gideon & Co., 1852.

———, *Letter from Hon. Edward Stanly, Military Governor of North Carolina, to Col. Henry A. Gilliam, Refuting Certain Charges and Insinuations Made by Hon. George E. Badger, in Behalf of the Southern Confederacy.* New Bern (?), 1862.

———, *Letter from Hon. Edward Stanly. His Reasons for Supporting Gen. George B. McClellan.* San Francisco: n.p., 1864.

———, *A Military Governor Among Abolitionists. A Letter from Edward Stanly to Charles Sumner.* New York: n.p., 1865.

F. Published Correspondence

Basler, Roy P. and others (eds.), *The Collected Works of Abraham Lincoln,* 8 volumes. New Brunswick, New Jersey: Rutgers University Press, 1953.

Battle, Kemp P. (ed.),, "Newbern in 1819. Letter of Hamilton C. Jones, the Elder," *North Carolina University Magazine,* New Series, XII (April, 1893), 212-220.

———, "Letters of Nathaniel Macon, John Steele and William Barry Grove, with Sketches and Notes," *James Sprunt Historical Monographs,* III. Chapel Hill: University of North Carolina, 1902.

Hamilton, Joseph Gregoire de Roulhac (ed.), *The Papers of William Alexander Graham,* 4 volumes. Raleigh: State Department of Archives and History, 1957-1961.

———, *The Papers of Thomas Ruffin,* 4 volumes. Raleigh: North Carolina Historical Commission, 1918-1920.

———, *The Correspondence of Jonathan Worth,* 2 volumes. Raleigh: Broughton Printing Company, 1909.

Hoyt, William Henry (ed.), *The Papers of Archibald D. Murphey,* 2 volumes. Raleigh: North Carolina Historical Commission, 1914.

Keith, Alice Barnwell and William Masterson (eds.), *The John Gray Blount Papers,* 3 volumes. Raleigh: State Department of Archives and History, 1952-1965.

Phillips, Ulrich B. (ed.), *The Correspondence of Robert Toombs, Alexander H. Stephens, and Howell Cobb* (volume II, *Annual Report of the American Historical Association for the Year 1911*). Washington: Government Printing Office, 1913.

Shanks, Henry Thomas (ed.), *The Papers of Willie Person Mangum,* 5 volumes. Raleigh: State Department of Archives and History, 1950-1956.

G. Memoirs, Diaries, Travel Accounts, and Reminiscences

Adams, Charles Francis (ed.), *The Memoirs of John Quincy Adams, Comprising Portions of His Diary from 1795 to 1848,* 12 volumes. Philadelphia: J. B. Lippincott and Company, 1874-1877.

Avary, Myrta Lockett (ed.), *Recollections of Alexander H. Stephens His Diary Kept When a Prisoner at Fort Warren, Boston Harbour, 1865; Giving Incidents and Reflections of His Prison Life and Some Letters and Reminiscences.* New York: Doubleday, Page & Company, 1910.

Bailey, William H., "Reminiscences of North Carolinians: Edward Stanly," unidentified newspaper clipping in North Carolina Collection, University of North Carolina Library, Chapel Hill.

Carr, John, *Pioneer Days in California: Historical and Personal*

Sketches. Eureka, California: Times Publishing Company, 1891.

Cole, Cornelius, *Memoirs of Cornelius Cole.* New York: McLaughlin Brothers, 1908.

Conway, Moncure Daniel, *Autobiography Memoirs and Experiences of Moncure Daniel Conway,* 2 volumes. Boston: Houghton, Mifflin and Company, 1904.

Greeley, Horace, *Recollections of a Busy Life.* New York: J. B. Ford & Co., 1869.

Green, John P., *Fact Stranger Than Fiction. Seventy-Five Years of a Busy Life with Reminiscences of Many Great and Good Men and Women.* Cleveland, Ohio: Riehl Printing Company, 1920.

Hilliard, Henry W., *Politics and Pen Pictures at Home and Abroad.* New York: G. P. Putnam's Sons, 1892.

Jones, John B., *A Rebel War Clerk's Diary at the Confederate States Capital,* 2 volumes. Philadelphia: J. B. Lippincott & Co., 1866.

Kip, William Ingraham, *The Early Days of My Episcopate.* New York: Thomas Whittaker, 1892.

Manly, Matthias E., "Memoir of Hon. William Gaston, Late a Judge of the Supreme Court of North Carolina," *North Carolina University Magazine,* X (November, 1860), 193-203.

Miller, Stephen F., "Recollections of Newbern Fifty Years Ago; With an Appendix, Including Letters from Judges Gaston, Donnell, Manly and Gov. Swain," *Our Living and Our Dead,* I (November, 1874), 239-252; (December, 1874), 338-352; (January, 1875), 449-467; (February, 1875), 583-586.

Pierce, Edward L., *Memoir and Letters of Charles Sumner,* 4 volumes. Boston: Roberts Brothers, 1877-1893.

Poore, Ben: Perley, *Perley's Reminiscences of Sixty Years in the National Metropolis,* 2 volumes. Philadelphia: Hubbard Brothers, 1886.

Rodman, Lida Turnstall (ed.), "Journal of a Tour to North Carolina by William Attmore, 1787," *The James Sprunt Historical Publications,* XVII. Chapel Hill: University of North Carolina, 1922), 5-46.

Sargent, Nathan, *Public Men and Events from the Commencement of Mr. Monroe's Administration, in 1817, to the Close of Mr. Fillmore's Administration, in 1853,* 2 volumes. Philadelphia: J. B. Lippincott & Co., 1875.

Seward, Frederick W., *William H. Seward: An Autobiography from 1801 to 1834. With a Memoir of His Life and Selections from His Letters, 1831-1846.* Second Edition. New York: Derby and Miller, 1891.

———, *Seward at Washington as Senator and Secretary of State. A Memoir of His Life, With Selections from His Letters, 1846-1861.* New York: Derby and Miller, 1891.

Shuck, Oscar T., *Bench and Bar in California. History, Anecdotes, Reminiscences.* San Francisco: The Occidental Printing Company, 1889.

Stewart, George R. and Edwin S. Fussell (eds.), *San Francisco in 1866 by Bret Harte. Being Letters to the Springfield Republican.* San Francisco: The Book Club of California, 1951.

Sumner, Charles and others, *The Works of Charles Sumner,* 15 volumes. Boston: Lee and Shepard, 1870-1883.

Tuckerman, Bayard (ed.), *The Diary of Philip Hone, 1828-1851,* 2 volumes. New York: Dodd, Mead and Company, 1889.

Weed, Harriet A. (ed.), *The Autobiography of Thurlow Weed.* Boston: Houghton, Mifflin and Company, 1884.

Welling, James C., "Reminiscences of Abraham Lincoln by James C. Welling," *Reminiscences of Abraham Lincoln by Distinguished Men of His Time.* Seventh Edition. Collected and Edited by Allen Thorndike Rice. New York: North American Review, 1888, pp. 519-557.

Wheat, Carl I. (ed.), "'California's Bantam Cock' The Journals of Charles E. De Long, 1854-1863," *California Historical Society Quarterly,* IX (June, 1930), 50-80.

Wheeler, John H., *Reminiscences and Memoirs of North Carolina and Eminent North Carolinians.* Columbus, Ohio: Columbus Printing Works, 1884.

Winthrop, Robert C., Jr., *A Memoir of Robert C. Winthrop.* Boston: Little, Brown, and Company, 1897.

H. Regimental Histories

Derby, W. P., *Bearing Arms in the Twenty-Seventh Massachusetts Regiment of Volunteer Infantry During the Civil War, 1861-1865.* Boston: Wright & Potter Printing Company, 1883.

Roe, Alfred S., *The Twenty-Fourth Regiment Massachusetts Volunteers 1861-1866 "New England Guard Regiment."* Worcester: Twenty-Fourth Veteran Association, 1907.

II. SECONDARY WORKS

A. General Works

Ashe, Samuel A. Court, *History of North Carolina,* 2 volumes. Raleigh: Edwards & Broughton, 1925.

Bancroft, Hubert Howe, *History of California,* 7 volumes. San Francisco: The History Campany, 1884-1890.

Hittell, Theodore H., *History of California,* 4 volumes. San Francisco: N. J. Stone & Company, 1885-1898.

Lefler, Hugh Talmadge and Albert Ray Newsome, *North Caro-lina: The History of a Southern State.* Revised Edition. Chapel Hill: University of North Carolina Press, 1963.

Moore, Frank (ed.), *Rebellion Record; A Diary of American Events, With Documents, Narratives, Illustrative Incidents, Poetry, etc; With an Introductory Address by Edward Everett,* 11 volumes. New York: Putnam, 1861-1868.

Moore, John W., *History of North Carolina; from the Earliest Discoveries to the Present Time,* 2 volumes. Raleigh: Alfred Williams & Co., 1880.

B. Monographs and Special Studies

Baldwin, Charles Candee, *The Baldwin Genealogy: From 1500 to 1861.* Cleveland, Ohio, 1881.

Barringer, Rufus, *History of the North Carolina Railroad* ("Papers of the North Carolina Historical Society at the University of North Carolina"). Raleigh: News and Observer Press, 1895.

Belz, Herman, *Reconstructing the Union: Theory and Policy during the Civil War.* Ithaca: Cornell University Press, 1969.

Brock, W. R., *An American Crisis: Congress and Reconstruction, 1865-67.* London: Macmillan and Co., 1963.

Burnham, Walter Dean, *Presidential Ballots 1836-1892.* Balti-more: Johns Hopkins Press, 1955.

Carman, Harry J. and Reinhard H. Luthin, *Lincoln and the Patronage.* Second Edition. Gloucester, Massachusetts: Peter Smith, 1964.

Carraway, Gertrude S., *Crown of Life. History of Christ Church New Bern, N. C. 1715-1940.* New Bern: Owen G. Dunn, Publisher, 1940.

Carroll, Eber Malcolm, *Origins of the Whig Party.* Durham: Duke University Press, 1925.

Cole, Arthur Charles, *The Whig Party in the South.* Washington: American Historical Association, 1913.

Coleman, Charles H., *The Election of 1868: The Democratic Effort to Regain Control.* New York: Columbia University Press, 1933.

Cox, La Wanda and John H., *Politics, Principle, & Prejudice, 1865-66: Dilemma of Reconstruction America.* New York: Free Press of Glencoe, 1963.

Creecy, Richard Benbury, *Grandfather's Tales of North Carolina History.* Raleigh: Edwards & Broughton, 1901.

Davis, Winfield J., *History of Political Conventions in California, 1849-1892.* Sacramento, 1893.

Dodge, Grenville M. and William Arba Ellis, *Norwich University 1819-1911. Her History, Her Graduates, Her Roll of Honor,* 3 volumes. Montpelier, Vermont: The Capital City Press, 1911.

Doherty, Herbert J., *The Whigs of Florida, 1845-18594*. Gainesville: University of Florida Press, 1959.

Eaton, Clement, *Henry Clay and the Art of American Politics.* Boston: Little, Brown and Company, 1957.

Ellison, William Henry, *A Self-governing Dominion: California, 1849-1860.* Berkeley: University of California Press, 1950.

Franklin, John Hope, *The Free Negro in North Carolina, 1790-1860.* Chapel Hill: University of North Carolina Press, 1943.

Giddings, Joshua R., *History of the Rebellion: Its Authors and Causes.* New York: Follet, Foster & Co., 1864.

Gilpatrick, Delbert Harold, *Jeffersonian Democracy in North Carolina, 1789-1816.* New York: Columbia University Press, 1931.

Hamilton, Holman, *Prologue to Conflict: The Crisis and Compromise of 1850.* Lexington: University of Kentucky Press, 1964.

Hamilton, Joseph Gregoire de Roulhac, *Party Politics in North Carolina, 1835-1860* (volume XV, *James Sprunt Historical Publications*). Chapel Hill: University of North Carolina, 1916.

———, *Reconstruction in North Carolina* (volume LVIII, *Columbia University Studies in History, Economics and Public Law*). New York: Longmans, Green & Co., 1914.

Hesseltine, William B., *Lincoln's Plan of Reconstruction* (number XIII, Wm. Stanley Hoole (ed.), *Confederate Centennial Studies*). Tuscaloosa, Alabama: Confederate Publishing Company, Inc., 1960.

Hoffman, William S., *Andrew Jackson and North Carolina Politics* (volume XL, *The James Sprunt Studies in History and Political Science*). Chapel Hill: University of North Carolina Press, 1958.

Hyman, Harold M., *A More Perfect Union: The Impact of the Civil War on the Constitution.* New York: Alfred A. Knopf, 1973.

Johnson, Guion Griffis, *Ante-Bellum North Carolina: A Social History.* Chapel Hill: University of North Carolina Press, 1937.

Jones, Jo. Seawell, *A Defence of the Revolutionary History of the State of North Carolina from the Aspersions of Mr. Jefferson.* Boston: Charles Bowen, 1834.

Kennedy, Elijah R., *The Contest for California in 1861.* Boston: Houghton Mifflin Company, 1912.

Kirkland, Edward Chase, *The Peacemakers of 1864.* New York: The Macmillan Company, 1927.

London, Lawrence Foushee, "The Public Career of George Edmund Badger" (Unpublished doctoral dissertation, University of North Carolina, 1936).

MacNeill, Ben Dixon, *The Hatterasman.* Winston Salem: John F.

Blair, 1958.

McCarthy, Charles H., *Lincoln's Plan of Reconstruction*. New York: McClure, Phillips & Co., 1901.

McKitrick, Eric, *Andrew Johnson and Reconstruction*. Chicago: University of Chicago Press, 1960.

Menefee, Campbell A., *Historical and Descriptive Sketch Book of Napa, Sonoma, Lake and Mendocino, Comprising Sketches of Their Topography, Productions, History, Scenery, and Peculiar Attractions*. Napa City: Reporter Publishing House, 1873.

Morgan, Robert J., *A Whig Embattled: The Presidency Under John Tyler*. Lincoln: University of Nebraska Press, 1954.

Murray, Paul, *The Whig Party in Georgia, 1825-1853*. (volume XXIX, *The James Sprunt Studies in History and Political Science*). Chapel Hill: University of North Carolina Press, 1948.

Nevins, Allan, *Ordeal of the Union*, 2 volumes. New York: Charles Scribner's Sons, 1947.

Norton, Clarence C., *The Democratic Party in North Carolina, 1835-1861* (volume XXI, *James Sprunt Historical Studies*). Chapel Hill: University of North Carolina Press, 1930.

Pegg, Herbert D., "The Whig Party in North Carolina, 1834-1861" (Unpublished doctoral dissertation, University of North Carolina, 1932).

Pessen, Edward, *Jacksonian America: Society, Personality, and Politics*. Homewood, Illinois: The Dorsey Press, 1969.

Phillips, Ulrich B., "The Southern Whigs, 1834-1854," (*Essays in American History*. Edited by Guy Stanton Ford. New York: Henry Holt and Company, 1910), 203-229.

Poage, George Rawlings, *Henry Clay and the Whig Party*. Chapel Hill: University of North Carolina Press, 1936.

Randall, James G., *The Civil War and Reconstruction*. Second Edition. Boston: D. C. Heath and Company, 1953.

Sabine, Lorenzo, *Notes of Duels and Duelling, Alphabetically Arranged, With a Preliminary Historical Essay*. Boston: Crosby, Nichols, and Company, 1855.

Shutes, Milton H., *Lincoln and California*. Stanford University, California: Stanford University Press, 1943.

Silbey, Joel H., *The Shrine of Party: Congressional Voting Behavior, 1841-1852*. Pittsburgh: University of Pittsburgh Press, 1967.

Simms, Henry H., *Emotion at High Tide: Abolition as a Controversial Factor, 1830-1845*. Richmond: William Byrd Press, Inc., 1960.

Simonds, William Day, *Starr King in California*. San Francisco: Paul Elder and Company, 1917.

Sitterson, Joseph Carlyle, *The Secession Movement in North Carolina* (volume XXIII, *The James Sprunt Studies in History and Political Science*). Chapel Hill: University of North Carolina Press, 1939.

Tatum, Georgia Lee, *Disloyalty in the Confederacy*. Chapel Hill: University of North Carolina Press, 1934.

Tilghman, Oswald, *History of Talbot County Maryland, 1661-1861*, 2 volumes. Baltimore: Williams & Wilkes Company, 1915.

Truman, Ben C., *The Field of Honor: Being a Complete and Comprehensive History of Dueling in All Countries*. New York: Fords, Howard, & Hubert, 1884.

Turner, J. Kelly and John L. Bridges, Jr., *History of Edgecombe County, North Carolina*. Raleigh: Edwards & Broughton Printing Company, 1920.

Van Deusen, Glyndon, *The Jacksonian Era, 1828-1848*. New York: Harper & Brothers, 1959.

Wagstaff, Henry McGilbert, *Federalism in North Carolina* (volume IX, *The James Sprunt Historical Publications*). Chapel Hill: University of North Carolina, 1910.

———, *State Rights and Political Parties in North Carolina— 1776-1861* (series XXIV, *Johns Hopkins University Studies*). Baltimore: Johns Hopkins Press, 1906.

Warren, Lindsay C., *Beaufort County's Contribution to a Notable Era of North Carolina History*. Washington: Government Printing Office, 1930.

Wheeler, John H., *Historical Sketches of North Carolina from 1584 to 1851*. Two volumes in one. Second Edition. New York: Frederick H. Hitchcock, 1925.

Yates, Richard E., *The Confederacy and Zeb Vance* (number VIII, Wm. Stanley Hoole (ed.), *Confederate Centennial Studies*). Tuscaloosa, Alabama: Confederate Publishing Company, Inc., 1958.

C. Biographies

Bancroft scrapbook, "Educated Men of California," Bancroft Library, University of California, Berkeley.

Chitwood, Oliver Perry, *John Tyler: Champion of the Old South*. Second Edition. New York: Russell & Russell, Inc., 1964.

Cleves, Freeman, *Old Tippecanoe: William Henry Harrison and His Time*. New York: Charles Scribner's Sons, 1939.

Connor, R. D. W., *William Gaston: A Southern Federalist of the Old School and His Yankee Friends 1778-1844*. Worcester, Massachusetts: American Antiquarian Society, 1934.

Dickey, Dallas C., *Seargent S. Prentiss: Whig Orator of the Old South*. Baton Rouge, Louisiana State University Press, 1945.

Dowd, Clement, *Life of Zebulon B. Vance*. Charlotte, 1897.

Hamilton, Holman, *Zachary Taylor: Soldier in the White House*. Indianapolis: The Bobbs-Merrill Company, 1951.

Hamilton, Joseph Gregoire de Roulhac, "Edward Stanly," *Dictionary of American Biography*, 22 volumes and index. Edited by Allen Johnson and Dumas Malone (New York: Charles Scribner's Sons, 1928–), XVII, 515-516.

–––, "Kenneth Rayner," *DAB*, XV, 416-417.

Julian, George W., *The Life of Joshua R. Giddings*. Chicago: A. C. McClurg and Company, 1892.

Ray, P. Orman, "John B. Weller," *DAB*, XIX, 628-629.

Robinson, Blackwell P., *William R. Davie*. Chapel Hill: University of North Carolina Press, 1957.

Schauinger, Joseph Herman, *William Gaston Carolinian*. Milwaukee: The Bruce Publishing Company, 1949.

Sellers, Charles Grier, Jr., *James K. Polk Jacksonian 1795-1843*. Princeton: Princeton University Press, 1957.

Simms, Henry H., *Life of Robert M. T. Hunter. A Study in Sectionalism and Secession*. Richmond: William Byrd Press, 1935.

Spalding, Thomas Marshall, "Lewis Addison Armistead," *DAB*, I, 347.

Steel, Edward M., Jr., *T. Butler King of Georgia*. Athens: University of Georgia Press, 1967.

Tucker, Glenn, *Zeb Vance: Champion of Personal Freedom*. Indianapolis: The Bobbs-Merrill Company, 1965.

D. Articles

Brier, Warren J., "How Washington Territory Got Its Name," *Pacific Historical Quarterly*, LI (January, 1960), 13-15.

Delaney, Norman C., "Charles Henry Foster and the Unionists of Eastern North Carolina," *The North Carolina Historical Review*, XXXVII (July, 1960), 348-366.

Dickson, Edward A., "How the Republican Party Was Organized in California," *Historical Society of Southern California Quarterly*, XXX (September, 1948), 197-204.

Dill, Alonzo Thomas, Jr., "Eighteenth Century New Bern–A History of the Town and Craven County, 1700-1800, Part VII, New Bern During the Revolution," *The North Carolina Historical Review*, XXIII (July, 1946), 325-359.

Fisher, George P., "Webster and Calhoun in the Compromise Debate of 1850," *Scribner's Magazine*, XXXVII (May, 1905), 578-586.

Gatell, Frank Otto, "Money and Party in Jacksonian America: A Quantitative Look at New York City's Men of Quality," *Political*

Science Quarterly, LXXXII (June, 1967), 235-252.

Gilpatrick, D. H., "North Carolina Congressional Elections, 1803-1810," *The North Carolina Historical Review*, X (July, 1933), 168-185.

Hamilton, Holman, "'The Cave of the Winds' and the Compromise of 1850," *The Journal of Southern History*, XXIII (August, 1957), 331-353.

———, "Democratic Senate Leadership and the Compromise of 1850," *The Mississippi Valley Historical Review*, XLI (December, 1954), 403-418.

Hoffmann, William S., "The Downfall of the Democrats: The Reaction of North Carolinians to Jacksonian Land Policy," *The North Carolina Historical Review*, XXXIII (April, 1956), 166-182.

———, "The Election of 1836 in North Carolina," *The North Carolina Historical Review*, XXXII (January, 1955), 31-51.

———, "John Branch and the Origins of the Whig Party in North Carolina," *The North Carolina Historical Review*, XXXV (July, 1958), 299-315.

Hurt, Peyton, "The Rise and Fall of the 'Know Nothings' in California," *California Historical Society Quarterly*, IX (March-June, 1930), 16-49, 99-128.

London, Lawrence Foushee, "George Edmund Badger in the United States Senate, 1846-1849," *The North Carolina Historical Review*, XV (January, 1938), 1-22.

McWhiney, Grady, "Were the Whigs a Class Party in Alabama?" *Journal of Southern History*, XXIII (November, 1957), 510-522.

Morrill, James R., "The Presidential Election of 1852: Death Knell of the Whig Party of North Carolina," *The North Carolina Historical Review*, XLIV (October, 1967), 342-359.

Newsome, Albert Ray, "Debate on the Fisher Resolution," *The North Carolina Historical Review*, V (April, 1928), 204-223.

Parramore, Thomas C., "In the Days of Charles Henry Foster," Chapter 13 of *The Roanoke-Chowan Story*. Murfreesboro, North Carolina: Daily Roanoke–Chowan News, n.d., pp. 146-156.

Raper, Horace W., "William W. Holden and the Peace Movement in North Carolina," *The North Carolina Historical Review*, XXXI (October, 1954), 493-516.

Roberts, A. Sellew, "The Peace Movement in North Carolina," *The Mississippi Valley Historical Review*, XI (September, 1924), 190-199.

Russel, Robert R., "What Was the Compromise of 1850?" *The Journal of Southern History*, XXII (August, 1956), 292-309.

Scisco, Louis Dow, "Baltimore County Records of 1665-1667," *Maryland Historical Magazine*, XXIV (December, 1929), 342-348.

Sellers, Charles Grier, Jr., "Who Were the Southern Whigs?" *The American Historical Review*, LIX (January, 1954), 335-346.

[Sumner, Charles], "Our Domestic Relations; Or, How to Treat the Rebel States," *The Atlantic Monthly*, XII (October, 1863), 507-529.

Vinson, John Chalmers, "Electioneering in North Carolina, 1800-1835," *The North Carolina Historical Review*, XXIX (April, 1952), 171-188.

Weeks, Stephen B., "The Code in North Carolina, Contributions to the History of the Duello," *The Magazine of American History* December, 1891), 443-456.

Whitford, John D., "Notes on John Wright Stanly, of New Bern, North Carolina," *Publications of the Southern History Association*, IV (November, 1900), 469-473.

Williams, Max R., "The Foundations of the Whig Party in North Carolina: A Synthesis and a Modest Proposal," *The North Carolina Historical Review*, XLVII (April, 1970), 115-129.

Williams, Max R., "William A. Graham and the Election of 1844: A Study in North Carolina Politics," *The North Carolina Historical Review*, XLV (January, 1968), 23-46.

Yates, Richard E., "Zebulon B. Vance as War Governor of North Carolina, 1862-1865," *The Journal of Southern History*, III (February, 1937), 43-75.

Index

Adams John Quincy: describes Stanly, 1; and gag rule, 42, 70, 75; criticized by Toucey, 43-44; mentioned, 22, 38, 40, 51-52, 54, 60, 63, 72, 78-79, 81, 83, 90, 95, 292n

Allen, Thomas, 37

Allen, Vine, 7, 20

Alston, Willis, 10, 24

American Literary, Scientific, and Military Academy, 23

Ames, Fisher, 27

Andrews, Landaff, 86

Antietam, battle of, 231, 253

Anti-Masonic party, 32

Armistead, General Lewis Addison, 14

Armistead, Captain Walker Keith, 14

Arnold, General Benedict, 251

Arnold, Thomas, 2, 78

Arrington, Archibald H., 89-91, 103, 295n

Ashe, W. S., 120, 138, 143, 156, 305n

Ashley, D. R., 181

Atherton, Charles, 47. *See also* gag rule

Atkin: member of North Carolina General Assembly from Buncombe county, 114-115

Atlanta campaign, 259

Atlantic Monthly: publishes Sumner article, 260-261

Austin, F. B., 190

Badger, George Edmund: birth and early life, 68; appointed Secretary of the Navy (1841), 69; anxious for Stanly's nomination for governor, 94-95; advises Henry Clay on Texas, 97; elected to Senate (1846), 105-106; ill feeling toward Rayner, 109-110; and slavery in the territories, 113, 121-122; reelected to Senate (1848), 113-115, 303n, 304n; favors Stanly as minister to Spain, 120-121; dislikes Mangum, 128; holds Webster in place, 134; vote on compromise measures (1850), 143; initially opposed to secession, 198-199; letter to Ely, 217, 223, 227; joins Conservative party, 225; mentioned, 66-67, 90, 117-119, 136, 138, 141, 161, 224

Badger, Lydia, 14

Badger, Thomas, 7

Baker, Edward D., 172, 175-176, 181-182, 196, 199, 318n, 319n

Baldwin, Cornelia (second wife of Edward Stanly), 195, 273, 275

Baldwin, Joseph Clarke, 195

Baldwin, Joseph Glover, 172, 186-187, 195. *See also* "Jack Cade, Jr."

Balls Bluff, battle of, 172, 319n
Bancroft, Hubert Howe, 269
Bank of Napa, 273
Bank of New Bern, 23-24
Bank of the United States: recharter sought (1811), 11-12; Jackson opposes, 32; charter sought for third national bank, 33, 74-80 *passim*, 97, 99
Bankruptcy act, 82, 103, 296n
Barbour, James, 59
Barringer, Daniel M., 66, 113-114, 120-121, 146
Barringer, Rufus, 92, 120
Bates, George C., 177
Battle, Kemp P., 154
Bayly, Thomas H., 129, 147
Beasley, Joseph, 88
Bedini, Monsignor Gaetano, 192
Bell, John, 37, 60, 133, 159, 195-197 *passim*
Bell, Samuel, 181
Belmont, August, 220
Benton, Thomas Hart, 39, 99, 128
Berrien, John M., 98
Biddle, Samuel S., 56
Biggs, Asa, 105, 112
Birney, James G., 67
"Black Codes," 264
Blackledge, William, 10-13 *passim*
Blair and Rives, 37
Blair, Francis Preston, 65
Blair, Frank, 270
Blair, Montgomery, 259
Bolton castle, 3
Bonaparte, Napoleon, 13
Boston *Atlas*, 56, 162
Boston *Journal*, 213-214, 218-219, 235
Botts, John Minor, 77-79. *See also* "Coffeehouse letter"
Bowen, Captain, 235
Bowie, George W., 188, 190-193 *passim*, 317n
Boyd, Linn, 129, 157, 186
Boyden, Nathaniel, 113
Bragg, Thomas, 224
Branch, John, 15, 24, 34
Branch mints: House debates, 62-63

Bray, Nicholas, 208-209, 214, 261
Breckinridge, John C., 195-197
Broderick, David C., 173, 176, 180, 194
Brooklyn Navy Yard, 52
Brown, Bedford, 67-68
Brown, B. Gratz, 259
Brown, Harvey, 176
Brown, Orlando, 140
Brown, William J., 128-129
Browning, O. H., 266
Brownlow, William G. "Parson," 96
Bryan, James W., 21, 79, 90, 94-95, 106-107, 114, 122, 124, 137, 140, 152, 160, 170
Bryan, John H., 17, 20-21, 24-26 *passim*, 51, 67, 94, 130-131, 198, 283n
Buchanan, James, 179, 193
"Bundelcumb" tariff essays, 144-145. *See also* Edmund Burke
Burch, John C., 197
Burke, Edmund, 144
Burnett, Peter H., 172
Burnside, General Ambrose E: occupies portions of eastern North Carolina, 201-202; mentioned, 202, 206-208, 212-213, 218, 220, 232, 236, 261-262
Butler, Gneral Benjamin F., 260, 269
Butler, William O., 2
Bynum, Jesse A., 17, 73, 288n, 291n
Caldwell, David F., 17
Caldwell, Green W., 156, 295n
Caldwell, Joseph P., 138, 143, 156, 305n
Calhoun, John C: supports Independent Treasury, 39-41; proposes resolutions on slavery and annexation, 42-43; mentioned, 22, 27-28, 31-32, 131
Cambreleng, Churchill, 37-38
Cameron, Duncan, 12, 16
Cameron, J. A., 12
Campaigns of a "Conqueror"; Or, the Man "Who Bragged High for a Fight," 90
Carr John, 177, 194
Carroll, Charles (of Carrollton), 175

Carter, David M., 154

Cass, Lewis, 112, 124, 134, 144, 162

Casserly, Eugene, 197

Central Whig Committee of North Carolina, 104

Chancellorsville, battle of, 253

Chandler, Joseph, 157

Charlotte and Danville (Va.) Company, 119-120

Charlotte *Hornet's Nest*, 124, 132 136

Chase, Salmon P., 255, 322n

Chenery, R., 182

Cherry, W. W., 300n

Cilley, Jonathan, 43

Civil Rights Act (1866), 264

Clark, Henry T., 217-218, 222, 224

Clarke, Henry S., 103

Clay, Henry: passed over by Whigs in 1840, 58-59; insists on special session, 73; outlines legislative program, 75; and Fiscal Bank bill, 76-77; remainder of legislative program passes, 82; North Carolina Whigs endorse for president (1844), 95; visit to Raleigh, 96; letter on the annexation of Texas, 97; and election of 1844, 99-101; North Carolina Whigs endorse for president (1848), 111; presents compromise plan, 132-134, 138-142 *passim*; mentioned, 24, 39-40, 128, 160, 261

"Clayton Compromise," 113-114

Clayton, John M., 97

Clingman, Thomas L: mentioned for Senate (1846), 105; controversy with Stanly and Badger, 109; candidate for Senate, 114-116, 303n; and slavery in the territories, 113, 124-125; reelected to House of Representatives (1849), 305n; in Whig caucus, 127; discusses secession openly, 131-132, 306n; and compromise measures, 138, 143; "scrimmage" with Stanly, 149-150; reelected to House (1851), 156; withdraws from Whig caucus, 161; leaves Whig

party, 164, 166, 170; mentioned, 128, 206

Clinton, DeWitt, 13

Cobb, Howell, 128-130, 138, 144, 156-157

"Coffeehouse letter," 78-79

Coffroth, James W., 180

Cogdell, Ann, 4, 6

Cogdell, Richard, 4

Cole, Arthur C., 2

Cole, Cornelius, 177-179, 182, 187, 272

Colfax, Schuyler, 168, 270

Collins, Josiah, 35, 73, 88

Colton, General David D., 257

Colyer, Vincent, 207-211 *passim*, 213, 261-262

Committee of Thirteen, 132, 138

Compromise of 1850, 141-143, 147-148, 150, 152, 154, 156, 159-168 *passim*, 176

"Confederate party," 225-227

Confiscation Act (1862), 228

Congleton, Abraham, 247

Connor, Henry W., 73, 288n, 291n

Conrad, Charles, 129

"Conservative party," 225-227, 234

Constitutional Convention of 1835, in North Carolina: denies free Negroes the ballot, 26; mentioned, 33

Constitutional Union party, 195-196

Cooper, James, 141

"Corporal's Guard," 1, 80

Corwin, Thomas, 142

Courts, Daniel W., 105

Cowpland, Jonathan, 4

Cox, Thomas, 179

Craig, Major James H., 6

Craven County Tippecanoe Club, 66

Crawford, George W., 140

Crittenden, John J., 97-98, 115, 120, 142, 163, 167, 197

Crocker, Charles, 177

Crocker, Edwin B., 177, 179, 181-182

Crockett, J. B., 197

Currey, John, 194

Dabble, C. B., 255

Daniel, J. R. J., 138, 143, 156, 295n, 305n

Davenport, Commander H. K., 238-239

Davie, William R., 10-11

Davis, Jefferson, 149, 156, 197, 225, 234, 255

Davis, John, 140

Dawes, Henry L., 248

Dawson, William C., 134

DeBerry, Edmund, 64, 138, 143, 156, 288n, 291n, 295n, 305n

DeLong, Charles E., 316n

Democratic national convention: in 1844, 98

Democratic party: in North Carolina, 33

Dimock, Henry, 108, 147, 151, 298n

Distribution: in North Carolina, 33; Clay introduces Senate resolution on, 75; Clay's bill passes Congress, 82; indorsed by North Carolina Whigs (1843), 95, 99; mentioned, 35, 37

Dix, General John A., 266

Dixon, James, 214

Dockery, Alfred, 156-157, 161

Donnell, John R., 20

Donnell, Richard Spaight, 102-103, 106, 113, 121-124 *passim*, 137, 154

Doolittle, James, 266

Doty, James, 137

Douglas, Stephen A., 141-142, 176, 185, 194-197 *passim*

Douglass, Frederick, 220

Dred Scott case, 181, 184-185, 187-188

Dudley, Edward B., 34, 67, 95

Duncan, Alexander, 49-51, 62

Edgerton, Henry, 199

Edmonston, Catherine Ann, 222

Edwards, Weldon, 15, 27, 114, 227

Ely, John S., 217, 223, 227

Emancipation Proclamation, 228, 231, 241, 244, 249-250, 257-258, 262

Evans, George, 72

Everett, Edward, 195

Ewing, Thomas, 76, 98, 140, 143

Farmer: member of North Carolina General Assembly from Henderson county, 114-115, 303n

Farragut, Admiral David, 259

Fay, Caleb T., 269-270

Fayetteville *Observer*, 132, 160, 227

Federal Judiciary Act of 1801, 10

Federalist party, in North Carolina: elects four congressmen (1800), 8; nearly crushed (1803), 10-11; stages revival (1808), 11; dismayed by Gaston's defeat (1810), 12; opposes War of 1812, 13; supports Clinton for president (1812), 13; critical of disunion, 15; excluded from high office, 15-16

Fillmore, Millard, 111-112, 141-142, 147, 158-161 *passim*, 163, 167, 169, 179, 193

First Bull Run, battle of, 258

First North Carolina Union Regiment, 244, 247

First Reconstruction Act (1867), 268

Fish, Hamilton, 140

Fisher, Charles, 73, 291n

Fisher, George P., 306n

Fitch, Thomas, 199

Folger, F. B., 318n

Foote, Henry Stuart, 124, 156, 172, 176

Force Bill (1833), 33, 154

Forts: Tejon and Miller, 172; Sumter, 192; Henry and Donelson, 253

Forward, Walter, 80

Foss, Reverend Andrew J., 164-165

Foster, Charles Henry, 202, 242, 244-248 *passim*, 327n, 328n

Foster, General John, 207, 236-237, 240, 243, 249, 251-252, 262, 329n

Fourteenth Amendment, 265, 267-268

Fowler, Orin, 157

Franklin, Walter S., 37

Franks, Elizabeth (wife of John Stanly), 7, 14, 25, 279n

Franks, Martin, 7

Fredericksburg, battle of, 253
Freedmen's Bureau, 264-265
"Free Labor Associations," 244-248 *passim*
Free Negro voters: in New Bern, 16, 19, 25-26; denied the ballot by Convention of 1835, 26
Free-Soil party, 112, 128
"Free suffrage," 111-112, 165, 170
Frelinghuysen, Theodore, 97
Frémont, General John C., 179, 193, 249, 259
Fugitive Slave Law of 1850, 146-147, 154, 162, 213-214
Gag rule: Pinckney's, 41; Patton's 42-43; Atherton resolutions, 47-48, 54-55, 60-61; "21st rule," 60, 70, 75, 90
Gales and Seaton, 37
Gales, Weston, 298n
Galphin claim, 140-141
Garrison, William Lloyd, 147, 220
Gaston, Eliza, 86
Gaston, William: defeated for House of Representatives (1810), 12; elected to House (1812), 13; elected to John Stanly's seat in House of Commons (1827), 23; replaces Stanly as president of the Bank of New Bern, 23; elected to House of Commons (1831), 25; favors free Negro suffrage, 26; pays tribute to John Stanly, 27; congratulates Edward Stanly on appointment, 30-31; political career and opinions, 31; declines election to Senate, 67-68; mentioned, 7-8, 14-17 *passim*, 20, 22, 24-25, 83, 86, 286n
Gentry, Meredith, 133, 160-161, 163
Georgetown college, 31
Gettysburg, battle of, 14, 254
Giddings, Joshua, 128, 142, 158, 186
Gilliam, Colonel Henry A., 217-218, 223-224
Goldsborough *Republican and Patriot*, 153, 155, 310n
Goldsborough *Telegraph*, 132, 153
Gooding, Jacob, 5-6

Goodloe, Daniel Reeves, 252-253
Goodman, John R., 24
Gorham, George C., 269-270
Grace Church (San Francisco), 172, 274
Graham, Edward, 7-8, 10, 20
Graham, James, 40, 63, 288n, 291n, 295n, 296n
Graham, Susan, 77
Graham, William Alexander: elected to Senate (1840), 67-68; elected governor (1844), 94-96, 98, 100; reelected, 103-104; declines appointment as minister to Spain, 121; appointed Secretary of the Navy by Fillmore, 142; nominated for Vice-President (1852), 163-166 *passim*; opposes secession initially, 198-199; joins Conservative party, 225; mentioned, 40, 69, 73, 77-79, 85, 87-88, 105-107, 109-111, 114, 119-120, 136, 146-147, 149, 152, 159-160, 167, 174, 206, 268
Granger, Francis, 98
Grant, General Ulysses S., 253-254, 259, 263, 270, 272
Graves, Calvin, 101
Graves, William, 43, 289n
Greeley, Horace, 229, 259, 274
Greene, General Nathaniel, 5
Guadalupe Hidalgo, Treaty of, 180
Gwin, William McKendree, 173, 176, 180, 194
Haight, Henry H., 269-270
Hale, Edward J., 160, 304n
Hall, Thomas H., 35-36, 53, 55
Hamilton, Alexander, 31, 175
Harris, Ira, 215-216
Harrison Hall (Raleigh), 66
Harrison, General William Henry, 58-59, 61, 64, 66-70 *passim*, 72-74, 298n
Hartford Convention, 15
Hastings, Serranus C., 172
Hatteras Island: Union government on, 202; satirized, 222; Foster elected to Congress from, 242
Hawkins, Micajah T., 64, 288n, 291n

Hawkins, Colonel Rush C., 202
Hawks, Cicero, 21
Hawks, Francis L., 20-21
Hawks, John (architect), 13
Hawks, John, 21
Hawks, William W., 172
Hayes, William, 172, 182
Haywood, William H., 98, 104-105
Hedrick, Benjamin, 242, 252
Hedrick, John A., 228, 242, 252
Helper, Hardie Hogan, 209, 211, 261
Helper, Hinton Rowan, 209, 299n
Henderson, Archibald, 10
Henry, Lewis, 14
Hickman, John, 211
Hicks, John Y., 118
Hill, General Daniel Harvey: contro-
    versy with Stanly, 250-251; men-
    tioned, 329n
Hill, John, 73, 291n
Hill, William Henry, 10
Hillard, George Stillman, 260
Hilliard, Henry W., 59, 61
Hillyer, Junius, 160
Hines, Richard, 95, 106-107, 146,
    300n
Hinton, Charles L., 120
Hitchcock, Dr., 274
Hodges, Wilson B., 30, 55, 291n
Hoke, Michael, 98, 100
Holden, William W., 112, 137, 139,
    146, 198, 225-226, 254, 256
Hone, Philip: describes Stanly, 82;
    describes dinner party, 98
Hooe, George Mason, 64
Hopkins, Mark, 177
House Committee on Elections, 242,
    248
Houston, John, 129
Howard, C. C., 236-237
Howard, Volney E., 131
Hunter, General David, 203-204
Hunter, Robert M. T., 60
Huntington, Colis, 177
Independent Treasury (also Sub-
    Treasury or Constitutional Trea-
    sury), 37-41 *passim*, 46, 53-54,
    64-65, 70, 75, 82, 103
Inge, Samuel W., 148-149

Ingersoll, Charles J., 81
Ingham, Samuel D., 24
Iredell, James, 23, 282n
"Jack Cade, Jr.," 186-187
Jackson, Andrew, 22, 24, 28, 32-34,
    68, 74, 98, 130, 153-154
Jackson, Claiborne F., 201
Jackson, Joseph W., 160, 312n
Jefferson, Thomas, 8, 10-11
Jenifer, Daniel, 47
Johnson, Andrew, 201, 205, 215,
    263-268 *passim*, 320n
Johnson, F. E., 274
Johnson, Guion G., 291n
Johnson, Herschel V., 195
Johnson, John Neely, 173
Johnson, Reverdy, 84-85, 98, 110,
    140, 198, 202, 268
Johnson, Robert W., 144
Johnson, William Cost, 2, 60, 81, 85
Johnston, General Albert S., 199
Johnston, General Joseph E., 263
Johnston, William, 225-227
Jones, Charles Lee, 149
Jones, George, 43
Jones, Hugh, 26
Jones, James C., 159
Jones, John B., 234-235
Jones, John W., 60
Jones, Julia (first wife of Edward
    Stanly), 26, 65, 69, 86, 195
Jones, William Watts, 19
Joyner, Andrew, 106-108, 110
Kansas-Nebraska bill (1854),
    175-176, 178, 180
Kendall, Amos, 49
Kennedy, Moses, 275
Kennedy, William L., 53
Kerr, John, 106, 165, 301n
King, Rufus, 20
King, Thomas Butler, 98, 126
King, Thomas Starr, 199-200
King, William, 165
Kinney, Charles R., 102
Kip, Bishop William Ingraham, 172,
    274
Know Nothing (American) party: ori-
    gin of, 173; in election of 1856,
    179; in California politics,

173-176, 178-180, 184-193
passim
Lafayette, Marie Joseph Paul Yves
Roch Gilbert Du Motier, Marquis
de, 17
Lake,Delos, 197
Lane, James, 211
Lane, Joseph, 195
Lane, William K., 106, 121, 123-124,
155
Larned, Daniel Reed, 206-207, 209
Latham, Milton S., 194
Lecompton Constitution, 194
Legaré, Hugh Swinton, 65, 80
Lee, General Robert E., 221, 230,
253-254, 257, 263
Lee, Admiral Samuel P., 238-241
Legislature, of North Carolina: passes
anti-duelling law (1802), 10;
repeals district system of choosing
presidential electors (1811),
12-13; debate on convention
question in House of Commons
(1821), 17-19; rejects penitentiary bill (1817), 19; rejects free
Negro exclusion bill (1825),
19-20; elects James Iredell governor (1828), 23; places Stanly portrait in House of Commons
(1830), 23; petitioned to deny
free Negroes the suffrage (1831),
26; elects Edward Stanly a state
solicitor (1835), 30; increases
state aid to railroads and estab-
lishes state free public school
system (1839), 34; senatorial election in (1840), 67-68; redistricts
(1842), 87; disinclined to pass
political resolutions (1844), 101;
senatorial election in (1846), 105;
redistricts (1846), 106; senatorial
election in (1848), 114-115; con-
siders Steele and Shepard resolutions (1848-1849), 116-118;
passes internal improvement measures (1849), 119-120; senatorial
election in (1852), 170; "federal
scheme" to elect peace men to
(1862), 226-227; purges state

officials (1862), 234; alleged to
favor reconstruction (1862), 235
Leigh, Benjamin Watkins, 98
Liberty party, 67, 101
Lincoln, Abraham: and election of
1860, 195-197; and secession
crisis, 198; views reconstruction
as primarily executive function,
201; appoints military governors,
201; offers military governorship
of North Carolina to Stanly,
202-205; interviews with Sumner
and Colyer, 210; interview with
Burnside, 212-213; appointment
of military governors debated in
Senate, 214-216; and Emancipation Proclamation, 228-229; interview with Stanly, 230-231;
assures Stanly of "entire approbation" of his conduct, 232; and
congressional elections in South,
241-242, 244; Free Labor Associations protest to, 246; meets with
Boston delegation, 249; Stanly
submits resignation to, 249-250;
interviews with Stanly, 252-253;
tactfully refuses Stanly's services,
255; and election of 1864,
257-260 *passim*; assassination of,
263; mentioned, 29, 219-222
passim, 270-271, 319n
Loan bill: passes Congress (1841), 82
Locke, Francis, 15
Loften, William C., 170
Lull, Louis, 176
McCall, George A., 127
McCarty, Colonel John M., 85, 297n
McClatchy, James, 178
McClellan Central Union Club of San
Francisco, 257
McClellan, General George B., 217,
221, 253, 256-260 *passim*
McClernand, William, 129
McCorkle, Joseph, 180
McDougall, James A., 172
McDowell, General Irvin, 258
McKay, James, 105, 114, 288n,
291n, 295n
MacKenzie's Rebellion, 294n

Macon, Nathaniel, 15, 33-34

Madison, James, 11, 13, 15

Mangum, Willie P: elected to Senate (1840), 67-68; presides over Whig caucus, 80; intermediary between Stanly and Wise, 84-85; votes against Texas treaty, 98; reelected to Senate (1846), 105; and slavery in the territories, 113; supports Waddell as minister to Spain, 120-121; dislikes Badger, 128; and compromise measures, 134, 138, 143; supports Scott for president (1852), 159-161, 166; declines nomination for Vice-President, 163; mentioned, 17, 95-96, 101, 106, 109, 114, 170, 300n

Manly, Charles, 66, 94, 107, 110-112, 139, 199, 224

Manly, Matthias E., 26, 30

Marshall, Humphrey, 160-161

Marshall, John, 7-8, 13, 27, 276

Martin, James G., 218

Mason, Armistead, 85

Mecklenburg Declaration of Independence, 99

Meeker, David, 184

Meredith, William M., 140

Mexican War, 104-105, 180

Miller, General Stephen, 30

Miller, Stephen F., 14, 24

Mining camps: in Calfornia, 171; Stanly visits, 186-187, 191

Mix, Colonel Simon S., 237

Mobile Bay, battle of, 259

Montgomery, William, 64, 73, 288n, 291n

Moore, Benjamin, 106, 301n

Morehead, James T., 156, 161

Morehead, John Motley, 65-66, 73, 87, 94, 97, 105-106, 111, 114, 225

Morris, Robert, 6

Morrissey, John, 269

Morton, Marcus, 60-61, 99, 292n

Mountain View Cemetery (Oakland), 275

Murphey, Archibald, 8, 16

Murray, Commander Alexander, 239-241

Napa County, 272-273

Napa Valley Railroad Company, 273

Nash, Henry K., 96

Nashville Convention, 131-132, 135, 137

National Republican party, 32

National Union Convention, 266-267

Neale, Abner, 16

New Bern Academy, 6, 20

New Bern committee of safety, 4

New Bern Masonic Lodge, 5-6

New Bern *Newbernian*, 94, 105, 123-124, 136

New Bern *North Carolina Sentinel*, 23, 25-26

New Bern *Progress*, 219-220, 224, 227, 234, 237, 242-247 *passim*, 327n, 328n

New Bern *Spectator*, 25, 35-36, 45, 66-67

New Bern Theatre and Thespian corps, 20-21

New York *Herald*, 205, 211, 237, 241, 247-248

New York *Times*, 167, 208-209, 227, 234, 241-243, 248-249

New York *Tribune*, 167, 213-214, 244-245, 259

North Atlantic Blockading Squadron: and licensing of coastal trade, 238-241

North Carolina Council of State, 6

Nullification: John Stanly opposes, 27; dismissed by Gaston, 31; in North Carolina, 33, 46; denounced by Edward Stanly, 28, 276

Nunes, Joseph A., 181

Oath of Neutrality: drafted by Stanly, 236, 325n

"Omnibus bill," 132-134, 138, 141-143

Order of the Star Spangled Banner, 173

Oregon, 103, 169, 181, 185, 199

Orr, James, 266

Outlaw, David, 108-110, 113, 127,

129, 131, 136, 138-139, 141, 143-144, 156, 160-162, 164, 166, 305n, 306n, 312n
Owen, John, 66-67, 69
Pacific Republic scheme, 197-199
Park, Treanor W., 181-182
Parmenter, William, 60-61
Partridge, Captain Alden, 23
Pasteur, Edward, 10
Patton, John, 42-43. *See also* gag rule
Peace Society: in North Carolina 254
People's Ticket: in North Carolina, 22
Pettigrew, Charles, 151
Pettigrew, Ebenezer, 30, 33-36, 39-40, 42-43, 46, 48, 51, 54-55, 63, 66, 68, 73-74, 76, 83, 85-86, 88, 91, 103, 288n, 294n
Pettigrew, William, 88, 151, 298n
Phillips, Wendell, 220, 249, 259
Pickens, Francis, 72
Pickering, Timothy, 27
Pierce, Franklin, 164-166, 172
Pigott, Jennings, 242, 244, 246-248
Pinckney, Charles Cotesworth, 11
Pittsburg Address, 178
Polk, James K., 37-38, 41, 47-48, 60, 98-99, 101-102, 104, 143-144, 180
Pomeroy, Samuel, 246
Pope, General John, 230, 253
Prentiss, Seargent S., 50-51, 65
"President's Plan," 130-131, 139, 141
Presidential reconstruction: theory of, 201; military governors appointed in Tennessee, North Carolina, Louisiana, and Arkansas, 201; in North Carolina, 201-253 *passim*; and Radical Republicans, 211-212; Senate debate on, 214-216; and Andrew Johnson, 263-264
Preston, William B., 126, 140
Preston, William C., 39, 65
Princeton, 14, 27, 31
Quitman, John, 156, 168
Raleigh *North Carolina Standard*, 86,

102-106, 108, 110-112, 121-123, 132, 136-137, 139, 146, 149,151, 155-156, 166, 168, 205, 223, 225, 227, 254, 311n
Raleigh *Register*, 49, 51, 53, 56, 59, 83, 87, 94, 96, 101-103, 106, 112-113, 119, 121-122, 124, 132, 136-137, 146, 149-150, 156, 160, 164, 166, 168-170, 202, 205, 221-222, 226-227, 292n, 298n
Raleigh *Star*, 12, 51, 132
Randall, James G., 228
Rankin, Ira P., 179, 181-182, 196, 318n
Rantoul, Robert, 99
Raymond, Henry J., 266
Rayner, Kenneth, 64, 66, 88, 94, 106-111 *passim*, 114, 116, 164, 170, 235, 291n, 295n
"Raynermander," 106
Reid, David S., 111-112, 139, 150, 165, 170
Rencher, Abraham, 288n, 295n, 296n
Republican party: origin of, 176-177; in election of 1860, 195-196; in election of 1864, 259-260; in election of 1868, 270-272; in California politics, 177-196 *passim*, 269-270
Respass, Isaiah, 240
Rhett, Robert Barnwell, 71, 156
Richardson, William, 143-144
Richmond: McClellan's drive on, 217, 221, 253; Confederate government at, 234; fall of, 263; mentioned, 257, 259
Ritchie, Thomas, 136, 144-145
Rives, William C., 65, 76, 78
Rodman, William Blount, 87
Root, Joseph, 133, 306n
Roulhac, Colonel J. B. G., 312n
Roulhac, Thomas, 273
Ruffin, Thomas, 151-155 *passim*, 170
Sacramento *Daily Bee,* 183, 185-186, 188, 192
Sacramento *Daily State Sentinel,* 188, 190

Sacramento *Daily Union*, 174, 179, 183-185, 189-195 *passim*, 269, 270-271

Saltonstall, Leverett, 92

San Francisco: early years of, 171; local Bar, 172; Whig party in, 172, 174-176; Know Nothing party in, 173; Democratic victory in (1855), 176; Republican delegation from, 183; Union mass meeting in, 197

San Francisco *Chronicle*, 179, 190

San Francisco *Daily Alta California*, 179, 182-183, 189-190, 198-199, 275, 317n

San Francisco *Evening Bulletin*, 171-172, 196, 199, 257-258

San Francisco *Herald*, 186, 190, 271

San Jose *Telegraph*, 177, 190

Sargent, Aaron A., 182

Satterthwaite, Fenner B., 107-108, 118, 137

Saunders, Romulus, 66, 99-100, 295n, 300n

Sawyer, Samuel T., 288n

Schouler, William, 162, 168

Scott and Graham Club of Raleigh, 166

Scott, General Winfield: and election of 1852, 158-168 *passim*, 172, 312n, 313n; mentioned, 58, 111

Secession: in lower South, 196-197; in North Carolina, 150-156, 198-199; mentioned, 27, 93, 131, 261, 276

Second Bull Run, battle of, 231, 253

Seddon, James, 131

Sengstack, C. P., 145

Settlers and Miners party: in California, 190

Seven Days Battle, 221, 253

Seward, Frederick, 65

Seward, William H., 65, 77, 126-127, 141, 147, 159, 162-163, 167-168, 177, 187, 195, 197, 202-204, 228, 239, 255, 265-266, 272, 313n, 315n

Seymour, Horatio, 270, 272

Shaw, William, 176

Shepard, Charles, 20-21, 25-26, 51-52, 56, 66-68, 73, 103, 288n, 291n

Shepard, James Biddle, 104-105, 114

Shepard resolutions, 117-118

Shepard, William B., 67-68, 105-106, 114-115, 117-119, 304n

Shepperd, Augustine H., 20, 24, 113, 134, 138, 141, 156, 288n, 295n, 296n, 305n

Sheridan, General Phil, 259

Sherman, John, 267

Sherman, General William T., 259

Simonton, James W., 196

Simpson, General Samuel, 16

Slade, William, 41, 49-50, 54

Smith, General E. Kirby, 224

Smith, Elias, 208-209

Smyth, William, 8-9

Spaight, Richard Dobbs, 7-10, 222

Spaight, Richard Dobbs, Jr., 16-17, 20-21, 23, 34, 103

Spaight-Stanly duel, 8-10, 280n

Sparrow, Thomas, 27, 110, 152, 154

Speight, Jesse, 288n

Spencer, John C., 80

Spruill, Hezekiah, 152, 155, 220, 236

Stanford, Leland, 177, 194, 200, 203

Stanley, Dancey (great-grandfather of Edward Stanly), 4

Stanley, Elizabeth Wright (great-grandmother of Edward Stanly), 4

Stanley, Major John (son of William and Mary Stanley), 3-4, 278n

Stanley, John, Jr. (son of Major John Stanley), 4

Stanley, Mary, 3

Stanley, William, 3-4

Stanly, Alexander Hamilton (brother of Edward Stanly), 14, 272

Stanly, Alfred (brother of Edward Stanly), 14, 24, 26, 206

Stanly, Ann (aunt of Edward Stanly), 6, 27

Stanly, Edward: described by Adams, 1; incident with Wise, 1-2; described by Cole, 2; described by

Wheeler, 3; personal appearance, 3; birth, 13; childhood, 14; attends New Bern Academy, 20; witnesses Stanly-Spaight canvass, 21; sent to University of North Carolina, 21; enrolls in American Literary, Scientific and Military Academy, 23; receives first taste of Washington society, 23-24; participates in Fourth of July celebration (1831), 25; announces for New Bern seat in House of Commons, and then withdraws, 25; becomes lawyer, 26; marries Julia Jones, 26; begins practice in Washington, North Carolina, 26-27; influence of John Stanly on, 27-29; elected state solicitor in second judicial district (1835), 30; influence of Gaston on, 31-32; becomes Whig, 33; and election of 1836, 34; nominated for House of Representatives (1837), 35; campaign, 35-37; appointed to Invalid Pensions Committee, 37; submits Sub-Treasury resolution, 38; votes for Patton "gag" resolution, 42; encounter with a "Connecticut nightingale," 44-45; speaks in Edgecombe county, 47; opposes Atherton resolutions, 47-49; controversy with Duncan, 49-51; clash with Shepard, 52-53; 1839 congressional campaign, 53-56; attacks "Van Buren abolitionists," 60-61; defends Harrison against charge of abolitionism, 61-62; assails Wheeler, 63; attends "Whig Young Men's Convention," 63; prepares Whig campaign documents, 63-64; stumps in New York and North Carolina, 65-67; secures cabinet post for Badger, 69; defends protective tariff, 70-71; exchange with Rhett, 71-72; challenged by Pickens, 72; 1841 congressional campaign, 73-74; appointed to Naval Affairs

Committee, 75; opposes gag rule, 75; and national bank question, 76-78; rebukes Arnold and Botts, 78-79; quarrel with Wise, 80-81; made chairman of Military Affairs Committee, 83; continues quarrel with Wise, 83-84; duel contemplated, 84-86; and Whig tariff of 1842, 86-87; 1843 congressional campaign, 87-91; unburdens self on slavery, 92; recalls difficulties with South Carolina delegation, 93; mentioned for governor, 95-96; advises Clay on Texas, 97; attends 1844 Whig convention, 97-98; "trial of strength" with Saunders, 99-100; elected to House of Commons, 100; chosen speaker, 101-102; meets Shepard in New Bern debate, 104; reelected to House of Commons, 104-105; chosen speaker, 105; mentioned for Senate, 105; elected state attorney general, 106; mentioned for governor in 1848, 106-108; rivalry with Rayner, 108-111; attends 1848 Whig convention, 111; debates "free suffrage" issue with Reid, 111; elected to House of Commons, 112; serves as Taylor elector, 112; and senatorial election, 115; opposes Steele resolutions, 116; opposes Shepard resolutions, 117-119; opposes "Danville connection," 120; candidate for diplomatic appointment, 120-121; nominated for House of Representatives, 122; 1849 congressional campaign, 122-124; opposes Toombs' resolution in Whig caucus, 127; uncovers Brown's secret negotiations with Free-Soilers, 128-129; compromise candidate for speaker, 129; favors Taylor's plan, 133-134; delivers major speech on slavery question, 134-135; press reaction, 135-137; urges friends to oppose

Southern Rights campaign, 137;
supports California statehood bill,
137-138; Taylor's choice for Secretary of War, 140-141; moves
into Clay camp, 141-142; vote on
Compromise of 1850, 143;
inquires into authorship of "Bundelcund" tariff essays, 143-146;
duel with Inge, 148-149; "scrimmage" with Clingman, 149-150;
1851 congressional campaign,
151-156; placed on Ways and
Means Committee, 158; supports
Scott for president, 159-163;
campaigns for Scott and Graham
in New York, Pennsylvania, and
North Carolina, 166; reasons for
supporting Scott, 167-168;
decides to retire from public life,
168; supports "Washington" as
name for new territory, 169,
314n; leaves for California, 169;
practices law in San Francisco,
172-173; active in church affairs,
172; refuses to join Know
Nothing party, 174; takes part in
Whig movement in San Francisco,
174-175; candidate for State Senate, 175-176; declines to address
Sacramento Republicans, 178;
Republican candidate for Senate,
180; Republican candidate for
governor, 181-194 *passim*; marries
Cornelia Baldwin, 195; wishes
Lincoln's administration to be
successful, 196; makes Union
speeches in California, 197-199;
appointed military governor of
North Carolina, 202-205; arrives
in New Bern and consults with
Burnside, 206-207; and closing of
Negro schools, 207-208; and
"Bray affair," 208-209; orders
Helper from department, 209;
supposed activities create "stir" in
Washington, 209-210; northern
abolitionists raise "hue and cry"
against, 210-211; subject of congressional inquiry, 211-212;

relates his side of controversy to
Stanton and Lincoln, 212-213;
effect of alleged behavior on
reconstruction legislation,
214-216; begins efforts to secure
North Carolina's voluntary return
to the Union, 216-218; policy of
state and Confederate governments toward, 218; visits Washington, North Carolina, 218-220;
visits Roanoke and principal
towns on Álbemarle sound,
220-221; letter to Gilliam,
223-224; suspected of "federal
scheme" to elect Unionists to the
state legislature, 226-227;
requests leave of absence, 228;
interview with Lincoln, 230-232;
interview with Vance, 232-234;
authorizes trade in North Carolina
waters, 235-236; gives "protections" to loyal citizens, 236-237;
dispute with navy over trade
licenses, 238-241; and union
election, 241-248 *passim*; submits
resignation, 249-250; controversy
with Hill, 250-251; visits Washington, D. C., and recommends
Goodloe as successor, 252-253;
offers services "not as Governor,"
255; supports McClellan for president, 256-258; controversy with
Sumner, 260-262; supports Johnson, 265-268; campaigns for
Haight, 269-270; campaigns for
Seymour and Blair, 270-272;
retires to Napa county, 272-273;
endorses Greeley for president,
274; dies in San Francisco,
274-275; abiding loyalties,
275-276; mentioned *passim*

Stanly, Elizabeth Mary (sister of
Edward Stanly), 14
Stanly, Fabius Maximus (brother of
Edward Stanly), 14, 25
Stanly, Frank (brother of Edward
Stanly), 14
Stanly, Harvey (cousin of Edward
Stanly), 23

Stanly, Hayes & Stanly, 272
Stanly, James Green (uncle of Edward Stanly), 6, 24
Stanly, James Green, Jr. (brother of Edward Stanly), 14, 104
Stanly, John (father of Edward Stanly): birth, 6; brief career as merchant, 6-7; marries Elizabeth Franks, 7; admitted to Bar, 7; formidable opponent in courtroom, 7; as conversationalist, 7-8; elected to House of Commons (1798), 8; elected to Congress (1800), 8; duel with Spaight, 8-10; defeated for reelection (1803), 10; elected to Congress (1808), 11; House speech on Bank of United States, 11-12; North Carolina Federalists take great pride in, 12; represents New Bern in House of Commons, 12; expresses preference for distinct Federalist candidate for president (1812), 13; advises brother to accept challenge, 14; deprecates disunion, 15; assists in electing Macon to Senate, 15; repeatedly elected to House of Commons from New Bern, 16-17; as Speaker, 17; an "Eastern" man on state issues, 17-19; advocates penitentiary bill, 19; speaks against bill to prevent free Negroes from migrating into North Carolina, 20; defeated for state senate (1822), 21; suffers paralytic stroke, 21-23; presented as candidate for governor (1828), 23; lingering illness, 24-25; death, 27; influence on Edward Stanly, 27-28; mentioned, 30-31, 68, 168, 276, 279n, 281n, 282n, 283n
Stanly, John, Jr. (brother of Edward Stanly), 14
Stanly, John A. (nephew of Edward Stanly), 272-274
Stanly, John Wright (grandfather of Edward Stanly), 4-6, 13

Stanly, Marcus Cicero (brother of Edward Stanly), 14
Stanly, Margaret Cogdell (aunt of Edward Stanly), 6
Stanly, Richard Dancy (uncle of Edward Stanly), 6, 14, 21
Stanly Thomas Turner (uncle of Edward Stanly), 6, 14
Stanly, Wright (great uncle of Edward Stanly), 5
Stanly, Wright, Jr. (second cousin of Edward Stanly), 20, 24
Stanton, Edwin M., 203-204, 209, 211-212, 217, 220, 228, 230-231, 233, 239-240, 250, 252-253
Stanton, Richard, 169
Steele resolutions, 116-117, 121-123 121-123
Stephens, Alexander H., 126-129 *passim*, 133, 141, 156-158, 162, 197, 266
Stephens, Linton, 158
Stevens, Thaddeus, 157
Strange, Robert, 67-68
Stuart, Alexander H. H., 77, 81
Sumner, Charles, 158, 210-212, 215-216, 260-262, 270, 322n
Sumner, General Edwin Vose, 199
Sutter's Mill, 171
Swain, David L., 19-20, 31, 69, 106, 115, 198, 206
"Swing around the circle": by Andrew Johnson, 267
Taney, Roger B., 175
Tarboro' Press, 47, 54, 89, 91
Tarborough *Scaevola*, 36-37
Tariff: compromise tariff of 1833, 70, 82; Whig tariff of 1842, 86-87, 90-91, 93, 99, 103, 166; Walker tariff of 1846, 105, 115; mentioned 33, 70-73, 75, 103
Taylor, John L., 157
Taylor, Marble Nash, 202, 222, 242
Taylor, Zachary, 111-112, 114, 124, 126-127, 129-130, 133-134, 137-141 *passim*, 147, 155, 172, 180, 306n
Terry, Davis S., 194
Texas, annexation of, 96-103 *passim*

Thompson, Waddy, 39
Ticknor & Fields, 260
Tilford, Frank, 176
Tippecanoe Club of Raleigh, 66
Toole, Henry I., 35, 74, 103
Toombs, Robert, 126-130 *passim*, 133, 141, 156-158, 162, 167
Toucey, Isaac, 43-45
Tracy, Frederick P., 180-181
Trumbull, Lyman, 214-215
Turner, James, 16
Turner, J. M., 181
Turner, Thomas, 5-6
Tyler, John, 1, 34, 58, 74, 76-80 *passim*, 82-83, 96, 101, 292n, 298n
Twenty-fourth Massachusetts regiment: band of, 207
Twenty-sixth North Carolina regiment, 225
Union army: depredations in North Carolina, 236-237, 251-252, 258, 262
Union election: in North Carolina, 241-248, 328n
Unionism: in California, 199-200; in Confederate North Carolina, 224-225, 234-235, 254-256, 319n
Vallandigham, Clement L., 256
Van Buren, Martin, 34, 36-37, 39, 41, 49-50, 62, 64, 66, 97-99, 112
Vance, Zebulon B: resigns self to secession, 199; elected governor (1862), 225-227; refuses interview with Stanly, 232-234; keeps Assembly from declaring for reunion, 234-235; contrasted with Stanly by Hill, 250-251; warns Davis of discontent in North Carolina, 255; defeats Holden for governor (1864), 256
Venable, A. W., 138, 143, 156, 305n
Vicksburg, seige of, 254
Waddell, Hugh, 3, 107, 120-121
Wade, Benjamin, 159, 162, 164
Wade-Davis bill (1864), 263
Ward, William T., 159
Warren, Edward J., 137, 154
Washington's Farewell Address, 118

Washington, George, 13-14, 27-28, 169, 210, 251, 261, 276
Washington *Globe,* 37, 50-51, 60, 62, 65, 97
Washington *Madisonian,* 37, 77-78
Washington *National Intelligencer,* 37, 49-50, 76, 84, 97, 231
Washington, North Carolina, battle of, 329n
Washington *North State Whig,* 91, 100, 105, 107-109, 122, 132, 137, 146-147, 153-155, 168-169, 298n
Washington *Republic,* 122, 135-136, 139, 144-145, 159-160
Washington (N. C.) *Republican,* 53-54, 87, 89, 91
Washington territory, 169, 314n
Washington *Union,* 136, 144-145
Washington (N. C.) *Whig,* 36-37, 53, 73, 87, 298n
Washington, William H., 87, 114, 151, 295n, 296n
Watterson, Harvey, 60
Webster, Daniel, 31, 39, 73, 79, 98, 133-134, 141, 158, 160, 163, 261
Weed, Thurlow, 58-59, 77, 140, 159, 167, 196, 266, 272
Weller, John B., 173, 180, 187-189, 191-194 *passim,* 317n
Welles, Gideon, 228, 238-241 *passim*
Welling, James C., 231
Wheeler, John H., 3, 63
Whig party: origin of, 32; in North Carolina, 32-33; in convention of 1839, 58; in campaign of 1840, 58-67 *passim*; and Tyler, 75-80 *passim*; in convention of 1844, 97-98; in campaign of 1844, 100-101; in convention of 1848, 111; in campaign of 1848, 112; and crisis of 1850, 126-142 *passim*; in convention of 1852, 163; in campaign of 1852, 164-168; in California, 172-173; in San Francisco, 174-176; persistent Whiggery, 275
Whitaker, Spier, 106
Whitford, John D., 6, 20, 26, 28

Williams, Henry, 60, 292n
Williams, Lewis, 64, 66-67, 288n, 291n, 295n
Williams, Captain William, 238
Willis, Stephen F., 244, 246-247
Wilmot Proviso, 113, 115-118 *passim*, 121, 123-128 *passim*; 132, 135, 142, 186, 189, 194
Windish, Colonel John, 224
Winthrop, Robert, 92, 127-130 *passim*, 133-134, 140, 158, 258, 260-261, 306n
Wise, Henry A: fight with Stanly in House chamber, 1-2, 80-81; continuing quarrel with Stanly threatens duel, 83-86; mentioned, 43, 47-48, 65, 73, 90-91, 110
Woodbury, Levi, 38-39, 46, 49
Woodfin, Nicholas, 206
Worth, Jonathan, 225, 254-255
Zabriskie, Colonel James, 189, 191